The publisher and the University of California Press Foundation gratefully acknowledge the generous support of the Lisa See Endowment Fund in Southern California History and Culture.

Boyle Heights

AMERICAN CROSSROADS

Edited by Earl Lewis, George Lipsitz, George Sánchez, Dana Takagi, Laura Briggs, and Nikhil Pal Singh

Boyle Heights

HOW A LOS ANGELES NEIGHBORHOOD BECAME
THE FUTURE OF AMERICAN DEMOCRACY

George J. Sánchez

UNIVERSITY OF CALIFORNIA PRESS

University of California Press
Oakland, California

© 2021 by George Sánchez

Permission to reprint has been sought from rights holders for images and text
included in this volume, but in some cases it was impossible to clear formal
permission because of coronavirus-related institution closures. The author and
the publisher will be glad to do so if and when contacted by copyright holders
of third-party material.

Library of Congress Cataloging-in-Publication Data
First paperback printing 2022
Names: Sanchez, George J., author.
Title: Boyle Heights : how a Los Angeles neighborhood became the future of
    American democracy / George J. Sánchez.
Description: Oakland, California : University of California Press, [2021] |
    Includes bibliographical references and index.
Identifiers: LCCN 2020034648 (print) | LCCN 2020034649 (ebook) |
    ISBN 9780520391642 (paper) | ISBN 9780520382374 (ebook)
Subjects: LCSH: Neighborhoods—California—Los Angeles—History. |
    Boyle Heights (Los Angeles, Calif.)—History. | Boyle Heights (Los
    Angeles, Calif.)—Race relations—History.
Classification: LCC F869.B69 S26 2021 (print) | LCC F869.B69 (ebook) |
    DDC 979.4/94—dc23
LC record available at https://lccn.loc.gov/2020034648
LC ebook record available at https://lccn.loc.gov/2020034649

Manufactured in the United States of America

29   28   27   26   25   24   23   22
10   9   8   7   6   5   4   3   2   1

*To my wife, Debra Massey Sánchez, for her ongoing
support and love,*

*And to the people of Boyle Heights, for their resiliency
and inspiration!*

CONTENTS

LIST OF MAPS AND ILLUSTRATIONS

MAPS

ILLUSTRATIONS

PREFACE

This book has taken close to three decades to complete. Through almost all that, my wife Debra Massey Sánchez was my constant companion, urging me to return to the project because she knew how much it meant to me. I do not think I would have finished this book if it weren't for her encouragement and sacrifice. It has filled so much of our twenty-three years of marriage. I am eternally grateful for your love, support, and partnership.

My parents, Jorge Reynoso Sánchez and Ninfa Sánchez Troncoso, both passed during the time it took to write this book, but they are the reason I was born in Boyle Heights and have always thought of it as home. It is through their vision for my future that I came to cherish my past, and they have given me my commitment to history and family. I miss them both terribly. But I am fortunate to have the support of my son, Adam Sánchez, his wife, Madelynn Katz Sánchez, and my precious granddaughter, Yemaya Sánchez, and to see that the future of activism and history is in great hands. Thank you for being such an important part of my life. And thank you to my adopted Massey family, Betty Jo Massey, Peggy Massey Wendzel, Paulette Baca, and the late Carol Massey, for supporting my journey and all the time I was working. Betty, I couldn't have finished without your dinners!

I have been fortunate to work at three different and wonderful universities during the time I have worked on this book. UCLA provided me the first opportunity to build on this project. It was there that I taught an undergraduate course in the history of Boyle Heights where we specifically recruited Chicano, Asian American, and Jewish student activists to interview past residents and discuss and debate their roles in shaping the neighborhood. The University of Michigan gave me my first opportunity to become an interdisciplinary American studies scholar and to think about this project in the broader history of multiracial communities across time and space. During my last 23 years at the University of Southern California, I have been supported to work on civic engagement projects in Boyle Heights through the Center for Diversity and Democracy, which has enhanced this project tremendously. Each university gave me teaching sabbaticals, leaves of absence, and research monies to work on the research and writing for this book; I appreciate this support immensely.

Specific colleagues at each of these institutions have shared their work with me and have intellectually pushed me to consider alternative approaches to the sources that have shaped this project. At UCLA, I learned much from Valerie Matsumoto, Bruce Schulman, Vilma Ortiz, Raymond Rocco, Richard Chabrán, and Sonia Saldívar-Hull. Moving to Ann Arbor, Michigan, enhanced my intellectual world by connecting me with Robin D. G. Kelley, Earl Lewis, June Howard, Kristin Hass, and Frances Aparicio. Returning to Los Angeles as a faculty member at the University of Southern California has allowed me to build long-standing scholarly connections to John Carlos Rowe, Natalia Molina, Lanita Jacobs, Francille Wilson, the late María Elena Martínez, Sarah Gualtieri, William Deverell, Philip Ethington, Lon Kurashige, Roberto Lint-Sagarena, Janelle Wong, Josh Kun, and Peter Mancall. I even learned a great deal as an administrator and vice-dean at USC from Lloyd Armstrong, Joseph Aoun, Howard Gillman, Dani Byrd, and Steven Lamy. And I thoroughly enjoyed the administrative work of launching new programs for racial equity and student success with Mary Ho, Katrina "Rissi" Zimmerman, Kimberly Allen, Christina Yokoyama, Felipe Hernández, Dolores Sotelo, Alisa Sánchez, and Disha Mahendro.

During those years, I have been blessed to have taught and mentored several generations of outstanding PhD students and undergraduate scholars, many of whom are now tenured and tenure-track professors with their own careers and published books. Almost all of them have served both formally and informally as research assistants for this book project, and I have gained much insight from their own research and scholarship. I want to thank Ernesto Chávez, Marc Dollinger, Linda Nueva España-Maram, John Nieto-Phillips, Miroslava Chávez-García, Catherine Pet Choy, Jaime Cárdenas, Omar Valerio-Jiménez, M. Lorena Chambers, Nhi Lieu, Anthony Macías, Daryl Maeda, John Mckiernan-González, Adrian Burgos Jr., Anna Pegler Gordon, Thomas Fujita-Rony, Pablo Mitchell, Nancy Mirabel, Anne Choi, Sharon Sekhon, Ana Elizabeth Rosas, Peter La Chapelle, Hillary Jenks, Laura Barraclough, Jerry Gonzalez, Emily Hobson, Gerardo Licón, Gustavo Licón, Rebecca Sheehan,

Perla Guerrero, Daniel HoSang, Christopher Jimenez y West, Michan Connor, Alex Aviña, Phoung Nguyen, Mark Padoongpatt, Abigail Rosas, Monica Pelayo, Julia Ornelas-Higdon, Rosina Lozano, Max Felker-Kantor, Gilbert Estrada, Genevieve Carpio, Ryan Fukumori, David-James Gonzales, Celeste Menchaca, Christian Paiz, Yushi Yamasaki, Jessica Kim, Yuko Konno, Alexandrina Agloro, Jessica Lovaas, Floridalma Boj-Lopez, Nic Ramos, Alfredo Huante, Yu Tokunaga, Roseanne Sia, Eunice Velarde, Charnan Williams, Anneleise Azua, Natalie Santizo, María José Plascencia, Felicitas Reyes, Krystal Cervantes, Michelle Vasquez-Ruiz, Cassandra Flores-Montaño, Laura Dominguez, and Yesenia Navarrete Hunter for their hard work on this project and the intellectual exchange that allowed me to apply new insights to this scholarship.

In my transition from UCLA to Michigan, Natalia Molina kept various intellectual and outreach programs going for me when she was my research assistant at the University of Michigan; now she is my valued colleague at USC. During much of my time as faculty at USC, two graduate students, Margaret Salazar-Porzio and Priscilla Leiva, kept this and several other projects going; without them my own work would have suffered considerably. Kathy Pulupa made sure I did not give up on this project as she blossomed as a scholar as both an undergraduate and a graduate student. Rachel Leah Klein entered my intellectual life as a research assistant when I needed her outstanding writing, editing, and organizational abilities to finish this project; I will always be eternally grateful for her friendship and passion for this book. It took a village for the final push to find photographs for the book through a pandemic and racial crisis, but this search was engineered by Rachel Leah Klein, Kathy Pulupa, Cassandra Flores-Montaño, and Michelle Vasquez Ruiz, with assistance from Margaret Salazar-Porzio, M. Lorena Chambers, and Priscilla Leiva.

This project was enhanced through civic engagement and public history projects throughout my time in Los Angeles, and each project educated me in seeing various viewpoints from present and past residents of Boyle Heights. The Japanese American National Museum began an oral history and exhibition project in the late 1990s that contributed mightily to our knowledge of Boyle Heights, and I am deeply grateful to my work with curators Darcie Iki, Sojin Kim, Claudia Sobral, and Clement Hamani. *Boyle Heights: The Power of Place*, which opened in 2002, became their most visited temporary exhibit to date, and I was blessed with numerous conversations with former residents who became docents for the museum exhibit. From that experience, I was able to connect with Stephen Sass, the director of the Jewish Historical Society of Los Angeles, who welcomed me into their "Breed Street Shul" project in Boyle Heights. I enjoyed working with them on a multiracial "History in a Box" project for elementary schools in the neighborhood, and specifically with Breed Street Shul project coordinator Sherry Marks. PhD students Carlos Parra and Monica Pelayo headed up the USC project, with help from undergraduates María José Plascencia, Felicitas Reyes, Krystal Cervantes, and Joseph Becerra.

My work with the L.A. Plaza de Culturas y Artes has enhanced this project, as I worked with them on revising their general historical exhibition on the Latino history of Los Angeles and creating their new La Plaza Cocina, and temporary exhibits, especially on the Chicano Walkouts of 1968 and the career of Edward Roybal. I want to especially thank CEO John Echeveste and board of directors chair Gloria Molina for their support and encouragement. My work with documentary filmmaker Betsy Kalin on *East LA Interchange* enhanced this project, and I especially appreciate Betsy's willingness to make her interviews available to me for this book. Throughout all my civic engagement work, I have benefited from the wise counsel and feedback from my peers in the organization Imagining America: Artists and Scholars in Public Life. I want to especially thank Timothy Eatman, Julie Ellison, Scott Peters, Jan Cohen-Cruz, David Scobey, Jack Tchen, Adam Bush, Maria Avila, Celestina Castillo, and Erika Kohl-Arenas for the intellectual climate of collaboration they have fostered.

My most important community-based work has come in collaboration with playwright Josefina López and her theater, CASA 0101, in Boyle Heights. Josefina and I began sharing our passion for Boyle Heights by exchanging writing on the neighborhood's history that would eventually be displayed on the theater stage. In 2016, we decided to form the Boyle Heights Museum, which would mount exhibitions on local history for residents, usually in concert with new theater offerings at CASA. I gathered a dedicated team of researchers, interviewers, curators, and educators who assembled four different exhibitions and opened my eyes to what was possible with sustained community engagement. I want to thank team members Michelle Vasquez-Ruiz, Kathy Pulupa, Alejandra Franco, Ivonne Rodriguez, Sami Sanchez, Ana Yaneiry Barrios, Matthew Carrera, Karen Kwon, Jorge Leal, Priscilla Leiva, Janine Vignes, Mary Fernandez, Rosa Noriega-Rocha, Isis Galeno, Eunice Velarde, Yesenia Navarrete Hunter, and Cassandra Flores-Montaño for all their hard work and camaraderie in shaping these meaningful exhibitions.

Neither this book nor the civic engagement work I have been a part of would have been possible without the support of affirmative action programs that gave me the opportunity to attend Harvard and Stanford University for my degrees and opened up employment to me as a professor at UCLA, University of Michigan, and the University of Southern California. I am a proud recipient of that targeted support for racialized scholars in financial need and am fully cognizant of the fact that universities did not open up to racial minority scholars on their own. Indeed, I have been able to keep open the door for future generations through my participation with two programs, the Mellon Mays Undergraduate Fellows Program and the Ford Foundation Fellowships for Diversity, that have continued in this tradition. I want to thank the Andrew W. Mellon Foundation and the Ford Foundation for their ongoing support for scholars and scholarship from underrepresented racial groups in the academy. I also want to thank the National Endowment for the Humanities, the John Randolph and Dora Haynes Foundation, the Rockefeller Foundation, and the UCLA Institute of American Cultures for their fellowship support for this project.

A book like this also requires strong support from a network of archivists and librarians that create and identify resources for scholars like myself to utilize in my research and scholarship. I want to particularly thank the staff at the archives at the Japanese American National Museum, the Jewish Federation of Los Angeles, the Southern California Library for Social Studies and Research, and the Huntington Library for their hospitality. Special Collections archives at UCLA, USC, the University of Michigan, Cal State Los Angeles, and Stanford University provided excellent homes for weeks of research, as did the Urban Archives Center of Cal State Northridge and the Oral History Program at Cal State Fullerton. I especially want to thank Roberto Trujillo of Stanford Library Special Collections, Clement Hamani and Shawn Iwaoka of the Japanese American National Museum, Ralph Drew of the *Los Angeles Times,* Annalise Welte of the Getty Research Institute, David Sigler of the Oviatt Library at California State University at Northridge, Claude Zachary of USC Libraries, Yurly Shcherbina of the USC Digital Library, Paul Spitzzeri of the Workman Homestead Museum, Molly Haigh at the UCLA Charles Young Research Library, and Xaviera S. Flores of the UCLA Chicano Studies Library for going above and beyond to help me track down images during the 2020 pandemic lockdown of archives and libraries.

I got the opportunity to present versions of this work in a variety of venues, receiving excellent feedback that was incorporated into the final product. I want to thank the Pacific Coast Branch of the American Historical Association, the California American Studies Association, the Latina/o Studies Association, the Organization of American Historians, the Association of Asian American Studies, the American Studies Association, the Western History Association, and the Oral History Association for providing scholarly opportunities for exchange of my ideas about Boyle Heights. Audiences at La Plaza de Cultura y Artes (Los Angeles), Ithaca College, the University of Vermont, the Japanese American National Museum, the University of Michigan, California State University at Northridge, Meiji University (Tokyo), Huntington Library, the Mellon Mays program in Cape Town, South Africa, the University of Texas San Antonio, UC Irvine, the University of Pennsylvania, the University of Houston, Middlebury College, the University of Iowa, Cal State Los Angeles, Occidental College, UCLA, the University of Notre Dame, Cornell University, Hawaii Pacific University, Autry Museum of the American West, UC San Diego, Columbia University, Duke University, Cal State Long Beach, and the Massachusetts Historical Society all provided excellent feedback on this work as I was developing it for publication.

Some scholars took the time to read draft chapters or the whole manuscript, and I found their input on my work to be invaluable. Over the years, Margaret Salazar-Porzio, M. Lorena Chambers, Kathy Pulupa, Lon Kurashige, Alisa Sánchez, Natalia Molina, and George Lipsitz read the manuscript and offered important comments and suggestions. Matt Jacobson and Josh Kun read the penultimate manuscript for the University of California Press and suggested important revisions. Bill Nelson provided his cartography skills to producing wonderful maps for the book. Lisa Colleen Moore of Glen Hollow, Ink was an amazing editor who helped me get the book in shape for publication. Rachel Leah Klein read the manuscript multiple times as an editor, a colleague, and the cheerleader I needed to complete this process. I want to thank Niels Hooper, my editor in the American Crossroads series from the University of California Press, and Robin Manley, editorial assistant, for their patience and support in bringing the book manuscript to fruition.

Finally, I want to thank the people of Boyle Heights, both current and past, for their resiliency and their inspiration as I worked on this project. Some are well-known political figures, like the late Edward Roybal, the first Mexican American elected to the city council in the twentieth century; Gloria Molina, the first Mexican American woman elected to the L.A. County Board of Supervisors, and Antonio Villaraigosa, the first Mexican

American mayor of Los Angeles since the nineteenth century. But most are little known, yet critical to this history of Boyle Heights. Some I encountered through other people's interviews: Emilia Castañeda, for example, who was banished from the United States as a child through the Mexican repatriation movement, and Ida Fiering, a Jewish leftist mother that one of my students interviewed to understand the forces that pushed Jews to leave Boyle Heights after World War II. Still others I got to know through my work with the Japanese American National Museum, among them Claire Orlosoroff, who witnessed the removal of her Japanese American classmates into internment camps; the incomparable Leo Frumkin, whose journey as a leftist organizer in Boyle Heights resonated across generations; and the late Mollie Wilson, who inspired the whole book with her personal protest against Japanese American internment through her letter-writing campaign as a high school student. And I was truly inspired by getting to interview Paula Crisostomo and Vickie Castro for this book, for these two critical Chicana activists took leading roles in the 1968 Chicano Walkouts of East L.A. schools, and their entire lives were dedicated to educational equity for the Mexican American population.

These are the lives that frame this book, and to whom this book is dedicated. But current residents of Boyle Heights continue to make history as they live their lives and stand up for their community in small and big ways in our present moment. They have influenced me, and I hope their stories will inspire you to live a life fighting for social justice and an equitable society that we can be proud of.

ONE

Introduction

A MULTIRACIAL MAP FOR AMERICA

IN 2002, THE JAPANESE AMERICAN National Museum hosted an exhibit called *Boyle Heights: The Power of Place*, which told the story of a multiracial Boyle Heights, today a mostly Latino neighborhood on the Eastside of Los Angeles. I was drawn to participating in the creation of this museum exhibition project in the aftermath of the 1992 Los Angeles Riots, when the rest of Los Angeles erupted in the wake of the Rodney King beating and the acquittal of four police officers. At the time it seemed as if many social commentators thought that the sheer existence of racial diversity in South Los Angeles and other communities in L.A. inevitably led to social conflict.[1] This only further reinforced the common perception that L.A.'s history is entirely one of intense segregation with distinct ghettoes, barrios, and lily-white suburbs, despite the many instances of working-class and middle-class neighborhoods where ethnic and racial groups were brought together. Thus I became interested in finding one particular area in Los Angeles where I could trace the changing levels of interaction—both positive and negative—over time among multiracial residents and could unearth what historical factors played into these relationships. My experiences as a Los Angeles native after the 1992 Los Angeles Riots, as well as my path as a historical researcher concerned with racial politics, brought me to Boyle Heights as a way to understand Los Angeles and the roots of its urban diversity.

Luckily for me, various organizations in Los Angeles had the same motivation at about the same time, and I ended up doing research for the *Power of Place* exhibition on the Boyle Heights neighborhood with a collective of four organizations. The lead organization was the Japanese American National Museum, where the exhibition opened ten years after the L.A. Riots. Other members of the collective were the Jewish Historical Society of

FIGURE 1. Mollie Wilson and Mary Murakami in front of Boyle Heights house. Japanese American National Museum (Gift of Mollie Wilson Murphy, 2000.378.2).

Southern California, Self-Help Graphics (a Chicano arts collective), and the International Institute, a social service organization that has served Boyle Heights for over 100 years. The organizing collective also held a variety of community forums, which brought together different generations of Boyle Heights residents that had rarely met before: today's largely recent Latino immigrants and an older group of white, Jewish, African American, Asian American, and Latino citizens who had first entered Boyle Heights in the mid-twentieth century but who no longer lived in the community.

In anticipation of one of these forums, Mollie Wilson Murphy looked into the back corner of her closet where she stored letters that she had held onto "for too long," as she later told us in one of the interviews conducted for the museum.[2] In this back corner she had safeguarded her correspondence with friends to whom she had written every day once they were taken away from Boyle Heights to internment camps during World War II. What she had carefully protected

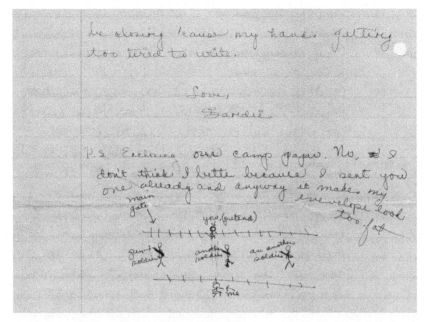

FIGURE 2. Letter to Mollie Wilson, sent by Sandie Saito (June 3, 1942) from the Santa Anita Assembly Center in Arcadia, California. Japanese American National Museum (Gift of Mollie Wilson Murphy, 2000.378.3A).

over the decades since were the return letters from five of her closest Japanese American friends. But the announcement of a community forum to be held at the International Institute in Boyle Heights prompted Mollie to finally dig out the letters and place them in two plastic grocery sacks to be donated to the Japanese American National Museum after more than a half century of conservation. Mollie Wilson Murphy represented the comparatively small African American community of Boyle Heights, but the letters she carried spoke to the power of multiracial interaction that this book hopes to capture.

These letters told us stories of young teenage friends from Roosevelt High School who came from different backgrounds but who sustained their friendships through consistent communication, despite the space that our government placed between them. In one letter, Sandie Saito (now Okada) told her friend Mollie what she could expect if she came to visit the Santa Anita Racetrack, where Japanese Americans from Boyle Heights were taken in 1942 before being sent to more permanent internment camps. She concluded the letter with a drawing that showed two young girls, separated by a barbed-wire fence, patrolled by soldiers with rifles.[3]

Despite the distance and confinement, Mollie never forgot her friends throughout this period. Indeed, when Japanese Americans were allowed back on the West Coast and Sandie enrolled at UCLA in 1946, she stayed with Mollie in Boyle Heights for a couple of months until she could get settled into a place of her own.[4] Fifty-five years later, Mrs. Wilson Murphy finally encountered a historical project that would tell this story to a wider public, and we would be entrusted with these precious memories. This simple but profound act of friendship, during one of the most hostile of periods, gave me hope regarding the possibilities of enduring relationships across cultures in times of war, as well as the importance of collaborative public history.

But Mollie's story raised larger questions: Why was she so adamant about maintaining these friendships via mail, writing consistently to her friends for three years, when so many others seemed to forget their neighbors amid wartime hysteria? Was there something unique to the way people grew up in Boyle Heights that created this powerful cross-racial friendship? Such stories plugged us into networks of friends from each Boyle Heights generation, many of whom stayed in extremely close contact with each other, sometimes for decades after they had physically moved away. This research also made me wonder about the similarities and differences between the almost completely Latino population that currently lives in Boyle Heights and the more multiracial community that made up Boyle Heights in the mid-twentieth century. In this way, this book addresses how this community came to be a thriving multiracial neighborhood, what challenges it faced in maintaining a sense of community over time, and how the legacy of this progressive multiracialism continued to exert a powerful influence over residents when the neighborhood became overwhelmingly Latino in the last third of the twentieth century.

But I also had personal motivations to conduct research on Boyle Heights. My own immigrant parents, Jorge R. Sánchez and Ninfa Troncoso Sánchez, had chosen to first settle in Boyle Heights when they arrived from Mexico in the late 1950s. After a brief stay with relatives in East Los Angeles, they rented a house, painted yellow with white trim, on City View Avenue, a typical Boyle Heights street with small stucco bungalows nestled next to each other on tree-lined lots. My parents found Boyle Heights inviting, familiar, and affordable. Interestingly, their arrival there occurred at just the time that Boyle Heights was making the transition from a multiracial polyglot neighborhood to one dominated by Latinos, particularly newcomers from Mexico. I believe that my parents rented a house from a Jewish family that had—like many of Boyle Heights' Jewish families in the fifties—recently moved out of the neighborhood. In fact, this couple gave my financially struggling parents their first dining room set, a white formica table with four chairs. It was on that table that I would learn to read and write, and it stayed with us for my entire childhood. Moreover, I was born just a few blocks from the family home, in 1959, at White Memorial Hospital in Boyle Heights, and my brother would arrive there a few years later. So the history of Boyle Heights and its political identity is a very personal story for me.

Yet even while growing up in this neighborhood in transition I knew little about Boyle Heights except that it was part of East Los Angeles and was a seemingly homogeneous Mexican American barrio. I was unaware of its rich history in Southern California and the larger transformation of the region's neighborhoods into more isolated barrios and ghettoes, separated from over-whelmingly white suburbs. Even though we moved from Boyle Heights to South Los Angeles before I entered school, and I would spend the next part of my childhood in a predominantly African American neighborhood, I grew up seeing segregation as normal, and living among people from all racial, ethnic, and national backgrounds as rather anomalous. However, as this book on the interracial history of Boyle Heights makes clear, I am interested in telling a different story, one of solidarity that helps inform the possibilities of a progressive, democratic culture in a city that tends to forget or erase this tradition.

MULTIRACIAL HISTORIOGRAPHY, SEGREGATED GEOGRAPHIES, AND RACIAL FORMATION

Having been trained as a twentieth-century American historian whose research focuses on immigration and race in urban areas, I consider the histories of communities like Boyle Heights as highly important. Since the 1960s, urban history has largely characterized inner-city areas as ghettoes and barrios, racially isolated from the rest of the urban landscape.[5] The history of Boyle Heights, however, indicates that alongside communities set apart by rigid racial separation were racially mixed neighborhoods that produced and sustained extensive interaction across racial and ethnic groups. Indeed, it was often in these interracial neighborhoods that newcomers learned the meaning of American identity, through their interaction with others from different backgrounds.

When I explored why the ghetto or barrio had become the standard depiction of urban inner-city space, I landed on the concept of "ethnic succession." This narrative to describe movement in urban neighborhoods was first developed by a group of sociologists, led by Robert Park and Ernest Burgess at the University of Chicago, who began to understand the growth and development of ethnic neighborhoods by looking at Chicago's immigrant communities of the early twentieth century.[6] They posited that immigrants were first attracted to concentrated settlements of their own kind in center cities where they were close to both working-class sites of employment and entrepreneurs from their own immigrant backgrounds who could cater to their consumptive and affective desires. The theory goes that their economic competition with other urban dwellers inevitably led to group conflict but would eventually dissipate as groups came to a gradual accommodation. Over time, they argued, well-established immigrants and subsequent generations in these families would leave the ethnic enclave for more suburban locations as they moved up the economic ladder to better-paying, more stable occupations. As they accelerated economically, they left their ethnic traditions behind and assimilated into American culture. This series of progressive stages of interaction—competition, conflict, accommodation, and assimilation—was in theory the same whether it involved immigrants or racial minorities, even though Park and his colleagues made some limited efforts to understand the prejudices that sustained the "Negro Problem" and the "Oriental Problem" over time.[7]

The power of this narrative of ethnic mobility and gradual economic and cultural assimilation, most starkly recognized in geographic terms, has become—through imitation, scholarly reproduction, and popularization—an enduring way to understand the path of virtually all immigrant groups, if not all nonwhite racial groups, in American society in the twentieth and twenty-first centuries. Its fortification in historiography has been a way for the largely liberal academic community to soothe the anti-immigrant sentiments of the greater public, if not the opportunistic politicians and policy makers, who often condemn the latest wave of poor, recent immigrants "yearning to breathe free."[8]

The inadequacy of that narrative is evident in the history of Boyle Heights, a community that was home to different populations of immigrant, ethnic, and racial minorities over the entire course of the twentieth century. Indeed, the group whose population would be concentrated in "minority ghettoes" in the post-1960 period—Latinos, largely from Mexico—was present in significant numbers earlier in the twentieth century as well. Therefore, rather than being an exemplar of ethnic succession, Boyle Heights was a multiracial community made up of Mexicans, Jews, Japanese, African Americans, Armenians, Italians, and scattered native whites for most of its history, well into the 1950s, only gradually becoming an almost all-Latino neighborhood in the last fifty years. At the height of Boyle Heights' multiracial history, in 1940, for example, the Jewish population totaled about 35,000, the Mexican population about 15,000, and the Japanese population approximately 5,000.

This reality tracks with much of the newer historical and sociological literature—which increasingly finds that although concentration and spatial clustering are critical to defining ethnic neighborhoods, communities described as "enclaves" or "immigrant ghettoes" are often made up of less than half, if that, of the specific ethnic group that has been said to define the space. Thomas Philpott's 1978 study *The Slum and the Ghetto* showed that the classic immigrant neighborhoods studied by Park and Burgess in Chicago in 1930 fit this characterization: the Swedish ghetto was only 24 percent Swedish; the German ghetto was only 32 percent German; Little Italy was less than 50 percent Italian, even though Italians were the "most segregated" white ethnic group.[9] In the late twentieth-century period, sociologist Min Zhou's *Chinatown* revealed that the core Chinese immigrant area of Flushing in New York City was only 14 percent Chinese, and John Horton's research on the Chinese in Monterey Park near Los Angeles found the suburb to be no more than 25 percent Chinese in the mid-1980s. In their own study of residential patterns of 15 groups in New York and Los Angeles in 1990, John Logan, Richard Alba, and Wenquan Zhang amended popular assumptions about spaces and set a minimum threshold of 15 percent to define "ethnic neighborhoods."[10]

Yet even in racially mixed areas like Boyle Heights, my research indicates that specific racial groups actually lived quite isolated from each other. A block-by-block analysis of a household survey conducted by the Works Progress Administration in 1939, for example, indicates that relatively few streets in the neighborhood were not dominated by one group or another. In fact, throughout Boyle Heights in the late 1930s, most residents lived on blocks in which over 80 percent of the residents were of the same racial group. Moreover, that Boyle Heights was a multiracial community did not mean it was immune from racism. Areas of Boyle Heights showed significant disparities in rents, housing conditions, and home ownership rates that were largely based on race. And although Boyle Heights was a solidly working-class area, the reach of poverty in the community was similarly dependent on one's race.

While ethnic groups mostly resided on separate blocks, they still had substantial interaction with each other in neighborhood institutions, businesses, schools, and playgrounds. But for too long, the actual social dynamics between groups living together in working-class communities have been less studied than the processes by which ethnic minorities leave these communities and "assimilate" into a wider, supposedly nonethnic, suburb.[11] Fortunately, new literature on racial formation has taken an alternative route, to explore this interface between different racial groups living in close proximity to each other.[12] Understanding race as a fluid but quite salient category, these studies have consistently shown that racialization is a historically grounded process in which groups form their own racial identities in relation to their neighbors. Along these lines, the various ways race and urban space have been made and remade in Southern California over the course of the twentieth and twenty-first centuries inform this book on Boyle Heights and contribute to this growing literature on racial formation, especially concerning the racial positioning of ethnic Mexicans and Mexican immigrants in US history.

STRUCTURING INEQUALITIES IN LOS ANGELES: URBAN APARTHEID AND FORCED REMOVALS

Since the 1990s, I have worked with the Jewish Historical Society of Southern California, partly to make sure that the Boyle Heights of the past is remembered, not simply as the old Jewish community that has since been revitalized as a Mexican neighborhood, but as a truly and long-standing interracial space. Nonetheless, while the multiracial lore of Boyle Heights is strong in some circles, residents of contemporary Boyle Heights sometimes forget that the reason an interracial community was able to thrive on the Eastside was that racism kept many of its residents out of most of the other neighborhoods that were growing in Los Angeles during the early twentieth century. Indeed, the multiracial Boyle Heights now remembered was a direct result of racially restrictive covenants that governed who could and could not buy a home in a particular neighborhood throughout the late nineteenth and early twentieth centuries. In Los Angeles, the general rules of segregation that governed most districts—what I call urban apartheid—enabled just a few areas to be racially mixed, including Boyle Heights.

Though the myth of ethnic succession looms large in US urban history, conveniently absolving responsibility for the segregated past in the United States, the terms of what George Lipsitz has called "the possessive investment in whiteness" were fundamentally altered in a twenty-year period from approximately 1935 to 1955. As Lipsitz makes clear, it was government policies, not simply the unfettered choices made by individual ethnic groups yearning to be "white," that were critical to racial formation in this period.[13] In my earlier work, I look at how Mexican immigrants and their children adapted to American life in ways that closely mirrored those of European immigrants in other settings.[14] In this book I hope to show how those options were systematically cut off from the growing Mexican American population and new immigrants from Mexico in the World War II and postwar periods.

In Los Angeles, urban apartheid was sustained via a private-public partnership between government officials and private industry, particularly the real estate lobby, a system that was certainly different but not separate from the Jim Crow system that produced intense segregation in the American South. As sociologists Douglas Massey and Nancy Denton put it in their classic work on the effect of segregation in American life, "Although America's apartheid may not be rooted in the legal strictures of its South African relative, it is no less effective in perpetuating racial inequality, and whites are no less culpable for the socioeconomic deprivation that results."[15]

Since the early twentieth century, local government officials had attempted to keep two discrete migrant streams—one for midwestern "folks" and another for arrivals who were distinctively nonwhite—carefully separated from one another in Los Angeles through an intricate web of residential segregation, which placed American-born Anglo newcomers on the Westside of the city while foreign-born and nonwhite residents found themselves largely confined to the Eastside and the Southside. As Lipsitz has argued, "People of different races do not inhabit different places by choice," meaning segregation is not inevitable but created and reproduced by state powers.[16]

The Eastside and Southside of Los Angeles were allowed to develop industrial sites, and immigrants and racialized newcomers flocked there, seeking residence near work opportunities. It was not until the late New Deal period that the government took notice of the particular racial makeup of these neighborhoods, instituting redlining in nonwhite and mixed communities through the Federal Housing lending program, which found these areas too "at risk" to qualify for mortgages. This meant that as the African American community swelled with migration to the city from the South for defense-related jobs and for refuge from racial violence, they could not get loans for homes in the only neighborhoods where they were allowed to live. On the Eastside, government policy actively worked to separate populations that had grown close to each other and eventually created social conditions that defined the Eastside, including Boyle Heights, as nonwhite territory.[17]

Most collective histories and individual stories about the reshaping of interracial districts like Boyle Heights in the post–World War II era describe tales of decision-making by white ethnics, like Jewish or Italian city dwellers, who would eventually move out of crumbling inner cities to newly accessible suburbs. This story of "white flight" fits narratives of upward mobility and advancement while allowing the contemporary spatial configuration of urban spaces to produce a certain amount of individualized white guilt, conveniently taking public policy and political officials off the hook. In other words, the narrative assumes US policy makers to be neutral or generic on the issue of racial separation. My research into the impact of the 1937 Housing Act makes clear that the government played a critical role in undermining the interracial community of Boyle Heights in the post–World War II era.

The result of this policy would be the widespread exodus of Jews from the Eastside and the shift of Jewish Los Angeles into a largely middle-class enclave, this time west of downtown. Previous work concerning the relationship of Jews to whiteness, even research on California communities, does not adequately address how whiteness came to be expressed in geographic terms, literally moving the center of the Jewish community from one side of the city to the other.[18] Moreover, this movement was not uncontested within the Jewish community, as some literally fought to maintain a Jewish presence in Boyle Heights and an immediate relationship with the nonwhite communities there.[19]

Put plainly, the history of Boyle Heights shows that a flourishing interracial community in the midst of a government committed to racial separation and white supremacy is deeply threatening and risks demolition from officials committed to a policy of urban apartheid. The issue of forced removal is therefore critical. Once I began to analyze these policies, the tangled history of forced removals in Boyle Heights became clear. Usually discussed separately by academic scholars, the "repatriation" of Mexican Americans in the 1930s, the internment of Japanese Americans during World War II, and the forced removal of urban residents to make way for public housing and extensive freeway construction all occurred within similar racially mixed neighborhoods. I argue that a certain ideology that linked racial depravity to urban space developed among city leaders and urban planners on both the conservative and the liberal sides of the political spectrum. This ideology associated particular neighborhoods like Boyle Heights with slum conditions and urban decay, and it prompted local officials to consider residents of these neighborhoods as utterly (re)movable in order to make way for their plans to improve social conditions and achieve urban progress. My argument is that historians of race in urban America should view these key events of the Depression and World War II periods as intimately linked in ideology and practice, even though they principally affected different racial groups who were often living next door to each other.[20]

These postwar developments rapidly transformed the community's demographics. By 1952, the Mexican American population of Boyle Heights had grown to over 40,000, forming close to half the population, while the Jewish population had shrunk to 14,000. The Japanese population remained steady at about 6,500 but showed no propensity toward growth. Increasingly, the non-Mexican population consisted of older persons with few children, while migration of young Mexican and Mexican American families into Boyle Heights dramatically increased, as Boyle Heights increasingly became a less desirable place to live, because of the government's actions.

ACTIVISM AND TENSION: CLASSIC BARRIOS, "*GENTE*-FICATION," AND THE FUTURE OF BOYLE HEIGHTS

When my parents moved into Boyle Heights in 1958, the neighborhood was well on its way to becoming a classic "barrio," with a population of poorer Chicano residents physically separated by freeways and a river, and subjected to racial housing restrictions and economic discrimination. The population of mostly Latino immigrants and their descendants very quickly became stratified and differentiated. As a neighborhood that welcomed newcomers, the residents included second- and third-generation Mexican Americans, recent immigrants from Mexico and Latin America in various legal statuses, and the remnants of other racial and ethnic populations that had long lived in Boyle Heights.

Yet exploring only the racist policies obscures the radical politics that was long a part of the Boyle Heights multiracial ethos. Indeed, during the 1950s

Boyle Heights was described as a "laboratory of democracy," a role that fit with its earlier progressive history of interracial labor unions, from the garment workers' union to the carpenters' union. The ability to live peacefully amid diversity while maintaining one's own ethnic and religious traditions was a vibrant memory for those who grew up in Boyle Heights, even as their metropolitan surroundings became more exclusive and discriminatory. These experiences and their related remembrances contradicted the main tenets of white supremacy, as well as the logic of ethnic succession: that a working multiracial neighborhood was an impossibility because of deep ethnic and racial hatreds, as well as the economic and social competition for resources embedded in the poverty of these communities. Instead, residents remembered neighbors helping neighbors and finding ways to communicate and organize across national and linguistic differences. Their experiences pointed toward an alternative way of living together, as they refused to fall in line with the highly segregated nature of society enacted by white supremacists and elites that governed the whole region. In this way, community memories and practices challenged the very assumptions underpinning the ideology of white supremacy.

The rise in numbers of undocumented immigrants from Mexico and Central America, who found the low-income housing and closeness to city center jobs in Boyle Heights attractive, was accelerated in 1964 by the end of the Bracero Program, a series of bilateral agreements with Mexico, initiated as the Mexican Farm Labor Agreement in 1942, that brought to the US over 4.5 million seasonal farm workers to fill in for World War II labor shortages. These *braceros* often developed strong ties to locations in the US, and their families and villages in Mexico often developed a critical dependency on the income that these laboring periods provided. The passage of the Immigration and Nationality Act of 1965 imposed for the first time a severe limit on the number of legal immigrants from Mexico and other Latin American countries. But the result was an exponential increase in undocumented immigrants, since migration patterns for seasonal work were now already established and the demand for cheap unskilled labor in other industries had also increased.

As the city of Los Angeles disinvested in the public housing complexes that now encircled Boyle Heights, more poor African American families from the South joined poor Mexican families, first from the Bracero Program, then directly from Mexico as undocumented immigrants, in those housing units as the last resort for shelter in the city. The history of labor and activism from the Latino families of the neighborhood, the growing local and national African American civil rights movement, and the similar economic conditions among Latino and African American families in the public housing complexes in Boyle Heights created opportunities for collaboration and competition between the two communities. These political forces, and the explosion of the Watts Riots in Los Angeles in 1965, fortified a solidarity among young people of color, which eventually led to a student walkout from local high schools in 1968 to protest discriminatory conditions in urban education in Boyle Heights and the surrounding East Los Angeles area.

Though Boyle Heights was over 90 percent Latino in 1970, differing legal statuses produced new tensions among residents. This occurred amid the backdrop of an increase in crime and gangs, cultivated by poverty-stricken environments, that led to local efforts to turn the tide toward positive community building, as in the creation of Homeboy Industries and Mothers of East Los Angeles. In the end, the long-standing history of community involvement and solidarity was able to unify the Boyle Heights neighborhood by the end of the twentieth century.

The history of Boyle Heights tells an important story about a neighborhood that was strong *because* of its diversity, and about the absorption of a constant stream of newcomers into the life of the city in ways that were both accommodating and complicated. It is clear that the residents of the neighborhood developed a unique identity that set them apart from the rest of the city, even while intense racialization was occurring among the various groups that made up the local population. Migrants to the United States learned in Boyle Heights what it meant to be American, as newcomers to Los Angeles learned what it meant to be Angelino. Even as the neighborhood changed dramatically over time because of larger racial and economic forces that fostered concentrated poverty and other unstable life conditions, a communal and progressive spirit prevailed in Boyle Heights that continued to define the promise of the American dream for all who lived there.

ORGANIZATION OF THE BOOK

This book is organized chronologically, with each chapter focusing on the interaction between different groups that made up the Boyle Heights population. Chapter 2 covers the longest period of the book, from the start of European conquest of Southern California in the eighteenth century to the end of the nineteenth century, when widespread urban settlement was about to begin. In general, the chapter charts the failure to turn Boyle Heights into an exclusive outpost for the white elite. Chapter 3 describes the development of Los Angeles as racially exclusive residential communities at the end of the nineteenth century and in the early twentieth century. Across the globe, however, the dramatic transformation of rural economies in the late nineteenth century propelled many worker activists toward communities similar to Boyle Heights in California. Many of these migrants came from societies embedded in revolutionary movements and brought with them ideologies of socialism, communism, or communitarianism and vast histories of organizing. While recruiting workers from abroad was critical to building a low-wage labor force for industrial production—and working-class individuals from Japan, Mexico, and Italy needed wage labor to survive—it was also dangerous because of the potential for organized resistance. By World War I Boyle Heights had become home to ethnic and racial working-class newcomers to the city, drawn to the neighborhood because of its relative racial openness, alongside economic opportunities in industrial Los Angeles.

The middle chapters of the book discuss the profound changes to the lives of Boyle Heights residents brought about by the economic and social convulsions and demographic transformations of the middle twentieth century, especially the Great Depression of the 1930s and the wartime society of World War II and its aftermath. Chapter 4 connects three attempts over a twelve-year period to remove from Boyle Heights populations that were seen by city leaders as "disposable": the "repatriation" of Mexican immigrants brought about by the pressures of the Great Depression, the internment of Japanese Americans at the start of World War II, and the pushing out of neighborhood residents by urban renewal and the placement of public housing units in Boyle Heights.

The book's fifth chapter then explores how an emerging working-class identity was reshaped by the upheaval of World War II, especially among non-Japanese members of the Boyle Heights community who witnessed Japanese American removal and incarceration and believed it to be unjust. As soon as Japanese Americans were forcibly disappeared from the region, the larger city of Los Angeles shifted to scapegoating young Mexican American youth as a societal threat. Chapter 6 focuses on the exodus of Jews from Boyle Heights during the war and especially in its aftermath, when other Southern California neighborhoods on the Westside, in the San Fernando Valley, and in eastern Los Angeles County opened up to them for the first time. This

process was fostered by the inclusion of Jews into whiteness, both ideologi-
cally and geographically, in the Southern California basin, while Jews that
remained in Boyle Heights simultaneously became only more politically leftist, committed to a multicultural radicalism.

Chapters 7 and 8 present the varied political responses from inside Boyle
Heights in the 1950s and 1960s. While chapter 7 explores the critical role of
city councilman Edward Roybal in bringing political representation to the
neighborhood in the post–World War II era, chapter 8 explores the struggle
for educational equity that brought about the student-led East L.A. Walkouts
of 1968. The ninth chapter of the book focuses on one critical aspect of diversity in the Boyle Heights neighborhood that has typically been neglected
once a majority-Latino population dominates the area: diversity of legal status and the particular place of the undocumented in the politics of Boyle
Heights. Just as high school students were leading walkouts in 1968, the
population of the Eastside was in the midst of tremendous transformation
as the urban economy lost skilled, unionized industrial jobs and replaced
them with low-wage service employment. In the 1970s undocumented
immigrants from Mexico and other parts of Latin America rushed in to take
these jobs and encountered widespread discrimination and anti-immigrant
sentiments.

The tenth and final chapter of this book explores the changing meaning
of community in twenty-first-century Boyle Heights. As Boyle Heights has
remained a hub for a low-income Latino population, both US and foreign
born, the generation that moved out of the neighborhood in earlier periods
has increasingly looked fondly to the community as a place where a diverse
population coexisted, unlike so many other locations in contemporary
Southern California. This chapter also explores the gentrification fears and
threats that have dominated recent politics in Boyle Heights, driven by the
history of urban renewal in the area, ever-rising rents and housing costs, and
the incursion into Boyle Heights of businesses from outside the neighborhood, such as art galleries and coffeehouses. The radical political tradition in
Boyle Heights, however, has also spawned new organizations, which have
fought gentrification efforts quite effectively, if still controversially. Much of
the neighborhood change has been driven less by white interlopers than by
higher-income college graduates from the Latino community returning to
East L.A., who still play a role in displacing lower-income residents.

What comes next for Boyle Heights will be contested, as community
members and activists fight for the neighborhood to remain open both to

low-income, immigrant newcomers, and to higher-income Latino college graduates, pushing local politicians and policy makers, urban planners and developers, to make inclusive decisions about the neighborhood's future. Fortunately, community organizations have a powerful historical record to build from as they decide how to move forward together and preserve what has made the neighborhood so unique over time.

TWO

Making Los Angeles

DURING THE SUMMER OF 2005, work crews digging a tunnel for an eastern extension of the Gold Line railway surprisingly uncovered the skeletal remains of 108 people, as well as 43 arms and legs, underneath First Street in Boyle Heights. Despite carefully avoiding the graves of Evergreen Cemetery, these workers had uncovered the unprotected vestiges of Los Angeles' original cemetery for the poor. Carbon-dating by archaeologists indicated that most of the remains dated back to at least the 1890s, and forensic analysis showed that most were Chinese laborers, who were ignored at that time by city officials. This evidence pointed to the fact that other city projects in the area throughout the twentieth century had probably also run across some portion of the remains and disregarded the find. While Metropolitan Transit Authority officials pondered how to properly re-inter the more-than-a-century-old bodies, Boyle Heights residents chalked up the mystery to a long-standing disrespect of their neighborhood by local officials, which spanned back to the nineteenth century. Months after the opening of the Gold Line extension, all the bones and artifacts found in 174 burial sites were re-interred in Evergreen Cemetery with the help of the Chinese Historical Society of Southern California, along with the dedication of a memorial wall and meditation garden in 2010.[1]

The burials and cemetery plots would remind residents of another era, when city leaders had associations with the Boyle Heights community, but only in death. As a section of Los Angeles set apart from the rest of the city because it was on the other side of an unruly river, Boyle Heights was often an afterthought to city leaders. Throughout the Spanish and Mexican periods, it was ignored as an area hard to get to and difficult to irrigate for agricultural purposes. In the period after the Mexican-American War, it would appeal only to speculators like Andrew Boyle who bet that they could buy land cheaply and get the growing city to eventually invest in irrigation and transportation networks that would open up the Eastside to development. Even with the building of bridges over the river, however, Boyle Heights would continue to lag behind the rest of Los Angeles. Racially restrictive covenants made other parts of Southern California more desirable for white newcomers to the region, and Boyle Heights came to symbolize a neighborhood that was compatible with immigrant newcomers and racial migrants attracted by a growing industrial base of jobs. And its location across the river meant that it could also be regularly forgotten by city officials eager to court white settlers into a new modern Los Angeles but still needing a place to bury those who had passed.

ORIGINS AND BOUNDARIES

The most defining landmark in Boyle Heights is the Los Angeles River, which emerges from underneath the Southern California basin, heads due east just north of the Santa Monica Mountains, and then turns abruptly south as it curls around the end of the mountain range. It is this river that divides Los Angeles into east and west. Yet from the earliest times, human beings depended on this river for survival. The Tongva-Gabrielino Indian village of Yang-na was set up along the river—near the current intersection of Alameda and Commercial Streets in downtown Los Angeles—to provide irrigation for rudimentary farming. When Spanish settlers first entered the region in 1781, they too followed those patterns, establishing El Pueblo de Nuestra Señora la Reina de Los Ángeles close enough to the river "to tap its waters yet high enough above it for protection against winter floods."[2] The 44 village settlers from northwestern Mexico formally settled the new *pueblo*—the Spanish word for "town" or "village"—on September 4, 1781. While only two claimed to be Spaniards, at least 26 *pobladores* (settlers) noted some African bloodlines, while the rest were either pure Indians or *mestizos* of various combinations. Each family had come to this northern outpost because of land they had been promised—seven acres of farmland and a 50-by-100-foot lot facing the planned Plaza—and the 36 square miles that encompassed the pueblo became the boundaries of the city when California was accepted into the Union in 1850. The unpredictable nature of the Los Angeles River would limit the growth of Los Angeles, and the development of the area that would be later known as Boyle Heights, until the late nineteenth century.[3]

From the start, the division between the west and the east sides of the river was substantial and reflected "markers of race-ethnicity, class, status, and prospect."[4] Indeed, the original Spanish settlers would move the Indian village to the east across the river to a new *ranchería,* indicating a settlement that they wanted to mark apart from themselves by both distance and hierarchy.[5] To make their new settlement self-sufficient, the early settlers of the pueblo built a communal water ditch, called the Zanja Madre (Mother Ditch), which would, in turn, provide water to the flatlands west of the river. No attempt would be made until 1855 to build an offshoot of the water ditch to offer irrigation east of the river, where the land abruptly jutted upward to the hanging white cliffs of El Paredón Blanco (White Bluffs). El Paredón Blanco was used primarily as communally owned pastureland for cattle because of the lack of an adequate water supply reaching the top. Taking care of cattle was mostly assigned to Indians who worked for (or were enslaved by) the pueblo. The Eastside, therefore, was a land inside the jurisdiction but set apart socially and economically from the emerging pueblo of Los Angeles.

BATTLING FOR LAND AND POWER

With a pattern of settlement and land ownership in place, other, less adventurous migrants came to try their luck in the frontier village. Twenty more families came to build new lives within the first ten years of settlement, including some of the most prominent names in Los Angeles history, such as Pico, Sepulveda, Figueroa, and Soto. By the turn of the century in 1800, the population had swelled to 315, with at least 30 adobe houses providing comfort to 70 families. Most of these homes were one-story, single-room houses, windowless with dirt floors, clustered around the Plaza. The town center, however, now contained a town hall, a guardhouse, army barracks, and granaries. Key to population growth and stability in the pueblo was the decision to grant grazing rights to retiring soldiers who had served in the presidios of California. Later these rights would be transformed into ownership of the lands and would become the basis for California ranchos of the nineteenth century.

Don Antonio Maria Lugo, who was at the founding of the pueblo attached to the presidio of Santa Barbara, and who would eventually serve as *alcalde,* or mayor, of Los Angeles from 1816 to 1819, was granted an area in 1810 that stretched between the Los Angeles and San Gabriel Rivers. In 1896, the reporter and historian H. D. Barrows described Lugo's importance in the area: "The flocks and herds of the venerable Don and of his sons, like those of the patriarchs of Scripture, ranged over 'a thousand hills'; and probably their owners did not know themselves, how many cattle they had. Don Antonio named over to me, all the governors of California, down to the coming of 'Los Americanos,' nearly every one of whom except of course, the first three, he knew personally."[6] Lugo's grazing area would become known as Rancho San Antonio and would encompass the southern boundary of the pueblo lands of Boyle Heights, now mostly within the city of Vernon. Coupled with the lands set aside for the San Gabriel Mission, which butted up against the eastern boundary of the pueblo lands, these two ranchlands encircled the mesa of Boyle Heights.[7]

The stability of this arrangement, especially for the Tongva-Gabrielino Indians, who did almost all the work on both the mission and rancho lands, would be upended by the Mexican War of Independence, although the lives of Californios (residents descended from Spanish settlers) were scarcely touched by the battles themselves. In March 1822, word finally reached Los Angeles that Spain had relinquished its western possessions, and the citizens of the pueblo of Los Angeles dutifully lowered the Spanish flag from all public buildings to signal the arrival of an independent Mexico. But the war had depleted funds for the newly independent country, and unpaid soldiers contributed to 25 tumultuous years of Mexican rule in California (1822–47), years that often left Californios on their own. By 1845, the secularization of the missions that accompanied independence had overwhelmingly put vast lands around the San Gabriel Mission in the hands of the Spanish-Mexican elite and Anglo-American newcomers to Southern California, while 400 Indians stayed on the land to work it, much as they had done under the mission system.[8]

One of these Californio elites was Claudio Lopez, who had been the *may-ordomo* of Mission San Gabriel for over 30 years and whose parents, Ygnacio López and María Facunda López, had migrated from Baja California and Tepic in 1771 to El Pueblo de San José de Guadalupe (San Jose), the first pueblo in California not associated with a mission or a presidio. López served as mayor of Los Angeles, and his son Esteban was a member of the *ayuntamiento,* or city council, of Los Angeles. In 1835, Esteban received a substantial grant of property within the boundaries of the pueblo located in El Paredón Blanco. Esteban, along with his wife María Jacinta del Sacramenta Valdez, built a house there and would eventually distribute some sections of this land to his own children.[9]

Mexico liberalized its immigration laws in 1824, allowing foreigners to settle in California more easily. A new naturalization law allowed for entry into Mexican citizenship after two years of residence as long as the foreigner was deemed useful and moral, as well as nominally joining the Catholic Church. The first foreigner who integrated himself into Californian society, Joseph Chapman of Massachusetts, actually had been captured as a pirate before this period in 1818. In 1828, John Temple also arrived from Massachusetts and along with fellow foreigner George Rice opened up the pueblo's first general merchandise store. Many of the other foreigners in the district came as merchants and peddlers, including both Anglo-Americans and European immigrants. Abel Stearns from New England trafficked in hides and wine, was involved in smuggling, and would become one of Southern California's largest landowners. Indeed, most historians believe that the 50 foreigners (outside of the Spanish) in the Los Angeles district dominated local business by 1840. But not all Californios were sympathetic to this takeover by foreigners, as was recorded by H. D. Barrows: "Don Antonio Maria Lugo ... looked upon the coming of the Americans as the incursion of an alien element, bringing with them as they did, alien manners and customs, and a language of which he knew next to nothing, and desired to know less. With 'Los Yankees,' as a race, he, and the old Californians generally, had little sympathy."[10] Others welcomed them, such as Esteban's son, Claudio López's grandson, Geronimo, who was living in El Paredón Blanco when the Butterfield stage wagons arrived. Eventually 29 of the area's 50 foreigners came from the United States, and most married into the elite rancho families of the region.[11]

By 1840, Los Angeles, recognized as a *ciudad* in 1835 by the Mexican government, had grown beyond a purely agrarian pueblo, attracting a growing number of craftsmen, retail shops, and saloons as a frontier city and a trading post for all the neighboring ranchos. With the growth of Los Angeles, rising tensions existed throughout the 1840s with both the central government—which had become less of a republic with the rise of General Antonio López de Santa Anna to power—and with the Northern Californians, who resented the growing political and economic pull of the southlanders. The Californio Juan Bautista Alvarado had led a bloodless coup rejecting Mexico's choice for governor in 1836 and instead claimed the position for himself. Yet this delayed the movement of the capital of Alta California ("Upper" California, roughly including the current states of California, Nevada, Utah, and some of Arizona, Colorado, Wyoming, and New Mexico) to Los Angeles until 1845 and further isolated Southern California from centralized power in both Mexico City and the Alta California capital of Monterrey.[12]

However, the struggles between Northern and Southern California would pale against the onslaught of a conquering army from the United States. In June 1846, word came from Sonoma that John Fremont had led a shoddy band of American-born soldiers in the Bear Flag Revolt to confront Mexican leadership and had imprisoned at Sutter's Fort in Sacramento the Californio general Mariano Vallejo, the highest-ranking military officer in Northern California. This caused the Mexican governor of Southern California, Pío Pico, to denounce all Americans as "adventurous pirates." By August, Commodore Robert Stockton's forces were anchored in San Pedro Bay and took Los Angeles without a shot being fired, as both Pío Pico and José Castro, governor of the North, fled to Mexico. Within two weeks, Stockton sailed to San Francisco and left Captain Archibald Gillespie in charge of the conquered territory of Los Angeles. Gillespie's unbridled corruption and violence toward the native Californios led General José María Flores to organize an effective opposition, taking back Los Angeles and marching Gillespie's troops toward San Pedro in October. In this shifting situation, Flores had turned his wrath against American-born rancheros of the region, imprisoning them in isolated adobes on the Boyle Heights mesa. They would be released only after the American forces of Stockton and General Stephen Kearny defeated the Californios on January 10, 1847, in the last battle of the war in California. It would take more than one year for the war between Mexico and the United States to end, with the signing of the Treaty of Guadalupe Hidalgo in 1848, but residents of conquered California would quickly have to adjust to the rule of a new power from the East.[13]

The conquest of California by the United States led directly to a torrent of fortune seekers from the East ready to take advantage of new opportunities. While much has been made of the California gold rush, historians have been less conscious of land speculators.[14] Land speculation in Southern California was critical to the demise of the Spanish-Mexican ranchero elite, as the 1851 Land Act put the burden of proving their ownership on the rancheros themselves. The Californios took on expensive lawyers with costly loans backed by their lands to validate their claims through the Anglo judicial system. And some recklessly gambled with their newfound prosperity by needlessly expanding their landholdings or succumbing to new forms of conspicuous consumption via horse raising or entertaining.[15] By the latter half of the 1850s, rapidly accumulated debt began to force more and more rancheros to sell off their properties. In the 1860s, severe floods followed by drought conspired with market forces to bring an end to "the age of the ranchos." Most rancheros, especially those of Spanish-Mexican origin, lost all their land as a result of the accumulation of debt, drought, and the Anglo legal system. Former Californio dons often became paupers on the streets of Los Angeles by the late 1860s.[16] The overall property holdings of the Mexican-origin population within the city boundaries were cut in half over the course of the decade, and violence against both Mexican newcomers and Californios increased dramatically as they began to be lumped together racially by the new Anglo elite.[17]

ANDREW BOYLE, WILLIAM HENRY WORKMAN, AND THE DEVELOPMENT OF BOYLE HEIGHTS

Andrew Boyle, an Irishman who had fought in the Texas War of Independence, who nearly died at the Battle of Goliad, and who ironically spent the next ten years as an entrepreneur in Mexico, moved to Los Angeles in 1857. He was captivated by the ruggedness and potential prosperity of the land. After surveying possible investments, he purchased the "Old Mission Vineyard" located along the river and the bluffs of El Paredón Blanco from one of Claudio López's sons, Francisco López, as well as Petra Barelas, Esteban's second wife and his widow, and another Californio elite, José Rubio, who had a stake in the area. Because of the lack of access to water, Boyle was able to purchase this land for as little as 25 cents an acre. In 1855, however, the Los Angeles Common Council had approved the construction of a private ditch on the east side of the river, the very first on the Eastside, that carried water to Rancho San Antonio south of the city limits but could also irrigate Boyle's new vineyard. Within a year he built himself a residence out of brick on the site overlooking the river and the growing pueblo. Parts of that residence, located at what would become 325 South Boyle Avenue, remained at that site until torn down to make room for an expansion of the Japanese Home of the Aged in 1987.[18]

The migration of Andrew Boyle presents an alternative story of how "the Irish became white" in mid-nineteenth-century United States. David Roediger and Noel Ignatiev concentrate on Irish American communities in the northeastern US, where Irish immigrants, considered a separate and inferior race by many Anglo-Saxons, rose in status by distinguishing themselves from African Americans through means that ranged from performing

FIGURE 3. Portrait of
Andrew A. Boyle. Herald
Examiner Collection/Los
Angeles Public Library.

minstrelsy in blackface, to competing for jobs and political power, to collectively rioting against blacks in 1863 New York City.[19] Frederick Douglass openly wondered "why a people who so nobly loved and cherished the thought of liberty at home in Ireland could become, willingly, the oppressors of another race here."[20] Yet Boyle, who arrived slightly before the massive Irish migration that resulted from the potato famine in Ireland, rose in social status by taking up arms for conquest against Mexico, then positioned himself to take advantage of the spoils of Western conquest. Indeed, by 1870 the Irish were the largest foreign-born population in the state of California, making up 25 percent of the state's total foreign-born.[21] Later in the century, other Irish immigrants like Denis Kearney would learn to claim his whiteness in relation to despised Chinese immigrants in California, but earlier, the conquest of Mexico became the historical opportunity that opened up elite status to European immigrants in California.

Speculation on the value of land in Southern California was critical to the rise of newcomers, and in this environment the Los Angeles City Council in

1865 sought to auction off its public land east of the river by dividing up the area into 35-acre lots. Andrew Boyle encouraged the auction, and most of the mesa that would later be known as Boyle Heights sold at $5 to $10 an acre in 1865, enabling both small and large investors to purchase property with the hope of future improvements.[22] According to historian Wendy Elliott-Scheinberg, it attracted investors who would become "the political and financial leaders of Los Angeles," since "they held vested interests in improving their Eastside property because with each refinement, value of their real estate increased."[23] Andrew Boyle, for example, would serve on the Los Angeles City Council and would push the city to establish municipal ownership of the critical water system, knowing that this would increase the chances of having water delivered to his 385 acres of land on the Eastside. Isaias W. Hellman, a 22-year-old Jewish newcomer to Los Angeles who held 420 acres of land scattered on the mesa in 1868, would eventually found the Farmers and Merchants National Bank in 1871 and serve as its president until 1920. Other landowner-investors on the mesa included a future California governor, Irishman John Downey, who owned 175 acres, as well as two future mayors of Los Angeles, French Canadian Prudent Beaudry, holding 60 acres, and William Henry Workman, who held title to 35 acres. Others who owned substantial plots of land on the mesa included a future city treasurer, a city auditor, and a superintendent of Los Angeles schools. Boyle's friend Matthew Keller, a fellow Irishman and Texas combatant, obtained 73 acres in hopes of expanding his citrus acreage, while Frenchman Antonio Labory owned 104 acres on the mesa to supplement vineyards for wine production that he owned elsewhere. Boyle lived on the mesa, but few others set up their permanent residence there, since most were interested in holding the land for agricultural or herding purposes, or for pure real estate speculation.[24]

One notable exception was William Henry Workman, whose English-born father David had brought his entire family to California from St. Louis, Missouri, in 1854. William Henry's uncle, William "Don Julian" Workman, owned Rancho La Puente and took William Henry under his wing when his father David died tragically in a riding accident soon after arriving on the West Coast.[25] It was William Henry's purchase of 35 acres of land atop the mesa in 1867 that would prove a critical step in the development of the Boyle Heights region. Indeed, later that year on October 17, 28-year-old William Henry married Maria E. Boyle, the daughter of his new neighbor on the mesa, Andrew Boyle. It seems that William Henry had both financial and personal reasons to purchase property on the mesa that year. The elder

FIGURE 4. Portrait of William H. Workman. Security Pacific National Bank Collection/Los Angeles Public Library.

Andrew Boyle built an additional wing onto his own house to accommodate the newlywed couple, and they lived there until 1878, when William Henry built a home on his own property at the very site where the first adobe house on the mesa had been located. William Henry and his wife Maria would raise seven children on that Eastside mesa, beginning with son Boyle Workman, who was born in 1868, just one year after their marriage.[26]

Like so many others, William Henry was initially a merchant, manufacturing and selling saddles and harnesses on Main Street. This occupation made sense for a man who had grown up on a rancho and now had to ride a horse to work, fording the Los Angeles River to get to his shop. In 1871, the elder Andrew Boyle died, leaving the future development of the mesa in the hands of his son-in-law. In the fall of that year, William Henry began his rise in Los Angeles city politics, becoming one of three school trustees.[27] He worked for three years to have the first bridge, a covered one, built across the Los Angeles River at Macy Street in 1873, an arduous process that required an act of the state legislature and a state appropriation for completion. During the rest of the 1870s, while leading efforts to develop the mesa in the city, he would name the region Boyle Heights after his deceased father-in-law in 1876.[28] His son Boyle would later describe this effort plainly: "Boyle Heights was laid out in 1876. Father subdivided and named the property in honor of Grandfather Boyle, who died in 1871."[29] In the 1870s and 1880s, William Henry would continue his efforts to develop Boyle Heights through direct involvement in city politics as a city council member and then as mayor of Los Angeles from 1886 to 1888.

Historian Wendy Elliott-Scheinberg makes clear that William Henry had to accomplish plenty of major infrastructural tasks in order to promote Boyle Heights as a prime residential location in late nineteenth-century Los Angeles: 1) providing a sustainable water source for the Eastside; 2) authorizing the construction of bridges across the Los Angeles River in order to overcome the city's geographical barrier to unity; 3) advancing streetcar lines, first horse drawn and later electric powered, to promote public transportation between Boyle Heights and downtown; 4) converting trails and unpaved routes to graded roads and paved urban streets to promote residential development; 5) providing public parks as amenities for potential urban residents; and 6) completing a utilities infrastructure by providing residential and business gas lines and electricity to the neighborhood.[30] Throughout the late nineteenth century, William Henry led efforts to accomplish these tasks and provide the needed infrastructure in an era where "the principal [sic] of 'conflict of interest' did not concern citizens."[31] In other words, William Henry and his fellow Boyle Heights landowner-investors used all means necessary to advance these projects politically, while benefiting from these developments personally.

For example, William Henry did not stop at constructing his own private reservoir and system of pipes to bring water to irrigate his land in Boyle Heights. When the city council refused his request to open a new *zanja* (ditch) to the Eastside, William Henry himself ran for and won a position on the city council in the mid-1870s and convinced his new colleagues to serve the upland area of Boyle Heights with a new irrigation ditch.[32] To ensure the profitability of the subdivision of his land, William Henry invested in the first horse-drawn car lines to cross into East Los Angeles in 1877 on Aliso Avenue, requiring the building of new suspension bridges to traverse the river and arroyo. The Los Angeles & Aliso Avenue Street Passenger Railway would

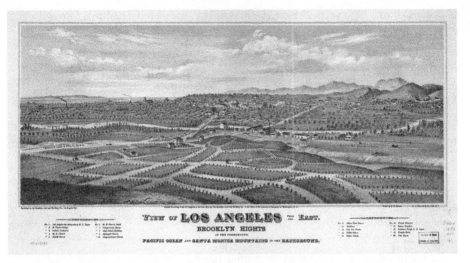

FIGURE 5. Birdseye view of Los Angeles and Brooklyn Heights from the east, ca. 1877. California Historical Society Collection, University of Southern California Libraries.

bring passengers out to baseball games that were set up on a makeshift diamond and to the newly opened Evergreen Cemetery on a five-acre plot near the end of the tracks. As his son Boyle would recognize, that carriage line was not constructed for its own profit, since "income was not even enough to feed the horses or pay the two boys (drivers) for their labor."[33] Rather, it allowed land that Workman and others had bought in 1867 for $5 and $10 an acre to be sold in the late 1880s for $200 an acre, with the subdividing of vacant land now "improved" for purchase. By the time this railway was abandoned in 1893, the Aliso line had accomplished its central task: rather than ever turning a profit, it had led to the solid and irreversible building up of several residential communities in Boyle Heights.[34]

William Henry Workman, therefore, was like many other Anglo pioneers of this era, such as Phineas Banning of Wilmington or Abbot Kinney of Venice, who promoted one neighborhood in Southern California before the rest to attract future residents and cash in on their investments in land. The late dean of California historians Kevin Starr equated this process with the completion of the Americanization of the region: "The Americanization of Southern California occurred in four stages. In the immediate post-annexation stage, first of all, the old Mexican elites held their own.... The drought of the early 1860s, together with a number of other factors ... ended this first state of Hispanic reconsolidation. The 1870s witnessed the falling into American hands of the

Mexican land-grant ranchos. In the 1880s many of these American held ranchos, especially those of Los Angeles County, were subdivided and sold as residential property. In the 1890s these subdivisions grew into towns and cities."[35]

What made these developments possible, especially the subdivisions of property, was a torrential influx of newcomers to Southern California, prompted by the completion of transcontinental railroads. While the Southern Pacific reached Los Angeles through San Francisco in the fall of 1876, it was the later railroad fare wars of the 1880s that actually led to the first true land boom in the region. When the Santa Fe reached Los Angeles directly in 1885, a rate war between it and the Southern Pacific brought a cross-country ticket down to as low as $15. Three years of intense real estate speculation followed, fueled by a city population that grew by 500 percent and totaled 50,000 by 1889. Indeed, estimates are that as many as 130,000 people took advantage of lower railroad rates to explore Southern California in the late 1880s. In Boyle Heights, the 1880 Census listed only 62 households holding 298 individuals, confirming Workman's initial belief that the neighborhood was "destined for agricultural and stock raising endeavors rather than a residential neighborhood."[36] Just ten years later, the Boyle Heights population was estimated to have grown close to 2,000 individuals, with at least 33 different residential subdivisions surveyed and plotted by developers.[37]

PLANNING FOR A WHITE LOS ANGELES

In the 40 years between the founding of Boyle Heights in 1876 and the beginning of World War I in 1916, the city of Los Angeles itself was transformed from a small Mexican town to a major American metropolis. Boyle Heights was a fundamental part of that development, with real estate speculation, political-economic consolidation of power, and the influx of newcomers all playing major roles in the newly founded suburb, just as they did in Los Angeles as a whole. At the beginning of the period, it seemed as if Boyle Heights was poised to become a sophisticated suburb for the growing Anglo elite of Los Angeles, as William Henry Workman sought to ornament the district with all the amenities that would foster gentlemen ranchers and businessmen to establish residences in the former Paredón Blanco. In particular, city leaders were hoping that Boyle Heights would serve as the first suburb of refined whiteness for the Anglo-American settlers from the East that they hoped to attract to Los Angeles.

Yet other land investors throughout Southern California were competing for the attention of exactly the same sort of incoming Anglo-American settlers that would make up these newly available suburbs. And the delay in getting an adequate water supply to the east side of the river, as well as bridges and adequate transportation networks to cross the river to downtown in the 1870s, put Boyle Heights at a disadvantage. For comparison, five hearty investors from Indiana purchased a tract just below the San Gabriel Mountains with incoming streams of fresh rainwater for $25,000, despite the national financial panic that year, and incorporated themselves into the San Gabriel Orange Grove Association.[38] In early 1874 they renamed the area Pasadena, and by June they had already laid out Orange Grove Avenue, including a water main, and had lined the street with orange trees. The group of former Hoosiers quickly built 40 houses, subdivided the large tract, and planted thousands of trees and grapevines at a frenzied pace, investing another $25,000 into the area in the first year. By 1886, Pasadena had been incorporated into a municipality, and by 1890 the first Tournament of Roses Parade marched along Orange Grove Avenue. Opulent hotels were built in this period to attract wealthy investors and upper-income future residents alike. Pasadena, supposedly an Indian name for "Key to the Valley," was one of the first instant neighborhoods built to satisfy newcomers with wealth. But it would not be the last.[39]

Boyle Heights rode the wave of this early expansive period because it was finally connected to the rest of the city by bridges over the Los Angeles River. The first permanent bridge in Los Angeles was built over the river by the San Francisco–based Pacific Bridge Company in 1873, and this initial bridge was followed by many others in the next 30 years, connecting the Eastside to the expanding downtown of Los Angeles and spanning the sometimes turbulent river at various points. The Southern Pacific and Santa Fe Railroads would follow closely behind, building expanses over the river to serve their trains, while the Los Angeles Cable Railroad built a viaduct in 1889 at Downey Avenue, connecting with First Street in Boyle Heights, to facilitate local public transportation and to conjoin the downtown populations to the Eastside.[40]

William Henry Workman and the other city leaders, hoping to develop Boyle Heights as one of the first suburbs inside of Los Angeles city boundaries, initially attempted to build homes for the growing elite of the town, now that they could easily cross the river over these new thoroughfares. Simon Francois Gless, a prominent French Basque rancher, built a large two-story,

15-room Queen Anne–style farm home in 1887 on land owned by his late uncle, Gaston Oxerart. This home reflected the desire to build opulence next to a working sheep ranch. The property was adjacent to William Henry Workman's own substantial home on Boyle Avenue. The Gless Farmhouse was an example of suburban Victorian homes, some of which are still standing, built in the late 1880s and 1890s to mark the elite standing of Boyle Heights, next to other well-known early suburban sites around the downtown area, such as Angelino Heights to the west of downtown and Victorian homes along Hoover Street, just north of the newly founded University of Southern California (1880).[41]

CREATING "RACIAL UNDESIRABLES" ON THE LANDSCAPE

From the start of the population boom, the elites of Los Angeles worried that the city's growth could be negatively affected by racial mixture, reflecting the disdain that Americans had for the nonwhite. In this context, city officials and those involved in land speculation (often one and the same) desperately tried to keep the Anglo newcomers away from both the poorer Mexican community that had remained around the Plaza and the new visible Chinatown that had established itself to the southwest of the Plaza. The Chinese become the first targets of formal government attempts at exclusion and segregation when the new California constitution of 1879 allowed incorporated cities and towns to remove and prohibit the creation of Chinese neighborhoods in the state. Newly appointed Los Angeles city public health officer Walter Lindley, while calling in 1879 for a new sewage system that would extend the city's primitive sewage lines to these new Anglo districts, contrasted them sharply with his description of the city's Chinatown as "that rotten spot," failing to advocate for similar improvements for that district. In the 1870s, both Los Angeles and San Francisco had passed "Cubic Air Acts," which allowed officials to regulate overcrowded boardinghouses and apartments. While these laws should have applied to all dwellings, officials consistently targeted only the Chinese.[42]

These efforts tended to be haphazard and idiosyncratic, but the late nineteenth century saw land developers in many American cities begin to take more systematic approaches toward residential restriction. Although restrictive covenants had been used as early as the mid-eighteenth century in

England by nobility seeking to subdivide but still control their property, they initially saw limited use in the United States in the nineteenth century by property owners hoping to preserve fashionable neighborhoods such as Boston's Lewisburg Square and New York's Gramercy Park. Until the 1880s, however, restrictive covenants looked no more legitimately promising than general nuisance law or design guidelines. But in the last decades of the nineteenth century, the US Supreme Court, and several state courts, removed the remaining legal obstacles to covenants through a strategic window.[43] In California, when Mr. Lee Sing sued the City of Ventura for attempting to disallow Chinese from living inside its jurisdiction, the response by federal courts in 1892 was to allow discrimination by private individuals, while barring state and municipal governments from discriminating themselves. With this green light, the first racially restrictive covenant filed in Los Angeles would occur in 1902, using the catchall term *non-Caucasians* to outline who could not purchase property. Within a few years, cities throughout Southern California applied restrictive covenants against Chinese, Japanese, Mexicans, African Americans, and sometimes Armenians, Jews, Italians, and other groups seen at the time to be racially undesirable.[44]

"Racial undesirables" were just one of many threats that land speculators sought to control in this period. Land speculation as a whole, however, could be a risky proposition in an unstable economic environment like Southern California. As the social commentator Carey McWilliams observed, out of more than 100 towns plotted in Los Angeles County between 1884 and 1888, "sixty-two no longer exist," making Southern California a series of virtual ghost towns in the aftermath of this boom.[45] Indeed, after 1889 in Boyle Heights, many of the plots that had been constructed for purchase stood idle as the late 1880s real estate frenzy went bust and a longer extended period of stagnation settled in. Empty lots throughout Boyle Heights were the most visible symbol of land speculation, as various developers hoped for a return to the explosion of buyers. Even though upper- and middle-class white Americans and Europeans still composed the vast majority of current residents in Boyle Heights at the end of the nineteenth century, major zoning decisions by the city at the turn of the century, as well as rapidly instituted restrictions of racial and ethnic populations away from other areas of growth in the city, forced Boyle Heights developers to open the district to newcomers from various parts of the United States and the world without much constraint.

Although the California courts had given individuals alone, and not political jurisdictions, the right to discriminate, widespread collective action and the interests of land developers and real estate agents would keep most Southern California communities segregated in the early twentieth century. The Los Angeles Realty Board, founded in 1903, led regional efforts to organize the real estate industry, professionalize its membership, and institute racially restrictive covenants in as many established neighborhoods and new residential developments as possible. They were also crucial in mobilizing the Los Angeles City Council to become the first city to pass an ordinance prohibiting industrial activities in a residential district. In 1908, Los Angeles led the national movement toward modern zoning by mapping out three large areas of the city in which almost all industrial operations would be forbidden to keep the majority of the city "a residential paradise of spacious homes in quiet, clean surroundings."[46] According to urban historian Natalia Molina, one effect of these ordinances was that city officials were able to solidify "the central role of race in the politics of acquiring and using space" by retroactively making it illegal for Chinese laundries to operate in all of these residential districts, even if they had been established before the passage of the laws.[47] The policy was enforced unevenly based on race, as city officials regularly gave exemptions to Anglo-American launderers, while consistently prohibiting Chinese launderers from working in most parts of the growing city.[48]

What effect did this growing restriction against selling or renting to families of color have upon their choices for living in Southern California? Outside of a few outlying rural districts, the traditional downtown residential communities around the Plaza and Chinatown remained a key starting point for Angelinos of color who first arrived in Los Angeles in the early twentieth century. In addition to these original "foreign districts," the neighborhoods remaining in the areas zoned as industrial, particularly those along the railroad tracks and the industrialized Los Angeles River, became racially and ethnically mixed neighborhoods, as did a growing Eastside Industrial District that stretched beyond the city limits to Whittier. New districts to the east and south that lay adjacent to or connected to these industrial zones by rail lines, including Boyle Heights, Watts, and Belvedere, were also relatively open to all. Each of these neighborhoods would become racially and ethnically mixed in the early twentieth century, containing not only African Americans, Asian Americans, and Latinos but also disparaged white ethnic groups like Jews and Italians. Even as these populations grew substantially in the wake of World War I and expanded the industrial labor force of Southern California, they remained isolated and restricted to this limited landscape,

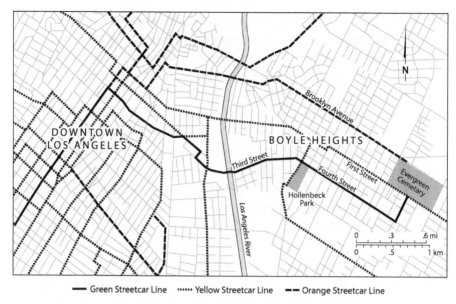

MAP 1. Streetcar railway lines to Boyle Heights, ca. 1906. Drawn by Bill Nelson.

thus producing substantial overcrowding and deplorable housing conditions in much of this region.[49]

But the restrictions did not keep racial minorities from trying to break their power and individuals from trying to circumvent their reach. One such case involved the Entwistle Tract, originally developed in 1905 by a woman named Lulu Nevada Entwistle Hinton Letteau. The tract, well south of downtown, around 41st Street and just east of Main Street, was originally developed as an all-white part of the city with restrictive deeds, including racial restrictions on occupancy. These covenants read that if the provision was violated the property would revert back to the original owners of the development. Since the area was so close to the growing African American community, many white homeowners sold some homes to blacks without incident, so others came. By the mid-1920s, blacks made up half the neighborhood. In early 1924, William H. Long and his wife Eunice, an ordinary working-class black couple, were able to buy their first bungalow in the neighborhood at 771 East 41st Street, putting a down payment of nearly $2,000 on a property that had been bought and sold several times since 1905. Days later, however, heirs of Mrs. Letteau brought suit against the Longs, arguing that the occupancy clause had been violated and that the title of the property should now revert back to them. Although the NAACP originally took up the Longs' defense, a superior court decision in December 1926 ruled in favor of the Letteaus, leading the heirs to sue every black homeowner in the Entwistle Tract, as well as the white owners who had been renting to African Americans. During these extended legal proceedings, Eunice Long saw her husband William deteriorate physically and mentally before tragically dying, and she herself became a semi-invalid. Nonetheless, the Los Angeles County sheriff served her with an eviction notice and she lost what little she had left.[50]

The growth of the commercial and industrial infrastructure of Los Angeles directly across the river from Boyle Heights and in the Flats area, and the zoning of the Eastside Industrial District, created a different path for Boyle Heights, as its developers were anxious to find prospective buyers for unimproved lots. In Boyle Heights, unlike the Entwistle Tract, private developers decided that trying to establish widespread restrictive covenants would only limit the possible customers to whom they might sell these lots, or to whom they might transfer ownership of existing homes. With the opening of beach towns in the first decade of the twentieth century—Hermosa Beach in 1902 and Venice in 1905—it appeared that the new rush of middle-class Anglo home seekers were more likely to move west toward the ocean than east across the river.[51]

The historical reference points that stratified the Eastside into a lower social rank than other parts of the city continued to play a role in the unequal distribution of resources and the placement of certain institutions that were deemed necessary for a burgeoning city but preferably kept out of main view.[52] As early as 1877, the city council had granted a permit to establish the city's first cemetery at the eastern edge of the city at Evergreen. At the conclusion of the real estate boom of the 1880s, the Daughters of Charity of St. Vincent de Paul, better known as the nuns of the Sisters of Charity, purchased property for the Los Angeles Orphans' Asylum at a new site in Boyle Heights. The asylum, which would house Catholic orphans until the 1950s, was moved across the river from the corner of Alameda and Macy Streets, and a massive facility was built for it at 917 South Boyle Avenue.[53] Increasingly, the institutions that reflected death, sickness, or individual tragedy, as in the case of orphans, were established or moved to locations east of the river. Los Angeles County eventually placed its first general comprehensive public hospital across the river in Boyle Heights in 1933, building upon the placement of 30 smaller public hospitals in East Los Angeles in the 55-year period since 1878.[54]

In this racially charged environment, María del Sacramenta López, the 19-year-old daughter of Boyle Heights landowner Francisco López, married

George Cummings, Austrian born and 20 years her senior, at the Los Angeles Plaza Church in 1869.[55] George Cummings became another Boyle Heights developer after marrying into his holdings. María, the great-granddaughter of Claudio López, had grown up on the family farm in El Paredón Blanco, located between present-day First Street and César Chávez Avenue. George and María decided to build Boyle Heights' first hotel at the corner of First Street and Boyle Avenue at a cost of $22,000; the completion of the four-story brick structure was timed to coincide with the opening of the Los Angeles Cable Railway in 1889. The Cummings Hotel was intended as a way station for white middle-class prospective homeowners interested in purchasing land in the nearby Mount Pleasant Tract, recently bought and subdivided by the couple.[56]

As it became clear that these were not the sort of immigrants that Boyle Heights would be enticing, and as the hotel's clientele become less and less elite, it was renamed the Mt. Pleasant Hotel and then the Boyle Hotel. By the turn of the century, George Cummings had moved away from Boyle Heights entirely, first to the Tehachapi Valley, then to Bakersfield, where in 1903 at the age of 75 he died a tragic death in a fire that engulfed the Kern Hotel. His wife María would go on to live until 1930 to age 80, but not before she rewrote her own family's life story in *Claudio and Anita* (1921), where she falsely claimed that her ancestors had come directly from Spain to Southern California, erasing her Mexican heritage. One analysis of this typical example of "Hispanophile Literature" notes that the author was trying to "separate its noble characters from others of lower stock" by "responding to social pressures that had codified recent Mexican arrivals as inferior and uneducated."[57] Imagine if María had learned that her Cummings Hotel would later be known as Mariachi Hotel, as Boyle Heights came to reflect modern working-class Mexican culture.

As railroad traffic into Los Angeles continued to grow and bring in prospective newcomers, both the Santa Fe and Southern Pacific Railroad Companies expanded their worker camps along the Los Angeles River. In the 1890s and the first decade of the twentieth century these camps housed an increasingly Mexican workforce in converted boxcars that had simply been moved off the tracks in the Flats area of Boyle Heights. Various European immigrant groups and African Americans from the US South would also find their way to the Boyle Heights community in the early twentieth century. And the 1906 San Francisco Earthquake would force many Japanese and Chinese families to relocate from the Bay area south and find new residences in Southern California, many settling in or near Boyle Heights.

Two multigenerational families discussed in this chapter represent the diversity of individuals and networks that became critical to the formation of the neighborhood of Boyle Heights and the development of its relationship with the larger Los Angeles community. Andrew Boyle is the central figure of this first family, an Irish immigrant to California in the mid-nineteenth century whose son-in-law, William Henry Workman, would name the region east of the Los Angeles River "Boyle Heights" to memorialize his departed father-in-law in 1876. The second family network is less well known but just as important. María del Sacramenta López's marriage to the Austrian-born George Cummings in 1869 inducted her family's Boyle Heights holdings into this ethnically mixed family. María came from a Mexican family that had long owned substantial property in the region, but this marriage would end tragically and push María to write a complicated family history in which she denied her Mexican roots and instead claimed Spanish origins. Andrew Boyle and María del Sacramenta López, albeit in different ways, both represented early attempts to find new meaning in the marginalized Eastside of Los Angeles.

Critical to this discussion is the topography of the Southern California region before the advent of human-made changes to the landscape. When most visitors arrive in Southern California, they are struck by what appear to be extensive flat coastal plains—stretching lengthwise for 275 miles—between the foothills of the majestic mountains and the shores of the Pacific Ocean. This land area, set apart from the southwestern deserts by the Tehachapi Mountain range and cooled by the ocean breezes, has been called an "island on the land" by novelist Helen Hunt Jackson, but its own internal ruggedness and ecosystem are often taken for granted by virtue of this framing.[58] Nowhere are the hills, valleys, and gullies that make up Southern California so pronounced as in Boyle Heights, which is etched into nearly the geographic center of that expansive plain.

But as this chapter shows, coupled with this geology, topography, and climate are human-made boundaries and their embedded meanings, spanning the political, racial, and more. By the time of widespread urban settlement of Boyle Heights in the late nineteenth and early twentieth centuries, white US-born newcomers to the region were directed to settle on the

Westside of the growing metropolis, and Boyle Heights would establish itself as a community open to a much more racially diverse population, with more class heterogeneity, than other parts of Los Angeles.

Furthermore, these layered meanings can be gleaned from the history of Evergreen Cemetery, as discussed in the opening vignette. When the Los Angeles City Council passed a resolution on August 23, 1877, establishing Evergreen Cemetery on the eastern fringes of the still small city, it seems as if the grateful owners of that burial permit provided the city with five acres south of the property to operate a potter's field for the poor and unclaimed. The county purchased the property in 1917 and built a crematorium there in 1922, but over the years city and county officials forgot about the existence of the original haphazard burials underneath what eventually became driveways, retaining walls, and tree-covered landscapes. Evergreen Cemetery had the unusual distinction of never banning African Americans from being buried there, and in 1917 it also had sections for Armenians, Japanese, and early white settlers, as well as a growing section of Mexican graves. Indeed, when William Henry Workman finally passed away in 1918, the former Los Angeles mayor would be buried at Evergreen Cemetery, just as Boyle Heights was transforming into a working-class, multiracial enclave.

THREE

From Global Movements to Urban Apartheid

LEO FRUMKIN'S FATHER LEFT RUSSIA in 1906 to escape a pogrom aimed at Jews by Cossacks and arrived at Ellis Island in New York City's harbor two years later. His mother, the youngest of five children, came with her mother from the Ukraine, migrating to New Orleans to join her older siblings. Frumkin's parents met at a Jewish colony for those with respiratory diseases near the Mojave Desert and decided to move to the fringes of Boyle Heights, where his father built their home around 1916. At the end of World War I, Frumkin's father arranged to have his parents join them from Russia. As other family members arrived in Southern California, and as children were born into the Frumkin household, Leo's father would simply add on rooms to the house, building additional space onto the lot or converting living rooms into makeshift bedrooms.[1]

But the Frumkin family also brought with them various and vibrant cultural, social, and political traditions. Leo and his siblings knew enough Yiddish to speak to their grandparents, because this was the only language the grandparents knew. His parents knew Yiddish but also spoke Russian to each other when they didn't want the children to understand what they were saying. Politically, the Frumkin clan was even more diverse. Leo's grandfather was a Stalinist and follower of the Communist Party, while his grandmother was a Labor Zionist. Both his parents were Social Democrat supporters of Norman Thomas, who ran for president six times as the candidate for the Socialist Party of America, until they switched to Franklin Roosevelt in the early 1930s. Both of his older sisters were socialists, but also Trotskyist members of the Socialist Workers Party at the time. One of his uncles started the second kibbutz in Israel, while two aunts were dedicated communists, one of whom went to Russia in the 1930s with her husband and was imprisoned in a

Siberian concentration camp.[2] Leo himself was influenced by all his family's perspectives but also by the world around him in Boyle Heights: "You grew up in a community that was a multiracial community, so you learned to appreciate—not tolerate, but appreciate—other cultures. You became socially conscious. . . . It was really a very large family. You slept in each other's homes. You'd eat at each other's homes. Kids in my block, their parents would give me tortillas and my mother would give them matzos two or three times a year. . . . It was a fellowship. I don't know what term you would use, except that you became internationalists. At least [that's] what I became."[3]

The Boyle Heights that was created in the early part of the twentieth century drew inspiration and strength from cultures and communities from around the world as newcomers arrived from Mexico, the American South, Italy, eastern Europe, Russia, and Japan. The dominance of immigrant families in the Boyle Heights district was reflected in data from the 1930 US Census, which showed that 56 percent of Boyle Heights residents in 1930 were foreign born. As Leo Frumkin indicated, "You were talking about families who, 99 percent of them, their parents had just come from the old country, Russia or Italy or Mexico, or wherever they came from."[4] While Leo's father had come from Russia to avoid pogroms against the Jews there, others arrived from Japan via Hawaii after industrialization impoverished the rural population. Similar agricultural pressure brought Sicilians, Calabrians, and others from southern parts of Italy. Revolution dislocated Mexicans, and African Americans who had the means fled the Jim Crow South in the face of lynching and political terrorism. Black Boyle Heights resident Mollie Wilson Murphy (who had harbored those letters from her interned Japanese American schoolmates) explained, "You'd do anything to get out of the South."[5] Mollie's father, Atoy Wilson, moved directly to Boyle Heights from Oklahoma when he was eight years old in 1896. Her mother, Kizzie Brown, came as a child at the turn of the century from Texas. By 1920, close to one million African Americans would leave the South as part of the first wave of the Great Migration to cities in the North, Midwest, and West.

Those who arrived in Boyle Heights had sought new homes in places where they could escape constant bouts of violence, displacement, and despair, but Los Angeles had structured its neighborhoods in such a way that new arrivals, who, by virtue of their race and national background, were limited in where they could land, ended up in the same Eastside neighborhoods. In Boyle Heights this brought them into dialogue with neighbors and coworkers across ethnic and national lines to envision and cocreate a new future for themselves. But these families rarely forgot where they had come from and drew inspiration from their various backgrounds and experiences, even as they experimented with new forms of resistance and survival.

TRANSNATIONAL PATHS AND RADICAL TRADITIONS

Eastern European Jews, like Leo Frumkin's parents, from Russia, Lithuania, Romania, and Poland, were often escaping pogroms that targeted their race. In 1880, 6 million of the world's 7.7 million Jews lived in Eastern Europe, with only 3 percent living in the United States. By 1920, such large-scale migration had taken place that 23 percent of the world's Jewry lived in the US.[6] But migration to Los Angeles for Jews was usually a secondary migration, bringing both the immigrant parents and children of immigrants west. In 1900, Los Angeles had only 2,500 Jewish residents, but estimates are that close to 2,300 Jews eventually arrived in the city directly sponsored by the Industrial Removal Office (IRO) of New York City, as part of a program intended to significantly disperse immigrant families west from the congestion of the Lower East Side.[7]

It was probably Yiddish-speaking socialists like Leo's parents, grandparents, aunts, and uncles who brought into Boyle Heights the most developed form of global radicalism. Many of the Jewish immigrants who settled in Boyle Heights during the early twentieth century had been part of the socialist movement in eastern Europe, but as the 1905 attempt at a Russian revolution failed and violent anti-Semitism rose, many of these leaders came to the United States as already committed leftists. Rather than a "Lower East Side" of proletarian migrants, Jews who came to establish the Yiddish neighborhood of Boyle Heights were largely American born or Americanized. But they made a political choice to establish a distinctive linguistic neighborhood based on the desire to create a Jewish working-class culture that stood out from the more assimilated Los Angeles community on the Westside. Their leaders, many of whom came from intensive schooling and some from wealth, saw Yiddish culture and language "as a vehicle for molding and mobilizing the Jewish 'folk masses' to bring about revolutionary change and for fostering socialist Jewish nationalism."[8]

Jews weren't the only ones escaping war and revolution in the period. The Molokan population, an ethnic group subscribing to a sect of Christianity considered heretical by the Russian Orthodox Church, fled Russia in the first years of the twentieth century to escape impressment in the Russo-Japanese War. Kate Boletin remembers that her parents left Russia in 1906 because they were pacifists, according to the tenets of the Molokan religion, "and they were beginning to take the boys into the service." They followed their elders, first to Canada, then south to Los Angeles and the Flats area of Boyle Heights.[9]

Violence and war led numerous exiles to settle in Boyle Heights. The Mexican Revolution of 1910, for example, pushed many individuals and families off their native land. Two of the most important newcomers to Los Angeles were the Flores Magón brothers, who had been expelled from Mexico in 1903 after critiquing the dictatorship of Porfirio Díaz. The growth of discontent against Díaz grew from a textile strike in Puebla in 1898 and a protest against Anaconda Mining and other US mining interests in 1906 in Cananea, near the US border town of Bisbee, Arizona. The protest blossomed into full-fledged revolution when they organized the Partido Liberal Mexicano (PLM) in St. Louis in 1905. In July 1907, Ricardo and Enrique Flores Magón moved the PLM headquarters to downtown Los Angeles, attracting *Magonistas* with fiery speeches in the Plaza against the semifeudal conditions in Mexico, particularly in Mexico's central plateau region, where modernization under Díaz saw hacienda owners and foreign investors expand their landholdings at the expense of peasant agriculture. The Flores Magón brothers faced criminal charges, arrests, and imprisonment but continued to publish the party's newspaper *Regeneración,* whose circulation grew close to 20,000.[10]

Like other migrants to Boyle Heights, Mexicans in the early twentieth century had firsthand experience with strikes and other labor agitations, but unlike other migrants, Mexican activists were often protesting against the same capitalists, whether they were in Mexico or Los Angeles, because of US ownership of agricultural, ranching, and mining interests south of the border.[11] Indeed, from their base in Los Angeles, the PLM organized an interracial group of mercenary fighters to invade Baja California and take up arms against the ruling elite at the start of the Mexican Revolution. Though they were ultimately unsuccessful, this action showed the transnational power of the Mexican Revolution and its influence on radicals on both sides of the border. After all, over half of those taking up arms for the PLM were non-Mexican.[12]

In the American South, another exploitative agricultural regime was implemented after Reconstruction: sharecropping, a system whereby tenant farmers paid landowners a portion of their harvest for the use of the land. The livelihoods of sharecroppers were tenuous at best, and economic transformations in agricultural production led many white family farms to shut down and pushed some ex-sharecroppers to Los Angeles. However, two-thirds of black migrants from the South were not from rural areas. Most African Americans who moved to Los Angeles in the late nineteenth century were motivated to escape discrimination and unbridled racial violence. Those from the large cities of San Antonio, New Orleans, and Atlanta dominated this migration, with one in five black newcomers being born in one of these three cities. Smaller cities in Texas and Louisiana, such as Austin, Galveston, Beaumont, Dallas, and Shreveport, also contributed many migrants to Los Angeles.[13] Mollie's grandparents, coming from generations of men who worked for the railroads, had the funds to purchase a home in Boyle Heights.[14] They were part of a middle-class African American generation of southern migrants that, in the words of historian Douglas Flamming, saw in the West "the opportunity for a kind of freedom that the South refused to offer them."[15]

The African American community of Boyle Heights also sparked the earliest rise of black nationalist organizing in Los Angeles through the efforts of John Wesley Coleman, whose mother and stepfather, moving to Los Angeles from Austin, Texas, in 1887, were the first black residents of Boyle Heights. His mother, Mrs. Harriet Owen-Bynum, became a real estate agent for African Americans, selling 65 lots and houses to black families and finding rental housing in the area for hundreds of others. John Wesley worked as a Pullman porter, landscape contractor, insurance and employment agent, and real estate salesman. With his mother, he developed Coleman Flats, an apartment building at 205 North Savannah Street in Boyle Heights, which served as an initial landing spot for many African American newcomers to the neighborhood in the twentieth century.

As an experienced entrepreneur, Coleman was instrumental in founding and leading the Los Angeles Forum, the People's Independent Church, and the Black Masons, Shriners, and Odd Fellows. In 1920, he called the first and only "National Convention of Peoples of African Descent" in Los Angeles, which produced Division 156 of the Universal Negro Improvement Association (UNIA). Coleman combined his interest in the economic well-being of African Americans with a devotion to Pan-Africanism. The *California Eagle* credited his employment agency with finding jobs for 50,000 persons by 1924. Despite schisms between the local branch and the national office, when Marcus Garvey visited Los Angeles in June 1922, the *California Eagle* reported that half of the African American community of Southern California, or 10,000 spectators, showed up for the UNIA parade through the city.[16]

Across the globe, the 1880s saw the beginnings of a dramatic transformation of rural economies. Industrialization in Japan, for example, separated many villagers from their family's farmland. To support the development of urban industry, the Meiji regime instituted the 1873 Land Tax, which required rural landowners to pay in money, rather than crops, as had been done previously. As the price of rice fluctuated, many small landowners were turned into debtors, forced to sell their land. Efforts to "modernize" local agriculture, privatize landholdings, and convert agricultural production to a market economy turned many farmers and villagers into a pool of working-class individuals in need of wage labor to survive and led to violent local uprisings. Although such newly landless laborers were initially drawn to contract labor in Hawai'i, and returned to Japan after a three-year period, many eventually found themselves in Los Angeles, since the average immigrant in California could make twice as much as a field hand in Hawai'i. From 1902 to 1907, about 38,000 Japanese moved from Hawai'i to the US West.[17]

Political motivations also spurred Japanese migration. The formation of the Socialist Study Society in 1898 marked the beginning of the socialist movement in Japan, and from the start a high percentage of anarchists and socialists who participated in this original organization had studied in the United States. Massive repression in Japan itself, including, in 1900, a wholesale prohibition of labor agitation for better wages and improved conditions, forced many of these leftist activists to migrate abroad. California was a prime location for Japanese socialists like Katayama Sen, who organized a group in 1902 that encouraged youth to emigrate to the United States. While combating the increasing anti-Asian sentiments within US labor unions, the Social Revolutionary Party did connect to the Industrial Workers of the World (IWW), which in the 1910s attempted to organize all workers, regardless of race, nationality, gender, or skill.[18] Japanese workers in Hawai'i had also begun to form unions across racial and ethnic lines in order to be an effective labor force.[19] Japanese laborers that moved into California and Boyle Heights from Hawai'i in the early twentieth century brought with them a recognition of the importance of these multiracial labor struggles.

Agricultural pressures affecting Italy in this period similarly pushed many Italians to seek work in the US and around the world. According to historian Donna Gabaccia, migrants represented almost one-third of Italy's 1911 population. "From 1876 to 1914, six million worked in other European nations, four million migrated, often cyclically, to the United States and Canada, and three million travelled to Argentina, Brazil, and other Latin American countries."[20] Unlike other European immigrants, three-fifths of whom headed to the United States, only one-third of Italians did. Most of this labor migration was intended to maintain subsistence agriculture throughout Italy, with people emigrating to make extra money to send back home to Italy so they could keep their land there. Return migration rates for Italy were as high as 50 percent, and this pattern of cyclical migration was deeply gendered, dominated by men. But conditions worsened in Italy as the global marketplace transformed agricultural production. California and Florida orchards outcompeted orange and lemon groves in Calabria, Sicily, and other parts of southern Italy, while French tariffs hurt the heart of the Italian wine industry. The rise in migration of Italian women, from one-quarter of the whole in 1876 to one-third in 1914, signaled a more permanent migration abroad, and with it the settlement of Italian families in Boyle and Lincoln Heights.[21]

There was a strong anarchist tradition among Italian immigrants to the United States, including those who eventually made their way to Lincoln and Boyle Heights. For example, Sicilian anarchist Ludovico Caminita would spend some of the 1910s editing an Italian-language column in *Regeneración*, one of the papers published by the Flores brothers. Ricardo Flores Magón had found some of the strongest support for the PLM among Italian anarchists, and it seems that Caminita's column led some Italians from the East Coast to fight in the Mexican Revolution in Baja California on the side of the PLM.

Caminita immigrated to the United States in 1902. He spent almost fifteen years trying to tie together anarchist movements from Italy, Mexico, Spain, and other nations, while challenging the racial color line in the United States, mostly working with members of an anarchist group known as Gruppo L'Era Nuova, or the "New Era Group." In 1910, Caminita relocated to Los Angeles to be closer to the PLM, and he recruited Italian anarchists to the movement, often speaking to workers from the newly constructed Italian Hall, on the corner of North Main and Macy, just off the Placita Olvera.[22] According to historian Marcella Bencivinni, the spontaneous protests "evolved into more organized struggles aiming at a fundamental political, economic, and social change."[23]

TRAVELING IDEOLOGIES MEET THE OPEN SHOP

What drew working-class migrants to Los Angeles from around the world was primarily the explosion of industrial development in Southern

California, marked by the development of corporate agricultural fields and industrial factories across the basin. However, migrants bound for Los Angeles brought with them radical belief systems forged by efforts to blunt the crippling effect of unbridled capitalist expansion in their home countries. The operating ideology of the open shop was promoted by the Merchants and Manufacturing Association (known as M&M), which was organized in 1896 and led by General Harrison Gray Otis, the powerful publisher and editor of the *Los Angeles Times*. The open shop led the business elite to make the city an industrial powerhouse, profiting from the complete lack of organized labor in industrial relations. By 1910, the industrial sector had grown so fast in Los Angeles that the proportion of the city's labor force defined as wage earners, 79.2 percent, was higher than in San Francisco. Ten years later, Los Angeles had surpassed San Francisco in the actual number of manufacturing establishments, becoming the largest manufacturing city in the West.[24]

Otis's goal "was to keep labor costs low, develop a nonunion labor force, and turn the city into an exemplar of 'industrial freedom.'"[25] In August 1890, Otis showed what his leadership would mean by firing every member of the International Typographical Union who worked for him when his employees refused to accept a 20 percent wage cut. This antiunion ideology was shared by Henry E. Huntington, nephew of Southern Pacific Railroad magnate Collis P. Huntington, who emerged as an industrial leader in Southern California at the turn of the century when he created L.A.'s interurban railroad network, known as the Red Car line, for the Pacific Electric Company. (One line operated near property John Wesley Coleman's parents had purchased in 1877 when they first arrived in Boyle Heights.) In 1902, Huntington fired all of his employees who tried to join the Amalgamated Railway Union, and when Mexican railway workers walked off the job in 1903 Huntington broke the strike by hiring Japanese and African American strikebreakers and enlisted large numbers of police to protect them. Otis's *Los Angeles Times* denounced the walkout, calling the workers "poor, ignorant peons employed in laying track ... stupid fellows, these peons, who don't know what a union is."[26]

But new Boyle Heights residents could recognize these antilabor narratives and practices, as they brought with them leftist ideologies of anarchism, socialism, communism, or communitarianism that would flourish in Boyle Heights in various labor unions and political organizations. While differing in doctrine and method, these political philosophies crossed ideological as well as national boundaries to promote the same goals: "to overthrow capitalism, emancipate the workers, and establish social and economic equality."[27]

In doing so, they produced a transnational generation of social rebels, or what the Italians called *sovversivi*.[28] Whether these political sentiments had been cultivated in the Russian Revolution, the Mexican Revolution, or various campaigns of the Italian Communist Party, in Boyle Heights they often merged in several multiracial trade union organizations.

For other populations streaming into Boyle Heights during the early twentieth century, nationalism was simultaneously emerging as a powerful force, reshaping a sense of belonging among the masses around the globe. As historian Allison Varzally argues, "Italians arriving in the late nineteenth and early twentieth century considered themselves Ligurians, Tuscans, or Calabrians."[29] At the time, strong regional identities were more characteristic of immigrants from various parts of the world than attachments to nation-states, which were then just in formation. Immigrants from Mexico were denigrated by elites from both Mexico and the United States, seen as lacking a firm nationalist connection to the Mexican state and instead possessing strong connections to family and their village of origin, a mind-set viewed as "pre-modern."[30] Similarly, Japanese emigrants of this period were often viewed as having few loyalties to the Meiji regime or the Japanese state, and their supposed disloyalty to Japan was a result of coming from rural areas characterized as backward.[31]

At the same time, each of these areas underwent an intense growth of nationalist sentiment during the era that immigrant communities were being established in Los Angeles. The Mexican Revolution spawned a new genera-tion of loyalists to the Mexican state, many of whom had fought for self-governance for the working masses through Emiliano Zapata or Pancho Villa before migrating north to avoid the violent aftermath. In the postrevo-lutionary society, Mexican immigrants in the United States would increas-ingly be seen as *Mexicanos de afuera,* acquiring skills and perspectives that made them more valuable to the Mexican state.[32] Japanese colonialist dis-course grew in the Meiji period as Japan built its own expansionist empire, increasingly seeing its migrants abroad as part of this imperialist develop-ment.[33] In either case, the active role of the consulates abroad in providing leadership and direction to the immigrant communities was motivated by the desire to promote nationalist connections to one's homeland. Consulates wanted migrants to not embarrass the country abroad and wanted to foster the potential for migrants' return to their country of origin with robust attachments and loyalties to the nation-state.[34] The leading historian of Italians in San Francisco, Dino Cinel, attributes the decline in regionalism and the rise of nationalism among Italians in California to the steady improvement of economic success in the community, the decline in the rate of return to Italy, the spread of nationalism in Italy itself that also reached Italians abroad, and the rise of fascism, which appealed to some as the culmination of Italian nationalist sentiment.[35] In addition, historian Michael Topp credits the anti-Italian slurs and police brutalization expressed against Italian American syndicalists in the 1912 Lawrence, Massachusetts, general strike and subsequent labor conflicts elsewhere as bridging the divisions between northern and southern Italians and forging a new national ethnic identity across the United States.[36]

The intense racism that immigrants suffered in Los Angeles also encouraged them to retain loyalties to their country of origin and to develop new passionate attitudes of belonging to the nation of their birth, even as they remained firmly planted in constructing a life on US soil. For some, like the Japanese and the Chinese, who were prohibited by the Alien Land Laws from obtaining US citizenship and owning land, their country of origin was the only logical place for their nationalist sentiments in the era of the rise of the nation-state. For others with more options, the growing nationalist views that were emanating from their home country—reinforced by active consular officials—often led to distinctive identities as ethnic Americans with decidedly "diasporic sensibilities."[37] While following political and economic developments in their place of origin through ethnic newspapers and word-of-mouth communication with newcomers, Boyle Heights residents began to see their birthplace through a racialized and/or ethnic lens, which helped shape their perspective in Los Angeles.

At least one scholar has argued that the radical ideologies of anarchism and socialism brought to Los Angeles from abroad joined with the fundamental multiracial nature of the working class of the city to shape an "antinational cosmopolitanism" within the racial and ethnic communities of Southern California in the first three decades of the twentieth century.[38] Although some radicals, especially in the Industrial Workers of the World (IWW) movement, could be called "antinational cosmopolitans," the vast majority of the working-class population of Boyle Heights balanced competing notions of internationalism with national identities. Moreover, as racial distinctions became a definitive marker of significance in the larger society, race often joined with national background to give Boyle Heights residents a sense of belonging and affiliation, even within a distinctly multiracial setting. Life in Boyle Heights made clear to most that they did not have to "give up" their immigrant national and ethnic identities to feel part of the community as a whole, at least in their own immediate neighborhood.

However, the multiracial nature of the Boyle Heights neighborhood also gave residents clear signals about what it meant to be "American." To everyone in Boyle Heights, the polyglot backdrop of the neighborhood and the multiracial dynamic of street life was what distinguished life in America from what they had known in their country of origin. Despite racialized job opportunities and restrictive covenants that limited housing opportunities, California appeared to be relatively open—a place without a hardened caste system, where their families could survive and eventually flourish through hard work and perseverance. Los Angeles' growing economy and the relative peacefulness of relations between different national and racial groups in Boyle Heights gave newly arrived residents a sense that American identity— even the hyphenated kind that predominated in the neighborhood—was possible for them and especially for their children. While national and local leaders may have had different ideas regarding American nationalism, Boyle Heights residents embraced diversity and inclusion as fundamental values in their adopted country, because this was what they witnessed immediately surrounding them.[39]

SEEKING LABOR, FINDING HOMES

What brought these immigrants and migrants together east of downtown Los Angeles in the first decades of the twentieth century was twofold: proximity to jobs and policies of racial exclusion from other housing options. Certainly, they were drawn to the booming city of Los Angeles by its burgeoning industrial economy, and Boyle Heights was close to such employment. In addition, as I detailed in chapter 2, the Los Angeles City Council became the first city to pass an ordinance excluding industrial activities from residential districts, which were almost entirely white, middle class, and on the Westside of Los Angeles.[40]

At the same time, the city council channeled industrial development into central city neighborhoods, inhabited by poorer racial and ethnic minorities, along both sides of the Los Angeles River. Already this area had been where the Southern Pacific and Santa Fe Railroads had set up maintenance shops for their railway lines, combining these with boxcar communities for some of their poorest Mexican workers. As new immigrants poured into Los

Angeles and filled the traditional downtown communities of Sonoratown and Chinatown beyond capacity, more newcomers sought residences across the river—still close to transportation networks and industrial jobs. By the early 1910s, the city had established an "industrial district" that stretched south from Chinatown and east from Main Street to the river. A 1915 amendment expanded the district across the river to the Flats area of Boyle Heights and extended it west beyond Main Street to encompass key markets for fruits and vegetables and flowers exchanges. Local residents had no say in these developments, and large property owners dominated the decision-making. More zoning changes in 1921 continued to funnel light and heavy industry into these central districts.[41]

Developers in the late nineteenth century had ensured that urban railway networks would reach east across the river so that working-class newcomers could now use public transportation to travel to jobs on the Westside in factories and at industrial sites that took advantage of this favorable zoning. By the early twentieth century, streetcar lines had been constructed along Brooklyn Avenue, First Street, Fourth Street, and Seventh Street, providing easy access to jobs and leisure activities across the river to downtown Los Angeles. Mexican and Jewish women, for example, could find employment in various garment factories that dotted the south downtown area, and also in food canneries set up to take advantage of new processes to can vegetables and fruits for a more distant market.[42] The transportation network also allowed laborers to get to jobs in construction and the growing service sector. Japanese American workers from Boyle Heights could easily get downtown to the retail produce market or floral exchange that sustained the emerging ethnic economy. Easy access to Little Tokyo's retail and service economy also made living in Boyle Heights relatively simple.[43] Further, access to Southern California's transportation networks from Boyle Heights made local agricultural labor, which was, until 1940, still the most significant industry in Southern California, a viable option for seasonal Mexican workers, who needed to get to the agricultural fields located close to urban settlement throughout the Los Angeles basin. Given the seasonal and migratory nature of this work, it was not uncommon for Mexicans living in the Flats area or farther east near Evergreen Cemetery to work in agriculture during the winter months and in industry during the other seasons when agricultural work was unavailable.[44]

By 1918, more than a third of industries in the city of Los Angeles were located in largely working-class districts in the central city near Boyle Heights.[45] As plans for an expanded civic center developed in the early 1920s, however, land pressure drove up costs in the central downtown area, so business and city leaders sought to expand the industrial zone to the east. The "East Side Industrial District," stretching from Main Street all the way east to Whittier, was established by the city council and the Los Angeles Regional Planning Commission. To supervise its development, the "East Side Organization" (ESO) was established, with members coming from the chamber of commerce, the Merchants and Manufacturing Association, and the Los Angeles Realty Board. Although the ESO called for widespread industrial development in the region, it also realized that these same neighborhoods housed its workforce.[46] As the California Commission of Immigration and Housing concluded, "Life cannot be normal in a district so much given over to industry, where there must of necessity be noise, grime, confusion, unpleasant odors, houses insanitary [sic] and dilapidated."[47]

Given the growing unpleasantness of residential districts butting up against industrial zones, it was more than nearby employment opportunities that kept these newcomers tightly housed in communities like Boyle Heights. As discussed in the previous chapter, Los Angeles would become the leading innovator in racial residential restriction in the United States. Neighborhoods to the east and south that lay adjacent to or connected to these industrial zones by rail lines, like Boyle Heights, Watts, and Belvedere, were relatively open compared to communities to the west. These racially and ethnically mixed areas were home not only to African Americans, Asian Americans, and Latinos but also to white ethnic groups disparaged at the time, like Jews and Italians. And even as these populations grew substantially with the evolution of the industrial labor force in Southern California, they remained isolated and restricted to this small area, therefore producing substantial overcrowding and deplorable housing conditions in much of the region.[48] As discussed by the foremost sociologists of US racial residential segregation, the practice of "apartheid" in US cities is comparable to its more well-known counterpart in South Africa, and not just in the Jim Crow South. Sociologists Douglas Massey and Nancy Denton argue that "although America's apartheid may not be rooted in the legal strictures of its South African relative, it is no less effective in perpetuating racial inequality, and whites are no less culpable for the socioeconomic deprivation that results."[49]

Despite the limited options, the Boyle Heights neighborhood offered a surprising range of housing for working-class and even middle-class families. Over 80 percent of the residences in the Boyle Heights/Hollenbeck area were single-family homes, but they were available at a variety of prices for rent and

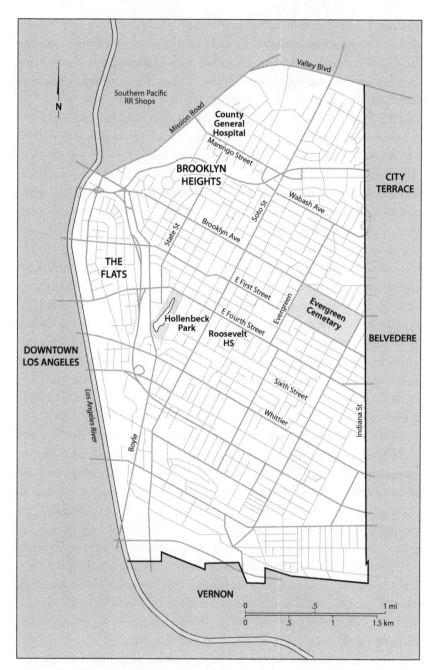

MAP 2. Boyle Heights neighborhoods and site locations. Drawn by Bill Nelson.

ownership, with few racial or ethnic restrictions. In the 1910s and 1920s, therefore, both wage earners and professionals, and even some doctors and nurses who worked in the neighborhood at White Memorial or Los Angeles County Hospital, would call Boyle Heights home. For those with means, large lots were available for purchase between $1,000 to $1,500 in "the hills" of City Terrace, as well as homes for rent for $35 to $40 per month. The Flats area of Boyle Heights offered cheaper lots for sale for $600 to $800, while smaller homes could be rented for under $10 a month.[50]

Albert Johnson remembered "the diversity of people that lived in the community" just west of Evergreen Cemetery. "I always had different kinds of friends. I had Japanese friends, I had Mexican friends, I had Chinese friends. There were other black kids in the community, in the neighborhood. So there was always a mix of people.... One of my earliest memories is hearing Spanish language music coming from homes around where we lived."[51] In fact, the census tract representing this area of Boyle Heights near the cemetery was by far the most diverse. Of the 253 individuals in the 1930 sample living there, 32 percent were white, 29 percent Mexican, 26 percent Japanese, and 10 percent listed as "Negro."

By 1910, this community was already recognized as one of the most significant African American neighborhoods in Los Angeles. Black cultural life had evolved there, anchored by Mt. Olive Baptist Church, located on Evergreen Avenue near Pennsylvania Avenue, and Caldwell's AME Zion Mission on Savannah Street near Brooklyn under Pastor J. R. Hambright. While other African Americans worshipped downtown, and self-help and racial solidarity clubs and other fraternal organizations were located near the routes of the streetcars, Boyle Heights had developed as a place that could sustain small businesses and entrepreneurs serving the black community. The mix of home ownership and rental units available for African Americans made the Boyle Heights neighborhood an appealing alternative for newcomers as the Los Angeles black community swelled in the 1920s.[52]

The Japanese community that migrated eastward from Little Tokyo along First Street into Boyle Heights eventually intersected with this African American community. Indeed, it is likely that Los Angeles realtors directed potential Japanese American home buyers to this Boyle Heights community specifically because it was an African American neighborhood and not a predominantly white neighborhood where Caucasian homeowners were likely to protest.[53] The first Japanese Americans who moved to Boyle Heights were professionals who were looking for family accommodations where they could plant extended families and escape the overcrowded conditions of Little Tokyo. Tract 214, the Evergreen section of Boyle Heights, provided this comfort because the typical unit was a detached single-family home. According to historian John Modell, what Japanese Americans were seeking when they sought to live in Boyle Heights was "the possibility of achieving an appropriately 'American' style of life, centering upon the home, consumption, and family living."[54]

Russian Molokan Kate Bolotin also remembers the Flats industrial area alongside the Los Angeles River as a place where her people interacted frequently with Mexicans, Armenians, and others. Her father "knew a little bit of Armenian; he knew a little bit of Turkish, so they were able to communicate." Her cousin Paul Zolnekoff remembered that parents got along because "they knew they were foreigners when they came here, and they were happy to be here, and everything was peaceful."[55] While the Molokans called the area Russian-town, the mix of other residents who lived in the neighborhood continued to call the area "the Flats." Most residents rented their homes in the neighborhood, but over time the Russian Molokans began to own homes, so much so that by 1920, 50 percent of the population were homeowners.

Just to the north of the Flats neighborhoods, in the northeastern corner of Boyle Heights along Mission Road, was the largest concentration of Italian immigrants, mixed with a significant number of Mexican immigrants. This section of Boyle Heights would blend into the growing Lincoln Heights neighborhood until the San Bernardino Freeway cut off this section from the north in the 1950s. As the Italian community expanded to the northeast from its original location near the central plaza, its members were often able to purchase the characteristic bungalows, since they were largely employed as skilled laborers and small entrepreneurs with stable employment prospects. This meant that in the first three decades of the twentieth century, 42 percent of Italian settlers could purchase property, becoming the city's fourth-largest group of homeowners and surpassing the rate of Italian home ownership in San Francisco (23 percent) and New York (21 percent).[56] A common Catholic faith prompted connections across national lines between Italian and Mexican newcomers.

However, most microneighborhoods in Boyle Heights had fairly strict racial boundaries. When asked about playing with kids from other races, Ray Aragon explained that he played with "mostly the guys on that street on Concord, mostly Mexican kids," because "our neighborhood, that was our world."[57] Growing up farther north in Boyle Heights of the 1930s, Hershey

Eisenberg remembered that "the street that we lived on, City View, was predominantly Jewish" and that "there was like a dividing line at State Street." He added, "On the other side of State Street was sort of a demarcation point where mostly Mexican families lived."[58] Indeed, all five of the census tracts that documented a more than 90 percent white population in my database were on the Jewish side of State Street. Eddie Ramirez, whose father sold fruit from a cart throughout Boyle Heights, remembered distinctly that his community was "mostly people from Mexico," while the Jewish area was "west of Evergreen."[59] Even though Boyle Heights as a whole had no single ethnic majority until the 1950s, the majority of individual blocks and sections were dominated by one group or another. As Claire Stein put it, "Everybody lived in their own little ghettos."[60]

The commercial districts along and between Brooklyn Avenue and East First Street, in this central part of Boyle Heights, were dominated by dozens of Jewish food-related businesses, including bakeries, delicatessens, restaurants, butchers, pickle barrels, fishmongers, and groceries. These businesses grew because of the particularities of kosher dietary laws and offered residents food that recalled eastern European and American Jewish specialties. Business was often conducted in Yiddish, and storefronts displayed Stars of David in their windows to draw in Jewish patrons. But as historian Caroline Luce reminds us, the commercial district was also home to a much more diverse group of business owners "offering an abundance of tempting treats that enticed the neighborhood's Jewish residents to violate kosher dietary laws and buy their food from non-Jewish business owners." According to her research, the blocks between 1500 and 2500 Brooklyn Avenue also housed two Japanese grocers, Armenian, Mexican, and Italian-owned bakeries, and several Mexican- and Mexican American–owned restaurants, alongside Jewish businesses. "Jewish residents could buy a nice rye from a grocery store or bakery, or opt for tamales or tortillas from Ismael Rodriguez or Jovita Campos, lavash from Joe Bajkowski, or rice noodles or dumplings from Orange Blossom Bakery."[61]

Away from the main thoroughfares of Brooklyn Avenue and Wabash Avenue, there was even more diversity among small businesses and entrepreneurs. In the Flats area, for example, Russian Molokans tended to open small grocery stores to serve the local community, but there were also a few Armenian grocers and a small section of Mexican retailers. Along First Street, dentists, doctors, lawyers, and realtors from Japanese American, African American, and other communities set up practices to serve a wide clientele. Thus the key to understanding Boyle Heights is that cross-ethnic interaction was often institutionalized, taking place not between equals but between an ethnic professional or small business operation and its customers, who included both a cluster of the business's own community and a wider range of multiple ethnic or racial groups. The locally based consumer class also had a range of options, including going downtown if they were unsatisfied with local options.

INSTITUTIONAL LIFE IN 1920S BOYLE HEIGHTS

Despite some mixture of consumerism, racial and ethnic segregation dominated daily activities for most adults in Boyle Heights, structured not only by their place of residence but also by highly segregated places of employment, business, and adult conviviality. With some rare exceptions—such as the Jewish and Mexican women employed by the garment industry—Jewish and Mexican adults had highly differentiated employment opportunities in Los Angeles and rarely had interaction at work.[62] Leo Frumkin, despite growing up in the predominantly Mexican Belvedere, recalled that "one reason it was hard to get to know the neighbors was because in many of the homes in Boyle Heights . . . [while] the kids spoke English . . . very few of the parents spoke English" in either the Mexican or the Japanese homes.[63] These language barriers, of course, also limited interaction across racial lines among parents in Boyle Heights. In addition, many of the clubs, prayer services, and other social gatherings were structured by distinct religious and ethnic institutions—largely limited to those of the same ethnic and linguistic background.

However, the fact that most institutions in Boyle Heights kept specific racial and ethnic groups apart from each other went beyond a lack of common language. The growth of ethnic-specific religious institutions and houses of worship in the 1910s and 1920s in Boyle Heights probably did more than any other part of institutional life in the neighborhood to keep neighbors separated. Jewish synagogues started to proliferate on the Eastside, beginning with the Talmud Torah Synagogue, otherwise known as the Breed Street Shul, which moved there from downtown Los Angeles in 1915. While this became the largest Orthodox place of worship for Jews west of the Mississippi River with the building of a new synagogue in 1923, at least nine other smaller Jewish houses of worship were distributed across the landscape of Boyle Heights. With services in Hebrew, and Orthodox practices limiting engagement with non-Jews on the Sabbath from sundown Friday night to sundown Saturday night, religious Jews spent a good deal of their weekends oriented inward toward family and the local Jewish community.[64]

The African American community similarly built their own places of worship in the evangelical Christian tradition in some of the most residentially integrated neighborhoods in Boyle Heights. Likewise, the Russian Molokan community built three small congregations, with services conducted only in the Russian language. In 1933, they consolidated these three groups into one large church serving 500 families, located at the corner of East Third and Bodie Streets in Boyle Heights.[65]

Japanese American congregations were first curated in Los Angeles by Protestant Christian congregations, given the Protestant "missionary" work in Asia, with Buddhist congregations trailing behind. Eventually both Protestant and Buddhist churches were established in Boyle Heights as offshoots to Little Tokyo–based houses of worship. Like other parts of the Japanese American community in Boyle Heights, these churches were concentrated along First Street, often attracting nearby residences and businesses to serve the local community. A large Buddhist congregation, located directly on the corner of East First Street and North Mott Street, joined Tenrikyo Church, a multipurpose congregation that combined Buddhism with Japan-based Shintoism and was the US-based home of a church started in Kobe, Japan. Each congregation had adjacent Japanese-language schools and sponsored community activities for nearby residents, expanding the ethnic reach from a religious foundation.[66]

One might think that the Catholic community would provide opportunities for Mexicans and Italians to worship together given their shared religion. But instead, Italian Catholic worship was solidified around St. Peter's Italian Church, which was created by the Irish-dominated Catholic Church in Los Angeles and its Bishop Thomas J. Conaty to offset the institutional church's disaffection for Italian immigrant Catholics. Father Tito Piacentini was instructed "to produce good Catholics in the Italian tradition" as early as 1904. This mission was solidified on July 4, 1915, when St. Peter's Church was relocated to North Broadway and Bishop's Road, slightly northeast of the downtown settlement but in a prime location to serve Italian Americans in Lincoln Heights and Boyle Heights. Although formally outside Boyle Heights, Italians living in that neighborhood, like those from around Los Angeles, would flock to this symbolic center of Italian Catholic life. By 1919, St. Peter's was designated the Italian national church of Los Angeles. Over the period from 1915 to 1932, more than 8,000 Italians were baptized and nearly 5,000 funerals were conducted there.[67]

Initially most Mexican Catholics in Boyle Heights continued to go to mass at the Plaza Catholic Church, the heart of the Los Angeles Catholic community for over one hundred years. But as the population grew east of the Los Angeles River, the first Catholic parish was created there on November 10, 1896, by Bishop George Montgomery, and was named for the Blessed Mother. It was dedicated one year later. St. Mary's Church was first a "stout red brick" building at the corner of Fourth and Chicago Streets. The founding pastor was Father Joseph Doyle, an Irishman who served until 1900. His successor, Father Joseph Barron, began the Holy Names Society in 1904. Three years later it opened a Catholic elementary school, which was only the third in the archdiocese. However, St. Mary's was overwhelmed by the number of parishioners it was asked to serve as immigration increased exponentially with the displacement from the violence of the Mexican Revolution and the Cristero Revolt of the 1920s against anticlerical statutes in the 1917 Constitution. In response, the archdiocese created a new parish, Resurrection Church, in the eastern part of Boyle Heights in 1923. But another church, Dolores Mission, formed in 1925 in the Flats area, utilizing the support of the priests from nearby St. Mary's Parish.[68]

Not all institutional life in Boyle Heights, however, centered on religious institutions. Indeed, Jewish radicals had worked hard to create a vibrant Yiddish public culture in Boyle Heights, and, as Luce makes clear, the "epicenter" was a five-block radius around the intersection of Brooklyn Avenue and Soto Street. Here the Labor Zionists had built their *folkschule* (or people's congregation) at 420 Soto, the Jewish socialists and affiliated organizations had set up the Vladeck Center at 126 North St. Louis, and the Yiddish communists had constructed their Cooperative Center at 2708 Brooklyn Avenue. But even more important, "The streets themselves became sites for debate, the corner of Brooklyn and Soto in particular serving as an impromptu pulpit for Yiddish orators espousing a variety of nationalist and socialist ideologies."[69] Yet as Luce herself argues, the socialist organizations in the Jewish community, at least until the 1930s, limited themselves to organizing Jewish radicals and maintaining a Yiddish tradition even amid the multilingual and multiracial Boyle Heights population.

A few immigrant-oriented institutions did try to serve a wide range of ethnic newcomers to Boyle Heights. Founded in 1914 and physically located in Boyle Heights as of 1924, the International Institute of the YWCA pledged to "serve the women and girls coming from Europe and the Orient and to assist the foreign communities in their adjustment to life in this country."[70] Early on in their work, they provided organized classes for English instruction or domestic homemaking that were multiethnic and tried to serve the diverse local population. But over time, even here, institutional priorities came to restructure classes and meetings into monoracial gatherings. Teachers found it easier to draw students together and teach them efficiently when they were all of the same ethnic group, and by the 1920s most Americanization and English language classes were made up by immigrants of the same ethnic background. Even when multiple classes were offered at the same location, they were often divided by ethnicity.

As religious institutions, consulate offices, and other ethnic organizations began to sponsor activities for the younger generation born in the United States, they also largely organized their activities along racial, ethnic, and national lines. For example, the ethnic-specific clubs aimed at young Japanese American girls were organized by Buddhist or Christian churches, or the pan-Protestant YWCA.[71] But one can also identify an intention among these clubs and organizations to loosen the cultural ties that bound immigrants to their home country and to advocate for increased assimilation into American life, encouraging cross-ethnic affiliations and friendships in the process. As the 1920s progressed, it was clear that US institutions were increasingly affecting the cultural affiliations and identities of US-born ethnic youth, and this worried both their parents and community leaders. But cross-ethnic connections only increased over time with the growth of unique American institutions, like the public high school, which brought together racial and ethnic youth in unprecedented fashion and added new generational tensions to the community.

YOUTH, SCHOOLING, AND THE RISE OF INTERETHNIC FRIENDSHIPS

In 1922, the Los Angeles School Board decided to organize a new high school to accommodate the growing number of young people who were living east of downtown Los Angeles. Up to that point, the teenagers of Boyle Heights attended Los Angeles Polytechnic High School at the corner of Washington Boulevard and Flower Street and had to travel five miles to continue their schooling after the middle grades.[72] Theodore Roosevelt Senior High School, named after the nation's popular 26th president just four years after his death in 1919, opened its doors in 1923. The new school's teams were named the "Rough Riders" after the regiment of soldiers that Roosevelt had led up San Juan Hill during the Spanish-American War in 1898. Those soldiers were known as quite a diverse group, including Native Americans, Ivy League students, white-collar professionals, and working-class ethnics.

There is a certain irony to the naming of the local high school in Boyle Heights after Theodore Roosevelt, known by his initials "TR." As president, he stoked fears around the idea of a "race suicide" of white Americans for not producing enough offspring, especially in relation to the immigrant masses flowing into American cities in the early twentieth century. Even before taking the presidency, TR had concerns about immigration and its effect on the US as a whole. In an 1894 article he authored, TR was an ardent advocate of Americanization: "We must Americanize in every way, in speech, in political ideas and principles, and in their way of looking at relations between church and state. We welcome the German and the Irishman who becomes an American. We have no use for the German or Irishman who remains such. . . . He must revere only our flag, not only must it come first, but no other flag should even come second."[73]

Despite the namesake of their school, many graduates remember Roosevelt High School as a "multiethnic utopia," where 61 different nationalities attended. In Boyle Heights as elsewhere, youth often played the critical role in initiating interethnic relations, whether through interracial marriage, political coalition building, or multiracial dancing venues, although young people who crossed ethnic and racial lines could, in the words of one author, "evoke both curiosity and fear."[74] The social, cultural, and institutional settings that frame these moments of border crossing also help underscore the long-term impact on families and communities.

Youth in Boyle Heights were often thrust into institutional settings, especially schools, where a multiracial setting was the norm. Because elementary grades were dominated by the same ethnic group that made up the immediate geographic area, many students experienced their first truly "multiracial" school environments in junior high school. At this level, several neighboring school regions were drawn together for middle grades, and individual students noticed the racial transformation of the student body.[75] Freda Mallow remembered her younger brother deciding to call himself García instead of Ginsberg at Hollenbeck Junior High, making a lot of friends for himself with his new identity.[76] On the other hand, many Mexican, Asian, and black

FIGURE 6. 1938 Hollenbeck Junior High School student body officers. Japanese American National Museum (Gift of Elma Takahashi, 2001.208.2).

children remembered junior high as the time when discrimination became visible to them, in practices such as the banning of Spanish speaking at school or the manipulation of student body officer elections to control who won.[77]

The reality was that for most, the student body at Roosevelt High School became less diverse and more segregated than the general teenage population of Boyle Heights. Children in Mexican American and Mexican immigrant families were disproportionately taken out of their schooling by parents in the 1930s and put to work after junior high school.[78] This happened not only because poor Mexican immigrant families needed their children's income but also because immigrants from Mexico came to the United States without established patterns or long-standing commitments to secondary school attendance, unlike those from Japan, which had featured compulsory education, or Jewish immigrants, who had a long history of religious education. Moreover, Mexican American high school students tended to be tracked into courses intended to prepare them for working-class jobs—like auto shop or industrial arts—or for domestic work, like home economics.[79] It was unusual that Mexican American children were left in the regular college preparatory

FIGURE 7. Roosevelt High School Spanish Club, ca. 1934, with future councilman Edward Roybal in first row. Shades of LA Photo Collection/Los Angeles Public Library.

curriculum, but some were able to excel despite teachers and counselors who often linked future economic and career opportunities to their racial background. Eddie Ramirez stayed in college prep courses only because certain teachers had fought the counselors and other teachers who had wanted to place him in an industrial arts curriculum.[80]

Many former students also remembered that extracurricular activities at Roosevelt were largely segregated by ethnicity. Ray Aragon recalled that elite Mexican kids—at least those aspiring to be elite—were in the Caballeros Club.[81] Hershey Eisenberg and Daniel Kawahara remembered separate clubs for other ethnic groups, including a Japanese Club and a Jewish Club.[82] Cedrick Shimo felt that "you could divide the sports activity by the race": varsity football was dominated by "huge Russians" and Jews, Mexicans and blacks were in varsity track, and "tall Slavics" were in varsity basketball. Junior varsity teams in football and track were where Japanese Americans were active, while debating was confined to "mostly the Jewish students."[83] Fifteen-year-old Leo Frumkin made the mistake of inviting Bobby Chavez to join a Jewish youth fraternity, AZA or Aleph Zadik Aleph, and left the group himself when he was informed you had to be Jewish to join.[84] While many

FIGURE 8. The Cougars Athletic Club from Evergreen Playground at Terminal Island, 1937. Japanese American National Museum (Gift of George Fujino, 2000.418.1).

students recalled the annual International Days when students dressed up in native costumes from their parents' homelands, and others recalled certain clubs like the World Friendship Club that fostered interethnic relationships, most former students remembered largely hanging out with those from the same racial or ethnic background.[85]

Groups organized outside school also proliferated during the teenage years, and these too were often racially divided. Most remembered that informal social groups, like the Saxons or the Jasons, and even some sports teams, like the Cougars, who played football and baseball in a Japanese league, considered themselves "gangs" at that time and were even called such by older residents. Most of these groups were male, although linked female social groups, like the Jesterettes, were formed as counterparts. These groups were usually residentially based, which meant that they were largely made up of one ethnic group but could involve other local youth if they lived nearby. Daniel Kawahawa remembered that both Manuel Ochoa and Atoy Wilson Jr., Mollie's brother, played with the Cougars when they practiced in the neighborhood but were not allowed to play in league baseball games because the league was officially Japanese only. In short, these groups were seen at the time to be much like the White Fence gang and other residentially based youth gangs that began to develop in Mexican American neighborhoods in the period.[86]

So even in a highly multiracial community like Boyle Heights, young people from different racial and ethnic groups were often separated structurally by school attendance, residential exclusivity, and differing interests. On the other hand, individuals did connect with each other across racial lines at various points in their lives, often in significant, life-altering ways. Claire Stein remembered entering a dance contest at Hollenbeck Junior High with a Latino classmate and winning the contest. Although she never told her parents because "they would not have liked that at all," the victory did appear in the Hollenbeck yearbook for all to see.[87] Mollie Wilson's friendship with Sandie Okada and Mary Murakami was forged when Sandie and Mary stood up for Mollie when she was denied a chance to run for student body president at Hollenbeck, and it endured even after they were taken to internment camps during World War II.[88]

Almost all of those interviewed acknowledged that, after junior high school, dating across racial lines was shunned. Indeed, Mollie Wilson remembered being pulled away from a white male roller skating partner by two white servicemen during World War II. As historian Mark Wild has also found, "The array of social forces opposing cross-cultural teenage dating helped to dampen its frequency."[89] While rarely a cross-racial partnership might flourish into marriage in that era, it was more common for young people to recognize and abide by the limitations placed on interethnic relationships in midcentury Boyle Heights.

However, clearly it was the American-born young people in each immigrant and racial or ethnic family that tended to bring other family members more decidedly into American culture and connection across racial and national lines. Whether it was young Mexican American women who brought cosmetics into their homes or took family members to American-made movies or US-born Jewish, Mexican, or Italian radicals who brought ethnic families in to support a localized union picket line, US-born young people were at the forefront of cultural experimentation across racial and ethnic lines in Boyle Heights.[90] These new affiliations and connections were not inevitable in Boyle Heights or in any other urban community; they had to be created through exploration, new institutional possibilities, and, most critically, people who overcame their prejudices and ventured outside their comfort zones. But a community like Boyle Heights was apt to nurture these new connections because of its multiracial neighborhood geography and ideologies of openness. This is how a neighborhood that was neglected by city leaders and intentionally marginalized became a multiracial ecosystem of coexistence and collaboration. For residents of the neighborhood, Boyle Heights became a microcosm of America.

In the early part of the twentieth century the world was undergoing profound disruptions to traditional patterns of economy and society, spurred by industrialization, global transnationalism, and imperial capitalism. Migrants to Los Angeles often came from areas of Latin America, Asia, Europe, and parts of the United States that were experiencing economic convulsions and violent political upheavals. They found in Boyle Heights a complex world of conflict, coalition, coalescence, comfort, and contestation shaped by racial and class segregation from the rest of Los Angeles. They also found a haven for those effectively exiled because of political or racial persecution and for workers who fled their places of origin for survival and for the sake of their family's future. Over the twentieth century, Boyle Heights became one of Southern California's most diverse neighborhoods, welcoming immigrants and racial and ethnic minorities from all over the nation and the world. This chapter has explored the place of Boyle Heights in the peopling of urban Southern California in the early twentieth century and in the global movement of peoples caused by dislocations, capitalist expansion, and imperialism around the world.

Most studies of racial or ethnic group migrants like those to Boyle Heights look only at cross-racial or cross-ethnic interactions with majority whites that eventually lead to the group's assimilation. This places each minority racial or ethnic group on a separate historical path and ignores their interactions with each other. But the tracing of a simple trajectory from country of origin to country of arrival and from alien status to inclusion obscures the multinational worlds that migrants inhabited, created, and sustained. In 1985 the perceptive Juan Flores, instead of focusing on cultural interactions that led to assimilation with the white center of power, recognized the polylateral relations among minority communities that created new possibilities for culture and expression in urban spaces: "This 'growing-together' is often mistaken for assimilation, but the difference is obvious in that it is not directed toward incorporation into the dominant culture. For that reason, the 'pluralism' that results does not involve the dissolution of national backgrounds and cultural histories but their continued affirmation and enforcement even as they are transformed."[91]

Historians of Los Angeles, too, need to move toward a similar multiracial perspective that is both relational and transnational to understand the zones of interaction between people, nations, and cultures in urban America.[92] What we uncover when we do this creatively is a hidden history of public and intimate relationships, neighborhood social and political alliances across racial lines, and both cooperation and conflict between groups marking much of American history. Migrants to Boyle Heights would share radical traditions from their various homelands, even while the rise of nationalist sentiments and segregated enclaves in the period led them to strengthen their own ethnic sense of self. Moreover, the experiences of transnational migration and expansion of empires made it possible for individuals from a wide variety of racial and national backgrounds to encounter each other in often-unexpected places. They sought new homes in places where they could escape violence, displacement, and despair, while pursuing new beginnings that would bring good fortune, if not to themselves, then to their sons and daughters. More often than not, their children would be the ones who formed more extensive connections with each other that would lead to profound transformations in mid-twentieth-century Los Angeles. Though this culture of collaboration would be tested during the Great Depression and World War II, it would make Boyle Heights a beacon for others regarding what was possible to achieve across racial and ethnic diversity and economic disparity.

FOUR

Disposable People, Expendable Neighborhoods

Well, I don't like [this whole idea of "repatriation"]. I don't think I'll ever like it, not after the way I was made to suffer. I feel that this country should have done something for its citizens instead of getting rid of them the way they did. It's the whole country that was involved. I'm sure it wasn't just one state. You can't just blame Los Angeles County or the State of California. The American Government said, "Let's get rid of the Mexicans since they're closest to their native lands."

EMILIA CASTAÑEDA DE
VALENCIANA, 1971 *Interview*

AT EIGHT YEARS OLD, Emilia Castañeda was able to see that her life was about to take a turn for the worse. Born in Boyle Heights in 1926, she had grown up in a loving Mexican immigrant household where she felt secure and taken care of by her mother and father. Her father, Natividad Castañeda, was a skilled stonemason from Ciudad Lerdo, Durango, who had immigrated around 1910. He was able to find plenty of work in Los Angeles because of the booming construction industry in the region during the 1920s. Emilia's stepmother Gregoria worked as a domestic for several Jewish families in Los Angeles.[1]

When the Great Depression hit Los Angeles, the Castañeda family collapsed. Suddenly, Natividad could not find work. Stonemasons like Natividad experienced over 25 percent unemployment rates by April 1930. If any jobs were available then, they went to Anglo Americans first; one out of seven Mexican men was already out of a job.[2] Natividad eventually adjusted—staying home and cooking, washing, cleaning, and taking care of neighbors' children—while his wife brought home the family wages. Without two incomes, though, they lost the house they owned and had to rent elsewhere in Boyle Heights. Eventually they went on county welfare to survive. As the only source of income, Emilia's stepmother Gregoria was forced to keep working despite a slight cold, until that cold turned into tuberculosis, or what Mexicans called *la gripa*. By the time she saw a doctor at County General Hospital, it was too late. Gregoria was confined as a TB patient to Sunland Sanitorium, where she eventually died in May 1934, on the same day that eight-year-old Emilia had her first Catholic Communion.[3] Emilia remembers, "After my mother died, I guess my dad was pretty sad. Here he was left with a family, no wife, no work, and living off of welfare. He had a trade and could work if the work was available. Maybe he thought he should go back to his country."[4] The decision faced by Natividad and his family was one faced by thousands of Mexican residents of Los Angeles and elsewhere in the wake of similarly desperate circumstances. Emilia's family returned to Mexico under Los Angeles County's so-called Mexican Repatriation Campaign, whereby Natividad accepted the state's offer of train tickets to Durango, Mexico, and thus was deemed "deported." No provision was made for his children's citizenship, who were effectively banished from their birth country.

The Mexican Repatriation Campaign was not the first time local officials had wanted to relocate a racialized immigrant population out of Southern California. As early as 1879, the newly appointed city public health officer Walter Lindley had suggested that the Chinese population of Los Angeles should be relocated to an unspecified destination because of the supposed health risk they posed to the city's population as a whole.[5] Aforementioned zoning laws, which kept racial "undesirables" away from white suburban communities, are another example. Utilizing historian Natalia Molina's concept of "racial scripts"—where patterns of dehumanization against one racialized group can be transferred into policy against another—I explore the linked logics and processes that undergird the forced movements of differing racial groups. This includes the "repatriation" of Mexican Americans in the 1930s, the New Deal progressivism that forced the removal of urban residents to make way for public housing and freeways, and the internment of Japanese Americans during World War II. At the same time, Molina outlines "counterscripts" as a mode of resistance and solidarity to this racialization, which allows us to understand how those racial and ethnic groups that were seen as disposable in Boyle Heights would band together to proclaim their worth as Americans who belonged.[6]

Boyle Heights had existed relatively undisturbed in the 1920s because the largely immigrant neighborhood supplied much-needed labor to surrounding industries in Southern California. All that changed with the collapse of the economy. With the stock market crash of 1929, the slump that was already in place in the agricultural sector became a prolonged and massive failure of basic economic networks and government safeguards. Unemployment soared, so that within one year, one out of every five persons seeking work in the city of Los Angeles had none. Many in Boyle Heights turned to ethnic-based charities, such as the Jewish Social Service Bureau, which helped indigent Jews "face our employment situation as a people and solve our problems within the group."[7] Others were sustained by strong ethnic-based economic networks, such as the Japanese cooperative industries of flowers and produce, which kept the Japanese in Los Angeles County off government assistance. Only 3 percent of Japanese in Los Angeles County were unemployed as late as 1940, compared to 12 percent of all workers in the district.[8] The Catholic Welfare Bureau was the largest private charitable agency in the city, serving both the Mexican and Italian populations. But as the funds were stretched by ever-greater needs, the Catholic Welfare Bureau adopted an anti-Mexican policy in their relief allocation. Food allowances for "American" families were reduced by 10 percent, while the allocation for Mexican families was reduced by 25 percent. The rationale given for this discrepancy was "differing food standards."[9]

The publicly visible suffering of the Depression spread and deepened dramatically during the early 1930s in Los Angeles. In addition to "Hoovervilles" taking root along the Los Angeles River, public bread lines appeared for the first time in June 1930. Yiddish socialists tried to address the needs of the unemployed through more programs at their Cooperative Center at 2708 Brooklyn Avenue, including child care services and a makeshift soup kitchen that operated out of the Cooperative Café and its adjoining bakery. While more radical Yiddish communists would adopt a daily "Fight for Bread" movement that called on forming unemployed councils, more moderate socialists started a cooperative movement that stressed buying clubs and self-reliance. Activists from all sides affiliated with the Cooperative Center aggressively fought evictions in the neighborhood and restored water, gas, and electric services when they had been turned off for nonpayment. These efforts led to the creation in 1930 of the left-leaning Jewish fraternal organization, the International Workers Order (IWO), which provided low-cost medical insurance, clinics, and other support for working-class immigrants. The IWO recruited non-Jewish members, including Hungarians, Ukrainians, Greeks, Italians, and others, and also established branches for African Americans and the Lazaro Cardenas Society, a Mexican branch, which often met at the Cooperative Center. It was involved in foreign-language newspapers (including those in Yiddish), union organizing, racial equality and integration, and advocacy for public policies such as the establishment of social security. On March 6, 1930, the IWO, affiliated with the Communist Party Los Angeles (CPLA), organized their first march for "Work or Wages" and began to have protests and rallies at least once a month.[10]

This leftist political activity drew the attention of the Los Angeles Police Department (LAPD) to Boyle Heights, especially the unit known as the "Red Squad" that was organized under the Intelligence Bureau of the Metropolitan Police Division. The police commissioner Mark Pierce expressed the philosophy of the unit during the Depression: "Communists have no Constitutional rights and I won't listen to anyone who defends them."[11] The Red Squad met the marches and protests with brutality, amassing 1,000 police to deter them with blackjacks and clubs. Even as Hitler took power in Germany and even as spies uncovered fascist organizing in Los Angeles in 1933, the preoccupation with communists led L.A. police chief James Davis to determine that "the greatest threat to democracy emanated from the Jewish-dominated Boyle Heights area."[12] A massive crackdown on left-wing activism included raids at the Cooperative Center; these eventually shut down the bakery and resulted in lifelong physical damage to several activists, including Isidore Brooks, manager of the Cooperative Café, who died from a police beating at a protest in 1932.[13]

For Boyle Heights and the rest of Los Angeles, the political response of city and county leadership to the challenges of rising unemployment, growing poverty, and economic collapse left much to be desired. By the end of 1930, when it became clear that the volunteer organizations were about to fold, Charles P. Visel was appointed head of the city "citizens'" committee, and began work on Christmas Eve 1930 to create a job placement service for unemployed city residents.[14] Almost immediately, Visel began to look for easy answers for Los Angeles' economic misfortune and for local scapegoats to blame. Visel noticed that William N. Doak, President Hoover's new secretary of labor, had promised to create jobs for US citizens by ousting any foreigner who held a job and deporting him from the country.[15] When Hoover appointed Colonel Arthur Woods as national coordinator of the President's Emergency Committee for Employment, Visel wrote a telegram to Woods on January 6 with a plan to generate jobs in Southern California by scaring local immigrants. Visel estimated that 5 percent of the 400,000 deportable "aliens" in the United States were in the Southern California district and requested advice on methods for getting rid of them. "We need their jobs for needy citizens," wrote Visel.[16] This contact began a series of communications between Visel, Woods, and Doak that eventually led Doak to send a set of immigration agents to Los Angeles to help enact a deportation plan.

By Monday, January 26, 1931, Visel sent a publicity release to local newspapers detailing the "alien" deportation plan, which targeted the first round of the 400,000 "foreigners" Doak had identified earlier that month. That Saturday, January 31, 19 federal agents arrived in Los Angeles and started their work identifying, apprehending, and deporting undocumented residents in various communities in Southern California. The climax of this effort was a very public raid of Los Angeles' central Plaza where—with the assistance of two dozen LAPD officers—the agents encircled the *placita,* questioning 400 individuals and eventually arresting 17 of them, 11 of whom were Mexican nationals. Meanwhile, in Boyle Heights and East Los Angeles, the publicity regarding the deportation campaign forced Mexican and Mexican American residents to go into hiding, avoiding public places altogether, including their places of employment.[17] The campaign to target and scapegoat the local Latino population had begun in earnest in early 1931 and would change the community's response to the economic downturn.

CRAFTING REPATRIATION AS A "NEW DEAL" FOR LOS ANGELES

The year 1931 was one of the most tumultuous in the history of the city of Los Angeles. As the city began to plan for the 150th anniversary of its founding, public officials were simultaneously struggling to respond to the growing economic crisis. As one of Los Angeles' most dedicated urban reformers of that decade, county supervisor Frank Shaw began in January 1931 to construct his own plan to reduce the welfare rolls in Los Angeles. He sought to ensure that more relief monies were available to local citizens to support his growing reputation and ambition as a politician who championed the interests of the "common folk." As chairman of the board of supervisor's charities and public welfare committee, Shaw knew that county relief funds would be quickly spent and would be unable to meet the exponential growth in the numbers of the region's poor due to the rapid rise of unemployment.[18] Mexican Americans had been among the first to require economic assistance from the government, since their unemployment that year rose to 60 percent, as many were banned from jobs because of their legal status and had few resources to fall back upon. Yet in January Shaw asked questions regarding the legality of transporting indigents outside the region at the county's expense. By February, Shaw had convinced his fellow supervisors to authorize the expenditure of $6,000 to transport indigents to their "place of legal residence wherein they will be officially accepted."[19]

Frank Shaw's efforts launched the largest organized repatriation campaign in US history, targeting Mexican immigrants and their American-born children in a city that their ancestors had founded 150 years before. By the end of 1934, when the last of the county's "repatriation" trains had left Los Angeles, over 13,000 Mexican residents and Mexican American citizens of Southern California—including Natividad Castañeda and his children Emilia and Frankie—had been sent to Mexico at a total cost of almost $200,000 to the taxpayers of Los Angeles County.[20] As Visel's scare campaign gained more publicity, Shaw's systematic efforts at removal would go on to affect a greater number of vulnerable families. Shaw worked with other civic leaders in both the city and the county who initiated parallel efforts to scare, cajole, deport, or encourage Mexican immigrants and Mexican Americans to leave the region. The county welfare department employed two Spanish speakers, Fernando España and Joseph Vargas, whose entire jobs in the period consisted of encouraging Mexicans to leave the United States.[21] Los Angeles lost nearly one-third of its Mexican population during the first half of the 1930s; Shaw used his aggressive and innovative actions to rise rapidly in Los Angeles politics.[22]

The actual implementation of Mexican repatriation by county welfare officials required a collective sense of racial urban geography, targeting specific areas in the region that, because of the city's segregation, housed particular populations. Nowhere in the city or county was more affected than the residential communities directly east of the Los Angeles River, in the Flats area of Boyle Heights. The Flats certainly came under intense scrutiny by urban reformers in the 1930s because of its visible poverty, spatially expressed in quite modest homes and rental units near industrial sites, that belied city leaders' claims of "progress" by being located within clear view of downtown office buildings. But it also became defined as a "slum area" in the region by virtue of its multiracial and immigrant populations, a demographic fundamentally at odds with the homogeneity of more middle-class sections of the city. Sociologist Pauline Young described the region in her 1932 book: "Life in The Flats is a strange conglomerate of immigrant peoples living side by side though speaking a veritable babel of tongues.... There is a conspicuous lack of American residents in The Flats. American families which owned homes here before 'the influx of foreigners' have left the district a long time ago. Negro workmen, Jewish merchants, Armenian truck drivers, Japanese gardeners, barbers, tradesmen, all contribute to life of The Flats. These diverse groups, elbowing each other in their daily life, have succeeded in accommodating themselves to each other to a certain degree."[23]

Not surprisingly, when county officials initiated their repatriation campaign they headed straight for Mexican indigents in the Flats area of Boyle Heights. From materials gathered from the Secretariat of Foreign Relations in Mexico, and connected to individual families identified in the 1930 US Census or Los Angeles City Directories, I have identified 567 individuals from 125 families repatriated from Boyle Heights from 1931 to 1933. Of these 125 families, 55 percent lived in the area described as the Flats, bounded by the Los Angeles River to the west, Boyle Avenue to the east, Brooklyn Avenue to the north, and Sixth Street to the south. Because my database of names and addresses is inevitably incomplete, it is likely that many more individuals were repatriated from the area. Nonetheless, I estimate that the Flats area remained the main zone of "repatriation" from Boyle Heights and one of the most significant targeted areas in all of Southern California.[24]

It is important to note that county social workers had long made home visits to the indigent to ascertain whether they were deserving of relief support. Eddie Ramirez remembers one such visit to his home when he was an adolescent:

> My grandfather, I saw him one day, he was in the living room, and the social worker came to talk with him. They wanted to confirm if he's still here, or what. And I was hiding in the closet there.... In Spanish, he was telling her. I don't know if the lady understood, but he was telling her, he says, "I don't want charity. I want to work." And he started to cry. And he raised up his arm and he showed her his muscle. He's got a big old muscle here. "Look. That's what I want." And he was crying. My grandfather was crying because he was on charity.[25]

On these visits during the 1930s, social workers were instructed to give Mexican indigents the option of a county-sponsored train ticket for each member of their family to travel to the interior of Mexico. If they refused, the social workers were told to cut off future relief for these families and take away all documentation that enabled them to receive food and other forms of sustenance.

The impact of this campaign on a single residential block in the Flats makes clear the extent of the targeting. On 151 Utah Street, north of First Street, county officials first convinced Trinidad García, age 46, to return to his birthplace, La Barca, Jalisco, on county funds in October 1931. He had arrived in the city nine years earlier in 1923 and had been employed as a baker before being forced out of work by the Depression. By April 1932, the Martinez family, two houses down from García at 143 Utah Street, was encouraged by county officials to leave on a county-sponsored train. Alberto Martinez had arrived in the US in 1905 and had worked as a boilermaker on the railroads, earning enough money to purchase his modest home in the Flats for $3,000. He had met his wife Altagracia in the United States, and when they left for Mexico City they took with them their six children ranging in age from 2 to 17, all American citizens born in the United States. By October 1932, the García family down the street at 255 Utah Street left Los Angeles for Guadalajara. This family included 35-year-old Apolinar, a common laborer, his wife Juana, their seven-year-old child Carmen, and Apolinar's 37-year-old brother, Paulino.[26] Virtually every block in the Flats contained similar stories of widespread relocation during these years.

This localized picture of "repatriation" in Boyle Heights shows that Mexican immigrant families were targeted despite their having been in the United States for years, if not decades. But understanding this campaign as immigrant focused masks how it swept up whole families, including children born in the United States. Indeed, estimates are that as many as 60 percent of those "repatriated" back to Mexico in the 1930s were US citizens who had their citizenship rights disavowed in the rush to deport them to Mexico— "back" to a country that many of them had never been to before.[27] At least one scholar has questioned our terminology of this program as "repatriation" or "deportation" when the majority of those expelled from the United States were actually US citizens. Mexican immigration scholar Marla Andrea Ramirez asks that we rename this forced expulsion as the "banishment" of US citizens of Mexican descent from their home country, highlighting the way local and federal officials emphasized racial criteria, versus nationality or citizenship, in their campaign.[28]

With the transfer of power in Washington, D.C., to Democrat Franklin Roosevelt in 1933, interest in "repatriation" among Mexican immigrants and their families in the region declined precipitously. Each county-sponsored train in 1933 had open spots, and several had to be delayed for lack of passengers.[29] This waning interest in "repatriation" was the outgrowth of a transformation in identity and the development of a "counterscript" among Boyle Heights' ethnic residents that challenged notions of themselves as Mexican outsiders and claimed all neighborhood residents as Americans who deserved regular employment and fair wages. This sentiment, forged in the very depths of economic decline during the Great Depression, was critical in bringing the Boyle Heights community together and expressed an overwhelming desire for political change in the United States to benefit working-class families in Los Angeles and beyond. It challenged the entrenched political establishment in the region, rooted in traditional Republican Party values of individualism and volunteerism and underscored by strong beliefs of white supremacy and US national exclusivity. Instead, a progressive alternative was shaped in Boyle Heights that—while drawing on radical traditions brought from abroad and grown domestically—coalesced to support the leadership of Franklin D. Roosevelt and the Democratic Party. While part of the commitment to the Democratic Party was shared with working-class communities throughout Southern California and the rest of the United States, it uniquely drew on the multinational and multiracial traditions embedded in Boyle Heights that were being recast as uniquely American.[30]

In particular, a widespread recognition that unemployment and poverty were results *not* of individual failure but rather of a systemic collapse of the US capitalist economy caused by corporate greed and political corruption connected directly to the appeal of Franklin Roosevelt and his call to bring a "New Deal" to Americans. Dorothy Tomer, a young teenager at the time that FDR began his Friday night fireside chats over radio at the start of his administration in 1933, remembers running errands for her mother who was keeping her family afloat in Boyle Heights as a seamstress. Because everyone's windows were open in the neighborhood, Dorothy remembers being able to listen to the whole radio program as she walked in the streets of Boyle Heights.[31] The connection that Boyle Heights residents had to FDR made them believe that new possibilities were available to them because of this national leadership that pledged broad access and compassion.

Boyle Heights became a Democratic Party stronghold in Southern California in this period, something made more extraordinary by the history of politics in the region. In the 1920s, the Democratic Party in California was a weak, fractious organization torn apart by the issue of Prohibition and divided between North and South, with only 20 percent of the state's population registered as Democrats by 1930. That same year, all of Los Angeles' 22 state assembly seats were held by Republicans, and the 1928 Democratic presidential candidate had garnered only 29 percent of the vote in Los Angeles County.[32] In 1932, the Democratic presidential vote in Los Angeles surged 248 percent from 1928, as Roosevelt garnered over 57 percent of the vote in Los Angeles County, a phenomenal protest decision in a region that had been consistently Republican for the previous three decades.

COUNTERSCRIPT: EQUAL PARTNERS THROUGH INDUSTRIAL UNIONISM

While the economic depression deepened after the November 1932 election, residents of Boyle Heights and other communities in Southern California began to see new possibilities for recovery and hope in president-elect Roosevelt. FDR's commitment to industrial unionism laid the foundation for the development of a counterscript to "charity" and "voluntarism," whereby working-class people could organize and contribute collectively to the "New Deal" as equal partners in the rejuvenation of the US economy. After FDR took office in March 1933, his initial policies encouraged workers in Southern California to stand up for a decent wage that could enable them to feed their families.

One of the first manifestations of this new consciousness emerged in the agricultural fields of Southern California, particularly in the El Monte area of eastern Los Angeles County, just ten miles east of Boyle Heights and easily reachable by train. In May 1933, the largely Mexican workforce of farmworkers began demanding a pay increase from 15 cents (approximately $2.84 in 2017 dollars) to 35 cents an hour, just as migrant workers began to pour into the region to pick that season's abundant harvest. The largely Japanese tenant farmers of the region rejected the farmworkers' demand, saying they could not afford it.[33] Out of at least 37 agricultural strikes between April and December that year in California, the El Monte Berry Strike became most known for the active involvement of both Mexican and Japanese consulate officials in devising a resolution. Ex-Mexican president Plutarco Elias Calles got deeply involved, and the battle became an international matter. The chair of the strike committee, Armando Flores, telegraphed President Franklin D. Roosevelt on Wednesday, June 14, to solicit his help: "Five thousand workers in Los Angeles county employed in vegetable and berry culture on Japanese farms on strike against wage scale of from six to fifteen cents an hour / Central Japanese Association of California with Takashi Fukami as secretary represents employers / situation acute with starvation threatening / respectfully request full investigation as soon as possible and prompt action toward relief under industrial recovery act authority."[34]

The telegram prompted the involvement of the US Department of Labor and eventually produced an intervention by federal mediators. Flores's telegram makes clear that local workers knew that the Roosevelt administration had been taking decisive steps toward a comprehensive industrial recovery act that would move the nation toward far-reaching economic planning. Indeed, by the date of Flores's telegram, the House had overwhelmingly passed and the Senate narrowly approved the National Industrial Recovery Act (NIRA), which the president signed into law on June 16, 1933, two days after the telegram.

The first union to take up the mantle of NIRA in Los Angeles was the International Ladies' Garment Workers Union (ILGWU), one of the few important unions in the American Federation of Labor (AFL) with a predominantly female membership. Seventy-five percent of the dressmakers were Latina, mostly Mexican and Mexican American, with the rest being Italians, Russians, Jews, and other "American-born" individuals, many of whom lived across the river in Boyle Heights.[35] The male cloakmakers, skilled immigrant craftsman, mostly Jewish and some Italian, were rhetorically interested in ILGWU but had done little over the previous decade to get women signed up in their union because, as they later expressed, "Mexican women could never be organized"—they would "work for a pittance and could endure any sort of treatment."[36] An early attempt to form a dressmakers' local floundered after ILGWU vice president Mollie Friedman toured the L.A. garment district in 1926, recommending that local efforts stay focused on trying to organize the minority of Jewish women among the dressmakers.[37] But by 1933, many of the Mexican dressmakers had become the sole breadwinners of their families and endured deplorable conditions, including long hours, widespread homework, and pay only for the time spent on garments, not on how many hours were actually spent at the factory.[38]

After ILGWU had launched several successful general strikes in New York City and other East Coast urban centers, leaders saw these victories as a sign that the West Coast was also ripe for further organizing, especially of its large contingent of dressmakers. ILGWU had a specific organizer in mind, Rose Pesotta, who knew the situation in Los Angeles and had the right energy and experience to organize in Southern California. Pesotta, a Russian-born Jew with anarchist sympathies who had spent 15 years learning labor organizing from the shop floor up in New York City, worked between 1932 and early 1933 behind a sewing machine in a Los Angeles garment factory until she was fired and blacklisted for union activity.[39] When she returned to Los Angeles on September 15, 1933, Pesotta set off on an ambitious agenda to mobilize the largely Latina workforce of dressmakers. She secured a short radio broadcast in Spanish each day that would reach Mexican women workers in their homes, broadcasting from a Main Street movie theater until management was pressured by local officials, a move that then forced the broadcast to amplify from a Tijuana radio station across the border. She also hired socialist Bill Busick to edit a four-page semiweekly newspaper, *The Organizer,* in both English and Spanish and produced leaflets addressed to workers in specific shops. Most important, Pesotta engaged nightly and on the weekends with Mexican families and culture at workers' homes in Boyle Heights, Lincoln Heights, and Belvedere. Through this work, she began to understand the communal fears of deportation, the family economy, which often included agricultural and industrial work, and the desire of women workers to live a more open life as Americans.[40]

On September 27, just 12 days after arriving in Los Angeles, Pesotta, with the growing support of Mexican women dressmakers, called a mass meeting that would be the "largest meeting of dressmakers ever held in Los Angeles" at Walker's Orange Grove Theatre on Grand Avenue. The women voted unanimously to authorize a general strike in the garment industry. Within days, the ILGWU had presented a series of grievances, including the discharge of workers for union activities and a pile of evidence that documented intimidation and violation of the state minimum wage laws. Pesotta explained the mass influx of Mexican workers into the union: "We get them because we are the only *Americanos* who take them in as equals."[41] Then on October 12, a general strike was called for the garment industry in Los Angeles, where mass picketing went on in front of dress factory buildings in the heart of the garment district, and Local 96 was established to represent the dressmakers of Los Angeles. Within a few days the Associated Apparel

FIGURE 9. Rose Pesotta being arrested during garment strike in downtown Los Angeles, July 29, 1941. Shades of LA Photo Collection/Los Angeles Public Library.

Manufacturers struck an agreement with the cloakmakers, and they withdrew from the dispute. Pesotta proved herself able to lead the dressmakers in innovative ways during the fight, getting too many picketers out in front of dress shops for the LAPD to arrest everyone, and even using Halloween as a time to get youngsters in costume to march with their mothers on the picket lines and attract press attention. Finally, on November 6, the strikers approved of an NIRA arbitration ruling that applied NIRA codes on wages and hours in the Los Angeles industry. But a lack of enforcement provisions in the NIRA meant that workers and the union found it difficult to implement those rules, as little work remained in the shops at the end of dressmaking season.[42]

Although Rose Pesotta and other garment labor leaders were disappointed by the arbitrated nature of the settlement, the ILGWU had proven that Mexican American women workers could be the backbone of the local in Los Angeles. Fundamentally, this strike, which was supported by community businesses and restaurants throughout Boyle Heights and East Los Angeles, was both a work site dispute and a community-based resistance against the open shop. It encouraged other union locals, such as the Jewish Bakers Union Local 453 based in Boyle Heights, to launch membership drives, reaching out to unskilled bakery workers, particularly women and racial minorities, and setting codes for fair competition that regularized protections and salary differentials and encouraged the hiring of a wider work force as well as the mass production of bread and other staples. As Carolyn Luce observed, "These strikes and actions successfully translated the solidarity cultivated in neighborhoods throughout the city through the 'Fight for Bread' and the cooperative movement into trade union solidarity."[43] Vitally, the 1933 Dressmakers Strike paved the way for a stronger linkage between industrial unionism and community-based efforts to enable a multiracial approach to combat the open shop in Los Angeles.

COUNTERSCRIPT: MULTIRACIAL AND PROGRESSIVE DEMOCRACY

The emerging first American-born generation in most of the racial and ethnic groups in Boyle Heights saw the future of the United States in the neighborhood's demographics. They imagined a new ethnic American identity for individuals of any background, who would have the opportunity to rise in American life to a comfortable social position with hard work and determination. This counterscript would often set Boyle Heights apart from other communities in Southern California and give it its unique self-fashioning as an American neighborhood. Together with the economic collaboration with FDR and the surge of industrial unionism, it would shape what historian Vicki Ruiz has described as "cannery culture" (referring to unionized food canning factories) in Boyle Heights. But more broadly, these three strands would make up what historian Gary Gerstle has called "working-class Americanism."[44]

In a community like Boyle Heights, trade unionism was tied to a transformation in local politics, which made more radical alternatives to traditional parties attractive to a large percentage of working-class voters. The 1934 gubernatorial race clearly showed that Boyle Heights residents were interested in more progressive options. Radical author and former Socialist candidate Upton Sinclair was surprisingly able to win the Democratic nomination for governor on a platform of "ending poverty in California," or EPIC. While EPIC and Sinclair lost the gubernatorial race, garnering only

37 percent of the vote compared to Republican Frank Merriam's 49 percent, Democrats with EPIC endorsements won 24 seats in the California assembly and the Los Angeles County seat in the state senate.[45]

By 1935, the counterscript of multiracial and progressive democracy was deeply rooted in the community of Boyle Heights through residents' commitments to labor organization, Democratic Party politics, and neighborhood empowerment. However, three major national and international developments also strengthened this position in the second half of the 1930s. Although the US Supreme Court ruled NIRA unconstitutional in late May 1935, within two months Congress replaced the defunct Section 7(a) with the National Labor Relations Act (NLRA), otherwise known as the Wagner Act, which reaffirmed the right of workers to organize and bargain collectively. This time, a new National Labor Relations Board was given the power to enforce its order, and because the Wagner Act was upheld as constitutional in 1937, the power of organized labor was fortified in the latter half of the 1930s.[46]

John L. Lewis led a group of dissidents out of the AFL in 1937 to fight for industrial unionism, and in Los Angeles the Congress of Industrial Organization (CIO) organized a rival central labor body to the AFL that directly competed to organize workers in the same industries, especially in steel, automobiles, rubber, garment, and construction.[47] In Boyle Heights, the rise of the CIO meant that US-born ethnics from immigrant families would take leadership roles in the developing political and cultural context of the New Deal, especially in Mexican and Jewish communities. A US-born Mexican American generation emerged in industrial labor throughout Southern California and produced a cadre of leaders in CIO locals. Frank López and Jack Estrada were union members in the carpenters' AFL local who went beyond it to organize furniture workers, and Anthony Rios and Jaime Gonzalez would become recognized forces in the Steel Workers Organizing Committee (SWOC) in Los Angeles just as steel manufacturing took off in the basin. Bert Corona would migrate to Los Angeles from El Paso to attend the University of Southern California (USC) on a basketball scholarship but would become a stalwart organizer with the International Longshoremen's and Warehousemen's Union (ILWU). The experienced union organizer Luisa Moreno would take over the reins of the United Cannery and Agricultural Packers and Allied Workers of America (UCAPAWA) from local Jewish communist Dorothy Ray Healey in 1939, organizing cannery workers, who often lived in Boyle Heights and worked in the Flats or just across the river.[48]

In addition to providing an avenue for leadership, the CIO created a mechanism to combat the discrimination that Mexican Americans often felt when trying to move up in an industrial plant from a menial job to a more skilled and better-paid position. By organizing across the industry and fighting for the average working man and woman to have the opportunity to compete, the CIO created space for self-empowerment for the average worker. According to historian Douglas Monroy, "Because 'Mexican' no longer automatically equaled 'helper' such unions also represented simple dignity to Mexicanos.... Now in an industrial union no strata or skill level could so easily dominate another. Most importantly, Mexicanos won some victories over their employers. Workers proudly wore their union buttons on the shop floor, exulting in this new seemingly simple slap in their employers' faces."[49]

The dignity in the workplace that CIO locals enabled for ethnic workers in Los Angeles also translated into different approaches to issues of racial and ethnic identity in organizing and politics in the community. For the CIO generation of Mexican Americans, it meant that this locally grown leadership in American unions could push the Southern California CIO to take up issues related specifically to the Mexican American community, such as matters of citizenship or educational equity. Nowhere was that more important than the key role of CIO locals in promoting El Congreso, the Congress of Spanish-Speaking Peoples, which met in Los Angeles in 1939 and supported a growing agenda of ethnic empowerment and entitlement to New Deal programs for Mexican American workers. According to El Congreso's platform, the trade union movement was "the most basic agency through which the Mexican and Spanish-speaking people became organized."[50]

But this "Americans All" approach was not limited to Mexican and Mexican American workers. The Yiddish Socialists, who had usually restricted themselves to Jewish organizing in the 1920s and early 1930s, took a broader approach in the late 1930s to form a "Popular Front against Fascism." Communists, fearful of the rise of Nazi Germany, also advocated a Popular Front. At its Seventh Congress in Moscow in 1935, the Communist International reversed itself and instructed party members to disband independent trade unions and work with formerly despised "bourgeois" reformers, such as socialists, social democrats, Democratic Party members, and other labor organizers. This period lasted until the Nazi-Soviet Non-Aggression Pact of 1939, and during it, in Los Angeles as elsewhere in the United States, some of the most effective and inclusive labor organizers were released to participate in some of the largest organizing campaigns in local history just as industrial plants of significant size were being opened in Southern California. The Popular Front drew on a wider coalition of unionists, activists, and writers, both Jewish and non-Jewish, to defend democracy against the rise of totalitarianism, using Boyle Heights as their base. As the fascist direction of Nazism became clearer in Germany, the growth of fascist groups in Los Angeles strengthened the resolve of the Los Angeles Jewish community to fight fascism both at home and abroad. As historian Michael Denning has argued, this "Popular Front" on the West Coast led to a substantial "cultural front" of artists, filmmakers, and ethnic leaders that saw commonality in producing new leftist cultural materials for a broad public through Hollywood and local cultural institutions.[51] In 1935, the Hollywood Anti-Nazi League commissioned Carey McWilliams to write *It Can Happen Here!*, a pamphlet that was published to proclaim the dangers of fascism rising in Los Angeles.

These political efforts were coupled with a drive to expand Yiddish cultural activities in Boyle Heights, including new programs for children and teens in the neighborhood, as a response to the dangers posed to Yiddish cultural survival in Europe. The Jewish Labor Committee established coalition efforts with both the AFL Central Labor Council and the CIO to spread awareness of the threats of Nazism to organized labor in Germany and the dangers of fascism to American democracy. Their efforts reached a peak in a massive protest in Boyle Heights in November 1938 to honor the victims of Kristallnacht (Night of Broken Glass), a wave of violent attacks on Jewish communities in Germany. Fifteen thousand people marched down Brooklyn Avenue to the steps of the Breed Street Shul for a massive rally that included representatives from CIO locals, El Congreso, the NAACP, the Los Angeles Urban League, and the Civil Rights Congress.[52]

The growth of a CIO leadership that was often rooted in the Boyle Heights neighborhood produced a powerful counterscript to the forces in Los Angeles that tried to marginalize local immigrants and their children from their right to US citizenship and civil rights during the Great Depression. It took a multiracial neighborhood to turn labor agitation and racial and ethnic justice into a claim of belonging to a "quintessential American community." But Boyle Heights would still be confronted with the challenge of city officials' plans to turn the neighborhood into something else—into a vision for the future of Los Angeles that did not include many

FIGURE 10. Demonstration against Nazism in Boyle Heights, 1938, sponsored by United Anti-Nazi Conference. Los Angeles Daily News Negatives Collection (Collection 1387). Library Special Collections, Charles E. Young Research Library, UCLA.

of its current residents. That battle would endure throughout the 1930s and 1940s and would continue to mark Boyle Heights as a unique community in the Southern California landscape.

REMOVAL FOR THE "PUBLIC GOOD"

Local officials did not view attempts to improve the lives of Boyle Heights residents through multiracial labor organizing for a living wage as a base for progress during the New Deal in Los Angeles. Instead, they believed poverty was to be remedied by removing poor people from their homes. Using the logic that underwrote Mexican Repatriation, politicians on both sides of the political spectrum associated neighborhoods like Boyle Heights with slum conditions, racial depravity, and urban decay best eradicated through neighborhood demolition. The Flats were an obvious eyesore for local officials attempting to show how the city was successfully weathering the economic downturn, so when federal officials made available public funds for both slum clearance and public works jobs, the city's elite initiated plans to obliterate the entire community for the sake of "progress" and the "public good." As discussed by the best study of housing in Los Angeles, Dana Cuff's *Provisional City*, "While housing activists in the thirties or forties might generally have agreed that the worst housing in the city was located northeast and especially southeast of downtown, specific sites for slum clearance were politically determined." But Cuff goes on to argue "that site selection was relatively arbitrary, and then backed by subsequent surveys rather than originally determined in some scientific way," and "that condemnation and slum clearance policy 'created' areas to demolish."[53] With one of the Flats' major ethnic populations already decimated by "repatriation" policies, city housing and transportation officials, along with private architects and housing activists, would now target the neighborhood for a complete urban overhaul, requiring further ethnic cleansing.

Encouraged by the new mayoral administration of Frank Shaw, a group of prominent Los Angeles architects in 1934 formed the Utah Street Architects Association to obtain a commission for an enormous housing project in the Flats under the newly constituted federal Public Works Administration. This group lobbied officials in Washington, D.C., and utilized their political ties to promote low-income housing programs and seek federal funding for their extensive plans to revolutionize housing for the poor in the region.[54] This group did not get a green light for its project until passage of the 1937 Federal Housing Act, almost eight years after the site had been initially identified as the place for Los Angeles' first public housing project. Although rumors of the planned destruction of the community circulated from at least 1934, it took the block-by-block appraisal done in October 1940 to confirm to all residents that they would be asked to vacate their homes. By that time, of course, many homeowners had already sold their properties and left, and those that hadn't certainly saw their property values plummet, creating a zone of blight that public housing was intended to remedy.

By the time ground was broken for Aliso Village in February 1942, the modernist plan for improving the lot of housing for the poor had also changed considerably. The 54 acres of housing north of First Street originally planned in 1934 had shrunk to 34 acres because of the addition of a new elevated highway that was added with federal and state highway construction funds for slum clearance purposes.[55] The new village would now be separated on its northern and eastern edges from the rest of Boyle Heights by the juncture of the new Santa Ana and Ramona Highways, currently known as the 101 Freeway. This would isolate the new residents, making them more appropriate subjects for the modernist vision crafted by urban planners. In addition, as Cuff has argued, because of the new highways "a visitor virtually soared into Los Angeles unaware—above the river, the railyards, the public housing, and any remnants of the working class neighborhoods below."[56]

This pattern of highway construction would severely affect Boyle Heights over the next twenty years. By 1960, four other freeways had been built through Boyle Heights, carving up neighborhoods and placing disruptive barriers throughout the area. The massive East Los Angeles interchange, which connected three major thoroughfares, was built in the 1950s in the southernmost part of the Flats, displacing another 5,000 residents. Altogether, almost 15 percent of all the land in Boyle Heights would be taken up by freeways by the time construction was completed. For some, like James Tolmasov, whose family was forced out of the Flats by the building of Aliso Village and the Santa Ana Highway, displacement would occur several times over. After leaving the Flats, his family bought a home on Lanfranco Street in the eastern part of Boyle Heights, only to have that two-story home taken over by the state in the 1950s when Highway 60 was built.[57]

The onset of World War II prompted officials to erect more public housing projects in the city. Of the ten housing projects that opened for residents in 1941 and 1942, nine were located in East Los Angeles or South Los Angeles, areas that were increasingly minority occupied. Indeed, Boyle Heights alone would house five of the city's ten public housing projects completed in this period. Ramona Gardens—located at the northern fringe of Boyle Heights on 32 acres cleared by extensive Mexican American "repatriation" and banishment—would be the first project to open, just after the new year in 1941. Estrada Courts, along the southern edge of Boyle Heights, would be the tenth and final site selected by city housing officials, replacing the only planned West Los Angeles site, known as San Vicente Village, which was abandoned after local homeowners and clergy in Westwood complained that the housing would bring "undesirable" poor minority residents to the neighborhood and probably integrate the public schools.[58]

Moreover, almost all of the former residents of the affected areas were ruled ineligible for actually occupying the new housing for the poor. The eligibility requirements had originally, and not surprisingly, required US citizenship, so most of the Mexican adult residents of the region in 1940 were deemed unworthy of federal support. However, once the war broke out in

1941, ill-housed defense workers earning $1 or less were given priority. With a long waiting list for spots in the new housing complexes, and widespread discrimination against racial minorities in the defense industries, few former residents of the Flats had the possibility of returning to their neighborhood. This was also the case for the other nine public housing projects completed in 1941 and 1942. When the war ended in 1945, veterans were given priority positions on the waiting lists. So although housing activists celebrated the fact that the City Housing Authority officially envisioned these projects as racially integrated, residents during and immediately after the war were narrowly restricted to the American born and the military involved.

Public housing, of course, was seen in the 1930s as the epitome of New Deal reform politics. In Los Angeles, it generated opposition from real estate moguls, including their supporters on the Los Angeles Chamber of Commerce, and from their spokesmen in the *Los Angeles Times,* who felt that any government interference in the housing market threatened their profits and freedom. And although most of the advocates for public housing were New Deal liberals, many socialists and even a few communists could be counted among them. Indeed, by 1952 the waning of liberal political power in Los Angeles would lead to the reversal of support for public housing there, so that sites like Aliso Village were deprived of continued levels of support.[59]

But it is intriguing that the logic that was central to Los Angeles politics in the 1930s and 1940s across the right, center, and left of the spectrum, and among both detractors and supporters of public housing, supported the designation of certain neighborhoods as "slums," a label that justified their clearance. As Ira Katznelson makes clear in his book *When Affirmative Action Was White,* New Deal policy was shaped by the political realities of bringing an activist government to bear on regions fundamentally shaped by racial inequalities. Katznelson convincingly argues that Democratic congressmen from the US South were able to structure all the foundational New Deal and World War II programs to ensure that state and local officials would retain their ability to administer the new infusion of federal dollars in ways that aligned with local customs and statutes of rigid segregation, as well as unequal distribution based on race.[60] This same uneven racial political reality, which barred agricultural and domestic work from provisions of Social Security legislation, would produce the administration of federal housing statutes that classified Boyle Heights, according to a 1939 Federal Housing Authority survey, as a region full of "subversive racial elements" that was "hopelessly heterogeneous."[61]

Race played a central role in the formulation of urban reform during the decade, but in unique ways because of the diversity and complexity of California's population. Whereas in East Coast cities the particular spatial ramifications of race in urban renewal could often be described in terms of a strict white-black racial binary, racialization took on a fundamentally different form when applied to areas like the Flats and were more entangled with the racialization of citizenship—that is, the understanding that citizenship belonged to those identified as white.[62] As we know throughout American history up to the contemporary moment, perceptions of foreignness intersect with racial categorization, which is often heightened by nativist anti-immigrant rhetoric at a time of intense economic competition or conflict. This engenders a particularly volatile form of racism that extends well beyond the imposition of a rigid color line.

The racialization of citizenship that historian Mae Ngai recognizes in the federal immigration policy of the early twentieth century defined Asian Americans and Latinos in the US as "alien citizens." This was localized by city and county officials in Los Angeles through the categorization of some neighborhoods as slums, whose populations could therefore be indiscriminately moved because they did not possess full rights as citizens either of the United States or of local communities.[63] Even leftist supporters of public housing in Los Angeles bought into this argument, believing somehow that the state could construct better housing for the *deserving poor* on land occupied largely by the *undeserving poor,* categories thoroughly racialized in the housing shortages of the Depression and World War II eras. In Los Angeles, the "undeserving" were most often Mexican and Japanese residents born abroad but also included their American-born children in this era when citizenship rights were still thoroughly racialized and exclusionary in the public imagination.

The Mexican and Japanese residents of Boyle Heights were directly targeted by this form of nativist racialization, even though the communities they lived in during this period were multiracial and multiethnic. White ethnic groups that lived among them, including many who had been born abroad and had just recently arrived in the United States, were spared the direct assault of targeted removal based on national origin and foreignness. However, the Jews, Russian Molokans, Armenians, Italians, and others who lived alongside these racialized immigrants were indirectly affected by this form of racialization by virtue of their neighborhoods becoming stigmatized as urban slums. They were also given incentives to flee to all-white areas and penalized for remaining in Boyle Heights. The stigmatization would force these white ethnic groups to find shelter elsewhere or continue to live in a community increasingly targeted for decline and eventual destruction. Some would become slumlords, subdividing their former residences and renting out apartments at exorbitant rates to newcomers.

African Americans, on the other hand, were almost exclusively limited to living in areas denigrated as "slums," even when their population exploded in the World War II era in Los Angeles. While leftist organizers of public housing often heroically promoted white/black integration of public housing complexes in the city, they were fairly ineffectual in opening up the private stock of housing in Los Angeles to black residents outside the Central Avenue corridor and were unable to place many public housing units outside minority communities. The continued use of restrictive covenants would keep the housing options of African Americans limited. Indeed, when the Great Migration to Los Angeles tripled the size of the black community in L.A. during World War II, the best new housing option available was the abandoned Little Tokyo neighborhood, renamed "Bronzeville," which instantly began to be described in "slum" terms.[64] In other words, leftist public housing advocates and administrators usually succumbed to the dictates of the wider discriminatory housing market in Los Angeles, even while promoting "democratic housing for the poor."

LINKING REPATRIATION TO INTERNMENT

To understand local government actions, accelerated by the emergencies of the Great Depression and World War II, that targeted racial and ethnic populations in Los Angeles, it is critical to recognize the particular processes of racialization at work in Los Angeles. As I have recounted thus far, racial targeting of particular populations was superimposed onto the geographic landscape of Los Angeles, making certain neighborhoods like the Flats, or the larger Boyle Heights area, susceptible to "urban reform" efforts aimed at moving out populations and restructuring urban spaces to fit the racial nativist sentiments of city officials, elite civic leaders, or protected middle-class populations. So this pattern of dealing with urban populations was well established by World War II and was a fundamental source of accumulated knowledge that would be utilized to process the removal of Japanese and Japanese Americans after the bombing of Pearl Harbor.

Of course, the causes of Japanese American internment have long been debated by some of the nation's leading Asian American historians.[65] Most historians see local officials and populations on the West Coast as playing a role in encouraging the president and the military to remove the Japanese-ancestry population under the banner of wartime emergency and a need to check for the possibility of espionage. However, that argument has usually focused on the most virulent anti-Asian groups in the West Coast, including those that would benefit economically from their removal in certain key industries, such as agriculture and fishing. I am less interested in the role of these racist groups in promoting Japanese internment and more interested in why politicians and leaders who were more moderate or liberal in their outlook didn't step up to oppose or provide alternatives to Japanese removal.[66] I would argue that their stunning silence and overwhelming acquiescence derive less from a specific anti-Asian sentiment that was triggered when Pearl Harbor shocked the nation and more from a well-established history of racialized population removal for urban restructuring that normalized this measure and its accompanying justifications for later use.

The actions of two of Los Angeles' most noted liberal politicians of the period, Mayor Fletcher Bowron and County Supervisor John Anson Ford, seem to epitomize the role of urban reformers in sustaining a consistent policy of population removal and ethnic cleansing for the purposes of "progress." Both Bowron and Ford were well known in the Japanese American community during the 1930s, seeking endorsements from the organized groups for their campaigns against the supposedly corrupt Shaw administration. As historian Lon Kurashige has shown, they were active participants in many events in the Japanese American community, particularly those sponsored by the second-generation Japanese American Citizens League.[67] Ford had Los Angeles' Little Tokyo in his own district, as well as Boyle Heights, and probably represented more Japanese Americans than any other elected official in the city.

But from the time he was elected to the board of supervisors in 1934, Ford was a major supporter of renewed attempts to sustain Mexican repatriation efforts in Los Angeles. There was a series of ongoing attempts by Los Angeles County to restart Mexican repatriation, including a 1938 agreement between County Supervisor Gordon L. McDonough with the Lazaro Cardenas administration to resettle Los Angeles deportees on Mexican rural lands for colonization.[68] Supervisor John Anson Ford's efforts had even included several trips to Mexico to convince Mexican officials to renew their cooperation in moving Los Angeles residents south of the border. During late 1941, Ford had been working with Wayne Allen, the county's chief administrator, on a plan to initiate a new Mexican Repatriation Campaign by cutting off all further assistance to indigent immigrants from the county, while providing $100 from county funds if a family agreed to return to Mexico immediately. On Tuesday, December 2, 1941, John Anson Ford was able to convince his fellow supervisors to initiate this plan once Allen testified that the amount of compensation amounted to less than two months of what it would cost the county to sustain the family on welfare relief. With the positive vote, Ford immediately went to Mexico to meet with officials there and work out the particulars of the program. However, that Sunday, when news of the attack on Pearl Harbor reached Los Angeles, John Anson Ford had to hurry home from south of the border.[69]

Both Ford and Bowron, in the weeks immediately following December 7, 1941, were quick to publicly defend the loyalty of the local Japanese American population to the United States and to ask all American citizens to refrain from racial attacks on this local population. This was to be expected, given their histories with the local Japanese American community and more generally with efforts at racial conciliation in Los Angeles. Yet by the end of January 1942, both these representatives would take official positions to call on President Roosevelt to physically remove Japanese immigrants and Japanese Americans alike from Los Angeles and other West Coast cities. Bowron, in particular, became a national spokesperson for questioning the allegiance of Japanese Americans on purely racial grounds, while advocating for their removal or incarceration.[70] Most historians have argued that this turnaround was due to the stress of seeing the United States losing badly to Japan in the Pacific War. But while this may have played a part, the reversal was also fueled by local concerns that reproduced earlier narratives and apparently justified a new round of population removal.

Indeed, years later when interviewed in 1971, Ford acknowledged that his support of "repatriation" of Los Angeles' Mexican American residents during the 1930s was part of the "same piece of cloth" or "mistaken psychology" that had also resulted in the internment of Japanese Americans during World War II. Ford explained, "It's all part of the same philosophy, the failure to recognize citizens' rights and human rights."[71] As the elected representative of the area where both ethnic groups were concentrated in eastern Los Angeles County, John Anson Ford failed to recognize the citizenship rights of the Mexican American or Japanese American residents in his district, choosing instead to prioritize local officials' concerns about burgeoning welfare rolls or the safety of white Americans.

The fate of many Japanese Americans in Boyle Heights speaks to these local concerns. Seventeen-year-old Ruth Matsuo (Brandt) met with repercussions from the bombing of Pearl Harbor immediately. She had spent December 7 with her family and her closest friends, whose son, almost a brother to her, was building the Matsuo family a brick barbecue in the backyard of their City Terrace home. When they heard the newscast about the Pearl Harbor bombing, they thought, "What's Japan thinking of? How could they attack the United States? We're so much bigger." It wasn't until that evening, however, that Ruth understood the full impact for her family. The FBI came to their house to take away her father, who was quite ill at the time and had very high blood pressure. Her father, Sei Fujii, was the editor of the *Kashu Mainichi,* a local Japanese-language newspaper, a position that defined him as a respected community leader and put him high on the list of FBI targets for immediate incarceration. An FBI doctor thought he was too seriously ill to be moved, so Sei stayed in his house for an additional week until he could no longer bear hearing the pleas for help from abandoned wives in the community. Ruth remembers being scared and hearing her parents speak in Japanese all week, which she could not understand. Finally, her father volunteered to go and was taken to Tujunga. He immediately called his wife to bring him pajamas and toiletries for at least six men who had been taken from the streets before they could pack anything. From there, Ruth's father was quickly taken to Missoula, Montana, then transferred to Lordsburg, New Mexico.[72]

By the end of December 1941, the immediate incarceration of those most under suspicion as "enemy aliens"—by virtue of their prominent role as Japanese editors, teachers, or community leaders—had left their families in precarious positions of destitution. The same county welfare departments that had, for years, been attempting to move Mexican immigrants south were now confronted with the almost immediate impoverishment of Japanese families, a community that had rarely sought county assistance before.[73] This group was significantly large in Boyle Heights and Little Tokyo and led local officials to begin asking whether the federal government would assist local governments in dealing with the indigent situation created by removing so many wage earners at one time. Throughout January 1941, administrator Wayne Allen was sent to Washington, D.C., to plead the county's case for help, despite the nation's immediate mobilization for war.[74] As it became clear that little federal support would be forthcoming, John Anson Ford and other local officials responsible for providing local welfare assistance began to advocate that families of these potential "enemy aliens" be sent to join their incarcerated heads of households, rather than left under the care of Los Angeles County.

What initially might have appeared unthinkable became reality and was even rationalized as maybe being "for their own good," from the perspective of a wartime emergency and from the precedent of previous forced population movements for the supposed long-term "benefit" of the affected people and areas. Within the month, John Anson Ford would provide the fifth vote to make unanimous a resolution of the Los Angeles County Board of Supervisors to encourage the president to physically remove the Japanese-origin population from the West Coast of the United States. When President Roosevelt made his decision in late February, and the evacuation was begun later that spring, Boyle Heights lost a significant number of its residents. Jews, Mexicans, and Molokans in the region saw neighbors and classmates sell their possessions and leave their homes as many others had done in the past. But this massive movement of people had been effected under the direct sponsorship and control of the US military, which had helped craft and then implement the president's executive order.

Ironically, this movement initially sent these families only thirty miles inland in Southern California, as more permanent sites at Manzanar, in Owens Valley, California, and elsewhere were still being built. Through the summer of 1942 Boyle Heights residents were housed at the Santa Anita Racetrack in the San Gabriel Valley, in stalls originally built for the thoroughbred horses that raced there before and after World War II. Many classmates and friends of the internees went to visit them that summer, but more often they maintained friendships through letter writing, just as Mollie Wilson had with Sandie Saito and Mary Murakami. One particular set of letters begun on May 21, 1942, interests me for what it reveals about reactions to this unjust incarceration. "War weaves strange patterns and, at present, with 110–120 other thousands of Japanese extraction, I am now in a concentration camp—American style. They say it is a military necessity so we acquiesce quietly," wrote Kay Sugahara from the Santa Anita Relocation Center to Supervisor John Anson Ford.[75]

The motivation for Sugahara to write his old friend and political confidant John Anson Ford that May was urgent, if a bit complicated. Sugahara had been president of the Los Angeles chapter of the Japanese American Citizens League (JACL) before the war and had had a personal and political relationship with Ford since 1934, when they met each other as political reformers trying to unseat the administration of Mayor Frank Shaw. Ford had long been a political supporter of the work of the JACL, having spoken at many of their dinners and events, even nominating a county employee for "Nisei of the Year" in 1940. As Sugahara began his third month in captivity, still in Los Angeles County awaiting the building of permanent relocation centers in the California desert, he decided to write his old friend Ford to inform him of "anything about camp life or conditions which you wish to know, the mind and the attitudes of people here."[76]

But Sugahara also wanted to make clear to Ford that the actions of both federal and local officials in supporting and carrying out "evacuation" of both Japanese immigrants and American citizens of Japanese ancestry had been unwise and potentially destructive of American values to decency and democracy. He certainly was aware that Ford, as part of the Los Angeles County Board of Supervisors, had been part of the unanimous vote in favor of a January 1942 resolution calling for the transfer of all Japanese internees "from coastal areas to inland points." Sugahara wrote to Ford as a "conscientious and conspicuous public official" whom he had personally witnessed "taking the so-called unpopular side of many issues . . . with great deal of courage." Although voting against Japanese internment had not been among Ford's political actions, Sugahara felt that he could tell Ford directly that the ongoing evacuation would have potentially serious repercussions for the future of race relations in Los Angeles:

> Is there not a danger that certain democratic rights have been infringed and race discrimination placed above law by segregating for evacuation Citizens of a certain ancestry? Is there not a possibility that this may lead to wider types of discrimination after the war in which the fever of hatred would not have yet cooled? Namely I mean the Jew and the Negro groups in certain sections of the country. . . . While pointing out of these facts may not be popular at this time, when the heat of war has cooled and people look with sane eyes upon the entire picture, the men who point [out] these things will be looked upon with regard by the people.[77]

Ford wrote back to Sugahara's rather frank letter on May 26. His reaction was sympathetic but cautious. Addressing his friend as "Dear Kay," he immediately told Sugahara that he appreciated his communication and "the tolerant spirit in which you refer to the problems involved in this unprecedented situation. . . . Perhaps you and your friends do not realize the significance of the chapter which those of your ancestry are writing in their extraordinary adaptation to restraints and regulations and in their almost unparalleled acceptance of imposed conditions for the sake of this government." Only weeks into the evacuation of Japanese Americans from the Pacific Coast, and months from his own vote in support of these efforts, Ford was willing to concede to a close friend that a mistake might have been made. "While battling a foe that has disregarded many of the accepted international procedures," he wrote, "we ourselves cannot afford to disregard the basic principles on which our own citizens rely." But he struggled to find the words that could morally justify the actions undertaken by the federal government. As he explained to Sugahara, he was "sure that retrospect will reveal some errors and injustices in the present program, but it will also show a high purpose to reconcile and ameliorate what many believe a desperate reality with the broad principles of our democratic government."[78] For years, Ford would argue that strong public opinion against the presence of Japanese Americans in California had forced him and other legislators to act as they did.

Boyle Heights, and particularly the Flats neighborhood, experienced the pain of a series of removal policies. These policies employed an overarching logic that rationalized displacement to make room for "progress" or "security." The individuals and families who lived together in Boyle Heights were seen as disposable, and the neighborhoods that they had created and nurtured were seen as expendable for the "greater good" of Los Angeles, at least in the minds of urban reformers of that era. After being repatriated from Los Angeles in 1934, Emilia Castañeda would spend ten years as a child and teenager in the villages, towns, and small cities of Durango, mostly working for other families as a babysitter and domestic worker, while her father struggled and migrated throughout Mexico to find work as a stonemason. While her brother never returned to the US, Emilia returned in 1944 during World War II to Boyle Heights, where she had to relearn English and restart as a young adult in a changing East Los Angeles. Her father Natividad never returned to the US, living out his life in Durango, with a family split across the border by virtue of the US's racialized immigration policy.[79] But the Los Angeles Emilia came back to had changed dramatically. Because of Mexican repatriation, Japanese internment, and the restructuring brought about by urban renewal and public housing, Boyle Heights residents now knew that their community was not immune to racial practices and that they were all vulnerable to future displacement and removal.

Yet at the very same time, residents of Boyle Heights had crafted a counter-script about themselves and their community that conceived of their collective neighborhood as the "most American" of communities because of their diversity, their immigrant backgrounds from around the world, and their dedication to local democracy and working-class social justice. On the eve of World War II, residents of Boyle Heights had spent a decade crafting an alternative vision of their community through industrial labor unions fighting against the "open shop" policy and fulfilling the social and economic promise of FDR's New Deal on a local level in Los Angeles. From the communist Left to social democrats to more traditional working-class FDR Democrats, Boyle Heights residents had a deep faith in their own contribution to US society and a sense of belonging to this particular neighborhood. The second-generation ethnic Americans that made up the bulk of young people in Boyle Heights saw themselves as the future of this country, without having to feel that they needed to abandon relations with the Old Country of their parents or with their racial and ethnic compatriots in Southern California.

This battle between the civic nationalism in Boyle Heights and the racial nativism of so much of Southern California's social and political elite would be tested dramatically during World War II.[80] Starting with the shock of Japanese America internment, wartime Los Angeles would witness heightened tensions between these two forms of Americanism. Boyle Heights residents, would once again be forced to respond to inescapable pressures on their neighborhood from the world around them, but by adhering to a collective sense of identity and purpose they would emerge from the war with a more developed sense of belonging to a special neighborhood of committed progressives and activists.

FIVE

Witness to Internment

I was so surprised, the way they treated those Japanese people, because they were Americans. What if we had a war with Mexico? They would have thrown me out too? ... I was angry that they'd have to pack up and leave. I was angry. I like them. They were my friends. ... And I felt for them, and I missed them, and I thought it was unjust.

LUIS SANCHEZ,
Boyle Heights resident, 2002 interview

CLAIRE ORLOSOROFF, A JEWISH STUDENT at Hollenbeck Junior High School in December 1941, could vividly recall the coming of World War II to Boyle Heights nearly sixty years later. She remembered the Japanese American students at Hollenbeck as "very studious. They were always in administration [and] in leadership positions. [They were] very highly thought of. They were bright." Orlosoroff remembered that the school administration put President Franklin Roosevelt's address to the US Congress declaring war on Japan, broadcast live on December 8, over the school's PA system. She had been sitting in Mrs. Sharp's drama class, and she recalled how uncomfortable it was for the Japanese American students who had been allowed to come to school that day by their parents—especially for Kei Ozawa, the student body president of Hollenbeck, who was not sure how to respond when the US national anthem was played at the conclusion of Roosevelt's speech. "He was really kind of torn. I remember that the national anthem was being played, and he didn't know what to do. He stood up, but he just didn't know what to do. It was very heart-breaking, because we were good friends ... all of us, and they were all sent away."[1] African American Mollie Wilson enacted her own personal protest by writing letters to her Japanese American friends taken to internment camps, as we learned at the beginning of this book: "I had a lot of emotions, but one was the unfairness and stuff. That really got to me. ... But there was pain, and there was a feeling of. ... See, I have to always think, if they can do it to them, they can do it to me too."[2]

Racialized citizenship was not new to the country and particularly not to Boyle Heights, as the Mexican Repatriation Campaign had prepared the way for the internment of Japanese Americans. The varied memories of Luis Sanchez, Claire Orlosoroff, and Mollie Wilson regarding the incarceration of Japanese Americans help us remember that the entire interracial community of Boyle Heights was dramatically affected by internment and the war. The Jewish community of Boyle Heights, who knew intimately experiences of persecution that stretched back to the Russian pogroms, certainly supported US involvement in the fight against Nazis and fascists. However, Leo Frumkin remembered real tension within their communities regarding how to respond to Japanese Americans preparing for evacuation. Leo's left-leaning politically diverse family was furious that "one of my parents' friends bought a drugstore on First and Soto, which was [previously] owned by Japanese people. And I remember my parents angrily telling them how could they have done this to these people; I'm assuming they bought it for a song because people just had to leave.... And I remember that my parents were just furious that they would take advantage of a situation like that. You know, 'Why didn't you rent it from them?' I remember that was the discussion, why didn't you rent it, or something like that."[3] Clearly there was a wide range of opinion regarding how to treat the sales of merchandise, houses, and businesses that resulted from evacuation orders.

With the departure of working-age men sent abroad to fight in the war, L.A. needed workers, and industry opened its doors once again to Mexicans (and women, and the growing black community). Soon, however, Mexicans were linked to the Japanese as the sheriff's department drew connections between the two populations that were steeped in biological racism. Deputy Sheriff Edward Duran Ayres reasoned that the prevalence of Indian blood in the Mexican "is evidently Oriental in background—at least he shows many of the Oriental characteristics, especially so in his utter disregard for the value of life."[4] Police targeted Mexican American youth throughout the war years, eventually leading to the Zoot Suit Riots of June 1943, when white US servicemen attacked youth of color in downtown neighborhoods including Boyle Heights. From the violence unleashed on zoot suiters during the riots to the day-to-day insults against Boyle Heights residents from the police in Southern California, local officials attempted to contain the freedom that wartime prosperity and demographic movement had unleashed in Los Angeles. These strategies of containment were highly racialized, as issues of national patriotism, identity, and adherence to wartime values became the currency of Americanism during World War II.

With the end of war in late 1945 and the return of its beleaguered Japanese American residents, Boyle Heights was radically transformed. These stories of transformation and an emerging civil rights consciousness created a lasting legacy from the war years, but one coupled with economic and political changes that turned a diverse and multiracial neighborhood into an increasingly isolated ethnic enclave.

WITNESSES TO INCARCERATION

Almost all interview respondents had vivid recollections of how they heard that the nation of Japan had attacked the naval base at Pearl Harbor. Dan Kawahawa, an energetic 22-year-old transplant from Hawaii, had plans to go dancing at the Hollywood Palladium that night with a buddy and their dates. After morning baseball practice at Evergreen Playground, he rode with his friend, a fellow graduate from Roosevelt High, to deliver vegetables to a market across town. His friend's father was in the produce business, and the son had been assigned the task of delivering the merchandise before using the truck to get to Hollywood later that night. But two blocks before getting to the market, the friend flipped the truck on its side to avoid hitting another car that had failed to stop at an intersection, and this sent the produce all over the street. The young men were not hurt, but they thought it odd that no one came out to help them, only to rush for the fruits and vegetables. It wasn't until they righted the truck and came home to change clothes that Kawahawa's parents, worried all day about their son, informed him of the bombing of Pearl Harbor that morning and the resulting curfew all over Los Angeles. Dan Kawahawa remembers calling his date to cancel and staying at home with his parents for several days listening to the radio.[5]

Most Japanese American residents of Boyle Heights experienced similar forms of alienation and distrust when they ventured outside Boyle Heights in the days and weeks following the bombing of Pearl Harbor. But inside the community of Boyle Heights itself, many felt at home and protected by their neighbors, often comforted by close relations with people who were not Japanese. Ruth Toshiko Matsuo (now Brandt) remembers the varied reactions from her racially mixed City Terrace neighbors: "The Mexican family next door was very sympathetic," but "the Caucasian family, a little aloof; they weren't quite sure."[6] And in the first few weeks of US entry into World War II, Mayor Fletcher Bowron and other local officials also expressed sympathetic messages of support for local Japanese Americans, calling on all American citizens to show expressions of unity and solidarity with this population that for decades had been so loyal to the United States.[7]

By the last days of 1941, however, regional pressure groups in California—especially those that competed against Japanese American economic interests and had long called for anti-Asian measures—vocally questioned their allegiance to the United States, increasingly portraying US-born Japanese Americans as tied to Japan because of their "blood" and heritage.[8] Bending to this pressure, the city and county governments of Los Angeles fired Japanese American employees during the early months of 1942, as official Los Angeles began to abandon its Japanese American constituents.[9] Now that these previously self-sufficient constituents were largely unemployed, local county officials began to realize the strain on local resources that their loss of employment created, and county officials halted public pronouncements of support. In the Boyle Heights community, however, both fellow Japanese Americans and non-Japanese increasingly aided displaced and often unemployed Japanese American families by sharing food and assisting in any way they could.

The US Justice Department, which was in charge of the alien-enemy control plan launched immediately after Pearl Harbor, remained steadfastly against incarceration but lost control of the discussion because of its inability to quell public suspicions about a "fifth column" of enemy support from within the United States. The major responsibility for the decision, therefore, fell to Lieutenant General John DeWitt, in charge of the defense of the West Coast from the San Francisco Presidio. He initially opposed mass evacuation but shifted from this position under pressure from figures within the military, local politicians, who were requesting federal assistance as county welfare expenditures ballooned, and a report advocating widespread incarceration from the Los Angeles Chamber of Commerce, the same organization that had played a key role in Mexican repatriation efforts ten years earlier.[10] DeWitt's first step was to designate "strategic zones" from which "enemy aliens" could be excluded: these were determined for California on January 21 and for Arizona, Oregon, and Washington on February 3.

On January 25, the Roberts Commission, tasked to investigate the Pearl Harbor disaster, erroneously charged that there had been widespread espionage in Hawai'i by Japanese consular agents and resident Japanese. This turned the tide. In early February, President Roosevelt made "military necessity" the governing rationale for any evacuation plan, and on February 14,

DeWitt recommended to the War Department a mass evacuation of all Japanese, foreigners and citizens, as soon as possible, in order to "protect" the Pacific Coast. Although he admitted that many second- and third-generation Japanese Americans were Americanized, "the racial strains [remain] undiluted. . . . It therefore follows that along the vital Pacific Coast over 112,000 potential enemies, of Japanese extraction, are at large today."[11] Both departments drew up the evacuation proclamation and presented it a few days later to the president for his consideration.

Meanwhile, residents in most parts of Los Angeles allowed decades of prejudice against Japanese Americans to turn the Pacific War into a "race war," with the circulation of images of crafty and bloodthirsty Japanese in both military and domestic propaganda.[12] Moreover, some Angelinos began to worry that they would be attacked next. Civil defense planners in Los Angeles had their first scare on Christmas Eve 1941, when a Japanese submarine attacked an American lumber carrier in the Catalina Channel, exposing the vulnerability of maritime shipping along the Pacific Coast.[13] Two months later, a Japanese submarine off the Pacific Coast fired twenty-five shells at oil tanks twelve miles north of Santa Barbara. Los Angeles, as a whole, believed itself to be on the front lines of imminent attack, and reports on February 23, 1942, that alleged the spotting of Japanese aircraft over the Southland (later revealed to be weather balloons) led to more Japanese residents being picked up by the FBI.[14]

When President Franklin Roosevelt called for the removal of "enemy aliens," including all Japanese, from the West Coast on February 19, 1942, the tone in the community changed dramatically. In the months between the evacuation orders and actual relocation in May 1942, Japanese were forced to sell furniture, household appliances, cars, and even homes at "dirt cheap" rates in an environment that was described by one interviewee as "chaos." Daniel Kawahawa, who had spent three years in Japan going to school and working for his uncle since graduating from Roosevelt High School in 1937, threw away all pictures and mementoes he had from that period of his life as his family prepared for evacuation: "Everything I had of Japan, I dumped it."[15]

Close neighbors of various ethnic groups were entrusted to take care of or manage property in the absence of their Japanese owners. Mollie Wilson's brother, Atoy Wilson Jr., then a recent African American graduate of Roosevelt High School, remembered his aunt taking care of a mom-and-pop store on Fresno Street for the Japanese American family who owned it. Though they never actually ran the store in their absence, they made sure that all the family's possessions were returned when they were allowed to return after the war.[16] Similarly, the Japanese American congregation at the newly built Tenrikyo Church on First Street entrusted the property and its contents to the parishioners of the largely African American Baptist Church nearby, who returned it unscathed at the war's conclusion.[17] James Tolmasov, a Russian Molokan resident of the Flats, whose father hauled away rubbish, remembered his father being given a fancy, well-trained canary to care for. As Tolmasov recounts, "We saved it for them. Basically, we bought it, but 'When you want it back, let us know,' attitude, because they were friends. You don't just take advantage of a friend."[18] Similarly, the African American writer Chester Himes and his wife cared for the downtown home of an interracial Japanese-white family, the Oyama-Mittwers, when that family was "evacuated" for the duration of the war.[19] It was this experience that led Himes to write into his first novel, *If He Hollers, Let Him Go,* a reference to the youngster Riki (Richard) Oyana:

> Maybe I'd been scared all my life, but I didn't know about it until after Pearl Harbour. . . . Maybe it had started then, I'm not sure, or maybe it wasn't until I'd seen them send the Japanese away that I'd noticed it. Little Riki Oyana singing "God Bless America" and going to Santa Anita with his parents next day. It was taking a man up by the roots and locking him up without a chance. Without a trial. Without a charge. Without even giving him a chance to say one word. It was thinking about if they ever did that to me, Robert Jones, Mrs. Jones's dark son, that started me to getting scared.[20]

There was also no obvious method by which Japanese Americans could secure their possessions in the midst of this chaos and uncertainty. Ruth Matsuo (now Brandt)'s mother made arrangements for her very good white friend to stay in their City Terrace home and care for their belongings, but upon arriving at Heart Mountain internment camp she learned that this family had decided not to stay there anymore because they feared being a target for air bombing.[21] The fate of the belongings of the Shimo family offers another example. Tamori Shimo, a martial arts instructor, was picked up almost immediately after Pearl Harbor and first sent to Tujunga, then Bismarck, North Dakota. It was left to his wife, Yoshiko Shimo, to dispose of the family property in the wake of evacuation orders, and she would eventually be sent to Manzanar. Bargain hunters offered her only ten dollars for all her furniture and appliances in their rented home, which left her so furious that she decided to leave everything at the house for the next tenant.

Indeed, she buried several items, including vases from Japan, in her garden for safekeeping.[22] Her landlord and neighbor, the Reverend LeRoque, allowed her to store books and photo albums in his garage, all of which were returned to the Shimos in fine condition after the war. Other personal items were stored at the Boyle Heights Nichiren Temple for safekeeping, but the temple was vandalized during the war and all these items were lost.[23] In 1990, as part of the first class I taught on Boyle Heights, a UCLA Asian American studies graduate student, Glen Kitayama, interviewed his grandfather, who had grown up in Boyle Heights and vividly remembered the chaotic period when Japanese American residents were forced to sell many of their belongings. I'll never forget Glen coming to me after his interview, shocked by what he perceived to be his grandfather's anti-Semitic feelings toward Jews as a result of Jewish neighbors trying to get a bargain from his misfortune. His grandfather had been so angry that he decided to sell his belongings only to Mexicans, even if this meant giving them away.[24]

For many in Boyle Heights, accustomed to the vast diversity of individuals and families that made up the community, the differential treatment toward their vulnerable neighbors made them realize, often for the first time, the harshness of US racialized policy and practice. Russian-born resident Kate Bolotin, for example, felt bad about the removal of her Japanese friends, but "As I thought about it, well, if they're going to be that way, then round up the Italians and the Germans, because they were all our enemies too."[25] Initially General DeWitt had wanted German and Italian removals, but he saw the Japanese as "an enemy race," a perception that overrode those broader sentiments. And by April 1942, General DeWitt reported that he saw no need for any full-scale evacuation or relocation of German or Italian aliens.[26] Thus it was clear to Kate and others that the Japanese were singled out for persecution and discrimination. Like many others, she never used the term *race* or *racism* to explain this disparity, but there was no mistaking that national and ethnic differences were driving US policy. In this way, local Boyle Heights residents of all backgrounds were getting a lesson on racialized citizenship, the kind that had served to banish Mexicans in the Mexican Repatriation Campaign. While hundreds of suspected German and Italian nationals were arrested by the US Justice Department in the wake of the bombing of Pearl Harbor, their cases were treated individually, and most were eventually released within weeks. The actions taken against Japanese Americans, with all of them being labeled as suspected enemy aliens, and then the entire West Coast Japanese-origin population incarcerated en masse, made clear to all

FIGURE 11. Japanese Americans arrive at Santa Anita internment camp, April 14, 1942. Los Angeles Herald Examiner Collection/Los Angeles Public Library.

Americans that racial background, not citizenship nor individual views, was the defining determinant of removals and internment. As Earl Warren, then attorney general of the state of California, explained: "We believe that when we are dealing with the Caucasian race we have methods that will test the loyalty of them. . . . But when we deal with the Japanese we are in an entirely different field and cannot form any opinion that we believe to be sound."[27]

Most Japanese Americans from Boyle Heights were sent first to Santa Anita Racetrack and then to camps in Arizona or to Manzanar in California.[28] Between May 7 and October 27, 1942, Santa Anita Racetrack housed over 18,000 Japanese Americans from all over Southern California in flimsy barracks constructed from former horse stalls.[29] The rest from the region were housed at the Pomona Fairgrounds. During the summer of 1942, when Japanese Americans were restricted to these inland Southern California locations while more permanent internment camps where being built in the interior of the nation, several Boyle Heights classmates and friends went out to visit and renew their relationships face to face through the fences of the racetrack. The actions and reactions of individuals to the challenges brought during 1942, and the experiences of widespread discrimination and fear for the future, would continue to live vividly in the minds of everyone in Boyle Heights as they saw profound changes in the community.

LOS ANGELES MOBILIZES FOR WAR

Although the removal of Japanese Americans was the most climactic and wrenching event after the bombing of Pearl Harbor for residents of Boyle Heights, the mobilization for war in Los Angeles would affect everyone in the region in crucial and surprising ways. Many male Boyle Heights residents, particularly the young adults, had their futures transformed by the unfolding military needs of World War II. Guy Gabaldon, along with his closest Japanese American friends, the Nakano brothers, tried to sign up for the National Guard the day after the bombing of Pearl Harbor, but Gabaldon was turned away immediately for being underage. Later Gabaldon would enlist in the Marine Corps at age seventeen and would become famous for capturing over 1,300 Japanese soldiers holding out in Saipan and Tinian, utilizing the pidgin Japanese he had first learned on the streets of Boyle Heights.[30] For him, as for so many others, the war provided an escape from the neighborhood that allowed him to see the world and offered experiences that would profoundly affect the rest of his life.

Bud Weber remembers that the war took "everybody that I knew out of the Heights, except three of our people: Charlie, Johnny, and Louie, who could not pass the physical."[31] This widespread military recruitment of almost all young men in the neighborhood produced for many a set of difficult decisions and forced them to grow up fast. Weber remembers seeing one of his friends off:

> My best friend and I were going to go into the marines together, but he got tired of living at home. His mother was hassling him, so he said, "Buddy, I need to go." So he quit Roosevelt in the 11th grade . . . to go into the marines. So I met him early in the morning. We walked up State Street to the B Car on Brooklyn Avenue. He had his little satchel in his little hand with his little shaving kit. He looked so young. My god—going into the marines. He got on the streetcar and he looked back at me like, what am I doing? I hope I know what I'm doing. I watched that streetcar go by.[32]

It was clear from the start of World War II that Jewish residents of Boyle Heights would lead efforts to combat Nazism and fascism, both abroad and locally, because of the direct threat that Hitler posed to them. Since 550,000 Jewish men and women served in the United States armed forces during World War II—11 percent of the total Jewish population of the US—the war had immediate and dramatic effects on neighborhoods with a large Jewish population like Boyle Heights. In particular, 50 percent of the male Jewish population in the US aged 18 to 44 were in uniform during World War II.[33] However, Jews from Boyle Heights likely exceeded this national average, as evidenced by the steady stream of Roosevelt High School graduates enlisting in the armed forces.

The youth clubs that had started to develop among Jewish teenagers in the late 1930s, such as the Saxons, would send almost all their members to the battle front during World War II. "Out of the 37 [who were Saxons then], 36 went into the service," remembered Gene Resnikoff, who had graduated two months after Pearl Harbor. "One was out because he had a punctured ear drum. And we only lost one," recalled Resnikoff, acknowledging Willie Goldberg, who was killed in Germany on a volunteer scouting mission.[34] Before heading to basic training, this group would often visit their former Japanese American classmates, detained at Santa Anita Racetrack in the summer of 1942 before they were sent to permanent internment camps. "We couldn't go in and they couldn't come out, so we would visit through the fence," remembered Israel Levy over 50 years later.[35] It's telling that before leaving for battle, the newly enlisted Jewish US soldiers did not find it incongruous to visit long-standing Japanese American friends, held in confinement by the US government because of supposed fear that they would sabotage military plans in favor of Axis ally Japan.

This outward flow of young men from Boyle Heights affected not just their own lives but also the lives of many young women of the neighborhood. Florence Coutin, for example, got married in 1942, just in time to see her newlywed husband, George, drafted into the army. For the next three years, George was stationed in an army air force base in Oklahoma, while Florence stayed close to her own parents still living in Boyle Heights. Finally, in 1945, Florence moved to Oklahoma to be with her husband, living there for six months as he concluded his wartime enlistment. When they returned to Boyle Heights in 1946, they moved back in with their family and lived there for the next three years, until 1949, when the young family was financially stable and able to leave the neighborhood.[36] The Coutins were not alone. The

FIGURE 12. War bonds sale at Boyle Heights Victory House at corner of Brooklyn and Soto, with Abraham Maymudes, chairman of Jewish Fraternal Order of IWO, presiding, 1942. Shades of LA Photo Collection/Los Angeles Public Library.

war's disruption pushed many individuals and families to leave Boyle Heights in the early 1940s—often for the first time in their lives. For most this was seen as temporary, but it quickly became clear how difficult it would be to resume normal life once the war ended.

At the local level, young women of every ethnicity saw their world expand beyond the borders of Boyle Heights, with the influx of servicemen, the growth of the Jewish community, and new work opportunities for teenagers. Claire Orlosoroff (now Stein) remembered joining the Jesterettes at Hollenbeck Junior High School with her other Jewish girlfriends and continuing with that female club throughout the war years as she attended Roosevelt High School. The club, which functioned much like the Jasons or the Saxons for young men in that era, gave Claire a protective environment to explore Southern California on the weekends with her peers, including trips to the beach, the Huntington Library, and the movies. She maintained this active social life as a teenager on top of working at the Famous Department Store downtown on Broadway and participating at the Soto-Michigan Jewish Community Center. In addition, with her Jesterette teenage cohort, Claire was busy working at the USO, or United Services Organization, for "coffee and companionship" for lonely servicemen stationed in Los Angeles. By age 17, and while still finishing up high school at Roosevelt, Claire would go on to marry her longtime boyfriend before he headed into the service.[37]

On virtually every street in Boyle Heights, families hung little banners painted with stars in their windows, indicating they had a family member serving in the armed forces overseas. When someone was killed, that star turned gold. Those remaining in Boyle Heights were mostly younger children and teenagers, and a much older contingent of parents and grandparents that sustained the neighborhood synagogues, shops, and cultural institutions. Yet the passion regarding the fight against fascism pervaded Jewish Boyle Heights among those of every age. Hershey Eisenberg remembers older men getting into fervent arguments about war strategy late at night in some of the 24-hour restaurants near the corner of Brooklyn and Soto.[38] Myer Pransky, president of the regional American Jewish Congress, led a 21-day drive in December 1942 and January 1943 and was able to raise $300,000 for war bonds. This gave the neighborhood the honor of funding the first bomber plane sponsored by a specific community, which was then christened *The Spirit of Boyle Heights* and, according to Congressman Chet Hollifield, demonstrated "the unifying force of democracy" in the neighborhood as "proof of their patriotism."[39]

CIVIL RIGHTS IN THE "ARSENAL OF DEMOCRACY"

Older men and almost all women of Boyle Heights, because of either their age, their physical condition, or their gender, were not called to serve in the armed forces and were instead recruited into the growing war industries of Los Angeles. During 1942 and 1943, Los Angeles became one of the most important manufacturing locations for weapons of war, particularly the building of ships and airplanes, as well as all the necessary steel, rubber, and mechanical components. Aircraft manufacturing, in particular, increased rapidly and, as an industry, led the efforts in Los Angeles toward wartime production. At the beginning of 1939, 13,300 workers were employed by aircraft companies in Los Angeles County; by the fall of 1943, the industry reached a peak employment of 228,400.[40] During this period Los Angeles officials enthusiastically accepted the moniker "Arsenal of Democracy" to describe the region.

Before these jobs could be filled and wartime production ramped up, the aircraft and shipbuilding industries and their unions had to confront their racist and gendered hiring policies that had kept these well-paying jobs exclusively male and white. Indeed, before Pearl Harbor these Los Angeles firms had been pressured to change their practices when the newly formed Fair Employment Practices Commission (FEPC) decided to have its first open hearings in Los Angeles in October 1941. Building off Executive Order 8802, which outlawed discrimination on the basis of race, creed, or national origins by firms holding defense contracts with the US government, President Franklin D. Roosevelt had intended to underscore the need for a wider workforce since signing the order on June 25, 1941. But it took the NAACP, the Urban League, and the Japanese American Citizens League to publicize discriminatory practices by local industries and unions and to push for change under the pledge to fight fascism collectively. With US entry into World War II after December 7, and the mobilization of most healthy white male workers to the ranks of soldiers and sailors, the urgency of equal employment hiring became a national priority.[41]

By mid-1942, the aircraft industry had lost almost 20,000 workers to the armed services, while there were 550,000 newly created defense jobs awaiting employees.[42] Billboards in English and Spanish were plastered all over East Los Angeles, including Boyle Heights, seeking women and men of all ethnicities, with no experience required. One of those that responded to this call was Margarita ("Margie") Salazar, a 25-year-old beautician from Boyle Heights, who had constantly heard from her customers in the beauty shop on Brooklyn Avenue about the good money to be made. Margie was excited to contribute to the war effort, since she came from a Mexican American family, originally from New Mexico, and already had two brothers who had signed up for the service. Working for Lockheed on Seventh and Santa Fe downtown under the bridge over the Los Angeles River was one way she could contribute directly to the war effort, but she also went beyond that by joining the Civilian Defense Corps, where she would coordinate communication with air raid wardens throughout the city in case Los Angeles was attacked.[43]

Margie Salazar's actions were like those of many young women in Boyle Heights who saw an opportunity to expand their worlds by joining the inflated employment market during wartime Los Angeles. Many entered a defense industry with other family members or friends. Irene Molina secured positions with her sister at O'Keefe and Merritt, a stove company turned ammunition shell producer in the period. They worked as an inspector and a

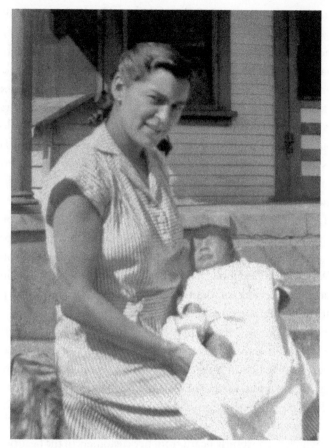

FIGURE 13. Margarita (Margie) Salazar with newborn son in front of her Boyle Heights home on Fourth Street and Mott, 1948. With permission of Margaret Salazar-Porzio.

welder respectively and saw many of their girlfriends from Roosevelt High School also join the payroll.[44] Mexican American young women from Boyle Heights could combine their commitment to patriotism with a larger paycheck. By January 1944, at Lockheed's two Los Angeles plants, 10 to 15 percent of the total workforce became Mexican, and 80 percent of the Mexican workforce were women.[45]

The growing labor demands of Los Angeles also encouraged newcomers to pour into the city. By the summer of 1942, the wartime industry in Southern California began to draw African Americans from all over the South, but particularly from Texas and Louisiana. The paternal grandmother of Albert

Walter Johnson, for example, came to Los Angeles from Houston, Texas, in 1941 for a job cleaning the railroad cars that transported troops to and from Southern California. Given Boyle Heights' close proximity to Union Station, she chose to live around Fourth Street in the Pico-Aliso district in the Flats area of Boyle Heights, eventually providing a home there for her son when he got out of the navy in 1946.[46] Young men and women of Boyle Heights also took advantage of increased opportunities for African Americans in the war industries. Mollie Wilson's brother, Atoy Wilson Jr., left his Boyle Heights job as a school gardener to work in the navy shipyards in Vallejo in Northern California until he was drafted in 1943.[47] The integration of African Americans into the ranks of defense industry employees, combined with a massive black migration to Los Angeles, made this a critical time for the racial restructuring of Los Angeles. Douglas Aircraft hired 2,200 African American employees by February 1943, while North American employed 2,500 and Lockheed Vega hired 1,700.[48] This increased the African American share of Los Angeles' war-related production work from a meager 1.1 percent in May 1942 to more than 5 percent in 1944.[49]

Labor unions also grew substantially in membership during World War II as part of an agreement with the Roosevelt administration to support labor union representation during the war in exchange for a no-strike pledge. This membership growth occurred largely because workers were entering industries at a time when union contracts were already in place. At one level, this meant that in a predominantly open-shop setting like Los Angeles, the increase in union workers, which more than doubled from 170,000 to 382,333 between 1939 to 1945, was significant. In 1945, 25 percent of the wage workers in Los Angeles were unionized, the highest percentage ever in Los Angeles, though this figure still lagged behind the rest of the United States by 11 points.[50] From communist organizers to AFL moderate union leaders, solidarity behind the war effort dominated the political commitments of labor activists during the early 1940s. Civil rights activists could now more regularly depend on CIO officials, as well as some AFL leaders, to join with them in pushing efforts to increase opportunities for racial minorities in defense industries, particularly for African Americans. Local unions in the aircraft industry, once they realized that women and minority workers were there to stay—at least through the duration of the war—welcomed these new members and largely were able to quell objections from white male workers about this move toward integration.

This development would have a profound effect on Boyle Heights residents, many of whom had their first union experience during wartime work in defense industries. Hope Mendoza, for example, had worked in the Los Angeles garment industry as a teenager but found a position as a riveter on the Lockheed assembly line during the war. Since all Lockheed employees were required to join the International Association of Machinists Local 727, Mendoza was able to join her first union. Even after she was forced out of the defense industry at the conclusion of the war, she became more politicized as a union organizer for the ILGWU and was one of the initial founders in 1947 of the Community Service Organization (CSO), which advocated for Latino civil rights. Mendoza eventually became chair of the CSO labor committee.[51]

Despite the progress in labor opportunities for ethnic minorities, white Los Angeles still resoundingly objected to living next door to African Americans, Mexican Americans, and other racial minorities during World War II. The black migration to the "Arsenal of Democracy" would not be met with the opening up of new residential communities, so the migration led to major overcrowding in the established black communities, from downtown to Central Avenue to Watts. Located just across the river from Boyle Heights, what was Little Tokyo and now "Bronzeville," would become the new port of entry for black migrants to Los Angeles. Largely white property owners compensated for the swift departure of their former Japanese residents and business owners by quickly converting and subdividing their properties into small apartments and "kitchenettes" to house black newcomers with few other housing options. A convenient entry point for migrants who had just disembarked from Southern Pacific trains from New Orleans or Houston at Union Station, the neighborhood also quickly became notorious for its substandard housing conditions and dangerous overcrowding. By 1944, 80,000 people lived in "Bronzeville" in a community that had housed only 30,000 before the war.[52] Howard Holtezendorff, a Los Angeles housing official, who testified in 1944 before a congressional committee, described these crowded conditions by citing records that showed "families piling up . . . four, five, and six persons to a bedroom. In one case a family of five was living in a dirt-floored garage with no sanitary facilities whatsoever. In an abandoned storefront . . . twenty-one people were found to be living—and paying approximately $50 a month for these quarters."[53]

Given the enormous housing shortage for African Americans that created these deplorable conditions and the strain it produced on the community, it is fascinating that almost all of the African American interviewees from Boyle Heights remember themselves or close relatives taking care of homes or businesses for interned Japanese American families. Black families in Boyle Heights who had taken on the responsibility of caring for the vacated homes and businesses of Japanese American neighbors apparently did not rent or otherwise open these spaces to black newcomers to the city. Perhaps reflecting a shared understanding and experience of racism among people of color, they, like Mexicans and other ethnic families who assumed these responsibilities, took special care to guard and protect these properties throughout the war despite the severe shortage of housing. Most Japanese American families would return to Boyle Heights to find their entrusted dwellings in perfect condition.

Since many of the new wartime manufacturing plants were constructed in geographic areas of the region far from minority communities, the residential segregation endemic in Westchester or Burbank, for example, became a major factor in limiting defense employment opportunities to those deemed Caucasian, including the white ethnics who had made up such an important part of the Boyle Heights community. Increasingly, Jews, Italians, Russian Molokans, and other white ethnics of Boyle Heights would move out of the community to take advantage of these economic opportunities and the newly constructed residential communities that now welcomed them as "Caucasian."

On the other hand, civil rights activists in Los Angeles had to fight for the expansion and integration of public housing and the opening of private housing opportunities in Boyle Heights and elsewhere on the Eastside and Southside of Los Angeles. The city's premier public housing project, Ramona Gardens in Boyle Heights, was opened in January 1941 to much fanfare around its supposed integration. While new white migrants from the South objected to this mixing, labor activist Bert Corona established a Mexican Subcommittee of the CIO Industrial Council to fight for more public housing options for Mexican American war workers.[54] Indeed, the stated priority for integrated city public housing was abandoned during the war in favor of prioritizing housing for wartime laborers and returning veterans amid the Los Angeles housing shortage. After a tense meeting with the City Housing Authority in August 1942, Mexican families were given permission to live in city-owned public housing only if at least one of their children was a US citizen and if someone in the family had a defense-related job.[55]

So while opportunities in the workplace advanced dramatically for residents of Boyle Heights during World War II, especially for Mexican Americans, racism outside the workplace continued unabated and could even be said to have increased under the pressures of the war. According to historians

Elizabeth Escobedo and Naomi Quiñonez, "In their memories of World War II, most interviewees recounted little or no discrimination on the job, and instead focused on discriminatory experiences in society at large."[56] But the restrictions stipulating where Mexican Americans and African Americans could live in Los Angeles, as well as discrimination in education, leisure activities, and consumption, increasingly seemed outdated to racial minority groups and contradicted the opportunities these minorities were given on the mixed factory floors under wartime employment.

THE NEW RACIAL SCAPEGOAT

Most Chicano historians of the period identify the removal of the Japanese Americans from Southern California at the end of the spring of 1942 as the beginning of increased antagonism toward Mexican American youth. This was primarily in the context of heightened tensions coming from the local white population and the servicemen awaiting assignment in the Pacific War, who needed a new population to direct their racial animosity against. As Carey McWilliams remembered in the 1940s, "It was a foregone conclusion that Mexicans would be substituted as the major scapegoat once the Japanese were removed."[57] This anxiety was a result of both a growing demand for conformity during the war on the part of the local population and a direct concern expressed by local officials and newspaper columnists regarding the possibility of disgruntled minority youth being recruited for enemy support.

In particular, law enforcement officials in Southern California made immediate connections between Japanese Americans and Mexican Americans when assessing the onset of what was perceived to be a "crime wave" among *pachucos* and "zoot suiters" in the Mexican American community. Los Angeles sheriff Eugene Biscailuz told a reporter that "the Japanese left instructions with these hoodlums before they were forced to leave their homes," claiming that "a group of these Mexican youths were known to frequent a certain Japanese grocery store in the Eastside where Mexicans and Japanese were in preponderance."[58]

This racial linking of the two populations, outside of the highly hysterical wartime environment of 1942, was odd because the youth of both populations had experienced such a different set of life circumstances up to this point, at least in Boyle Heights. While most of the Japanese American youth of Boyle Heights before World War II could look forward to completing high school at Roosevelt and often going on to college, most Mexican American young people in Boyle Heights left school before high school graduation. As one former Boyle Heights honors student of Jewish background explained about the racial attitudes of local educators of the period: "I think they were grouping kids in those days ... if not overtly, mentally. I know they did it with testing. ... I don't know whether the Hispanic kids got what they should have gotten."[59] The *pachuco* population of East Los Angeles evolved almost exclusively from the Mexican American youth who had dropped out of school before or during high school. Most had already begun working, which actually gave them the additional income necessary to purchase a fine "zoot suit," a flashy exaggeration of dance-hall elegance, including high-waisted wide-legged pants, a long fancy jacket with padded shoulders, a watch chain to the knees (or longer), and a wide-brimmed hat. The style, likely originating with African American jazz artists and the jitterbug culture of the 1930s, represented a cross-ethnic urban style that transcended the barrios, ethnic segregation, and working-class constraints.[60] For the young men of Boyle Heights and other parts of working class Los Angeles, the zoot suit advertised their newfound income and signaled a refusal "to concede to the manners of subservience."[61] As British scholar Stuart Cosgrove long observed of the zoot suit: it was "an emblem of ethnicity and a way of negotiating an identity."[62] This defiant and extravagant look by young men of color was even more oppositional in this wartime era when contrasted to "the neat trim look of the servicemen," which "placed a high value on the conservation of basic materials such as cloth" and emphasized "unity and conformity in order to defeat the common foe," according to historian Edward Escobar.[63]

Young Mexican American women also donned their own version of the zoot suit by matching a cardigan or V-neck sweater with a long fingertip coat, a skirt considered relatively short to just above the knee, bobby sox pulled high, and huarache sandals, saddle shoes, or platform heels. Women further emphasized their distinct look with dark lipstick, plucked eyebrows, and hair lifted high into a pompadour.[64] A public sensuality was intended to mark a gendered display of rebellion, toward both authorities and restrictive immigrant parents, as the greater independence of young women during the war bucked the sensibilities of more conventional notions of womanhood and respectability. In many ways, young *pachucas* were making greater claims to participation in public life than all other women during World War II now seeing more of the city through work life and leisure activity across the Southland.

FIGURE 14 (Left). Young man wears his drapes, a variation on the zoot suit style of the 1940s. Shades of LA Photo Collection/Los Angeles Public Library.

FIGURE 15 (Right). Ramona Fonseca poses in a zoot suit, June 26, 1944. Shades of LA Photo Collection/Los Angeles Public Library.

Many young women combined new jobs in the defense industry with fresh looks and sociality as *pachucas*. Historian Elizabeth Escobedo tells the story of 17-year-old Ida Escobedo, who started her first job in a small defense factory in Los Angeles in the summer of 1942 to earn money for her family after her brothers went overseas to fight. Although her mother "didn't approve of [zoot] clothes or anything about it," Ida dreamed of using her share of earnings for a tailor-made fingertip coat and matching skirt. She went with her sister to a men's clothing store once she had collected the money to buy the coat and wore it flamboyantly at her high school graduation ceremony. Ida remembered her mother being "ashamed of me," but she was marking her independence and asserting agency over her own life.[65]

But the growing societal tension was not just a result of young minority women and men affirming themselves. The Los Angeles Police Department was also undergoing a significant transition in wartime Los Angeles. Since the LAPD had stopped its former antilabor activities because of pro-union New Deal policies, its new invented enemies, replacing radical communists and unionists, were defiant racialized youth. A corruption scandal also created intense pressure for the LAPD to reform and reestablish its relationship with the broader public. They fixated on a new population of potential criminals, declaring a crime wave by Mexican American youth to gin up support from the white community of the city. The white population gave police officers great leeway in how aggressively they could govern the spatial movement of minority youth in the city. Historian Edward Escobar has shown that arrests, especially juvenile arrests, were way up in 1942, the year of the alleged "Mexican crime wave," but citizens actually reported 25 percent fewer crimes that year than in the previous one. "Arrest statistics for juveniles show an inverse relationship to reported crime: juvenile arrests rose as reported crime fell."[66] Escobar's statistical analysis also reveals that the LAPD increasingly and disproportionately arrested Mexican American youth from the mid-1930s on, so that by 1942 Mexican Americans accounted for 56 percent of all juvenile arrests. Indeed, during the war years Mexican Americans and African Americans accounted for between 77 and 83 percent of all juvenile arrests in Los Angeles. However, a very low number of these arrests led to actual prosecutions, which dipped during the war to an average of 56 percent of adult arrests and as low as 27 percent of juvenile arrests.[67] Overall, the alleged "Mexican crime wave" caused by *pachucos* was largely a myth, but what was real was a new aggressiveness by the police in terms of surveilling and harassing Mexican American youth.

This tension erupted on the morning of Sunday, August 2, 1942, when a Mexican American man named José Díaz was found unconscious by a dirt road near a gravel pit called Sleepy Lagoon, just south of East Los Angeles. When he died of head trauma later that day, police arrested a score of Mexican American boys associated with Henry Leyvas, who had gotten into a fight on Saturday night near that same location. No physical evidence tied Leyvas or his friends to the death of Díaz, yet police arrested at least 59 young people for his death and beat many of them to obtain confessions about their alleged role in the killing. With the police vowing to launch an "all-out war" against this "zoot suit menace," newspapers attributed the "Sleepy Lagoon murder" to "Mexican Boy Gangs" and reported that a "Boy Gang Terror Wave" was sweeping the city.[68]

The aftermath of these mass arrests in the wake of the Sleepy Lagoon case only served to heighten tensions throughout the city, but particularly in the barrios of Boyle Heights and East Los Angeles. Racialized stories connecting the contemporary Mexican American population with Aztec Indian blood rituals and Oriental despotic practices fueled the narrative of juvenile delinquency. County prosecutors filed murder charges against 22 youths, and the criminal trial that followed in December 1942 and January 1943 was the largest mass trial ever held in the state of California. Put plainly, it was a travesty of justice. The presiding judge did not allow the defendants to bathe or shave and consistently showed prejudicial conduct against their defense. Although three young women—Frances Silva, Dora Barrios, and Lorena Encinas—were originally charged with murder, when those charges were eventually dropped they were still held as material witnesses for the trial. Angelinos following the trial were fascinated by the spectacle of combatant *pachucas*, and though no women were ever found guilty of a crime, these three and five others were declared wards of the state and sent to the Ventura School for Girls, a juvenile correctional facility well known for violence and abuse.[69] Although the prosecution presented no evidence in court that any defendant had assaulted José Díaz, on January 13, 1943, the jury found three defendants, including Henry Leyvas, guilty of first-degree murder, nine others of second-degree murder, and five of assault. Judge Fricke sentenced those convicted to life imprisonment, five years to life, and six months in the county jail, respectively.[70]

Los Angeles liberals and leftists from both the white and Mexican American communities were moved to action by the trial, conviction, and sentencing of the Sleepy Lagoon defendants. Under the leadership of Josefina Fierro de Bright, who had helped organize the Mexican American advocacy group El Congreso, and LaRue McCormick, of the International Labor Defense (ILD), initial meetings around the case produced the Citizens' Committee for the Defense of Mexican-American Youth, which eventually became the Sleepy Lagoon Defense Committee (SLDC). This group was worried about how the negative publicity generated from this miscarriage of justice would affect support for the war from Latin American nations, but it also focused on raising funds for the actual defendants as they worked toward an appeal of their convictions. Rather than focusing on curtailing juvenile delinquency, this group specifically attacked the prejudicial criminal justice system and sought to rid Southern California of the biases against Mexican American youth.[71]

Unfortunately, the racial hysteria against Mexican American youth and the supposed crime wave kept growing in early 1943. Coupled with mixed results of the Allied efforts in the Pacific and the European front, the local crime wave story kept white Angelinos feeling that they were fighting a battle at home even while the war was raging overseas. Local newspapers continued to bombard the population with racialized stories about crime, identifying culprits as "Mexican hoodlums" and decrying "Zooter crime."[72] By the time of the so-called Zoot Suit Riots of June 1943, young people who had grown up in Boyle Heights had witnessed much abuse by police and servicemen stationed nearby. Indeed, the constant migration of new servicemen into Southern California, as many as 50,000 a week, alongside more white migration from the Midwest and the South, created communities of newcomers in Los Angeles unaccustomed to the fluidity of race and difference that was typical in places like Boyle Heights.[73] Increasingly, many Mexican youth learned to stay closer to home, especially avoiding those downtown establishments visited by sailors.[74] Others, however, continued to push at the boundaries of the barrios in East Los Angeles, and it was this spatial and social conflict that sparked the next explosion in the city.

As historian Edward Escobar has observed, "The Zoot Suit riots that raged in Los Angeles between June 3 and June 10, 1943, were the direct result of the anti-Mexican hysteria of the preceding year."[75] Thousands of servicemen stationed in and around Los Angeles were profoundly swayed by the news coverage of a "*pachuco* crime spree" that was depicted as uncontrollable by local police and that allegedly threatened the safety of their families. It was in this context that servicemen decided to deal with the zoot suiters themselves, probably sparked by a confrontation in the Alpine district near Chavez Ravine where a cluster of sailors confronted zoot suiters after a group of off-duty LAPD officers had attacked *pachucos* in a vigilante action. Escalating from an initial confrontation on May 30, by Thursday, June 3, several dozen sailors were beating every zoot suiter they could find and pulling Mexican American boys out of downtown theaters, stripping them of their clothes, brutalizing them, and leaving them naked in the streets.[76]

Over the weekend, the confrontations escalated, almost always involving sailors and marines looking for opportunities to attack zoot suiters and sometimes any Mexican American, no matter how he was dressed. By Sunday night, June 6, servicemen were moving into Boyle Heights and East Los Angeles looking for zoot suiters to attack, despite an additional 300 LAPD and sheriff's deputies on patrol. For example, one group of sailors chased zoot suiters into a dance hall on First and State Streets in Boyle Heights, leaving the Mexican American youths "crawling about with battered heads and smashed noses."[77] As was the pattern of law enforcement personnel throughout the riots, the LAPD adopted an informal policy of allowing the violence to continue as long as the servicemen had the upper hand; when zoot suiters tried to defend themselves or fight back, police officers intervened and arrested the Mexican American youth.

On Monday, June 7, however, the dynamics of violence changed as Mexican American and African American youth decided, after days of unmitigated attacks on them, to defend themselves and retaliate in organized and unprecedented fashion. Rudy Leyvas, brother of Sleepy Lagoon defendant Henry Leyvas, reported on a battle that occurred in downtown Los Angeles, on the corner of Central Avenue and Twelfth Street, where African Americans lent Mexican Americans their cars to gather zoot suit combatants, almost 500 deep. From hiding places in alleys, 20 were sent out onto the street to draw out the US Navy personnel, and when they came out to fight, the others appeared and engaged in a violent battle with fists and baseball bats. When servicemen crossed the Los Angeles River and entered Boyle Heights, they even entered people's homes. That night, it was later reported, Mexican Americans were attacked in the Meralta Theater, just 300 feet from the LAPD's Hollenbeck Division headquarters, but the officer in charge refused to send in officers to stop the violence.[78] The battle had been elevated to a major race war in neighborhoods throughout the city, including Boyle Heights.

The next day, on June 8, the navy declared the city of Los Angeles out of bounds for sailors and marines. Although violence persisted in the city that night, and in surrounding suburbs over the next couple of days, the naval order was the major turning point in the de-escalation of the crisis.[79] Almost immediately, it was clear that these events had shattered the outside notion that Los Angeles was immune to the racism and discrimination that marked other parts of the United States. Still, city officials, especially Mayor Fletcher Bowron, tried to deny that race had anything to do with the disturbances and instead blamed juvenile hoodlums and rambunctious servicemen. But the events of early June 1943 would forever change the future of civil rights in Southern California. First Lady Eleanor Roosevelt, speaking at a press conference on June 16, said that she believed that the riots resulted from "long-standing discrimination against Mexicans" in California and the Southwest. Mrs. Roosevelt felt that "race problems" were increasing throughout the United States and worldwide and declared, "We must begin to face it." Although these comments set off a firestorm of protest from prominent Angelinos and conservative institutions like the *Los Angeles Times,* they also indicated that it would be impossible for the region to avoid confronting its own legacy of racism and discrimination.[80]

In the wake of the Zoot Suit Riots, new organizations of interracial unity were formed throughout Southern California and older ones were reinvigorated. The short-lived Committee of Civic Unity was formed in the summer of 1943 and contained key individuals who had been active previously but would now lead efforts at racial reconciliation well into the postwar period. These included author and activist Carey McWilliams, president of the California CIO Philip "Slim" Connelly, Mexican American activist Eduardo Quevedo, African American newspaper *California Eagle* editor Charlotta Bass, director of the Los Angeles Urban League Floyd L. Covington, Jewish activist Harry Braverman, and *Eastside Sun* editor Al Waxman. Some of this group would later form the Eastside Interracial Committee, which explicitly fought the rise of fascism and "fifth column" racism in Los Angeles. The Sleepy Lagoon Defense Committee also revived and was eventually successful in getting the defendants' convictions overturned and securing their release from jail on October 23, 1944. Eventually, the Los Angeles County Board of Supervisors established the County Committee for Interracial Progress, while the city was forced to create a Human Relations Commission to identify and combat racial prejudice and discrimination.[81] Cooperation across racial lines, so evident in the neighborhood of Boyle Heights, now became a standard operating practice to confront the problems of the city as a whole, and Boyle Heights residents and officials would be critical to this mission.

FIGHTING NAZISM IN LOS ANGELES

In the Jewish community of Boyle Heights, the energy that had been focused on labor agitation among the political Left turned to racial civil rights during World War II. At Roosevelt High School, Leo Frumkin organized the Socialist Youth Club when he was in eleventh grade in 1944. Coming from a very socially conscious family and witnessing the growth of anti-Semitism around the world and in Los Angeles in particular, Frumkin was outspoken against racism, even as a teenager, as detailed in last chapter's story of how he rejected membership in a Jewish organization because it wouldn't admit one of his Mexican friends. When Gerald L. K. Smith, a known fascist and anti-Semite, came to speak at Polytechnic High School in 1945, Frumkin and the Socialist Youth Club organized a protest against him that led nearly 600 students in a walkout from Roosevelt High School. In addition, he got students from Hollenbeck Junior High School next door to participate, as well as African American students from Jefferson High School to protest at the board of education offices downtown. At Jefferson, Frumkin jumped on a lunch table and said, "If you want to ride in the back of buses like they do in the South, then don't do anything. But if you're opposed to that, then come out with us and protest this guy who wants to put you on the back of buses and who is anti-black." In the end, about 1,000 students ended up protesting downtown, and Frumkin and several other students were arrested by the LAPD.[82]

For Jews in Boyle Heights, the end of World War II brought into focus the enormity of the Holocaust and the ongoing threat of fascism. In the organized Jewish community, however, the realization that European Jewry had been devastated by the Nazis and that local Southern Californian fascists and Nazi sympathizers continued to operate in Los Angeles forced Jewish leadership to adopt a different strategy toward community relations. From the time of Adolf Hitler taking power in Germany in 1933, Jewish leaders in Los Angeles, led by Leon Lewis, the Southern California representative of the Anti-Defamation League of B'nai B'rith (ADL), had organized the Community Relations Committee (CRC)—called the Community Committee until 1941—to closely monitor Nazi activities in the US, especially in Los Angeles. The committee's work included an undercover operation to spy on fascist and right-wing local maneuvers.[83] This intelligence task force uncovered, for example, a 1934 plot for a mass killing of Jews in Boyle Heights with automatic shotguns after the killing of the 20 most prominent Jews in Hollywood and Los Angeles.[84] Because of the incompetence and unwillingness of surveillance efforts by the FBI and LAPD, Lewis's team was the major intelligence-gathering operation on internal Nazi efforts in the US, and on allied organizations such as the Silver Shirts and the Ku Klux Klan, up until the eve of US entry into World War II in 1941.[85]

It took the bombing of Pearl Harbor and US entry into World War II to force the FBI to take seriously the threat to the security of the United States posed by right-wing individuals working under Nazi direction. Only then did FBI director J. Edgar Hoover utilize the many reports and lists provided to him by Lewis and his protégé, Joseph Roos, uncovering the nefarious activities of Nazi sympathizers in Los Angeles trying to promote Hitler's agenda and undermine US war preparations. The arrests, using the information provided by Lewis and Roos, of local Nazis and German and Italian immigrants who posed a threat to the US and the enhanced surveillance put into practice during World War II finally forced the FBI to take over the intelligence operation that had been launched by the CRC eight years earlier.[86] While this gave the committee the ability to look at a broader set of issues, it also forced them to confront a dangerous development in American attitudes toward the influence of Jews in US society. It seemed as if large portions of the American public were increasingly agreeing with the anti-Semitic attitude that Jews had forced the US into war. When asked in April 1940 if "Jews have too much power and influence in this country," a majority of Americans answered affirmatively. Following the US entrance into World War II, that number increased. Near the war's end in July 1945, the percentage of Americans answering that question affirmatively had risen to 67 percent.[87] Since "blame the Jews" was a major argument to keep the US out of the war put forward by Nazi sympathizers, anti-interventionists, and the "America First" campaign, Lewis and Roos worried about its implication for a growing tide of anti-Semitism in the United States during World War II.

The answer by Lewis and Roos was to advocate that the CRC commit itself to moving from a principally Jewish "defense" agency to working as a community relations agency dedicated to fighting bigotry against any Los Angeles residents. In this way, anti-Semitism would be confronted as part of a broader project to combat all forms of racism and discrimination.[88] As early as the summer of 1942, Lewis had asked that all CRCs nationwide search for ways to convince Jews to "champion the rights of other minority groups."[89] According to historian Shana Bernstein, though this position often led to intense disagreements within Jewish groups during the war, "By the end of World War II, many Los Angeles Jewish community organizations had done an about-face on building coalitions with other, more racialized minorities."[90] In mid-1943, at the time of the Zoot Suit Riots, the CRC would participate in efforts to free the Sleepy Lagoon defendants, and the following year it would participate in aiding the return of the Japanese American internees. CRC members became one of the most active groups in forming multiracial civil rights coalitions, including community and human relations boards at both the city and county levels.[91] In many ways, the Boyle Heights setting of interracial cooperation spread to transform the outlook of the organized Jewish community leadership and affect multiracial efforts at racial solidarity throughout greater Los Angeles.

PREPARING FOR RESETTLEMENT IN THE BATTLE FOR CIVIL RIGHTS

While the aftermath of the Zoot Suit Riots, the growth of anti-Semitism, and the ongoing threat of fascism created a new context for the development of civil rights organizations on the Los Angeles home front, the last few years of wartime in Southern California continued to show how deep racial resentment lay in the hearts and minds of many Angelinos. Probably no better evidence of this exists than the decision by the *Los Angeles Times* in December 1943 to ask its readers to "send in your answer to the Jap problem." Through a series of "yes" or "no" questions, *Times* readers overwhelmingly expressed that the War Relocation Authority (WRA) had mishandled the problem of the Japanese and that the army should take control of the Japanese in the US for the duration of the war. Almost all opposed the release of "loyal Japanese," while most were willing to trade Japanese Americans for US war prisoners being held in Japan. By a nearly 10 to 1 margin, the readers wanted to deport Japanese Americans at the conclusion of the war, regardless of whether they were US citizens. While a few readers objected to the *Times* purposely fomenting racial hatred, an overwhelming readership sided with overtly racist positions against Japanese Americans in December 1943.[92]

According to historian Kevin Leonard, "In 1944 the debate about 'race' and Japanese Americans' loyalty shifted decisively."[93] What accounted for this pivotal change was an increasing number of powerful public officials, including army officers, speaking out against Japanese American discrimination. The most prominent figure was Secretary of the Interior Harold L. Ickes, who in a speech in San Francisco in April 1944 "called upon West Coast residents to quiet 'the clamor of those few among you who are screaming' for vengeance against former Pacific Coast area Japanese." Since the WRA was now under his jurisdiction, he spoke directly against those anti-Japanese agitators who wanted his agency to participate in "a lynching party."[94] By the middle of May, army officials reported that they had allowed 33 Japanese American women, with their children, to return to the Pacific Coast because they were all married to men who were not Japanese American or to US soldiers and therefore posed no risk.[95]

When the anti-Japanese activists attacked the decision to allow 19-year-old Esther Takai to leave internment to study at Pasadena City College in September 1944, 97 people wrote to the board of education supporting Takei. Protestant church groups rallied around Takei, as did a group of World War II veterans at UCLA. Finally, a group of citizens advocating "fair play" for "loyal Americans of Japanese ancestry" organized themselves into the Pasadena "Fair Play" Committee and invited WRA director Dillon S. Myer to speak to a standing-room-only crowd at the Pasadena Public Library. He argued against "fear and ignorance" and extolled the service record of loyal uniformed Japanese Americans in combat in the European front.[96]

Still, local officials and institutions continued to advocate for discriminatory measures against Japanese Americans returning to Los Angeles. Los Angeles police chief C. B. Horrall argued the police did not have the manpower to protect returnees, who would inevitably need it against hostile residents. Likewise, the *Los Angeles Times* editorialized against allowing Japanese Americans to return, asserting that wartime congestion in Los Angeles had left them no place to live, and especially pointing out how crowded the former Little Tokyo district was. When the army allowed 54-year-old Tadayuki Todah to return to his job operating the City Hall Grill in downtown, District Attorney Fred N. Howser exclaimed that "the second attack on Pearl Harbor has started!" "Fair Play" advocates, including an increasingly united religious community of Catholics and Protestants, called these remarks "un-American" and "un-Christian."[97]

On December 17, 1944, the army finally rescinded the exclusion orders. While the mayor and the police commissioner protested, almost all civil rights organizations applauded the decision, including the Catholic Interracial Council and Friends of the American Way in Pasadena. California governor Earl Warren accepted the army's decision and encouraged all California residents to honor and protect Japanese Americans' civil rights. And the day after the army's decision was announced, the US Supreme Court ruled that the federal government did not have the authority to detain American citizens who were loyal to the United States—a significant victory for some, albeit dangerously arbitrary and subjective.[98]

Slowly Japanese American families began to return to California, including families that had left Boyle Heights three years earlier. For most families that were able to return, getting back on their feet was quite difficult. With Southern California in a severe housing shortage, and many neighborhoods still very hostile to Japanese Americans, resettling in Los Angeles could often be an arduous process. Cedrick Shimo described visiting his friends in 1946 in Los Angeles, after he was discharged from the military: "Most of my friends came back penniless, so they were living in hostels, or . . . Bunker Hill. Little rooming houses, dirty, dingy places. Families were all living together, sharing rooms while trying to find a job. I remember visiting them and thinking, oh, my gosh, what a miserable condition they're in—no money, no job."[99]

Toshiko Ito remembered her family returning to her old neighborhood in Los Feliz in 1945, only to encounter signs that said "No Japs Wanted." The family had to get a court order to evict the renter who had been taking care of the house in their absence but who vandalized it and stole belongings before being forced to leave. Her Los Feliz neighbors put tacks in the family driveway, and none of the community grocery stores would sell any food to the family. This forced her mother to do all her shopping downtown in Chinatown or in the Grand Central Market and to drag grocery bags back home to Los Feliz. Her father hoped to get his job back as an insurance sales-man, but the company would not employ him, even in a demoted position. He was so upset by this treatment that he fell into deep depression and even-tually committed suicide.[100]

As Japanese Americans were released from the internment camps, many individuals and families came back specifically to Boyle Heights to recon-struct their lives, often with few resources other than the clothes they could carry. Former neighbors were crucial in helping them get resettled. Cedrick Shimo remembers Mrs. LeRoque, the matriarch of the family next door, wife of Reverend LeRoque as well as their landlord, taking him in after the war when he returned to Boyle Heights because he "had no place to go." He also recalls that every Christmas she would invite Cedric to attend their holiday gathering.[101] Even former acquaintances and friends from Boyle Heights who had moved out of the neighborhood offered critical means of support. Mollie Wilson provided shelter for her good friend and correspondent Sandie Saito when she decided to attend UCLA, where Mollie was a student.[102]

William Phillips, former sailor and owner of Phillips Music Store, a com-munity fixture on Brooklyn Avenue in Boyle Heights since 1937, went out of his way in the 1950s to support Japanese American entrepreneurship. When Kenji Taniguchi came to him with the idea of starting a sporting goods store to serve the Japanese youth sports leagues among the returnee community, Phillips did more than extend Taniguchi with a line of credit from the store. He cleared out a corner of the music store itself so that the fledging Japanese American entrepreneur could begin selling his wares from a high-profile location in the middle of Boyle Heights. From that start, Taniguchi was able to launch a successful sporting goods store on his own, which provided uniforms and sports equipment for the Japanese American community that had reconstituted itself in East Los Angeles.[103]

It is not surprising, therefore, that unlike many other neighborhoods throughout Southern California, Boyle Heights regained a substantial Japanese American population after the war that rivaled its pre–World War II community.[104] Indeed, as other non-Mexican populations were rapidly leaving Boyle Heights in the late 1940s and 1950s, many Japanese American newcomers settled into the community, joining the neighborhood alongside former residents who were returning to their homes upon release from the internment camps.

Housing continued to be an issue, but certain residences were converted into multiple household residences or collective living arrangements to respond to the overcrowding and new conditions of life postwar. The American Friends Service Committee and the Presbyterian Church transformed a former Boyle Heights boarding school into the Evergreen Hostel for emergency housing. It saw several thousand returnees pass through its doors in 1946.[105] The YWCA converted a large mansion on Third Street in Boyle Heights into the Magnolia Residence for Girls and ran it as a cooperative. The vast majority of the residents after 1945 were single Japanese American women, and the director from 1948 until the late 1950s was Toshiko Ito's widowed mother, who had returned from Heart Mountain internment camp with her family in 1945. However, during this period the Magnolia Residence also housed African American, Latina, and white women, all of whom worked as secretaries or clerks in nearby downtown offices and stores.[106]

In the war's aftermath, Boyle Heights returned to its history of interracial cooperation, now buoyed by newfound interconnections. Japanese Americans rekindled relationships with friends in the neighborhood and tried to restart their lives as best they could. Non-Japanese in Boyle Heights, somewhat embarrassed by their lack of protest at the initial internment, were satisfied that their deepened commitment to civil rights for all would help them overcome new challenges to interracial harmony in the future.

While many Asian American historians have vividly told the story of the internment of Japanese Americans from the West Coast of the United States, less attention has been paid to the reactions of the neighbors, classmates, fellow workers, and friends who watched these activities unfold. The histo-riographical depiction of Japanese American internment seems to assume that most Japanese Americans were highly segregated at the onset of World War II, residentially isolated in communities like Little Tokyo and within organizations and social settings where little communication and interaction occurred with non-Japanese. This chapter, however, shows a high degree of interaction at all levels and among all ages of Boyle Heights' Japanese American residents with others in the community.

Japanese American internment profoundly shattered the sense of peaceful coexistence that characterized the pre–World War II collective experience in Boyle Heights. Residents of all ethnic backgrounds quickly came to realize their own vulnerability to forces beyond their control, whether because of international events or domestic policies at home. The lives of almost all residents in Boyle Heights would be altered substantially by the forces of World War II—not as severely as those of Japanese American internees, but with a shared uncertainty about their personal and collective security. For many, watching one's neighbors and classmates suffer the indignities of incarceration because of their race left a lifelong impression that encouraged an active stance toward civil rights at the conclusion of the war itself.

Later, long after the war had ended and Japanese Americans had returned to Boyle Heights in large numbers, local residents seemed to have combined a quest for civil rights with a sentiment of guilt for not having acted more quickly or vocally to protect their Japanese American brethren. Even John Anson Ford, the liberal on the L.A. County Board of Supervisors who had voted for internment in January 1942, crusaded for civil rights, partly because by the 1950s he felt that Japanese internment had been a miscarriage of justice and should never be repeated. Future struggles would recall and be connected to Japanese internment, such as protests against "Operation Wetback" when Mexicans were deported. For the most part, the experience of living through the tumultuous World War II era, including the evacuation and internment of Japanese Americans, the fight against Nazis and fascists abroad and locally, the rising anti-*pachuco* campaign and the Zoot Suit Riots, and the return of Japanese American residents seemed to leave a distinct impression on many in the Boyle Heights community that would translate into their commitment to civil rights for all. In the postwar period, various organizations would emerge to lead new efforts to protect the rights of citizens, no matter what race or ethnicity. None would forget the legacy of Japanese American internment or the discrimination faced by zoot suiters in the midst of wartime Los Angeles.

Most of the stories I have gathered here point to the subtle, quite personal and quotidian ways that individuals protested Japanese American internment, even though this occurred far away from the eyes and ears of US officials. Leo Frumkin, for example, remembers running for student body president at Roosevelt High School in the fall of 1945 as the community was adjusting to the return of interned Japanese Americans. Already a union leader and a known rabble-rouser in Boyle Heights, he ran on "the program that a great injustice had been done to our fellow students, and we had to go out of our way to try to welcome them back and help integrate them."[107] After his five-minute speech for office at a school assembly, the principal called him into the office "very upset because I had used the term *concentration camp*," saying that it was simply what happened in a war. Frumkin, not one to back down easily, retorted, "No. What did these people have to do with the war?"[108]

SIX

The Exodus from the Eastside

JUST AS THE SCHOOL YEAR was starting in the fall of 1961, Ida Fiering confronted a painful dilemma for herself and her family. Her son was the only Jewish child left in his fifth-grade class at Malabar Elementary School. Mrs. Fiering, of course, knew that Jews had been leaving Boyle Heights since World War II and that in the last decade the community had become overwhelmingly Mexican. Yet to be faced with this changing demographic on such a personal level was jarring for Fiering, despite her commitment to understanding other cultures. Like many on the left in Boyle Heights during the 1950s, Ida had been involved in secular Jewish organizations, such as the Jewish People's Fraternal Order (JPFO) and the City Terrace Cultural Center, but she also had majored in Spanish at UCLA, participated in the State Assembly campaign of independent progressive Ida Alvarez, and claimed a Latina neighbor as her best friend. But the realization that her son was the last Jewish child in his class pushed her to weigh various personal, political, and ethnic factors against each other.[1]

Ida Fiering herself had been born in Boyle Heights in 1926 into a Jewish family with a strong socialist background, committed to the preservation of Yiddishkeit culture. Her parents, both born in Kiev, Russia, came to the United States in 1910 and into the City Terrace section of Boyle Heights in 1922. Her father had been among the charter members of the Painters' Union, Local 1348. After attending Malabar Elementary, Belvedere Junior High, and Roosevelt High School (class of 1945), Ida herself attended Berkeley and UCLA before marrying in 1949. After the newlywed couple lived in East Hollywood for one year, they decided to move back to Boyle Heights to start a family and raise their children in what remained of Yiddish culture in the area in 1950. In light of this strong desire to raise children in a Jewish environment steeped in tradition, the fact that her child was the only Jew left in his class came as a shock; Ida and her husband now decided to leave Boyle Heights. This move was done with reluctance and ambivalence, given the family's deep roots in the cultural and political history of working-class Jewish life on the Eastside, and signified a transition, not unique to Los Angeles, as postwar prosperity, the decline of anti-Semitism, freeways, and suburbanization transformed the place of Jews in Los Angeles urban life.

JEWS AND WHITENESS

Twentieth-century industrialization brought waves of Jewish immigrants (and Italians, Armenians, Russian Molokans, African Americans, and Mexicans) to Boyle Heights. While these ethnic groups lived in the same Boyle Heights neighborhood and intermixed, especially around unionization and other progressive and radical political issues, Jews in Boyle Heights were determined to keep a separate and unique Yiddish identity and culture. As we have seen in previous chapters, as Los Angeles' population grew in the early twentieth century, residential development kept "non-Caucasians and non-Gentiles" out of neighborhoods now populated by white Protestant newcomers from the Midwest. The Immigration Act of 1924 established quotas to further limit "undesirable" eastern and southern Europeans and Asian immigrants, but Boyle Heights' Jewish population continued to grow as Jews moved from other cities to Los Angeles, making the Jewish population in Los Angeles the second largest in the country outside New York. The Jews of Boyle Heights also witnessed firsthand the "repatriation" of their neighbors, American citizens of Mexican descent, during the Depression and the internment of their other neighbors, this time American citizens of Japanese descent, during World War II. A civil rights agenda began to emerge as Jews were galvanized by the horrors of the Holocaust to connect anti-Semitism (and racialized citizenship) to other forms of racism at home.

While working-class leftist Jews were located on the Eastside in their Boyle Heights homes, to the west, in L.A.'s Hollywood, film moguls and other entertainment elites created a more prosperous Jewish enclave. Much has been written about and debated regarding the ambivalence of Hollywood Jews toward their Jewish heritage and the impact of this disassociation on films during this period.[2] However, Jews in Boyle Heights had no such distance from their heritage and from issues of racial identity, which continued to be fraught and personal. At that same time, "Hebrew" as a racial category was eliminated from the records required by the Immigration and Naturalization Service in 1943, indicating a shift in official racial categories.[3] In 1945, the "Truman Directive"—which Congress passed in 1948—prioritized "displaced persons" (a term developed to describe those who had been denied citizenship in Nazi-occupied areas and therefore had no legal national affiliation). Jews once again poured into L.A. at the same time that Jewish professionals became powerful builders, architects, and real estate developers who welcomed these newcomers. "White" began to apply to those of European descent in a way that included Jews and reflected an overall unease about anti-Semitism as the world became aware of the human cost of the Holocaust. The old rules describing Jews as "aliens" gave way, and Jews—despite ongoing anti-Semitism in some quarters—now had access to "white" residential options.[4]

After the war, the working-class jobs from the war industries transformed into peacetime professionalism in a way that enabled a more affluent professional Jewish population to grow outside Hollywood. Jews had formed Jewish community centers and other social service organizations in the early twentieth century to serve the less fortunate in their community. Given their postwar prosperity and their rejection by mainline Protestant clubs, these centers became the centerpiece of Jewish community life after 1945. The loss of residential options in Boyle Heights also forced Jews to look for homes elsewhere, often outside Boyle Heights, particularly to the Westside or to less affluent but friendly neighborhoods nearby, including the Fairfax district and parts of the San Fernando Valley.[5] Meanwhile, the new Jewish immigrants streaming into Los Angeles at this time had little in common with the Yiddish working-class activists who had seen "repatriation" and internment tear their neighborhood apart in Boyle Heights. In broader society, a postwar cult of cultural conformity in the late forties and fifties associated Americanness with a homogeneous tradition that was fervently anti-communist, forcing ethnic groups of all stripes to find their way into this "melting pot." To be sure, many Boyle Heights Jews were not interested in this kind of assimilation and remained fiercely committed to progressive politics.

The exodus of Jews from the Eastside to the Westside became the dominant pattern of Jewish migration from inner-city neighborhoods out to suburban settings after World War II and was a national phenomenon in urban centers throughout the United States.[6] Almost all white ethnic groups achieved a certain level of social and geographic mobility after the war due to the booming interwar and postwar economy. The postwar decline of anti-Semitism, along with successful legal challenges to the practice of restrictive neighborhoods and to overt antiethnic prejudices, benefited Jews in particularly significant ways. As historian Gerald Sorin has observed, "By the late 1950s many of the urban Jewish neighborhoods of the interwar years were being abandoned, except for enclaves of mostly older and poorer Jews, and surrounded by mainly Black and Puerto Rican newcomers."[7] Although Boyle Heights experienced Mexican in-migration while Jews moved out, this Los Angeles neighborhood fit the overall pattern, which at first glance suggests a trajectory of ethnic succession, with one group replacing another.

But identifying this changing ethnic makeup begs the question: What processes were at work when a certain ethnic group, such as Jews, were able to move out of a given neighborhood in large numbers, while other groups, such as Mexicans or blacks, seemed confined to that community? Contemporary scholars have complicated notions of "ethnic succession," instead characterizing this process as one of "whitening" and specifically noting how descendants of European ethnic groups profited from economic restructuring and racial profiling in the post–World War II era to assume a "white racial position." Historian George Lipsitz recounts how liberal, social democratic reforms of the New Deal and World War II era "widened the gap between the resources available to whites and those available to aggrieved racial communities."[8] Early reforms such as public housing initially supported only white veterans, for example, and the idea of urban renewal was used to tear down multiracial residential areas. The Federal Housing Administration (FHA), created under FDR, required lower down payments for the home mortgages they underwrote. But the FHA also used supposedly "objective" criteria to codify race and urban locations as risk factors, making it harder for those who were considered "nonwhite" to get loans or for anyone to get a loan to live in a supposedly "decaying and dangerous" (nonwhite) urban area such as Boyle Heights. Lipsitz's work builds on previous research that delineates the insidious role that the federal government played in shaping racial discrimination in the postwar period. Long-standing racial zoning in Los Angeles was thereby exacerbated by these reforms, commonly known as "redlining" for the red line drawn on maps around the neighborhoods deemed too "at risk" for low-cost home mortgages. Redlining thus broadened the already large racial disparity in home ownership. "For perhaps the first time, the federal government embraced the discriminatory attitudes of the marketplace," wrote urban historian Kenneth Jackson. "Previously, prejudices were personalized and individualized; FHA (the Federal Housing Administration) exhorted segregation and enshrined it as public policy."[9]

Before the war in 1940, almost one-third of all Jews in Los Angeles—about 35,000—resided in Boyle Heights and nearby City Terrace, forming over 40 percent of the total population of Boyle Heights. In the early 1940s, the number increased dramatically, reaching a zenith of at least 50,000; some estimate even higher.[10] At the war's conclusion, however, the numbers of Jews in Boyle Heights plummeted. By 1955, Jewish residents in Boyle Heights had fallen to 14,000, a decline of at least 72 percent in less than 15 years. Jews now made up less than 17 percent of the area's population, while Mexicans had grown to constitute almost half of the residents in Boyle Heights by the same year. Further, the decline of Jews in Boyle Heights occurred while the Jewish population of Los Angeles nearly tripled, climbing to about 350,000 from a base of 130,000 just before World War II. In short, the place of Boyle Heights as a centerpiece of Jewish life in Los Angeles collapsed in the postwar period, replaced by the significant expansion of Jewish communities on the Westside of the city, a change that had major repercussions for the working-class multiracial political life and culture that had thrived in Boyle Heights in the first half of the twentieth century, and most especially for the Jews who left. By 1960, only 4 percent of all Jews in Los Angeles lived in Boyle Heights. By early 1994, only eight Jews remained in the neighborhood.[11]

EXODUS TO THE WEST

Neither the Boyle Heights neighborhood nor Los Angeles as a whole remained the same after the war. California, already known for its population growth, increased by two million people during the war itself—a 30 percent growth rate—and by 1946 the population reached nine million.[12] A large percentage of these newcomers were veterans, who had their first glimpse of the state in basic training or en route to the Pacific during the war.[13] But others were African American and Mexican American workers pulled into the state by jobs in the various war industries.[14]

In Boyle Heights, these newcomers were joined by returning Japanese Americans released from internment camps in 1945, as well as the seasonal farmworkers from Mexico making their way to urban centers from the San Joaquin and Imperial Valleys. The working-class neighborhood provided a safe haven for the newly arrived from throughout the nation and abroad, as it had done for previous generations. In short, Boyle Heights continued to attract various ethnic communities as newcomers and returnees took advantage of connections that existed in the community among family members and friends. It was not uncommon to see families doubling up temporarily in the immediate postwar period within the single-family residences that were so common in Boyle Heights. This overcrowding occurred throughout Southern California but was particularly acute in Boyle Heights.

As the population in the neighborhood ballooned, even those with strong familial ties to Boyle Heights began to look elsewhere for possible housing. With few private homes constructed during the war, many who first looked to return to Boyle Heights could find little to match their family needs or pocketbooks. Young servicemen, especially in the Jewish community, took advantage of the GI Bill to access higher education, loosening residential bonds to Boyle Heights and establishing new connections to locations throughout the Southern California basin.[15] But the building of middle-income housing on land made available by the depletion of oil fields on the Westside during the 1930s prompted Boyle Heights Jews to consider moving west. Other communities located on the Westside or in the San Fernando Valley were ready to take their positions as leading centers for permanent Jewish settlement. The Fairfax district—located in the midcity area west of downtown and close to the flourishing Miracle Mile shopping district—already housed four Jewish congregations in 1940, one of which was headed by the former spiritual leader of Boyle Heights' Breed Street Synagogue, Rabbi Solomon N. Neches. When the Metropolitan Life Insurance Company annexed the region from Fairfax to Cochran in 1941, their Park La Brea housing project opened up the neighborhood for widespread settlement. Ten other annexations followed this large one, creating new urban settlements in the middle of the city of Los Angeles. Compared to Boyle Heights, this community in 1940 encompassed residents with more advanced levels of education and higher incomes but also had more renters and fewer single-family residences.[16]

In the San Fernando Valley, residential development was even newer than in the Fairfax district. Planned communities sprouted up in Panorama City, North Hollywood, and elsewhere to take advantage of a geographic area almost the size of Chicago. In 1950, the *Valley Jewish Press* reported about 22,000 Jewish families living in the Valley, out of a population of over 400,000.[17] The San Fernando Valley, however, contained fewer than 5,000 African Americans and other "nonwhites" in 1950, so its growth was highly selective and uneven. Besides a small community of Mexican and Japanese

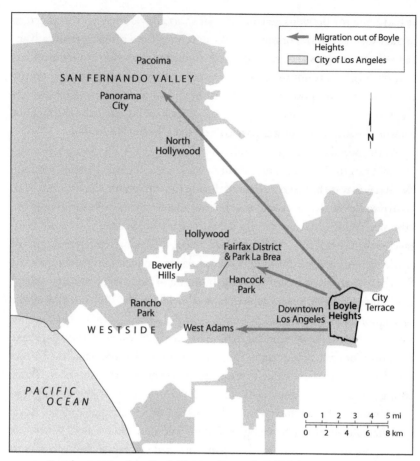

MAP 3. Jewish migration from Boyle Heights. Drawn by Bill Nelson.

residents in Pacoima that had existed prior to the war, most of the Valley housing was developed within strict racial boundaries.

Even after May 3, 1948, when the US Supreme Court ruled that racially restrictive covenants were discriminatory and could not be enforced by state agencies, the Hancock Park Property Owners Association prevented the singer Nat King Cole from taking possession of a home he had bought in an exclusive neighborhood of Los Angeles. Cross burnings, threatening phone calls, vandalism to property, and physical abuse were all components of enforcing racial restrictions before and after the Supreme Court decision, as was visible and organized opposition to blacks, Latinos, or Asian Americans moving into specific neighborhoods. Overt discrimination by real estate agents, property owner associations, and lending companies was on display in August 1948 when promoters offering "wonderful terms" to GIs in Allied Gardens refused to show floor plans to Julius Blue, an African American World War II veteran, instead giving Blue and his wife a mimeographed sheet reporting the following: "No person whose blood is not entirely that of the Caucasian race (and for the purpose of this paragraph no Japanese, Chinese, Mexican, Hindu, or any person of the Ethiopian, Indian or Mongolian races shall be deemed to be Caucasian) shall at any time live upon any of the lots in said tract 15010."[18]

An extensive December 1948 report from the Anti-Defamation League made clear that this was not an isolated incident in Southern California. Even after the Supreme Court decision, the San Gabriel Valley Realty Board passed a resolution stating that districts should be zoned racially: "We feel that our citizens are better off when allowed to congregate in districts or settlements, such as Irwindale for Mexicans. There is no reason why, in zoning, districts can't be set aside for our citizens to live and enjoy the pursuit of happiness, without upsetting the whole social structure." In El Monte, the realty board expelled member Maurice Curtis in August 1948 for selling a house to a Mexican American, in violation of the Realtor's Code of Ethics and the board's own constitution, which stated: "A realtor should never be instrumental in introducing into a neighborhood a character of property or occupancy, members of any race or nationality, or any individuals whose presence will clearly be detrimental to property values in that neighborhood."[19] However, these postwar legal and illegal restrictions did not directly affect Jews, who had, for the most part, moved across the line of exclusion by being absorbed into whiteness.

Of course, most Jews who purchased new homes in these areas, especially with the help of Veterans Affairs (VA) or FHA loans, which allowed them to put as little as 10 percent down, did not migrate from Boyle Heights but rather were complete newcomers to Southern California. By 1950, only 8 percent of adult Jews in Los Angeles had been born in the city. By the end of the decade, only one Jewish head of household out of six had been a prewar resident. Changing demographic realities because of newcomers were not new in Los Angeles. But for Jews on the Eastside this meant that the political and cultural importance of Boyle Heights significantly faded from public memory, and thus Jewish newcomers were not steeped in the historic connections Jews had maintained to a variety of ethnic groups in the Heights.[20] New families elsewhere in Los Angeles established communal institutions, from schools to synagogues, and for many in the postwar era there was no Jewish past in Los Angeles. Jewish institutions in Boyle Heights had to consider their own future, given the declining Jewish population and the role of these new suburban communities in Jewish life.

For the Jewish entrepreneurs of Boyle Heights, deciding what to do about the shifting Jewish population was a weighted decision that had direct economic consequences. Solomon's, an establishment that specialized in Judaica, was among the first to move directly to the Fairfax area in 1945. Leader Beauty Shop moved the following year. Canter's Delicatessen, an institution on Brooklyn Avenue, chose a different route. Its owners decided to open a Fairfax branch in 1948 but kept the original location in Boyle Heights until the 1960s.[21] Likewise, Zellman Clothiers remained in Boyle Heights, selling tailored suits to all who walked through its doors until 1999.[22] Phillips Music Store outlasted other music shops founded in the Great Depression, adapting its products to new populations in the Boyle Heights community. During the 1950s, many budding Latino musicians who came out of Roosevelt High School credited William Phillips, the store's owner, with introducing them to a wider network of musicians from Central Avenue or the Hollywood Studios.[23]

Part of the reason that some Jewish businessmen stayed in Boyle Heights was that certain groups of Jewish residents did remain in the community, despite its demographic transformation. Elderly Jews whose children had already left the family stayed behind in the community in which they felt comfortable and that had met their needs in the past. As one 1954 Jewish community report put it: "The population movement out of the area in the last several years has left most of the aging men and women with us. They resist the idea of moving out—they choose to remain in the area they know best and where their friends still reside."[24] But this was starkly generational, and over time the often poorly maintained property of these residents was rented out by their grown children from afar at unusually high rates, due to limited housing availability, and mostly to Mexican Americans. Therefore, for some, Jewish connection to Boyle Heights evolved from living side by side to the exploitation of misery in the neighborhood, which entailed exporting capital to the Westside and to the San Fernando Valley.[25] But the narrow slice of Jewish Los Angeles that remained consisted of committed leftists—either socialist, communist, or embedded in secular Yiddish culture—among whom established unions and leftist organizations had long been rooted. And these would become the most involved in interracial coalitions and interethnic dialogue.

Institutionally, disruptions over leaving Boyle Heights are best exemplified, not by stories of synagogue closures, but by the struggle over control of the Jewish Community Center. This institution affected all Jews in the neighborhood, both religious and secular, and potentially could reach beyond the Jewish community to serve all peoples in a given neighborhood. The Boyle Heights area had been served by a Jewish community center since the 1920s, after a group of community leaders presented the need to the Federation for Jewish Charities in 1923. In January 1924, a three-story building was purchased at the corner of Soto and Michigan Streets, remodeled, and formally named the Modern Talmud Torah and Social Center. It combined religious instruction with social service work, in a style reminiscent of other religious settlement houses. After religious instruction and service work were severed from each other in 1930, the Menorah Center in City Terrace emerged to offer Hebrew-learning programs for children, as well as Yiddish programs for adults. The Modern Social Center moved into a new facility at Michigan and Breed Streets, rapidly growing in membership and usage, and taking on, in particular, the problem of juvenile delinquency among Jewish young people in the neighborhood. In 1934, the center moved back to the Soto and Michigan address, renaming itself the Jewish Community Center and adding more Jewish content to its programming, along with its ongoing emphasis on serving wayward youth in the community.[26]

The importance of such centers is evident in residents' memories of the community. Many Jewish youth who grew up in Boyle Heights during the 1930s remember the Soto-Michigan Center with particular fondness. The building was notable for its California midcentury style, featuring a wall of glass windows in a simple open rectangular design. Hershey Eisenberg, who would go on to take a few social work courses in college, recalled that "if you were a social worker, you'd love to be put in a situation like that, where you had all these kids who wanted to learn and wanted to give. That was what was going on at the Soto Michigan Center."[27] One way that the commitment to working with youth became realized was by extensive athletic programs and facilities to sustain a variety of activities. Eisenberg remembered that "they had a lot of organizations, a lot of clubs, social athletic clubs in the main. . . . The best gym of all, even better than Roosevelt High, was Soto-Michigan's gym. It had a great floor, great bounce. We used to have terrific basketball

FIGURE 16. Eastside Jewish Community Center, formerly Soto-Michigan Jewish Community Center, 1938. J. Julius Shulman Photography Archive, ©J. Paul Getty Trust, Getty Research Institute, Los Angeles (2004.R.100).

leagues there. People would come from all over the city to play in that."[28] Indeed, Eisenberg spent so much time at the Soto-Michigan Center that there was where he met his future wife, while she was playing volleyball.[29]

In 1932, the first Jewish Centers Association (JCA) was established. Then in 1939–40, talks began under the sponsorship of the Federation of Jewish Welfare Organizations to consider the creation of an umbrella organization to coordinate activities, control finances, and set policy for all the Jewish community centers in Los Angeles.[30] By 1942, all the organizational funders—which included the Los Angeles Federation of Jewish Welfare Organizations, the National Jewish Welfare Board, and the Community Chest, a nonprofit organization that pooled community resources for charity—agreed that they would not entertain application for funds outside the JCA structure. This ensured that central authority for funding and coordination would run through the JCA board, but it remained unclear exactly what autonomy individual centers would have over their personnel and programming. In 1943, just as the Jewish population movement to the Westside

FIGURE 17. Children unloading from Eastside Jewish Community Center bus in Boyle Heights, 1952. Los Angeles Daily News Negatives Collection (Collection 1387). Library Special Collections, Charles E. Young Research Library, UCLA.

accelerated, the two centers on the Eastside, Soto-Michigan and Menorah, took their place as half of the collective merger that made up the JCA. The other two centers included an underfunded center in West Adams and a small, makeshift center at Beverly-Fairfax.[31]

For the next fifteen years, the leadership of the Soto-Michigan Center battled with the JCA of Los Angeles in an attempt to keep their center open while the Jewish population in the city moved westward. However, the tension between the Eastside center and the JCA was due to more than shifting demographics and the pull of limited resources. In the late 1940s, the Soto-Michigan Center became a target of the growing anticommunist movement in California that threatened the integration of Jews into the wider postwar Los Angeles community. On September 7, 1948, Joseph Esquith, the director of the Soto-Michigan Center, was summoned to testify in front of California's Un-American Activities Committee, chaired by state senator Jack Tenney, a right-wing Republican from Los Angeles. The California committee, which lasted from 1941 to 1949 under Tenney's command, shared information with the federal House Un-American Activities Committee (HUAC), utilizing many of the same tactics of public confrontation, humiliation, and red-baiting in front of media and public officials. Tenney, well known for his anti-Semitism by 1948, often equated communism with Judaism while interrogating Jewish witnesses. One could imagine what the director of the Soto-Michigan Jewish Community Center might expect having been summoned to appear before the Tenney Committee.[32]

Early in the hearings, Tenney accused the Soto-Michigan Center of allowing communist front organizations to operate on its grounds. Committee counsel R.E. Combs read into the record references from the *People's Daily World* where activities at the Soto-Michigan Center had been listed. The most damning evidence to the committee was that the center received substantial funding from the Community Chest, which Tenney spuriously alleged was being used by the Soto-Michigan Center to fund "communist propaganda." He chastised the center directly: "I want to point out to you that the... people of Los Angeles County who contribute to this Community Fund would be highly indignant if they thought the funds contributed by them were being utilized for the purposes of spreading Communist propaganda."[33]

Esquith, for his part, responded with eloquence and force, reminding the committee that the center "was a laboratory of democracy where free speech, free association, and free assemblage flourished."[34] The Soto-Michigan Center welcomed all groups through its doors, as part of a tradition that hearkened back to the social settlement period at the beginning of the twentieth century—its only explicit exception being overt political parties.[35] When the center's board met one week later on September 14, they unanimously passed a resolution protesting Tenney's attack, condemned the committee's action, and demanded an immediate public response from the JCA. As Al Waxman, member of the Soto-Michigan Center board and editor of the *Belvedere Citizen*, put it, "The entire Jewish community was on trial in not having made an immediate answer to the Tenney attack."[36]

However, a swift and supportive response did not come from the JCA. Instead, the association formed a special committee to investigate the situation, making clear the JCA's concerns about being smeared with the label "communist" or "communist sympathizer." One month later, on October 25, Leslie G. Cramer, president of the JCA, reported back to the Welfare Federation, concluding that over the past year, of the 110 groups that had used the Soto-Michigan Center, only 11 had been listed by the Tenney

Committee as communist or communist front. These organizations accounted for only 3 percent of the total attendance at the center from September 1947 to August 1948, with most using the facilities purely on a rental basis. Many in Boyle Heights recalled that the American Jewish Congress itself had been on Tenney's list before public pressure led him to remove this middle-of-the-road organization.[37]

That report, however, did not satisfy the Welfare Federation of Los Angeles, who continued to worry about being branded as a communist front organization. By the end of 1948, the Welfare Federation issued a directive to all its agencies, including the Soto-Michigan Center, to deny its facilities to any organization on the attorney general's subversive list that had been drafted by the Tenney Committee. The Soto-Michigan board rejected this demand, claiming that it infringed on its right to set its own policies and that it contradicted the open-forum philosophy of the Jewish Centers movement.

The wider Jewish community had already begun to purge perceived communists from their midst, however, and by 1949 the JCA further restricted the open-forum policy by requiring those renting center facilities to acquire JCA approval. The JCA also eliminated the distribution of unauthorized leaflets at the center and challenged the membership of the JPFO for its relationship with the Jewish fraternal organization of the IWO, a benevolent society for the working class affiliated with the Communist Party. The JPFO was the IWO's Yiddish-speaking section, sponsoring a Jewish summer camp in Los Angeles and meeting regularly at the Soto-Michigan Center with members who included those with roots in the Yiddish-speaking political Left in Boyle Heights—residents like Ida Fiering. It was considered "an integral part of the Jewish Community of Boyle Heights." But by early 1951, as the Cold War heated up in Korea and the red scare demonized the Left as un-American, the JPFO was ousted from the organized Jewish community for being subordinate to the IWO and, therefore, to Moscow.[38]

Within fifteen months of the Tenney Committee attack, another tension, this time internal to the Jewish center movement, added more stress to the relationship between the JCA board and their Soto-Michigan counterparts. In 1949 and 1950, the Los Angeles Jewish Federation board refused to negotiate a new union contract with social workers and other employees working in federation-sponsored facilities, such as the community centers.[39] By its board meeting of November 10, 1949, the Soto-Michigan Center had to consider its place in this growing labor dispute. Not surprisingly, it sided with the workers and against the shutdown of the centers by the JCA and the federation. At that meeting, the Soto-Michigan board passed the following resolution: "That the Soto-Michigan Board of Directors advise the Jewish Centers Association that this Board is seriously disturbed by the possibility that as a result of the impasse between the union and the Federation, a strike will occur; such a situation in the Boyle Heights area would seriously impair public relations between the Center and the community and the community and the Center parent bodies; that the Board therefore respectfully requests that the Jewish Centers Association intercede to prevent such an eventuality."[40] Despite this plea, a strike did occur in early 1950 that closed all centers in Los Angeles. Though the strike eventually ended at the conclusion of the year, the tension between center workers and the federation continued, placing the Soto-Michigan board uncomfortably in the middle.[41]

The struggle over the Eastside community center unfolded while the JCA leadership determined that a large, permanent Jewish community center on the Westside was needed. A temporary Jewish community center on the Westside opened in 1947, and planning and fund-raising began almost immediately for a much larger, stable facility. This effort dominated JCA discussions in the postwar period, but it would not be until 1954 that a new state-of-the-art facility opened to much fanfare along Olympic Boulevard—ultimately, with ominous repercussions for the Soto-Michigan Jewish Community Center.[42]

INTERRACIALISM AND THE FESTIVAL OF FRIENDSHIP

The struggle of the Soto-Michigan Center is emblematic of Jewish life in Boyle Heights. As Jewish adult membership and participation lagged in the late 1940s and early 1950s, Mel Janapol, as director of the Community Relations Committee, encouraged the board to take a wider look at the very meaning of community in Boyle Heights. Janapol began by inviting non-Jewish youth from outside the community to a model seder at the Jewish Center. At the same time, youth director Mark Keats organized the first Friendship Festival in spring 1949 at the Fresno Playground, to "bring together Mexican, Japanese, Negro, and Jewish youth in a cooperative venture."[43] By the following year, the "Festival of Friendship" had grown to include a three-hour formal arts program, a parade, food sales, and an art exhibit. Over 12,000 people attended, and over 1,500 participated in the parade alone. Keats quickly became acknowledged within the center as the general community relations person for his sustained work with the non-Jewish youth of Boyle Heights. In addition to the yearly summer festival, Keats set up an annual intercultural week in December, worked directly with youth and parent groups at the Pico Gardens public housing project, organized an intercultural teenage chorus, and coordinated celebrations of "Negro History Week" and Mexican Independence Day at the center. He also met regularly with a Mexican American boys' group at the center and was a principal organizer of the Hollenbeck Coordinating Youth Council, an activist group set up in the wake of the city's Zoot Suit Riots of 1943.[44]

This intercultural work on the part of the Soto-Michigan Jewish Center increasingly received praise from within and outside the Los Angeles Jewish community. After a particularly successful launching of a planned intercultural week in November 1950, when over 400 people attended the Japanese American night, the board of the Soto-Michigan Center unanimously passed a resolution commending Mel Janapol for "the finest job in intercultural activity being done in the entire city." By 1951, Director Esquith was asked to speak in front of the Los Angeles Community Chest Budget Committee regarding this intercultural work, which became a model for the committee as it sought to implement its own city-wide intergroup team. Moreover, the Soto-Michigan board received numerous commendations from various ethnic organizations following intercultural programming, such as one from Tats Kushida, regional director of the Japanese American Citizens League (JACL), in November 1950, "expressing pleasure in having participated in the intercultural program and offering future cooperation wherever possible." In 1951, letters of commendation followed from the Parents Group of Pico Gardens, the CSO, the Asociación Nacional México-Americana (ANMA), and Mayor Fletcher Bowron, all extolling various activities involving intercultural programming.[45]

While board members of the Soto-Michigan Center rightly took great pride in opening up new avenues for intercultural activity, they also worried about the repercussions of a dwindling Jewish community in Boyle Heights. For example, one board member, Mrs. Esther Werner, complained about "the complete lack of Jewish dance and music" in the first Friendship Festival, which—as center leadership explained—was due to a "slip up in planning" after the scheduled Jewish dance and choral groups fell through. Such a mistake would never be allowed to happen again, but it did reveal that that the Soto-Michigan Center was now relying on groups outside Boyle Heights to provide its Jewish cultural content.[46] By October 1951, these demographic pressures led the JCA to look at a consolidation of the two Eastside centers, and specifically the shuttering of the Menorah Center in City Terrace.[47] Neither Soto-Michigan nor the Menorah Center had suffered from a substantial drop in membership, since the curated programming by both centers to meet the needs of their changing populations had kept membership rolls high. But by 1952, a report on participation in center activity showed that almost 15 percent of participants at Soto-Michigan were non-Jews, who were most active in the various special programming at the Soto-Michigan Center where all ages were represented, and in the playground and gym.[48]

Nowhere was this concern for membership more evident than in the turnover at the Soto-Michigan board. Throughout the early 1950s, numerous committee members resigned because of active members moving out of the Boyle Heights area. This undoubtedly led to a certain flexibility regarding who was considered a legitimate member of the community, and the board allowed, and possibly even encouraged, Jewish entrepreneurs who no longer lived in Boyle Heights to assume and retain leadership positions. William Phillips, for example, owner of Phillips Music Store on Brooklyn Avenue, became a board member in April 1950, almost one year after he had changed his residence to Beverly Hills.[49] By January of the following year, the executive committee itself expressed worry over the depletion of the board of directors of the center, as more and more of its members continued to move out of Boyle Heights and were unable to fulfill their duties to the board.[50]

In addition, during this period, a new round of anticommunist hysteria rose in Los Angeles, including attacks directed at the Soto-Michigan Center. The city's real estate industry and the *Los Angeles Times* were already smearing public housing as communist inspired and preparing for an all-out assault on Mayor Fletcher Bowron. Beginning in June 1951, board member Eliezer Ettinger started to levy accusations about communist infiltration at Soto-Michigan. After complaining about the choice of speakers for the open forum and the showing of a film from Czechoslovakia, which he called an attempt "to push 'iron-curtain' material" into Boyle Heights, Ettinger forced the board to call a special meeting during which he accused two center workers of being communists and a fellow board member of spreading communist propaganda. This special committee presented its findings to the board, which voted unanimously (with two abstentions) against Ettinger, who had previously been ousted by the American Jewish Congress for similar behavior, and Ettinger resigned from his post.[51]

FIGURE 18. William Phillips, owner of Phillips Music Store, at his counter, ca. 1950. With permission of Bruce Phillips.

By November, Tenney's renewed attacks on the Soto-Michigan Center culminated in Tenney decrying donations to a Community Chest fund-raising drive because of the Community Chest's continued support for "Communist activities" at the Soto-Michigan Center. Walter Hilborn, a noted lawyer and long-standing Jewish member of the Community Chest executive committee, called the Soto-Michigan Center staff to his home, demanding to know whether, in fact, any of them were communists and threatening to ask the same of the entire board of directors.[52] When an Eastside Study Committee was organized by the JCA in late 1951 to advise the JCA on a plan of consolidation, members of the Soto-Michigan board prepared for the worst. But after heated discussion, the JCA decided to retain the Soto-Michigan Community Center rather than the Menorah Center against the recommendation of the Eastside Study Committee.[53] However, the Menorah Center was ready with its response: "We here at Menorah are as much interested in the promulgation of Jewish culture and Jewish values as in intercultural activities, but our emphasis is on Jewish content, because a Jewish Center which receives Jewish funds should emphasize what they were originally intended to do."[54]

While the Soto-Michigan board had won the battle, the struggle exposed the growing rift among secular and religious Jews on the Eastside and in Los Angeles as a whole. The rift between the two centers had also created a division of perspectives regarding the importance of intercultural activity among the Jewish population in the changing community of Boyle Heights, with one group deeply committed to these efforts and the other seeing it as peripheral to "Jewish culture and Jewish values." But without JCA funding, the Menorah Center closed its doors, and on September 9, 1952, the Soto-Michigan Jewish Community Center board formally changed its name to the Eastside Jewish Community Center. More was at stake here than a name change, however. That meeting also was the final meeting of Esquith as director of the center, a position he had held for five and a half years of stellar service, as he would go on to assume the position of director of the new Westside Center. Such leadership changes fundamentally altered the politics of the Eastside Center and put programming firmly in the direction that the JCA board preferred. In November, the executive director of the Jewish Centers invited members of the Eastside Center to groundbreaking ceremonies for a new center on the Westside. On December 7, the JCA also announced a cutback of services in "special interests areas" on the Eastside, as part of the effort to shift funding and priorities from east to west.[55] While intercultural activities continued, they no longer possessed the vitality they had in the past. Clearly the period of innovative programming and outreach at the Eastside Jewish Community Center had passed.

RADICALISM, RACE, AND IMMIGRANT PROTECTION

The story of the Soto-Michigan Jewish Community Center indicates that, in the postwar period, political radicalism increasingly became associated with promoting and defending multiracialism. Invariably, the combination of radicalism and diversity in a relatively small neighborhood like Boyle Heights made the two seem uniquely intertwined in Southern California, and various leftist organizations utilized this to defend their politics in the red-baiting McCarthy period. Boyle Heights, therefore, became something of an ideological bunker, somewhat protected by its geographic isolation, defending its residents from outside attack while nurturing a particular brand of radical politics and multiracial sensibility. Jewish radicals were central to this combination, even as Boyle Heights Jewry became more narrow and splintered in its political orientation, with more moderate or apolitical Jews rapidly moving out of the neighborhood, and various leftist organizations and individuals calling Boyle Heights home in the postwar period.

In working-class districts of Southern California, the anticommunist crusade hit directly against labor unions and ethnic community leadership. A series of legislative acts in the late 1940s and early 1950s targeted suspected and former communists, particularly those who had been born abroad, with deportation, denaturalization, and unlimited detention without due process. The 1947 Taft-Hartley Act reversed the federal government's alliance with American labor unions and made it more difficult to get federal support for union elections in the workplace. It also made it illegal for communists and those "calling for the overthrow of the U.S. government" to participate in American labor unions, with the Smith Act of 1940 assigning criminal penalties for advocating the government's "violent overthrow." The McCarran Internal Security Act of 1950 allowed the federal government to deport foreigners who admitted or were suspected of ever having joined the Communist Party or any affiliated group. But the law that solidified and expanded the reach of the anticommunist campaign was the McCarran-Walter Act of 1952, which changed immigration law in many ways, including the provision that naturalized citizens could be "denaturalized" if found to have been communist sympathizers at the time of their citizenship statement of allegiance. Not surprisingly, the US Justice Department almost immediately began to target union leaders, particularly those in Boyle Heights.

In response, the Los Angeles Committee for the Protection of the Foreign Born (LACPFB) formed in 1950. It was nominally a branch of the American Committee for the Protection of the Foreign Born, established in 1932, and the very different trajectories of the two organizations point to differences between East Coast and West Coast politics concerning radicalism, immigration, race, and multiethnicity. The American Committee was part of the Popular Front alliance fighting fascism and was labeled a communist front organization; it worked mostly with European refugees and Caribbean immigrants.[56] The Los Angeles Committee, formed in the 1950s, was a multiracial group of activists who were often targeted by the anticommunist McCarran-Walter Act.[57]

Most importantly for this book, the LACPFB emerged out of the multiracial communities of Los Angeles' Eastside and Southside, especially Boyle

Heights. Rose Chernin, from a strong Jewish radical tradition in Boyle Heights, became the organization's executive director in 1951. Rose moved to Boyle Heights in the mid-1930s, having been born in Russia and joining the Communist Party in New York City in the late 1920s before moving to Moscow with her husband. But Rose chose Boyle Heights after Moscow in the 1930s because the rest of her family had already moved there from New York. Her parents had moved to City Terrace as political liberals, and her mother Perle had evolved, near the end of her life, to become a "very outgoing, very social" woman who found "the *shtetl*" of her youth replanted in Boyle Heights of the late 1930s. Rose Chernin's parents had themselves moved there to be closer to Rose's sister Lilian and her husband, both members of the Young Communist League. Rose described Boyle Heights of the 1930s as a community of "working people, it had trade unionists, cultural groups, a synagogue, kosher stores, a place where you could buy a Yiddish newspaper and books."[58] Chernin was arrested the year she became the LAFCP executive director under the antiradical Smith Act. In 1954, the Justice Department led a failed attempt to "denaturalize" Chernin under judicial proceedings.

Though the L.A. Committee supported many ethnic groups, the largest national group that it sought to protect was Mexican, just as Attorney General George Herbert Brownell launched "Operation Wetback" in 1954 to apprehend "undocumented aliens" in the American Southwest. Boyle Heights, and the Eastside in general, probably led the count of those targeted for deportation and therefore attracted substantial attention from the L.A. Committee.[59] While the LACPFB maintained its major office in downtown Los Angeles, within three years of its founding it established an Eastside branch at 3656 East Third Street, where Josefina Yanez, the executive secretary of the Eastside branch, spearheaded activities for the Mexican community. The Eastside's branch contained active membership from both the Jewish and Mexican communities.

In May 1954, the LACPFB issued a call to "all democratic-spirited, fair-minded Americans" to protest the actions of the US Immigration and Naturalization Service (INS) in raids conducted throughout Los Angeles. Utilizing the recently approved provisions of the McCarran-Walter Act, the INS had launched mass detentions of Mexican nationals in open-air pens in Elysian Park in downtown Los Angeles under a campaign called Operation Round-Up. The LACPFB called this campaign a "concentration camp order," as well as "an insult to the 500,000 members of the Mexican-American community." But the LACPFB also used rhetoric in their call that asked specific ethnic groups to side with them in recognition of their shared history of oppression. Specifically, the committee addressed communities that had a history of living together in Boyle Heights and in other parts of the Eastside. First, it felt that these actions could be identified as harassment "by the 350,000 members of the L.A. Jewish Community who are reminded of other pogroms and other concentration camps when they saw or heard of the noon-hour sweep-down on Wilshire Blvd.'s Miracle Mile, wherein 212 young Mexican workers were carried off summarily." Clearly, this was a call to an ethnic community whose population center had moved to the Westside (Wilshire Boulevard), but one that the LACPFB felt could be convinced to side against this state violence because of a shared persecution.[60]

The LACPFB also connected the raids and Elysian Park Stockades to another US government effort and believed it could summon outrage and support from "the 110,000 Japanese-Americans who recall the shameful Relocation Camp round-ups and indiscriminate incarceration of thousands of Japanese nationals and Japanese-American citizens in World War II." While the American Committee based in New York during World War II had failed to speak out against Japanese American incarceration, the Los Angeles Committee had no problem linking these seizures to others they saw as similar. By associating the oppressive detention program of the US government during World War II with that of Germany under Hitler, pogroms in Eastern Europe, and the actions of the US Immigration Service in the 1950s against primarily Mexicans, the committee sought to remind "all other Americans who recoil to think that—in our America—people are sought out by the color of their skin; are followed, fingered and picked up on the streets, in their homes and their factories as 'alien,' as 'illegals,' and who can say how many citizens among them." In short, the shared racial histories of various groups that had made up Boyle Heights and other working-class communities in Los Angeles were now marshaled, by the LACPFB, to come together to support the latest victim of mass arrests and unfair jailings: the "thousands of defenseless Mexican nationals" being targeted by the INS.[61]

Moreover, the LACPFB made it clear that the rights of immigrants were intertwined with the civil rights of everyone, especially given that the mass deportations of "Operation Wetback" were fundamentally racialized and had wide impact. Josefina Yanez pointed in her description to how the raids struck "terror not alone to the non-citizen, but to Mexican American citizens of the first, second and third generations."[62] Even while the federal government worked to explicitly associate "illegality" with Mexican American identity, as it had done in the racialized citizenship of "repatriation" in the 1930s and in the zoot suit hysteria during World War II, the LACPFB called for solidarity across all racial groups and across all immigrant generations.

LACPFB fund-raising had this same intention. The "Festival of Nationalities" seemed patterned after the Soto-Michigan Center's "Festival of Friendship," with this one-day event held every year from 1950 until well into the 1960s at the Croatian-American Hall and Picnic Grounds just outside Boyle Heights at 330 South Ford Avenue. The Sunday event saw "garden and meeting turned into booths and squares offering the good, rare foods of many countries."[63] Even in the organization's own internal get-togethers, the spirit of multiracialism prevailed. When the seven-year deportation case against Edo Mita, the Japanese-born editor of the LACPFB's newsletter, *The Torchlight,* failed in 1958, the committee celebrated by sponsoring an "International Smorgasbord Dinner," with entertainment from West Indian, Mexican, and folk music. Furthermore, this event was one of the first sponsored by the "Victory Club," a newly formed committee of former targeted deportees who had won dismissal of their cases in immigration court.[64]

What the LACPFB could not prevent, however, was the growing tension within various communities over questions of radicalism in the 1950s, and particularly the ideological attacks that consistently linked communist infiltration with multicultural sensibilities. The pervasiveness of anticommunism in Southern California during the 1950s led local officials—at the behest of private citizens and organized elites—to expand their efforts not only within the suburban communities but also within ethnic communities trying to reposition themselves around a growing civil rights agenda that could be successful in more conservative times.[65] In no community was this ideological split more prominent than in the Los Angeles Jewish community.

On February 7, 1958, the *B'nai B'rith Messenger* reported that Marion and Paul Miller had been honored by the Los Angeles City Council for "their distinguished service to their country" during the past decade. This was the latest of a long line of commendations for the couple, who lived in Rancho Park on the Westside of the city, including naming Marion Miller "outstanding Jewish woman of the year." They were awarded for their contributions as paid informants to the FBI and various anticommunist government committees about the inner workings of the LACPFB from 1950 to 1955. Marion, at the encouragement of the FBI, had risen to become the recording secretary for the LACPFB in this period, earning $80 a month for her efforts.[66] As the *B'nai B'rith Messenger* reported: "The whole Jewish community has reason to be proud of these intrepid spirits. Their patriotic and self-sacrificing service performed in imminent peril of discovery and the summary vengeance of fanatics who hesitate at nothing, reflects the spirit of the Psalmist's words: 'The Lord is my light and my salvation, whom shall I fear?'"[67] Herman Gluck, who wrote the article, ended it with an emphatic ethnic ring: "The Millers are Jews—good Jews—and I, as a Jew, am as proud of them as I am of Einstein."

Even more telling was the fact that the citation was presented to the Millers by Rosalind Wiener Wyman, the first Jew elected to the Los Angeles City Council in the twentieth century.[68] From the Westside of Los Angeles, Wyman's politics articulated a specific brand of Westside liberalism. This liberalism was staunchly anticommunist, though it did include moderate support for civil rights efforts in the city. For example, Wyman joined Boyle Heights representative Edward Roybal, the first Mexican American to be elected to the Los Angeles City Council in the twentieth century, in support of public housing in 1953. But from 1956 to 1958, she also led efforts within the city council to hand over the Chavez Ravine neighborhood for demolition to Walter O'Malley to facilitate the move of the Brooklyn Dodgers to Los Angeles, ignoring the pleas of former Mexican American residents of the neighborhood.[69]

Not surprisingly, this honoring of the Millers incensed the LACPFB, especially its executive director, Rose Chernin, who clearly saw herself and her committee as exemplifying the righteousness of the Jewish tradition. She orchestrated a letter-writing campaign to the city council, and particularly Wyman, to protest the award. Indeed, one of the committee's biggest supporters, Charlotte A. Bass, editor of the *California Eagle,* Los Angeles' main African American newspaper, also wrote Councilwoman Wyman to dispute the celebration of someone "who would spy for a fee."[70] But no one wrote to the city council with more wrath than Rose Chernin: "We of the Committee are shocked at this action on the part of the City Council. It is our considered judgment that the Council acted very unwisely in choosing a paid informer to honor as an example for Young Americans. Considering also that the City Council could have picked a woman far more representative of the contributions that the Jewish community in Los Angeles made in the last year in the fields of Science, Education, the Arts, etc. It is our considered judgment that this can be construed as a slur on the Jewish Community."[71] This incident laid bare the bifurcation of the Jewish community in terms of which political ideologies best reflected Jewish life, as well as the geography of Los Angeles in the 1950s. Unfortunately, even the leftist Jewish tradition in Boyle Heights would come to a close with the aging of the population and the mounting pressures on individuals and institutions that remained.

Although Boyle Heights had a long tradition of working-class politics and was a home to various labor unions before World War II, it was only after the war that institutions in the area were specifically attacked for harboring communists, socialists, and sympathizers. In the politically conservative period in the early 1950s, both within and outside the Jewish community, Boyle Heights became increasingly seen as an anomaly in Southern California for being sympathetic to liberal and leftist causes, and it was attacked accordingly. But this growing reputation also led many leftists, including those in the Jewish community, to stay put in Boyle Heights, while it encouraged other leftists from Southern California to move into the community just as it was becoming known as a Mexican American "ghetto" neighborhood. On a larger scale, if one asks, "What became of radicalism in Southern California during the 1950s?" the answer would invariably lead one to investigate Boyle Heights and its continued reputation for racial tolerance and politically radical ideologies.

Along those lines, Leo Frumkin remembers the Jewish community of Boyle Heights of his youth in very specific political terms. Living with an extended family who ranged from social Democrat voters for Roosevelt to communists, Frumkin recalled:

> It was a secular community. And of this 80 or 85 percent who were secular Jews, I would say 10 or 20 percent of them were apolitical. Liberal, but apolitical. The balance of them, let's say 60, 70 percent of the Jewish population, were pretty evenly divided between communist and socialist. So there were discussions going on all the time. . . . People were always talking politically. We had the summer camp at the Arbiter Ring, Workmen's Circle, where all the kids would go to in the summertime, and that is where I learned all the socialist songs, labor songs—"Solidarity Forever," "Union Makes Us Strong," "Hold the Fort," "The International." You all learned these kinds of things. But the community was extremely political, extremely political.[72]

Frumkin already saw the distinction between his community of Boyle Heights and the growing Jewish community on the Westside in 1945. There was "an unspoken solidarity among all the neighbors" on the Eastside, including the 60 percent of his neighbors who were Mexican. "We never had a lock on our door, never had a key. You just didn't do it. I don't know if it was unspoken, but as poor as we were, nobody stole from anybody else." While Boyle Heights had this working-class solidarity, a certain level of contempt was reserved for the more middle-class surroundings on the Westside. As Frumkin said: "When we would smoke, for instance, we would keep the cigarettes in the car. We would never dump them out in East L.A. When we used to go to West L.A. to the Jewish Community Center to dances, we'd dump all our ashtrays out, because we knew the streets were going to be cleaned there. But we never did it here."[73] The anticommunist crusades of the Tenney and HUAC Committees of the late 1940s and 1950s only exacerbated this divide between working-class Jews in Boyle Heights and the growing middle class in emerging suburban communities on the Westside and in the Valley.

With few young people moving into the neighborhood, it was inevitable that the Jewish institutional presence would diminish rapidly, given the growing needs elsewhere in Los Angeles. Indeed, within five years of the 1952 merging of the two Jewish community centers on the Eastside, the JCA ignited discussions around shuttering its operations in East Los Angeles altogether. By the summer of 1955, the staff at the Eastside Center was reduced to just six full-time positions. Within a year, a new Eastside study was undertaken that led directly to talks with potential buyers of the property by 1957. Finally, on September 4, 1958, the Eastside Center's board met for the last time, formally dissolving after selling the property to the All Nations Foundation. The foundation, founded in 1914 on the social gospel of the interracial All Nations Church, became one of the largest welfare organizations in Los Angeles. One Latina employee, Lena Corrales, was the only staff member who stayed on to work for All Nations after the transfer.[74]

For the shrinking numbers of Jews who remained in Boyle Heights, life had been transformed. Leo Frumkin, who lived in the house he had been born in during 1928, finally moved out to Monterey Park in 1958 "because the house literally began to fall apart" and he was able to buy a tract home further east for $18,000. By this time, most of his friends, both Jewish and Mexican, had already moved out of the neighborhood to Lakewood and other lower-middle-class neighborhoods farther east near expanding employment opportunities.[75] Another Jewish family, who found themselves to be the last remaining Jews on their block in Boyle Heights, were concerned about their child remaining at his middle school as it gained a reputation for growing violence and tension. So the father picked the largest Mexican boy in his neighborhood and paid him to protect their son through junior high school in the late 1950s.[76] Jewish families were faced with difficult choices, and most of them would eventually move out of the neighborhood, no matter how committed they were to Boyle Heights.

The longest-lasting remnants of Jewish Boyle Heights were the businesses along Brooklyn Avenue. Phillips Music Store and Zellman Clothiers would remain in Boyle Heights as they adapted to meet the buying needs of the growing Mexican immigrant community. Jews would continue to venture back to the "old neighborhood," and specifically to these businesses, if they wanted to connect to a part of their youth, and to a time when Jews had lived in a working-class area in Los Angeles.

But, increasingly, Jewish Boyle Heights would become part of historical memory. Boyle Heights' transformation—from a partial Jewish enclave to a predominantly Mexican community with a selective Jewish population committed to multiracialism—created the conditions for neighborhood residents to see their fates as intertwined and to mobilize to protect the community against encroachments foisted on the area, such as the Golden State Freeway. Moreover, the Jewish community of Los Angeles as a whole was converted by this demographic shift, clearly becoming "white" in the racial hierarchy of the region, both geographically and politically. The Jews who decided to remain in Boyle Heights saw the institutional and collective Jewish community that they knew radically transformed by this newfound economic and social positioning, even while they battled to retain an ethnic community tied to its working-class origins and leftist sensibilities. As the 1950s continued, however, the whitening process of suburbanization made it harder for Boyle Heights Jews to reconcile their profound desires for a community that could be both Jewish and multiracial with their own personal futures.

SEVEN

Edward R. Roybal and the Politics of Multiracialism

ON FRIDAY, JULY 1, 1949, Edward Roybal was fresh from being sworn into office as the first Mexican American to serve on the Los Angeles City Council in the twentieth century and the only Mexican American to hold a major elective office in the state of California at large. He had left his job as a social worker to run two bruising political campaigns over the previous two years. Now, as a 33-year-old with a wife and family, he was searching over the holiday weekend for a new home in his district that would be more appropriate for a member of the political elite. His family had moved from the multiethnic Flats area of Boyle Heights to a slightly larger home outside his Ninth District in El Sereno after his 1947 loss, but the family moved back temporarily to the district in late 1948 to position Roybal for another run for the council seat. Joining a city council made up of thirteen white Protestant men and one Irish Catholic, Roybal must have been feeling the weight of his words at his swearing-in ceremony, where he pledged to "represent all the people in my district—one of the most cosmopolitan in our city."[1]

That following Monday, on the Fourth of July, as the Roybal family searched for their own personal independence from the toils of the past two years, they were attracted to a new housing development in the Ninth District advertised for "GI Housing" that would allow him to utilize benefits from his service during World War II. Ready with a check for a $250 deposit on the house "of their dreams," the Roybals were taken aback when the salesman responded, "Well, I'm sorry, young man, it's not my fault, but I'm instructed that I cannot sell to you because you're a Mexican." Incensed, but realizing his newfound responsibilities prohibited him from physically or verbally retaliating against this blatant discrimination, Roybal said nothing but handed the salesman his newly printed city council business card and walked back to his city car parked in front of the sales office. Roybal, like many other potential home buyers of color, probably realized that the previous year's landmark decision by the US Supreme Court in *Shelley v. Kramer* to outlaw state enforcement of racial housing covenant restrictions had not produced any effective government mechanisms to prevent private housing discrimination.[2]

The salesman at this housing development, however, quickly realized that it did not make sense to alienate this district's councilman. Before Roybal was able to get his car started, the salesman ran over and said, "I'm sorry, but I can sell to you because you're different." It is unclear whether this change of heart was due simply to Roybal's new political position or to his light skin. Later, Roybal would claim that this salesman had said that although "we can't sell to Mexicans, if you say you are of Spanish or Italian descent we will sell you a house." Whatever the reason for the change, Roybal refused the offer on principle and decided to make housing discrimination a fundamental part of his political agenda during his first few months in office. The very next day, on his second workday as a councilman, he addressed the city council and recounted his experience with racism, thereby garnering nationwide publicity. In light of this event, the Community Service Organization (CSO) set up a picket line outside the housing development, protesting racial discrimination. The protest convinced the head of the company to negotiate a solution with Roybal and the CSO that would end his discriminatory practices while the CSO withdrew their picket line. Later that summer, a survey indicated that only six developers in Los Angeles County did *not* discriminate against racial minorities and that eleven would sell only if the prospective purchaser claimed to be of Spanish descent instead of Mexican.[3]

This story of Roybal's tumultuous first few days in office reveals the challenges of being the first person of color to serve on the Los Angeles City Council in the twentieth century. But Roybal's ascension to public office was the product of being involved in organizations that had both mobilized the growing Mexican American community of Boyle Heights and constructed one of the strongest multiracial political coalitions to date. In various concrete ways, Roybal represented a liberal-Left coalition in the city of Los Angeles that cut across race in a time of conservative politics and cultural retrenchment during the Cold War. Moreover, that a Mexican American would rise as representative of that multiracial coalition speaks to the changing political and cultural life of Boyle Heights, which remained a key part of the Ninth Council District and of Los Angeles as a whole.

After nearly a century of civic silence, [Mexican Americans are] learning to make use of the most effective channel open to democracy's cultural minorities—the ballot.

LOS ANGELES DAILY NEWS, July 1, 1949

Edward Roybal was born in 1916 in Albuquerque to a long-standing Hispano family who traced their ancestry in New Mexico back to the seventeenth century. The family came to Boyle Heights in 1922 to start a new life and eventually built their house near the newly opened Roosevelt High School on Fifth Street. Roybal graduated from Roosevelt in 1934, then joined the New Deal's Civilian Conservation Corps (CCC) and attended UCLA and Southwestern University Law School briefly before settling in as the director of health education for the Los Angeles County Tuberculosis and Health Association.[4] After his discharge from the army during World War II, he transitioned into politics. Roybal used his summer vacations in 1945 and 1946 to travel to Chicago and study community organizing under the independent radical Saul Alinsky, who had founded the Chicago-based Industrial Area Foundation (IAF) in 1940 to train community organizers. Alinsky himself had spent the summers of his youth among Jewish relatives in Boyle Heights and had an active interest in the fate of the community and what he saw as the important rise of Mexican American empowerment in the district. The group that organized to establish political clout for Mexican Americans on the Eastside selected Roybal to run for the Los Angeles City Council in the fall of 1946.[5] Indeed, the door-to-door canvassing Roybal had done around the menace of tuberculosis gave him experience in waging a campaign and forging a community coalition.

In his initial unsuccessful run in 1947, Roybal was surrounded by a larger group that included those US-born Mexican Americans who had just recently fought in World War II and an emerging labor union leadership of second-generation Mexican Americans. Anthony Rios, local president of the Steel Workers Organizing Committee, and his wife Lucy were part of this cohort. Gilbert Anaya had also begun his career as an organizer in the 1930s for the United Steel Workers of America (part of the CIO federation of unions). Henry Nava had worked with Roybal in the Tuberculosis Association, and Lito Tafoya, originally from New Mexico, was a cook at a local hamburger grill. Maria Duran sat on the board of the local International Ladies Garment Workers Union (ILGWU), and Hope Mendoza had also been part of that union, with a stint as a Lockheed riveter during World War II. Collectively, they represented the postrepatriation community of Mexican American activists, deeply connected to the Los Angeles labor movement.[6]

Yet this group alone, organized as "the Committee to Elect Edward Roybal," had gotten him only to third place in the 1947 race, with 15 percent of the total vote in the Ninth District. Roybal finished 375 votes behind the incumbent, Parley P. Christensen, a Utah transplant who had been the Farm-Labor Party presidential candidate in 1920. Christensen had gotten most of the endorsements of organized labor as well as the local newspaper the *Eastside Sun* and the liberal *Daily News*. Downtown public relations consultant Julia Sheehan, a Democratic Party official supported by Governor Earl Warren and the conservative *Los Angeles Times,* hoping to be the first woman on the council, had finished second. Although 75 percent of Roybal's votes came from the Eastside's Mexican American neighborhoods, he was frustrated by what he saw as a community pattern of Mexican immigrant parents who had never become citizens living with their adult children who did not bother to register to vote. Only about 4,000 of 25,000 potential Mexican American voters in Boyle Heights were registered to vote in 1947, and overall in the Ninth District, Latinos were only 34 percent of the population, with whites being the largest group at 45 percent and African Americans numbering 15 percent. It was a disappointing finish and illustrated that something needed to be done to mobilize the wider community to elect an ethnic Mexican.[7] Alinsky wrote a telegram to Roybal the day after the 1947 defeat and asked: "What are you going to do next?"[8]

The CSO was formed after Roybal's 1947 defeat to coordinate civic empowerment in the growing Mexican American community and to elect Roybal to the district's city council seat in the next election. Roybal was its president, but the CSO was a culmination of more than homegrown Mexican American activism. Along with the Mexican American generation that emerged after World War II, the organization depended on the interracial coalition building that had solidified after the Zoot Suit Riots. This leftist community dedicated to interracial cooperation and advancement was key to the creation of the CSO, and their ideological dedication is probably best represented by Fred Ross, who would become the CSO's lone paid organizer.

Fred Ross was born in San Francisco in 1910 but grew up in Echo Park in Los Angeles. He graduated from the University of Southern California and was first introduced to social activism by a Jewish classmate, Eugene Wolman, who would perish in the Spanish Civil War.[9] But Ross's pathway to becoming

FIGURE 19. Edward Roybal, Fred Ross, and CSO registrars, 1949.
Edward Roybal Collection, UCLA Chicano Studies Research Library.
With permission of the Roybal Family Trust.

a committed organizer was predated by his work as a government relief
worker for the Farm Security Administration in the 1930s, where he witnessed the misery of the migrant worker camps in California and Arizona
and gained the trust of the Mexican workers, encouraging them to organize
to improve their conditions. He subsequently managed a camp for Dust Bowl
migrants outside Bakersfield and worked as part of the War Relocation
Authority with Japanese Americans. After the war, he helped ease racial tensions exacerbated by the Zoot Suit Riots as part of the American Council for
Race Relations, organizing Mexican and black Americans to fight segregation. Ross went on to organize Mexican Americans into Unity Leagues in
rural areas of the Inland Empire and Orange County.[10] From the start, Ross
impressed Ignacio López, editor of *El Espectador,* in the Citrus Belt in

Southern California by his dedication to organizing Mexican Americans. According to historian Rosina Lozano, "What made Fred Ross special as an organizer was his ability to empathize with the community he was serving. He emulated the active, informed, and compassionate citizen demanding the right to the 'good life.'"[11]

Notwithstanding Ross's organizing history, apparently the initial meeting between him and Roybal was filled with tension. In the summer of 1947, following Roybal's electoral defeat, the aspiring politician did not believe that a full-time organizer was needed in Boyle Heights, especially one who wore cowboy boots and was a racial outsider to the Mexican American community. Despite these concerns, Roybal invited Ross to meet with the larger circle of supporters, who had recently named themselves the Community Political Organization, or CPO. Ross convinced Roybal and the larger group to change their name to emphasize civic action, not just politics. It took Ross a whole summer of listening to this group of dedicated local Mexican American leaders, wary of Ross and his background, before they trusted him and thought his interests in seeing their community advance were sincere. Finally, at a meeting in September 1947, the group, now named the CSO, unanimously voted Fred Ross into the organization and accepted him as their only full-time organizer, a position paid for by Alinsky's IAF.

Once voted in by the leadership of the CSO, Fred Ross wasted no time in moving forward with his ambitious plan to increase the membership of the CSO and to mobilize the entire Mexican American community toward civic participation. In a strategy he had learned during his work in the Imperial Valley, Ross asked three of the most experienced volunteers in organizing, Maria Duran, Lito Tafoya, and Anthony Rios, to invite their friends over to their homes to discuss critical issues to the CSO and to enlist a larger group of volunteers.[12] Ross also organized a respected advisory committee made up of professionals, businessmen, and community leaders to build a strong backbone to the organization. And he met with the Catholic hierarchy, union leaders, and fraternal organizations to establish robust ties of support that would be influential across the entire Los Angeles community. Although the CSO was clearly a working-class organization, Ross developed support from middle-class sectors in a way that would not dilute the will of the people or try to take over the organization.[13]

At this point, Fred Ross convinced Hope Mendoza to get more heavily involved. Born in Miami, Arizona, in 1921 to immigrant parents from Mexico, Hope had been drawn to the committee that formed around

Roybal's first campaign. Her parents had moved to East Los Angeles when she was just one year old, and she was one of nine children in a family that converted to Protestantism because of her mother's divorce and remarriage.[14] Mendoza translated her given name, Esperanza, to "Hope" to reflect her identity as part of the "Mexican *American*" generation. She attended both Garfield and Roosevelt High Schools in the 1930s before dropping out during the Great Depression because of discriminatory treatment and her family's destitution. "You'd try to hide the fact that you were eating tortillas instead of a sandwich," she recalled.[15] So Mendoza left school at age 16 and entered the garment industry as a seamstress, marrying at 19 to get out of the house, before taking advantage of wartime opportunities to work for Lockheed as an assembler from 1942 to the end of the war. Her exposure to labor unions at Lockheed got her interested in becoming an in-house organizer for ILGWU when she returned to the garment industry in 1945. As a labor organizer and community activist, Mendoza was drawn to work with the Community Relations Conference of Southern California, a multiracial committee of Los Angeles County. The experience expanded her network and knowledge of the problems across the region affecting all racial groups. In her own words: "You can't be effective if you don't know about the community, where the pressure points are."[16] Eventually, this community education would propel Hope to chairperson of the CSO's labor committee, and to an ongoing commitment to civic engagement and liaison work through the immense labor union network in Los Angeles.

Between 1947 and 1949, Mendoza was pulled in multiple directions. In this period, she went to Harvard for leadership training in labor organizing, became a paid business agent in the garment industry, and emerged as a labor organizer for the ILGWU in 1948, being placed on the Central Labor Council in Los Angeles. Ross relied on her organizational skills to get union laborers registered to vote, and to raise monies from labor unions across Southern California in support of Roybal, but even more important was her commitment to representing community democracy. Mendoza became an important face of this burgeoning CSO group.

The most critical part of the organizing of the CSO were the weeknight rendezvous where Ross—accompanied by one of the original CSO members—visited families in the community to recruit them to get involved in voter education and to become official CSO members. By 1949 the CSO had enlisted nearly 1,000 active and semiactive members, at least 65 of whom were now empowered to register others to vote, up from a total of 4 in Boyle

Heights in 1947. While Ross and his CSO partners would listen to the needs of the families they visited, their solution would often center on the urgency of registering voters, and in general they attempted to engage the large Mexican American community in electoral political participation. However, the CSO leadership also learned a great deal about other issues in the community, ranging from the need for more accessible public housing to the fight against police brutality. Through word of mouth and from these labor-dominated grassroots campaigns emerged a dedicated group of local activists who could be counted on to educate others about the importance of voting to address a myriad of societal problems. Working throughout 1948, the group would grow with a goal of eventually registering as many as 25,000 new voters. Since voter registration efforts could not start until two and a half months before each election, this effort at increasing registrars eventually was able to register some 15,000 new Mexican American voters in 1948 and 1949, up from only 4,000 in 1947.[17] According to Roybal, the "get out the vote" campaign was highly effective and successfully mobilized over 95 percent of those previously registered to participate in actual voting.[18] The unprecedented voter registration effort on the Eastside enrolled 17,000 new voters of all backgrounds ahead of the 1949 election.

While the emphasis was on creating new Mexican American voters, the organizing effort had other tangible results in Boyle Heights. Lead organizers were first identified and encouraged via small gatherings in family homes in Boyle Heights, a house meeting style that had evolved out of Ross's early experience with migrant workers. Over several weeks, attendees would learn about each other, listen to grievances, align with CSO goals, and forge strong bonds that involved not just increasing voter registration but learning about the needs of the community in the tradition of Alinsky-style civic engagement. In this way, a brand-new civic leadership emerged around the effort to elect Roybal to the district's city council seat.

Ross, in many ways, reflected the importance of the "bridge" organizers who had been critical to every successful Southern California movement for social justice since the loose coalition of leftist organizations in the Popular Front period of the late 1930s.[19] He served as a "bridge" between communities of color on the Eastside of Los Angeles and the wealthier leftist community around Hollywood and the culture industries on the Westside. He also helped the CSO gather crucial support from key bishops in the Southern California Catholic Church and was able to solidify the support of labor unions with strong Mexican American members without being labeled "com-

FIGURE 20. CSO ad, "Help Build This Bridge!" March 1, 1952. *Los Angeles Daily News*, M0812, Fred Ross Papers, Box 10, Folder 12. Courtesy of the Department of Special Collections, Stanford University Libraries.

munist." While the staunch anticommunist organizational stance that both Ross and Alinsky promoted pushed the CSO away from more radical organizers who backed Henry Wallace for president in 1948, it also served the CSO well in withstanding the persecution of communist organizers in Los Angeles during the McCarthy period. Ross advocated for the creation of an Advisory Committee for the CSO that would amplify that the CSO was a homegrown group dedicated to democracy with widespread support among local institutions, including the Catholic Church and the business community—a depiction that was critical in gaining trust among other potential Los Angeles supporters.[20]

In addition, Alinsky urged the Jewish community to support Roybal and the CSO. The Jewish community, both inside and outside Boyle Heights, was critical to the development of the CSO between 1947 and 1949, bringing

Roybal together with a broad, multiracial coalition of backers. Moreover, Alinksy had wanted to involve himself actively in the strengthening of the Los Angeles Mexican American community ever since the 1943 Zoot Suit Riots but had failed to find an effective organization until this point. It was the veteran social activist Carey McWilliams who was able to connect Alinsky with the Los Angeles Jewish network through alliances he had developed in the Sleepy Lagoon Defense Committee (SLDC). McWilliams introduced Alinsky to Isaac Pacht, a prominent Jewish leader who eventually became the first West Coast IAF chairman. Pacht helped connect the CSO to other important allies. McWilliams knew Pacht because one of his law partners, Clore Warne, had been on the SLDC and the Los Angeles Committee for American Unity.[21] Despite this networking, McWilliams would eventually be dropped from consideration to serve on the CSO Advisory Committee because of his ties to the leftist community that could tarnish the CSO with a "communist" label.

Historian Ken Burt describes in vivid detail the way that Alinsky, working with Harry Braverman and Seniel Ostrow, owner of the Sealy Mattress franchise, buttonholed friends at the Hillcrest Country Club to extract donations for the CSO. Braverman, who had worked with McWilliams on the SLDC and chaired the Los Angeles Committee for American Unity, eventually raised the initial $9,000 in seed money to help finance the CSO.[22] Fred Herzberg, who served on the CSO Advisory Committee, secured a $7,500 pledge of support from the Jewish CRC, where he was executive director, replacing Leon Lewis in 1947.[23] Though all this money raised from individual Los Angeles Jewish individuals and organizations went to Alinsky in Chicago, Alinsky redirected it back to Los Angeles to the CSO, though this arrangement was not advertised in either community.[24] This fund-raising helped Alinsky pay Fred Ross a $3,000 yearly salary from 1947 to 1952.

The reasons for Jewish support of the CSO were varied and complex. The threat of violence in Los Angeles was made evident with the 1943 Zoot Suit Riots, and this had a particular resonance for Jews because of the history of anti-Semitic violence in the US and Europe. To see violent attacks on a minority population in Los Angeles brought home the notion that this sort of outbreak could happen anywhere and against any group, including Jews. Moreover, fears of violence coming from oppressed minority groups themselves was a specific concern, especially as the Jewish population began to integrate itself more into white suburban Los Angeles and leave behind minority ghettoized neighborhoods and barrios. Jews feared resentment because of this exodus, especially against Jewish neighbors who continued to live and work in large numbers in communities like Boyle Heights. Jewish support for the CSO was therefore based not only on altruism but also on a concern to ease potential tensions and improve Jewish relations with other minority populations in Southern California.[25]

For example, Jews did more than support Roybal and the CSO financially; they became a critical part of his 1949 electoral coalition by voting for him in the Ninth District. In the March 1949 primary election, Roybal was able to win 36.7 percent of the total vote (11,271 votes), of which 71 percent came from the Eastside, forcing the incumbent Parley Christensen into a May general runoff election. Anglos in 1949 continued to be the largest group in the Ninth District and were undoubtedly an even larger percentage of the voting constituency. But as the last chapter showed, Jews, now grouped in with whites, made up a major portion of this "Anglo" population and turned out substantially for Roybal. And they did so even more in the general election, especially after the Roybal campaign, in its final two weeks, announced the formation of a Boyle Heights support committee cochaired by William Phillips, prominent owner of Brooklyn Avenue's Phillips Music Store, and Jack Y. Berman, a theater chain operator on the Eastside. Both men had been active for years in the Soto-Michigan Jewish Community Center and were widely respected Boyle Heights businessmen. Roybal won the general election with 59 percent of the 35,106 total votes cast, 62 percent of his votes coming from the Eastside. Roybal had also been able to win a majority of the votes cast in the South Central and Bunker Hill areas of the district, a clear sign that his following had grown well beyond Eastside Latinos.[26]

Jewish support for Roybal would continue to solidify after the 1949 victory, and this would be particularly vital to his first reelection campaign in 1951 when Irving Rael, Jewish owner of an Eastside furniture business and president of the Community Business Men's Association, ran against him. Indeed, directly after Roybal's 1949 victory, one disgruntled civic leader thought that splitting the Roybal coalition would be key in defeating him: "If Roybal runs on that unification of minorities claptrap again, we'll hang him with it. We'll buy ourselves a Negro, a Mexican, and a Japanese for a thousand bucks each, and we'll run them all. We'll split that vote so wide Gerald L. K. Smith [the ultra-right-wing America First founder] could get through."[27] But rather than split Jewish votes away from Roybal, Rael's weak candidacy seemed to only harden support for Roybal among Jewish voters. Roybal's 1951 campaign had its kickoff banquet at the San Kwo Low Restaurant on

February 19, sponsored by the Citizens Committee to Re-Elect Roybal, whose chair was once again Jewish record store owner William Phillips, and whose master of ceremonies was Dr. E. I. Robinson, Southern California chair of the National Association for the Advancement of Colored People (NAACP). The Boyle Heights community newspaper, the *Eastside Sun*, reported that both Mexican and Jewish folk songs were performed at the multiracial event.[28] This time the *Eastside Sun,* which had supported Christensen in 1949, endorsed Roybal, and its editor, Joseph Eli Kovner, actually attacked Rael in print for engaging in desperate, emotional election tactics.[29]

Edward Roybal easily won reelection in 1951 with 70 percent of the total vote, garnering majorities in each of the four major areas of the Ninth District: Eastside, Downtown, South Central, and Bunker Hill. However, in this landslide victory, 10,000 fewer votes were cast than in the contentious 1949 campaign. Roybal had run his own grassroots campaign in 1951; the CSO had pulled out of electoral campaigns immediately after the 1949 victory, so the on-the-ground mechanism to get out the vote in the district simply was not there.[30] Even before the 1949 general election, the CSO had begun to concentrate its efforts in other parts of the Eastside, from Lincoln Heights to Belvedere, and by 1951, new chapters had been organized in these Mexican American communities in Southern California. In 1952, Fred Ross would leave his position as an organizer for the CSO, and the organization would become a statewide advocacy group. It was left to the ingenuity of Edward Roybal and his local supporters to sustain and nurture a multiracial coalition not simply for winning elections but also for improving conditions among residents of Boyle Heights and the rest of the Ninth District.

COALITION OF THE DISPOSSESSED

The election of Edward Roybal to the Los Angeles City Council made other politicians in Los Angeles pay attention, sometimes for the first time, to the emerging Mexican American electorate. Fred Ross, in his unpublished memoirs, tells the story of the CSO being contacted by Los Angeles mayor Fletcher Bowron following Roybal's 1949 primary victory by 2,000 votes over incumbent Christiansen: "The day after the Roybal victory in the Primary, the Mayor's Public Relations man, Dave Apter, is on the line: 'The Mayor's been hearing a number of good things about the CSO, recently[,] and he'd like to come out and talk to some of the leaders. You know, get a little insight into some of the East Side problems ...'"[31] Apparently Bowron, despite having been mayor since 1938, had never held a public meeting anywhere east of the Los Angeles River during his tenure. The historic meeting was set up at St. Mary's Parish Hall in Boyle Heights, and the CSO had a large number of its committee workers show up, to the surprise of Bowron, who thought he would be meeting with only a select group of "leaders." "That's who these folks are, Mr. Mayor," responded Henry Nava, who had replaced Roybal as the local CSO chapter president to allow him to run for public office. "They're the ones who do the work in the organization. Way we look at it, every worker is a leader, so we invited 'em all." Having heavily prepared for this momentous meeting, CSO officials then grilled Mayor Bowron for an hour on his inattention to the Eastside and ended the meeting with a call for a citizens' committee to review police misconduct in the district.[32]

While Bowron's attention had been refocused because of the participation of Eastside residents in the election cycle, it took the actual placement of Roybal as an energetic member of the city council and representative of the Ninth District to direct increased resources toward improvements in the area. In her extensive study of Roybal's political career, Katherine Underwood stresses that Roybal was an effective legislator in three key areas: constituent relations, symbolic resolutions, and the obtaining of material benefits for the district.[33] Roybal, upon his swearing-in in July 1949, held regular open office hours in his district each week to hear constituent complaints and suggestions and used the local press to disperse information to district residents about important council actions. As an active councilman, he also sponsored honorary council resolutions acknowledging individuals and organizations for their service to the community. Roybal prepared citations recognizing prominent Latinos and Jews, welcomed visiting union delegations to Los Angeles, and commended progressive actions by the local Hollenbeck Division of the LAPD. But it was the concrete action of delivering, according to the *Eastside Sun,* "22 new traffic signals, 23 new pedestrian cross walks and 18 boulevard stops," as well as more street lighting, sweeper service, trash pickup, and ambulance service, that truly signaled improvements in the daily lives of residents of the Ninth District.[34] And it was exactly these achievements in a district that had largely been ignored, including by its own political representatives, that marked a major turning point, which the *Los Angeles Daily News* would call an "awakening" by the "bypassed islands of L.A."[35]

Edward Roybal had learned his approach to governing through his leadership and involvement in the CSO, where he had been educated on the

FIGURE 21. Edward Roybal and family enter campaign headquarters after election victory, 1949. Edward Roybal Collection, UCLA Chicano Studies Research Library. With permission of the Roybal Family Trust.

importance of direct action, a method he was first trained in by Alinsky and the IAF. Besides the CSO Membership Committee, the first three committees that were organized by the CSO in the fall of 1947 revolved around health, housing, and civil rights. The work directly reflected the needs of members. The Health Committee, for example, immediately started on a diphtheria program for immigrants in Boyle Heights, a decision that came from listening to constituents about their concerns and was a follow-up to the tuberculosis eradication campaign that Roybal brought to the city council from his previous position.[36] The Housing Committee met with the race relations adviser of the Federal Housing Administration (FHA) to discuss the widespread issue of housing discrimination. The Civil Rights Committee immediately took up cases of police brutality by the LAPD and would eventually hire lawyers to help individuals take cases to court to seek damages and compensation.[37] Watching and participating in these CSO committees not only gave Roybal insight into democratic practice in action but also prepared him to be the kind of politician he wanted to become upon taking office.

So at his swearing-in he already had much experience defending the rights of his constituents. From the first days of his tenure, numerous residents approached Roybal with harrowing stories of police brutality by the LAPD, and he often sought official inquiries into what he saw as miscarriages of justice. Roybal understood the injustice of police brutality on a personal level, having been a victim of police profiling and brutality growing up in Boyle Heights, most notably when a police officer purposefully and violently pushed him while he was on a date so that he would drop the food he and his date were sharing on the street, humiliating him in front of his future wife, Lucille Beserra.[38] But he also tried to approach the local division at Hollenbeck in a positive manner, believing that plenty of police officers tried their best to serve the multiracial community fairly. Yet the rise of William Parker as chief of police in 1950 made accountability for LAPD brutality nearly impossible, as Parker himself routinely made racist statements against Mexicans and African Americans and spearheaded a reign of police terror on minority communities.

Nonetheless, to Roybal and the CSO's credit, they were able to get the LAPD to acknowledge the problem of police brutality and obtain convictions against specific officers for the first time. In December 1951, for example, five officers were convicted of assault, with an additional 38 suspensions and 54 transfers, after the Bloody Christmas incident. The incident, fictionalized in *L.A. Confidential* by James Ellroy, occurred on Christmas Day when police stormed the jail to avenge two officers who had been involved in a bar brawl the night before. The brawl had begun when two officers demanded several men leave the Showboat bar because of complaints that they were minors, though none were. Later the officers picked up the men who had been in the bar and hauled them from their homes to jail. In the incident, seven Mexican American men were brutally beaten, resulting in punctured organs, broken bones, and blood transfusions. Another such example was the case of two officers who stripped, beat, and jailed a leading CSO official, Anthony Rios, in 1952 for intervening as plainclothes police were beating a man outside a bar. Rios was acquitted. Despite these successes, Roybal, and the CSO, among others, were unable to obtain broader punishment for the higher-ups who had condoned such conduct for years.[39]

However, it was in the area of broad public policy that Edward Roybal would gain his most important backing from multiple constituencies in Boyle Heights, in the Ninth District, and throughout Los Angeles, even though in this area he was consistently on the losing side of council votes. Through his entire period on the city council from 1949 to 1962, Roybal had to contend with a deeply conservative majority on the fifteen-person council, buoyed by a fervent anticommunist ideology that saw a leftist conspiracy behind virtually any attempt to achieve racial and social justice. In this environment, Roybal represented one of the few districts that was proudly racially diverse and consistently left of center in its political leanings. Yet he also had to contend with the fact that the majority of both Republicans and Democrats who served on the city council represented areas much more conservative and unwilling to move forward on initiatives to democratize local decision-making and achieve some semblance of equity in social policy.

However, Roybal did not shy away from defending and promoting unpopular minority opinions. After only one month in office, Roybal sponsored a bill to have the council establish a Fair Employment Practices Commission (FEPC) in Los Angeles to actively administer existing but unenforced laws that made it illegal to racially discriminate against employees for firms doing business with the city. Since World War II, support for federal, state, and local FEPCs had been a standard demand from progressive Jewish groups, African American organizations, and Mexican American organizations, but most white voters and politicians in California had rejected these efforts consistently on the grounds of infringing on individual liberties. The *Los Angeles Times* argued in 1949 that "such a law tends to rob an individual of his freedom to choose his associates in work, as business partners or employees, and stirs up a train of resentments and conflicts."[40] The council eventually rejected Roybal's proposal for a commission that provided oversight for employment discrimination in an 8 to 6 vote, but Roybal gained enormous political backing from African American and progressive Jewish organizations for having spearheaded the effort.[41]

In the next few years, he would continue to work on the losing side of major issues intended to help working people in his district. In 1950, Roybal tried to stop the city council from removing rent control legislation across the city, a policy that had kept rent hikes in check against the inflationary pressures unleashed during wartime and its aftermath. Under intense lobbying from the real estate industry, the council voted overwhelmingly to deregulate rents, but Roybal nonetheless worked to soften the blow for his constituencies by documenting hardships and trying to forestall subsequent evictions. He would once again run up against the real estate lobby by being the most consistent supporter of public housing on the council, even as many of his more moderate peers switched positions in the early 1950s, a shift that eventually led to the collapse of support for public housing in the city council itself. At the end of 1951, when the city council voted to cancel the city's public housing contract with the federal government, Roybal continued to fight for its reinstitution, and later for continued support for public housing, as his Boyle Heights district encompassed three of the largest public housing complexes.[42]

The issue that probably got Roybal the most acclaim from progressives throughout the nation, but that showed the lonely position he occupied on the city council, was the issue of communist registration. After a week of carefully consulting with many friends and organizations in his district, Roybal decided to oppose an ordinance proposed in September 1950 by conservative councilman Ed Davenport to require all members of the Communist Party living or entering the city of Los Angeles to register with the chief of police or face fines, imprisonment, or both. All other liberal members of the council, seeing the futility of opposition, decided to vote in favor, but Roybal was the lone legislator to hold his ground on a 13 to 1 vote. In registering his negative vote, Roybal stated that he was concerned about the "thought-control" aspect of the ordinance, particularly its effect on "a large number of little civic organizations in my district and elsewhere who are interested in their own neighborhood problems . . . [and] with the preservation and advancement of our Democracy" that would get caught in its enforcement.[43]

The political and personal bravery of that vote cannot be overstated. A crowd of 500 people had jammed the council chambers to hear speaker after speaker rail against supposed communist conspirators and witness the vote count. When Roybal left the chambers with his family afterwards, he was mercilessly booed. His daughter, Lillian Roybal-Rose, remembered, "We

FIGURE 22. Edward Roybal and *Eastside Sun* editor Joseph Kovner, 1949. Edward Roybal Collection, UCLA Chicano Studies Research Library. With permission of the Roybal Family Trust.

were walking, and people [were] screaming at my dad, 'Go back where you came from, dirty Mexican!'" She recalled that her father just instructed the children to look straight ahead, to keep walking, and not to look at anyone. "And I remember they spit on us and I had spit running down my face and I was too scared to wipe it off my face," said Lillian Roybal-Rose, who at the time was only seven years old.[44]

While Roybal acknowledged that his vote might leave him "dead politically," it in fact had the opposite effect. Local newspaper editor Joseph Kovner wrote that Roybal deserved a "badge of courage" for his vote, while a *Daily News* editorial thought that his principled stance "took the kind of courage that great patriots and martyrs of all ages have demonstrated when they took positions in opposition to the popular view."[45] Within ten days, Roybal had received over 800 letters commending him on his stance against anticommunist hysteria, including one from the assistant director of the

American Civil Liberties Union (ACLU), George Rundquist, from New York. Rundquist wrote: "I am certain that because you have taken a firm stand based on principles about which you felt strongly, you will have the courage to maintain your stand for the ideals you believe in whenever the occasion again arises." In response, Roybal concurred, writing that "I shall continue to fight for . . . the right of all people to speak their minds in a true democracy for the advancement of common views by free association."[46]

At the end of 1950, the IAF decided to end their direct support of the CSO, which meant that their payment of the salaries of organizer Fred Ross and secretary Carmen Medina would come to an end. By June 1951, the IAF formally severed its relationship with the CSO. During 1951, CSO leadership tried desperately to find a new funding mechanism for the organization, including enacting a dues-paying membership scheme and becoming an affiliate of the ACLU. None of these plans worked, and the CSO was left in a precarious financial state.[47]

Partly because of these financial troubles, Fred Ross announced in late 1951 that he would take a new position in 1952 as the executive director of the California Federation for Civic Unity in Northern California. Councilman Roybal hosted a send-off celebration in his home for Ross, as leaders from each of the three CSO chapters that Ross had started in Southern California—Boyle Heights, Lincoln Heights, and Belvedere—praised his accomplishments. Later that year, Ross would go on to discover a new aspiring organizer, César Chávez, and would bring him into the CSO fold. The CSO, for its part, would establish a statewide federation of CSOs in 1952, with Anthony Rios as its president, expanding until it consisted of 30 chapters in California and Arizona by 1965.[48] In Los Angeles, however, Edward Roybal would carry on in the city council as an advocate for democratic action from Boyle Heights without direct support from CSO organizers but with a contingent of supporters as a result of five years of organized collaboration and locally based political activity.

DEFENDING A DISTRICT FROM "REDEVELOPMENT"

When incumbent mayor Fletcher Bowron lost his mayoral reelection campaign to conservative Norris Poulson in May 1953, the forces promoting rapid development of the city through the use of public funds for private development came to dominate Los Angeles. Even though that election also resulted in two additional liberal candidates elected to the city council, Everette Burkhalter and 22-year-old Jewish Rosalind Wiener (later Wyman), these two represented, not geographic concentrations of working-class progressivism such as the Ninth District, but rather a liberalism born of homogeneous suburbia and white flight.[49] In many ways, the successful campaign of the Committee Against Socialist Housing (CASH) that had defeated public housing in Los Angeles and led directly to the defeat of the reelection of Bowron, now had advocates for rapid urban renewal and public expenditure of funds to create a "new Los Angeles." This movement for renewal saw much of the Ninth District as slums to be eliminated and—with the *Los Angeles Times* as their mouthpiece—began a decade of unbridled urban redevelopment that would barely take into account the needs of Roybal's constituents.[50]

After 1953, Roybal increasingly sought to protect his district from a marked form of brutality: the land grab of urban redevelopment for "progress" in Los Angeles. In 1956, he fought the relocation of his working-class constituency from Bunker Hill by the Community Redevelopment Agency (CRA) to make way for a new tourist, business, and cultural district intended to "upgrade" the downtown area. But because the progrowth majority on the city council favored the interests of redevelopment, Roybal was not able to do much to counter the decision by the CRA to completely destroy the multiracial Bunker Hill neighborhood. The 30-block, 136-acre Bunker Hill project was the largest real estate transaction in Los Angeles history, and residents were evicted from their homes mainly through eminent domain. Roybal was able, however, to obtain council approval in 1957 for an antidiscrimination ordinance governing CRA redevelopment projects, and he later helped oversee the finding of new homes for 9,500 displaced residents of Bunker Hill, many of whom were retirees on fixed incomes. Defining the area as a slum that had to be cleared, Roybal's colleagues on the city council went along with the CRA in favor of downtown development even though this land swap took away the homes of some to serve the commercial interests of private developers.[51]

Similarly, the fate of the few remaining residents of Chavez Ravine was settled in 1958 by the overwhelming forces who wanted to build a stadium to bring a major league baseball team, the Brooklyn Dodgers, to Los Angeles. While Roybal was the staunchest opponent of the sweetheart deal with Dodger owner Walter O'Malley and vehemently protested the forced removal of the Arechiga family from their home, he could do little to shift public opinion or that of his council colleagues.[52] After the plans for public housing in the area were forever shelved with the election of conservative Poulson in 1953, he could do little besides attempting to convince others to side with him. The turn against public housing and toward private redevelopment and urban renewal pushed almost all the city council, including the newly elected liberals and moderates like Wyman, to support the luring of the Brooklyn Dodgers to Los Angeles, onto the land of Chavez Ravine, taken from residents who had been promised public housing. Indeed, the first live telecast of local news in Los Angeles history became the 1959 broadcast of the forced removal of the Arechiga family from their Chavez Ravine homes to make way for the bulldozers that would clear land for Dodger Stadium. Roybal physically went to bear witness to these forced removals even though this was outside his district, and he sought adequate compensation for all affected residents, as he had done for residents of Bunker Hill.[53]

The most unreported story regarding this change in local housing policy in the 1950s, however, was the rapid decline of support for the maintenance and upkeep of public housing already built and the subsequent transformation of the population supported by government housing. Boyle Heights had been significantly altered through the construction of Aliso Village, Ramona Gardens, and several smaller public housing projects in the late 1930s and early 1940s. Even though the City Housing Authority intended for housing projects to be built throughout the city of Los Angeles, Boyle Heights and South Los Angeles ended up with the bulk of the constructed units in the city. Originally, the City Housing Authority was adamant about making these projects interracial examples of equitable living and ensured that the first residents were demographically diverse, pulling from the white, black, Mexican, and Asian communities. Then, during World War II, the Housing Authority reprioritized defense workers in order to meet the enormous housing needs of the burgeoning wartime population that needed to be close to employment. Finally, directly after the war, the Housing Authority once again switched gears to focus on meeting the housing needs of returning war veterans and the acute housing shortage they faced in Southern California.[54]

In 1951, when the city council canceled the public housing contract with the federal government, they did more than refuse to build any additional housing units like those at Chavez Ravine, or the additional 10,000 units whose construction was already in motion by a city council resolution. City officials were so quick to get out of the public housing enterprise that they even sent back to the federal government money earmarked for the maintenance of the existing public housing that already had residents and had been functioning well. This led to a rapid decline in the quality of public housing in Los Angeles and a serious deterioration of existing housing stock, especially those large units that had been operating in Boyle Heights for about a decade. Not surprisingly, and to the delight of the *Los Angeles Times* and the private real estate lobby that fought against public housing, those who could purchase private homes or rent elsewhere in Los Angeles quickly left what had been integrated housing communities to enter privatized, highly segregated neighborhoods in the 1950s.

Those left behind, who were abandoned in existing public housing communities or who had no other options when they entered Los Angeles, were largely poor African American residents and newcomers and recent Mexican immigrants entering as *bracero* farm workers or undocumented immigrants into Boyle Heights. To get the eviscerated City Housing Authority to take care of maintenance issues, to improve deteriorating conditions, or to even listen to residents' complaints took enormous grassroot efforts in the 1950s, even with a sympathetic city councilman like Edward Roybal on their side. The neglect of the public housing projects in Boyle Heights is generally seen as part of the reason why the quality of life in Boyle Heights declined over the course of the 1950s and 1960s, making it less attractive for those Jews, Italians, and Japanese Americans who had other options. However, this deterioration did lead to the opening up of spaces in public housing, which in turn led to the movement of working-class people into Boyle Heights, into this housing of last resort. Public housing in Boyle Heights would produce some of the most well-known African American athletes to emerge from Roosevelt High School in this period. But the decline of public housing would also bring greater poverty to the Boyle Heights neighborhood, as well as serve as a launching pad for alienated youth to seek refuge in gangs. The substandard quality of public housing in Boyle Heights was only one factor in the decay of the neighborhood, as the expansion of the freeway system also played a critical role.

Probably the most meaningful, yet most frustrating battle over land use in the Ninth District was the battle over freeway routing and construction that dominated the last ten years of Edward Roybal's city council career. What made this struggle so meaningful for Roybal and his constituents was the ways it left Boyle Heights permanently scarred and divided and its residents angry over the destruction of many private homes and businesses by five major freeways. At the end of the process, more than 15 percent of all the land in Boyle Heights was taken up by freeways, largely to serve the suburban

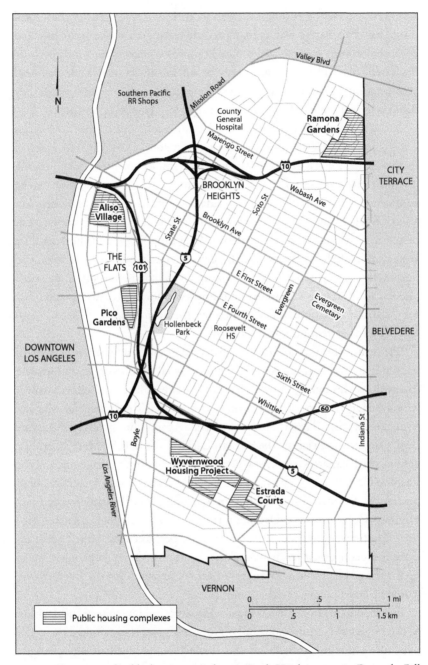

MAP 4. Freeways and public housing complexes in Boyle Heights, ca. 1960. Drawn by Bill Nelson.

commuters traveling through metropolitan Los Angeles rather than local residents. This battle was even more frustrating to those most affected because they were up against the State Highway Commission, a purposefully insulated government agency with broad authority and little political accountability. Commission members were appointed, not elected, and they could largely dictate the routing of freeways despite local opposition.

In the summer of 1953, the Highway Commission notified the Los Angeles City Council that it intended to place a portion of the Golden State Freeway in the Ninth District directly through the middle of Boyle Heights in a north-south direction. The $32 million project was a continuation of the Santa Ana Freeway that would lay a wide concrete barrier between the main area of Boyle Heights and the smaller Hollenbeck Heights area to the west, bisecting a shared commercial district along First Street and shearing off a large section of Hollenbeck Park. This construction would also destroy 1,400 homes, displacing 5,000 Boyle Heights residents. In response, an Anti-Golden State Freeway Committee was formed by local residents in September 1953, chaired by Councilman Roybal, with *Eastside Sun* publisher Joseph Kovner leading its fund-raising efforts.[55]

The committee was able to gain nearly unanimous support from individual residents and businesses in the region, as well as from organizations and institutions throughout Boyle Heights. A truly multiracial effort ensued, which included support from entities as diverse as the College of Medical Evangelists, the Jewish Home for the Aged, the Brooklyn Avenue Businessmen's Association, the Russian Catholic Church, St. Mary's Catholic School, the Japanese Methodist Church, the Breed Street Synagogue, and the Eastside Community Center. A rally was held at the Second Street School to protest the freeway in preparation for a second public hearing by the State Highway Commission on December 15, 1953. Edward Roybal facilitated protest via letter writing and at least one citizens' petition amassed 15,000 signatures from concerned residents and organizations. Over 350 people showed up for the public meeting to suggest alternative routes for the freeway so it would be less disruptive to the community.[56]

In the end, however, all this organizing work did not change the decision of the Highway Commission, and on June 24, 1954, they adopted the original route through Hollenbeck and Boyle Heights without any changes. Months later, on March 7, 1955, Edward Roybal cast the lone dissenting vote in the city council for approval of the agreement between the City of Los Angeles and the State Highway Commission for closing the streets for the construction of the Golden State Freeway. Two years later, the same commission unveiled plans for the Pomona Freeway to cut through the southern portion of the Eastside, and Roybal helped organize protests again, but to no avail. While Roybal was successful in helping individuals get compensated for their property from the State of California, he was unable to stop the bulldozers. The question remained, as Joseph Kovner wrote in 1957, "How do you stop the State from continuing to butcher our town?"[57]

MOVING OUT, MOVING UP

Some Boyle Heights residents, rather than stay and watch the "butchering" of their neighborhood, packed up and moved out in the 1950s, particularly Jews, as the last chapter has shown, reflecting changes in racial restrictions and the housing stock of the new suburbs after World War II. The rapid decrease of the Boyle Heights Jewish population in the 1950s has been discussed widely; less discussed, however, is the movement of Mexican Americans and Japanese Americans out of Boyle Heights. As these populations improved their economic situation, they moved to suburbs to the east, such as Monterey Park and Pico Rivera. Indeed, local CSO chapters were started in some of the areas of eastern Los Angeles County precisely because of the movement of CSO members out of the city, and these individuals often led efforts to integrate these eastern suburbs.[58] While some Boyle Heights residents were forced to leave because their homes stood in the way of coming freeways, others moved voluntarily to escape the deterioration and neglect of the neighborhood, the disruptive freeways, or undersupported public housing.

New Mexican immigrants often filled the void of these departures, renting the houses that were formerly owner-occupied. In addition, the growing African American community established an increased presence in Boyle Heights, some taking advantage of falling rents or home prices, while others at the lowest economic levels moved into the public housing developments.

This demographic shift changed the nature of the Eastside electorate. Although Mexican-origin people were the majority of the Boyle Heights residents for the first time in the census of 1960, they had fallen throughout the 1950s in terms of the number of eligible voters in the area, given the increase of noncitizens and recent immigrants. Indeed, in Roybal's last election for city council in 1961, only 9,632 votes were cast on the Eastside, about half the voter turnout in 1949.[59] The African American population, on the other hand, had grown to 14 percent of Los Angeles' total population by 1960 and now represented the single largest demographic group in the Ninth District overall. This transformation was accomplished not only by an increase of African Americans living on the Eastside but also by the changing boundary lines of the Ninth District itself. In 1952, the city council had eliminated parts of Lincoln Heights north of Main Street from the Ninth District, while expanding it southward along Central Avenue to Jefferson Boulevard. In 1956, the council further expanded the district's southern boundary to Slauson Avenue to encompass more of the African American community. While the Latino population in the district had been 19 percent larger than the African American population in 1950, by 1960 the Ninth District's African American population was 4 percent higher than the Latino population. In both of Roybal's last two elections for city council in 1957 and 1961, many more votes came in from South Central than from the Eastside.[60]

Edward Roybal adjusted to these demographic changes in his district by increasingly and proactively incorporating African Americans as a significant part of his governing coalition. When he first won office in 1949, when only 15 percent of the district's population was African American, he responded to why African Americans should support him with the answer: "Our skin is also brown—our battle is the same. Our victory cannot but be a victory for you, too."[61] As time progressed, his consistent support of a municipal FEPC gained him the endorsement of the *California Eagle* and its editor, Charlotta Bass, and he regularly called for the investigation of police brutality against both African Americans and Mexican Americans. In the late 1950s, he was the most active council supporter of the NAACP's crusade to desegregate the city fire department, and his popularity among black voters grew in each election during the 1950s.[62] But despite the Ninth District's growing constituency of African Americans, no African American had yet been elected to the Los Angeles City Council.

Given all of his community work, it is not surprising that Roybal's decision in February 1962 to declare his candidacy for the newly created 30th District in the US Congress would set off a scramble to replace him in the city council. Indeed, Mexican American candidates had lost so many close races in California throughout the 1950s that many perceived a broad lack of support from the state's Democratic Party. The Mexican American Political Association (MAPA) was formed in 1960 to more successfully compete for public office, often garnering support from the same businessmen who had financially supported Edward Roybal.[63]

But African Americans had also long waited for adequate representation in local government, and as their numbers swelled in Los Angeles, city officials actively thwarted these aspirations in order to maintain white electorate majorities and white leaders. In 1959, they had moved one district from South Central to the San Fernando Valley rather than leave a majority-black city district, and in 1961 they appointed a white real estate salesman, Joe Hollingsworth, in a heavily African American district, ignoring many well-qualified black candidates. Gilbert Lindsay, a black deputy to Supervisor Kenneth Hahn, was the first to petition the city council to replace Roybal, while Richard Tafoya, a cousin of Roybal's and an aide to Mayor Sam Yorty, the colorful and conservative Democrat who succeeded Mayor Poulson, also expressed interest.

After Roybal's November 1962 congressional victory, the city council decided to appoint Gilbert Lindsey to Roybal's council seat in January 1963, just three months before the scheduled election for the post, where Lindsey would defeat Tafoya by over 3,000 votes. Thus the first appointment of an African American to the Los Angeles City Council also resulted in the absence of a Latino from the council, and this situation would remain the same until 1985 with the election of Richard Alatorre. The April 1963 elections, on the other hand, would see two other African American candidates, Tom Bradley and Billy Mills, win election to the city council. Lindsey would use much of Roybal's strategy to maintain this multiracial coalition, appointing a Latino to be his chief aide and fostering open dialogue to his office and an equitable distribution of services to all parts of the Ninth District.[64]

Roybal, for his part, although publicly supporting his cousin Tafoya for the position, also criticized the way in which the Mexican American political elite had tried to hold onto the seat. He challenged the decision by MAPA to unilaterally select Tafoya to replace him, which both incensed black leaders and split the Mexican American vote. He thought that both Mexican Americans and African Americans should have sat down and backed a single candidate acceptable to both groups. "I told them they should select someone who would represent all groups—not just Mexican Americans. I even went so far as to say I would prefer a liberal Republican candidate for the post than a reactionary democrat." To the end, Roybal tried to encourage multiracial politics, even in an era when representation politics seemed to carry the day.[65]

The legacy of Edward Roybal's time in the Los Angeles City Council is a blueprint for building multiracial political coalitions anchored by principled political practice, as well as a deep desire to adequately represent the needs of all constituents in a district. At his funeral in October 2005, generations of politicians and city leaders of all backgrounds came to tell stories of the multiple ways Roybal had inspired them to seek a better life for themselves and others. Then 32-year-old city councilman Alex Padilla told those assembled at the Cathedral of Our Lady of the Angels how his immigrant parents had looked up to Roybal as their representative. Harry Pregerson, a longtime judge on the US Ninth Circuit Court of Appeals and a former resident of Boyle Heights, 50 years Padilla's senior, said that Roybal had "inspired many of us to take up the cause of social justice."[66] There was, and is, no contradiction in being both a Mexican American political trailblazer and the recognized leader of a multiracial coalition of progressives fighting for social justice for all.

On the surface, it might appear as if Edward Roybal's successful electoral climb to city council in the late 1940s was simply a result of the maturation of a Mexican American political elite that mobilized its own community to participate, register, and vote for one of their own. But Roybal's constituency was diverse ethnically and economically. It included Mexican American veterans and Mexican American labor leaders, who also enlisted leftist organizers dedicated to interracial cooperation, African Americans, and Jewish Angelinos. All of these played significant roles in building a multiracial coalition best represented by the membership of the CSO. Roybal's years on the city council (1949–62) reflect his commitment to serving his district's multiracial community, even as its demographics were changing over this key period. The CSO that had launched Roybal's political career and secured his victory in the late 1940s went on to organize other California communities as Roybal nurtured his own multiracial group of supporters to raise important issues for the Boyle Heights neighborhood. As an elected official who owed much of his electoral success to Mexican American organizers, Roybal was forced to walk a fine line between serving a multiracial constituency and being a spokesperson for the emerging Mexican American political movement in Los Angeles.

EIGHT

Black and Brown Power in the Barrio

I know the tension had heightened, activity had heightened district wide, a lot of schools were talking about it, everyone knew it was going to happen, everyone was waiting for the sign. But I remember the atmosphere was absolutely tense, I mean it was just electric in school. This had been building for so long, and everyone knew it was going to happen and everyone was just waiting and waiting.

PAULA CRISOSTOMO, *Lincoln High School*
1968 Walkout leader, quoted in Delgado Bernal,
"Chicano School Resistance"

Students walked out with dignity, with their heads held high as Chicanos!

SAL CASTRO, *Lincoln High School teacher*
and Walkout leader, in the film Chicano!

SEVENTEEN-YEAR-OLD PAULA CRISOSTOMO had not been able to sleep the night before the planned walkout from Lincoln and other East Los Angeles high schools on Wednesday, March 6, 1968. Though it had been strategized over several months in the spring of 1968, Paula was still concerned about her safety and that of other high school students at the forefront of the organization. And one of her biggest worries was that her classmates would not follow her out the door. At the appointed time of 8:30 a.m., set to have an impact on the school's enrollment figures for that day, Paula got up, yelled, "Let's walk out!" and went for the classroom door. Once in the Lincoln High School's hallways, she looked for the older college students who were waiting for them, making noise, and helped guide them toward the doors of the school. Once outside, Paula was relieved to see her mother, who had told her she would be waiting for her out front. Now, finally feeling safe, Paula took the picket sign her mother handed her, and they began to march in protest of conditions at Lincoln and other East L.A. schools. They continued to march that first day until teacher Sal Castro told them all to go home for the day because they had not constructed a plan for further action until the second Walkout day, when they marched to Hazard Park, where the Los Angeles Unified School District (LAUSD) regional offices were located. On this first day, they were just happy that most students, 1,700 of Lincoln High School's student body of 2,000, had followed them out of the classrooms.[1]

During the first two weeks of March 1968, over 10,000 high school students walked out of their classrooms in all five of the East Los Angeles high schools to protest inadequate educational conditions. This largely Latino student body was also joined by students from several predominantly African American schools in South Los Angeles and a few predominantly Anglo schools in West Los Angeles. The Walkouts of East Los Angeles high schools are seen by most participants and historians as the beginning of the urban uprising known as the Chicano Movimiento, which would transform the politics and culture of the Mexican American community of Los Angeles and beyond. Following on the heels of the emergence of the United Farm Workers in the rural landscape of California in the mid-1960s, this urban uprising of young people led directly to political activism against the Vietnam War, electoral challenges to the status quo, and a cultural renaissance of ethnic pride and self-assertion. But it also occurred toward the end of a decade that was marked by widespread protests, youth empowerment, and a powerful African American civil rights and black nationalist movement that helped propel this student activism.

This chapter focuses on the intimate relationship between Chicano student activism and the African American civil rights movement by looking at the connections between these two communities in Boyle Heights in the post–World War II period. The growth of the black population in Boyle Heights, especially in the public housing in the district, engendered overlap and connections between Mexican American and African American families in several key neighborhoods and contributed to a new set of relations between students at local schools and playgrounds. Moreover, community leadership and individual families learned political strategies, shifting ideological positions, and even styles of protest and self-assertion from the growing black civil rights movement, both nationally and locally. Although newfound ideologies of Chicano nationalism late in the decade often masked this impact, a localized exploration of the role of community connections in Boyle Heights will reveal the important ways in which student activism among Chicano and African American young people was a shared experience that mobilized a strong movement for self-empowerment among Chicanos in the late 1960s and reverberated long afterwards.

Boyle Heights had always had a small African American community. The earliest black people to move into Boyle Heights had fled the Jim Crow South at the end of the nineteenth century and the beginning of the twentieth, forming a small, largely lower-middle-class enclave near Evergreen Cemetery. For example, Mollie Wilson Murphy, who at the beginning of this book described the treasured letters from her interned Japanese American schoolmates, said her parents had been brought as children to the burgeoning city of Los Angeles at the turn of the century "to get out of the South."[2] These black pioneers often worked as Pullman porters on the railroads coming into Los Angeles and took advantage of the availability of homes for purchase by buying real estate east of the river. Since Boyle Heights was one of the few locations in Southern California not closed to African Americans by racially restrictive covenants, real estate purchase and occupancy were somewhat accessible to the migrants who founded this small enclave. Some of the families of these early settlers rented rooms or apartments to other individual African Americans and sometimes whole families, thereby consciously growing the community.[3]

The explosion of Los Angeles' African American population during World War II and in the immediate postwar period put new housing pressures on multiracial neighborhoods like Boyle Heights. The city's African American population doubled during the war to 133,082 by 1946, then continued to grow to 171,209 by 1950. In the 1950s, the African American population in Los Angeles almost doubled again, reaching 334,916 by 1960, and rising to 12 percent of the overall city population.[4] Because housing continued to be highly segregated, it was often the neighborhoods already established as multiracial in the city that had to absorb the new migrants from the South, and largely into overcrowded conditions. During World War II, the abandoned Little Tokyo was transformed into a congested "Bronzeville," but with the return of the Japanese American population after the war, the historic Central Avenue community swelled and expanded to the south.[5] Communities in South Los Angeles that had long been multiracial, such as Watts, became almost completely black by 1960. At the outbreak of World War II, Watts had approximately equal numbers of whites, Mexicans, and blacks in its population, but by 1958, blacks made up 95 percent of Watts' residents.[6]

In Boyle Heights during this period, private housing stock was being reduced by the onset of highway construction and public housing. Population pressures were intense because of wartime migrations, including the movement of *braceros* and their families during the war, and then, after the war, returning servicemen of all racial groups, as well as Japanese American internees. Boyle Heights, however, benefited from much of the public housing built by the City Housing Authority (CHA) during the period. The first and only public housing project built before entry of the United States into the war, Ramona Gardens, had opened in January 1941 with 610 units. Three more projects were built quickly during 1942 in Boyle Heights to house war workers, Estrada Courts (opened June 1942), Pico Gardens (August 1942), and Aliso Village (December 1942), incorporating 214, 260, and 802 units respectively.[7] Even with the pressure to prioritize the housing of war workers during the war itself, the CHA kept its policy of trying to maintain racially mixed housing despite the discriminatory practices of wartime industries.[8]

At the conclusion of the war in December 1945, the three Boyle Heights public housing projects were the most racially mixed in Los Angeles. Ramona Gardens had 20.6 percent white residents and 16.8 percent black residents. Similarly, Aliso Village had 37.2 percent white residents and 23.3 percent black residents. The "other" category, which included Americans of Mexican, Japanese, Filipino, or Chinese descent, was large, composing 62.6 percent of the Ramona Gardens population and 39.5 percent of the Aliso Villagers. In contrast, many of the housing projects built in Watts and South Los Angeles were almost completely black, while several in predominantly white neighborhoods were made up of almost 100 percent white residents.[9]

The real transformation of the public housing population in Boyle Heights did not occur until the collapse of support for public housing in Los Angeles from 1949 to 1953, when little new housing was being built and whites and Asians moved out of public housing in droves. During this period, the *Los Angeles Times* and the chamber of commerce attacked public housing as "communist," in a campaign that led to the defeat of pro–public housing mayor Fletcher Bowron and the election of *Times*-sponsored candidate Norris Poulson in 1953.[10] But overlooked in this transformation was the fate of thousands who already lived in public housing in Los Angeles built in the post–World War II era.

The most vulnerable public housing residents were often newcomers to the city, such as black migrants from the US South and former *braceros* from Mexico trying to establish more permanent roots in Los Angeles. One such

FIGURE 23. Children and parents pose during Cinco de Mayo celebration at Ramona Gardens, 1948. Housing Authority Photo Collection/Los Angeles Public Library.

family was the Crisostomos, who moved into Ramona Gardens in the mid-1950s, after having their application for public housing accepted. Paula, who was born in 1951, had an immigrant father from the Philippines who worked the graveyard shift as a janitor for the phone company. Through an acquaintance, her father, José Fumar, met Paula's mother Frances, a local US-born Mexican American woman, and they eventually married and would go on to have eight children of their own. Growing up in Boyle Heights, Paula remembers that "Ramona Gardens was very racially mixed.... There were lots of African American families, some Asian families and some white families, and of course a lot of Mexican families."[11] She remembers that her mother developed close friendships with several African American mothers in Ramona Gardens, one whom she called "Miss Dorothy" because that was a southern custom. Paula remembers families sharing and borrowing food from each other, especially because it was difficult to create nutritious meals on limited budgets since all the families were poor. "So it was a community, a family," as Paula remembered.[12]

This was also the period in Boyle Heights when African American residency was at its height, and several black high schoolers from the neighborhood became well known for their athletic achievements. Mike Garrett grew up in the Maravilla public housing during this period and would eventually letter in several sports at Roosevelt, graduating from high school in 1961. From there, he would make it to the University of Southern California, where he would become a star running back for the football team, emerging as the University of Southern California's first Heisman Trophy winner in 1965. Another stalwart in baseball and track at Roosevelt High School was Willie Davis, whose family had migrated to Estrada Courts from Arkansas. Davis would graduate from Roosevelt and sign with the Los Angeles Dodgers in 1958, becoming their starting center fielder for a 13-year period beginning in 1960 in the era of Hall of Famers Sandy Koufax, the left-handed "Left Hand of God" pitcher for the Dodgers (1955–66), and "Big D" Don Drysdale, who pitched his entire career for the Dodgers (1956–69) before becoming a sports commentator.

CIVIL RIGHTS AND MATERNAL INFLUENCES

The influence of African Americans on Boyle Heights was not limited to athletics but strongly affected attitudes toward self-worth, political activism, and racial pride amid the ongoing civil rights movement. For Mexican Americans, as for other Americans, much of this information was conveyed through television coverage in the living rooms throughout Boyle Heights. There they witnessed the violence directed at civil rights activists and the oppositional struggles waged by Martin Luther King Jr. and the college students in the Student Nonviolent Coordinating Committee (SNCC) as they worked to upend segregation in the American South. But many of the future student leaders of the Chicano Walkouts also remember political discussions with their families about the events taking place in the US during this period. Vickie Castro, for example, remembers family dinners in the early 1960s when she was a student at Roosevelt High School, where her father, Peter Castro, a foreman at a furniture factory, would gather her mom and her four brothers, as well as various uncles, around the dinner table and "always talk politics."[13]

Discussions surrounding the civil rights struggles of African Americans were often combined with other issues traditionally seen as central to the political lives of Mexican Americans in East Los Angeles, such as the fate of fellow Catholic and president John F. Kennedy. On a local level, Vickie Castro remembers that her "father talked about the Roybals a lot and we lived in the Roybal area," even though she often had "no interest in any of that as a teenager."[14] Beyond electoral politics, César Chávez had been selected as executive director of the Community Service Organization (CSO), and from 1958 to 1962 he and Dolores Huerta were organizing for the CSO in the Boyle Heights community, which was also the location of its national headquarters, to enact a more progressive agenda for local activists working to empower Mexican Americans in East Los Angeles.[15] Increasingly, political discussions among Boyle Heights families had to incorporate the changing landscape of racial justice that civil rights activism of the 1960s had introduced on a national scale, and children began to realize the fundamental changes that were unfolding in the United States because of the strength of the civil rights movement, as it affected both Mexican American and black young people.

Yet in almost all the families of future Chicano Walkout activists from Boyle Heights, the activist role of the mother was central to the political education of the children. Vickie Castro remembered her mother Carmen Chávez Castro as very active in the garment industry union when Vickie was a child in the 1950s, and she reported that she'd sometimes accompany her mother at the picket line. "All I can remember is 'Don't buy Judy Bond blouses,' that was the chant. I don't know who 'Judy Bond' was but I just remember they were all chanting—that was very significant in my mind."[16] The mother of Tanya Luna Mount, who was a junior high school student at Roosevelt during the 1968 Walkouts, was a union leader in the garment industry during the 1930s and 1940s. Julia had been involved in one of the largest massive walkouts and pickets in 1939 as part of the strike against the California Sanitary Canning Company (Cal San). She and her Anglo husband George got involved early in the black civil rights movement, the Mexican American Political Association (MAPA), and the Peace and Freedom Party (PFP), which advocated for farm workers, black liberation, women's liberation, and gay rights, and against the Vietnam War.[17] Many Boyle Heights students, especially the young women, first developed an interest in politics and activism through their mothers long before their own activist periods as students in the 1960s.

Paula Crisostomo's mother, Frances Crisostomo, had entered political activism through her work with black women organizers in the public housing and welfare rights battles in Ramona Gardens that pitted combative mayor Sam Yorty against the black and brown activists of Los Angeles. After moving to Long Beach for three years for her father's work, Paula remembers moving back to Ramona Gardens in 1964 with a new sense of purpose as she entered Lincoln High School.[18]

The Economic Opportunity Act of 1964 proposed by President Lyndon Johnson and passed by Congress set in motion Johnson's War on Poverty agenda, which introduced Head Start, Youth Corps, Job Corps, Work-Study, Volunteers in Service to America (VISTA), and the Community Action Program (CAP), among other programs. CAP was intended to foster "maximum feasible participation" among the poor in the implementation of programs to eradicate poverty from the United States. In other words, the stated goal was to have poor people represented on every committee set up to address poverty. The effect was a different story. Because of the struggle over its meaning in a local context, historian Kazuyo Tsuchiya believes that "Los Angeles was at the forefront of the antipoverty struggles of the 1960s."[19] Here local activists and Democratic congressmen, including Edward Roybal and Augustus "Gus" Hawkins, the first African American from California to serve in Congress (1963–91), challenged the Youth Opportunity Board (YOB), set up by Mayor Yorty in 1962, for control of funds for CAP in order to ensure participation by local antipoverty activists. Creating the Economic Opportunity Federation (EOF) in September 1964 in the wake of the passage of the act, these anti-Yorty forces enlisted civil rights leaders, including Anthony Rios of the CSO in Boyle Heights, to fight for expansion of participation of the poor through an organization called the Community Anti-Poverty Committee (CAPC).[20]

Frances Crisostomo was enlisted to participate in massive protest demonstrations on behalf of the poor, welfare activists, and public housing advocates in the summer of 1965, under the leadership of Reverend H. H. Brookins of the United Civil Rights Committee of Los Angeles. Over one year had passed since the enactment of the Economic Opportunity Act, and Los Angeles had still not received any War on Poverty funds because of its inability to create its own Community Action Agency. For all involved, the War on Poverty in Los Angeles had reached a crisis point, and both African American and Latino activists in public housing, stretching from South to East Los Angeles, were in the middle of the debate about the future of poverty programming in the region.[21]

In 1964, Paula Crisostomo entered Lincoln High School at age 13, and her personal experiences with racism would profoundly alter her outlook on student empowerment and civil rights. In the three years since her family had moved away from Ramona Gardens, she had what she refers to as "my enlightenment, my awakening."[22] Her family had moved to Long Beach both because of a job opportunity for her father and because of her parents' concern over the influence of gangs in East Los Angeles. Paula entered middle school there as one of the few Latinas in advanced courses and was subjected to anti-Latino comments from teachers and students. She became best friends with a white girl with the same initials as her, Paula Carson, who would invite her over to her house to watch television while her parents were away at work. When her friend finally invited her over on a weekend and she met Carson's parents, Crisostomo was told on Monday that "she couldn't hang around with me anymore 'cause her mother said I wasn't the right kind of girl for her." Once her former friend stopped talking to her, Paula Crisostomo marked that as "the day where it all came together." From that day forward she realized that she was discriminated against because of the color of her skin—a product of both "classism and racism."[23]

The Boyle Heights that Paula returned to in 1964 was becoming more Latino and African American. The changing demography of Boyle Heights led to radical shifts among the student population at Lincoln and Roosevelt High Schools and their feeder junior highs, which in turn fundamentally changed the context of racial interaction. Because of improved economic opportunities after World War II, Mexican-descent families more often kept their children in school after junior high, so by the 1950s Roosevelt's student body increasingly became Mexican. This development led its principal to suggest in 1955 that the high school should become primarily a vocational school, since most teachers, almost all white at the time, believed Mexican American children were never going to go on to college. Only interventions from the CSO and Lucille Beserra Roybal, wife of Councilman Edward Roybal, kept this from happening. Systematically placing Mexican American children into vocational programs continued and expanded in this period, as college prep courses were dominated by the remaining Jewish and Japanese students.[24] Such widespread discrimination against Latino children would lead directly to the complaints of student activists who organized the East

L.A. Walkouts, the Chicano Blowouts, of 1968. As two Roosevelt High School graduates, Ray Santana and Mario Esparza, expressed it, "Chicanos had reached the boiling point at which we could no longer tolerate the inferior quality of education which we were receiving and people decided to do something about it, which were the blowouts."[25]

For Mexican American children, staying in school through high school in this period often meant encountering greater gradations of racism as they moved up the educational ladder, especially for those in the college prep curriculum. For example, Vickie Castro was one of only four Chicanos in an advanced course, segregated from the vast majority of her friends, with whom she walked to school or hung out with in the neighborhood. This led her to ask, "How come our other friends aren't in our classes?" It also led Vickie to feel that she and the handful of Chicanos were "like the tokens in those rooms," which only reinforced that they "were different."[26]

While the white ethnics moved out in droves, many in the Japanese American community remained or supported the Japanese American institutions that endured in Boyle Heights, such as the Tenriyko Buddhist Church. Some learned to live within an increasingly Mexican-dominated community. Don Nakanishi, for example, the future director of UCLA's Asian-American Studies Center, was a Boyle Heights resident in the 1960s. His final years at Roosevelt High School are indicative of the transformations occurring in the Boyle Heights community. Although Mexican Americans formed a majority of the Roosevelt student population by the mid-1960s, they continued to be concentrated in non-college-track courses and were largely absent from extracurricular activities like student government. Launching his campaign for student body president in 1965, Nakanishi ran against one of the most popular Japanese American students in the school, a charismatic individual who would eventually become a Buddhist monk. Nakanishi devised a strategy of having a standard stump speech that he would deliver in English, Japanese, and Spanish, primarily to students taking courses in automotive repair, home economics, and other nonacademic subjects. These students, predominantly Mexican American, had never participated in student elections before but were moved enough by Nakanishi's trilingual appeal to vote for him. Although Don Nakanishi was elected as Roosevelt High School's new student body president, he would also be the last Asian American to hold that title, ending a string of nine consecutive Japanese Americans, as Mexican Americans now mobilized for participation and inclusion.[27]

As young Mexican American students became aware and endured the often-blatant racial discrimination from teachers and administrators, these experiences pushed them into student activism. In Vickie Castro's senior year at Roosevelt in the early 1960s she began to realize the prejudices that affected her educational future. Because she had two older brothers in college, had good grades, and had become involved in student government, Vickie went to see Mrs. Nichols, the college counselor, about applying to Mills College, an all-female Catholic college in Northern California. But Mrs. Nichols was discouraging. She told her: "Well, I think you should go to East L.A. [Community] College, and then if you do well, then you can go." Vickie remembers thinking, "She had my records. . . . She knew more about me than I knew about me. So, I thought I wasn't qualified.[28] It wasn't until later, when Vickie discussed this encounter with her other talented Chicana friends, that she realized that this was the standard "advice" Mrs. Nichols gave to all the Mexican American students regardless of their situations. With the help of her friends and without her counselor's assistance, Vickie figured out how to apply to California State University, Los Angeles, and was admitted to the then mostly white campus.[29] In the end, Vickie Castro was one of the fortunate students who actually went on to college. During the 1960s, Chicano youth had the highest dropout rates of any ethnic group, with over half of all Chicanos dropping out of high school by the time they reached 16 years of age. Moreover, of the Mexican American teenagers who did manage to graduate from high school in the Los Angeles Unified School District (LAUSD), only a quarter would attend college.[30]

As a senior, Vickie Castro was one of five Mexican American students from Roosevelt High School selected to attend the very first Mexican American Youth Leadership conference retreat at Camp Hess Kramer in the Malibu Mountains in 1963. These weekend retreats were begun by Rabbi Alfred Wolf, chair of the Los Angeles County Commission on Human Relations, and were often the first time any of the youth had ventured beyond downtown and East Los Angeles. Rabbi Wolf had administered Camp Hess Kramer for the Wilshire Boulevard Temple since 1952, and made it available for Mexican American high schoolers in Southern California to come together "for a weekend of introspection, growth, and leadership training." Tobias Kotzin, a Jewish trouser manufacturer who employed hundreds of Mexican American women at his Los Angeles factory, was the major financial sponsor.[31] The five from Roosevelt were all in student government and were selected by Mrs. Macias, the student government adviser, as part of her plan to nurture her students' leadership qualities. Mrs. Macias had herself participated in this retreat when she attended Sacred Heart Academy. After graduating from high school, Vickie Castro was selected to be a peer counselor for these retreats and would make the annual event a regular occurrence. After her second conference in 1964, a group from East Los Angeles met at Laguna Park and formed the Young Citizens for Community Action (YCCA), electing Vickie as the group's first president. The YCCA would focus on two issues, education and police brutality, and Vickie would concentrate on educational issues, serving on two or three advisory councils created by President Johnson's Title 1 initiative, a program to inject federal funds into the educational system to support low-income students in meeting their educational goals. Vickie focused on work at Malabar and Second Street elementary schools in Boyle Heights.[32]

THE WATTS RIOTS AND THE
RADICALIZATION OF YOUTH

Developments in the wider Los Angeles community transformed the political context for all youth of color in 1965. The arrest of 21-year-old African American motorist Marquette Frye on August 11, 1965, by a white highway patrol officer at 116th and Avalon near the Watts district of Los Angeles sparked an angry confrontation. It lasted for six days, changing the trajectory of racial organizing in Los Angeles, and led directly to a broad radicalization of urban youth. The Watts Riots would eventually leave 34 people dead, 1,032 injured, and 3,952 arrested, while damaging approximately 600 buildings and destroying $200 million in property. Moreover, it would fundamentally recast police-minority relations, amplifying the daily realities of vulnerable people in South and East Los Angeles as they faced an occupying army willing to brutalize young people of color. The Watts Riots invigorated the rise of black and ethnic nationalism across the country, while also generating a white backlash against urban politics and minority youth that stalled the War on Poverty efforts in Southern California.[33]

In the households of Boyle Heights, the sentiments toward the Watts Riots could vary tremendously. In the Crisostomo household, Paula describes her parents' "mixed reactions." Unlike the other civil rights issues covered on television, she explained, "The Watts Riots was very different because it was happening live and down the freeway." Paula recalled the strong sentiments of her parents: "My father said they were all breaking the law and deserved what they were getting. My mother didn't agree . . . [arguing] that the Los Angeles Police Department was out of line." But Paula's activist mother was careful never to contradict her husband directly, instead giving her dissenting opinion directly to Paula.[34]

These differences also marked varied reactions in the larger Los Angeles community. Everyone in city government blamed the lack of antipoverty funding in Los Angeles as a cause of high black unemployment in Watts and surrounding communities. But people focused their blame on different actors—the divisive mayor Sam Yorty, Congressman Gus Hawkins, a middle-class black leader who was represented as out of touch with the needs of poor, the federal government as represented by Sargent Shriver, to whom President Johnson had entrusted the federal government's antipoverty efforts as director of the newly created Office of Economic Opportunity (OEO). Councilman Tom Bradley harshly criticized Police Chief William Parker, as did Martin Luther King Jr. in his visit to Los Angeles after the riots. Bradley subsequently helped the city council establish a human relations board for the city. President Johnson dispatched representatives to force a compromise among city officials, and Leroy Collins, undersecretary of commerce, was able to get an agreement on a 25-person board, the Economic and Youth Opportunities Agency of Greater Los Angeles (EYOA), that would now govern antipoverty funds coming from the federal government. Within two weeks, the federal government approved the agreement and announced over $12 million in grants to Los Angeles.[35]

Mexican American youth and adults in East Los Angeles took note of the attention given to black grievances by the local and federal government and adopted more activist positions in their own attempt to combat poverty and address educational inequities in their neighborhoods. As teacher Sal Castro recalled, "Watts showed me that only dramatic action could capture the attention of officials and the public . . . [and] how far behind and how ignored were Mexican Americans and their problems."[36] The organization that Vickie Castro helped found changed its name from Young Citizens for Community Action to Young Chicanos for Community Action (remaining YCCA) and became more militant in its posture against police brutality and toward the Los Angeles Police Department (LAPD). When David Sánchez took over from Vickie Castro as president in 1965, one of the first groups he met with in 1966 were representatives of the Black Panthers, who embodied the revolutionary black nationalist ideology that was growing among African

American youth and served as an inspiration to Chicanos. Sánchez embraced the militant posture of the Panthers to create the Brown Berets, whose members wore uniforms and berets like the Panthers. This group recruited politically conscious Chicano youth from throughout East Los Angeles—some of whom were enrolled in college while others were full-time workers.[37]

In the fall of 1964 Paula Crisostomo had returned to Ramona Gardens and entered Lincoln High School, where she immediately felt more comfortable, made friends easily, and was put on the college preparatory track. She became class president and president of the girls' club and had mostly supportive teachers. But her harrowing experience in Long Beach had awakened her sense of the inequality embedded in the school districts of Southern California. "I had a different point of reference and I saw other schools. . . . I just knew that schools over at Long Beach looked a lot better than the school we have here." After the Watts Riots in August 1965, Paula met Sal Castro for the first time during her sophomore year, finding him charismatic and outgoing. Castro was the adviser to the boys' organization, so she interacted with him on the student council. When she found out that in her second semester of sophomore year she could do work for a teacher or counselor as an elective, Paula signed up to work for Sal Castro in his role as a guidance counselor.[38]

Sal Castro had begun his career as a social studies teacher at Belmont High School after a stint in the US Navy. He had long noticed how the educational system in LAUSD had mistreated Chicano/Latino youth, so he had made efforts to reach out to Mexican American students from the beginning. When he encouraged a Mexican American student running for student council to give her speech partially in Spanish because most students would interpret it as an act of pride, LAUSD transferred him, reassigning him to Lincoln High School.[39] Paula started working for Sal Castro in 1966 and probed him with lots of questions as he guided her toward more advanced reading that they would discuss. At one point, Paula remembers Castro handing her the 1948 classic *North from Mexico,* Carey McWilliams's multicultural antidote to the story of Los Angeles in which McWilliams points out, "Mexicans have never emigrated to the Southwest: they have returned."[40] From this interaction, Paula remembers, "I started putting the pieces together and connecting all the dots . . . not only racism but classism and everything else."[41]

Later that spring, Castro invited Paula to attend the Mexican American Youth Leadership weekend retreat, where she would meet Vickie Castro, other Mexican American college students, and high school leaders from throughout Southern California. By this point her mother was a volunteer with the Human Relations Commission, which facilitated her entry into the retreat, even though her father was still against her participation for fear "she would come home pregnant." According to Paula, attending the retreat was transformative: "To meet other bright students like me who were from all over, all over this part of the county was amazing. . . . I had no idea." Paula quickly joined the YCCA back home and began to join the protests against the Vietnam War and for the burgeoning United Farm Worker movement, with regular meetings at Obregon Park. Vickie Castro became a mentor for Paula, driving her to YCCA meetings with the support of her mother. By this time, Vickie had become a part-time student, a part-time worker, and a full-time activist, mentoring younger local organizers like Paula and Rachel Ochoa, a Roosevelt high school student. According to Vickie, it was a "sister-hood relationship" that extended to older women mentoring Vickie, including Paula's mother, who had a strong reputation as a community activist.[42]

The regular meetings of the YCCA at Obregon Park and the related discussions at Piranya Coffee House in a building on Olympic Boulevard and Atlantic Avenue were intense. The "coffeehouse" never actually had any food or drinks served; it was more of an open space with tables, chairs, and a jukebox to listen to music. The students would center their discussions on what was happening at their various high schools, involving both current high school students and recent graduates who were now at local colleges but who were invested in their home community's future. Paula Crisostomo remembers that everybody was "sort of saying the same thing. . . . Today we call them micro aggressions, you know . . . but a lot of macro aggressions too." She recalls telling others about how she had asked a question in geometry class at Lincoln and her teacher Mr. Thompson had responded very loudly so the whole class could hear: "Oh, come on, Paula. Why are you wasting my time? We all know you and your girlfriends are going to be pregnant before the end of the summer. You're not going to college. Why are you even in this class?" Because Paula had heard that all her life from her father, she had internalized that sentiment, but now she had a group where she felt comfortable to share her insecurities, as well as react to this act of verbal discrimination. For Paula, as for others in the group, teachers and counselors at their high schools, rather than offering information or encouragement, had discouraged and ridiculed them for even considering college.[43]

Vickie Castro remembers meeting Sal Castro for the first time at a meeting at Father Luce's Church of the Epiphany when he came to discuss how their community was negatively portrayed in an article in *Time* magazine that had described their streets as smelling like wine. Castro encouraged them to demonstrate against these kinds of descriptions and to show that they were more than that by getting a college education. Through the YCCA the young people received summer training in organizing, including a guest lecture by César Chávez, who was then leading the United Farm Workers (UFW) battle against grape growers in the San Joaquin Valley, and who spoke to them about his organizing techniques. They put these tactics in motion, as some of the students joined picket lines with the UFW during the summer of 1967, while others protested against the Vietnam War by picketing the local army recruiting center.[44]

While being trained as activists, the high school students were also all campus leaders who believed that they could improve their schools and provide important information to local leaders, so they collectively decided to develop a survey to be distributed at each East Los Angeles high school. The 1967 Camp Hess Kramer meeting generated that idea, and they met consistently in 1967, organizing the survey, conducting it at their individual high school, and analyzing its results, which detailed a pattern of constant racial discrimination against Mexican American students by teachers and counselors. The first people they approached with the results of their surveys were their high school principals, because, as Paula Crisostomo makes clear, they believed that the principals would say, "You guys are right! We're going to get rid of these racist teachers." Instead, the schools' leadership attempted to pacify them, saying how smart they were and that they should keep going, without any action or accountability on the schools' end. The students then talked to elected officials about their survey results, including members of the Los Angeles School Board, and received a similar reaction. Their growing frustration at not being taken seriously at their schools and in their communities led them to consider more activist measures by the end of academic year in 1968.[45]

THE WALKOUTS AND THE RISE OF REBELLION

As they pondered their next move, everyone agreed that they had to attract significant media attention to the issues they had uncovered in their survey and the daily injustices and acts of discrimination they had all faced in their high schools. Sal Castro argued that the only way to get the attention of those in power was to cause a stir, and he understood that it had to be "something dramatic, like Watts."[46] But both Castro and the student leaders were fearful that they could be susceptible to the same violent response from the LAPD that it had showed the young protesters in Watts. So the students agreed on a peaceful protest that they believed would get maximum attention. With the knowledge that school funding was dependent on enrollment for each day, the students came up with the idea of a mass walkout from their schools before daily attendance was taken. The Walkout then would grab the attention of school board officials and school administrators because it would affect capital and the resources allocated to each school.

Sal Castro hoped that the warning of a massive walkout would be enough to get the attention of local officials and that the threat itself would not have to be carried out. He pushed the organizers to schedule the potential Walkout for late in the school year in May near final exams in order to minimally disrupt the education of the students.[47] The college students who were involved in the planning were more anxious to see the Walkouts happen because they hoped that these efforts would help the overall Chicano empowerment movement that was growing inside universities. In the time leading up to the Walkouts, Vickie Castro, for example, had seen the creation of the United Mexican American Students (UMAS) organization at Cal State Los Angeles and other Southern California colleges. During that academic year, the Movimiento Estudiantil Chicano de Aztlán (MEChA) began to replace the various UMAS chapters as one way in which college students were getting more emboldened for direct action. Already anticipating widespread police suppression, older graduates who had joined the Brown Beret chapters were willing to offer protection to the younger students and to be buffers between them and the police.[48]

The high school students had organized themselves into school committees, and each one had specific responsibilities for spreading the word among other high school students, drawing posters, and relegating roles for the day of the action. Very quickly word spread to high schools outside East Los Angeles regarding the plan, and other students saw the action as a call for student empowerment in their schools as well. The main group of organizers met with representatives from high schools from South Los Angeles at Café Piranya and agreed to coordinate their actions. African American student leaders from Jefferson High School and Jordan High School had long had open communication with their counterparts from Roosevelt and Lincoln High Schools, and this was a continuation of these efforts. More surprising was the interest of a few schools from West Los Angeles, especially Hamilton High School, where students agreed to walk out in coordination with the students from East Los Angeles.

FIGURE 24. High school students walk out and march across Breed Street in Boyle Heights, March 1968. La Raza Collection, UCLA Chicano Studies Research Library.

Despite months of careful planning, unanticipated events pushed the organizers to launch the Walkouts early. The principal at Wilson High School canceled a school play production of *Barefoot in the Park*, in which several Mexican American students were scheduled to perform, because he found the play sexually inappropriate. The committee at Wilson decided to walk out in protest, early, on Friday, March 1, 1968. Then, encouraged by the action at Wilson, students at Garfield High School walked out on Tuesday, March 5.[49] The student committees from the other schools, along with Sal Castro, decided that they had to take advantage of the momentum generated by the successful Walkouts at Wilson and Garfield and scheduled the other schools to do a walkout the very next day.

Vickie Castro was selected to go to Lincoln High School to meet with the principal that morning on the pretext of applying for a teacher assistant position. Because she was seen as "someone who is going to pass and not be threatening," her job was to set up an appointment with the principal, go that morning to his office, and keep him busy. So Vickie got dressed up in her nicest outfit and went that morning for the interview. As the principal came out of his office, he said, "I will be right with you, young lady," but he kept going in and out of his office, saying, "I just have to check on this." He led her into his office from the waiting area, then had to excuse himself, but was eventually forced to come back to his office because Vickie was in there wait-ing. Both were performing, trying not to let the other in on what was unfold-ing outside the office among students—a situation Vickie remembers as "a little comical."[50] Those minute-long delays in the schedule of the principal that morning, facilitated by Vickie's presence, allowed for greater participa-tion in the Walkouts by Lincoln students.

As the beginning of this chapter makes clear, Paula Crisostomo was part of the core group at Lincoln High School, and her job was to shout "Walkout" at 8:30 a.m., bringing as many other fellow students with her as possible. College students familiar with Lincoln were to be in the hallways at that time to help the high school students lead all students out of school. The college students were on the stairwells and banging items against the walls to make noise and attract attention from the other students. Once they were outside, picket signs were available, and the group marched in front of the school for about an hour before heading home. When the second walkout from Lincoln happened the next day, the group was more organized and marched to the regional offices of the LAUSD in Hazard Park.[51]

Importantly, Paula Crisostomo admitted that at the time she did not consider herself a leader of the Walkout committee, even though she was the only young woman who was part of the rotation of chairs for the Lincoln strike committee. Few women in 1968 were willing to speak in front of cam-eras or at a rally, and most were in the background support teams, reflecting how gender has often constructed visibility in activism.[52] Her good friend and fellow Lincoln High School alumna Moctezuma Esparza, who had graduated from Lincoln one year prior as class valedictorian and was now a first-year student at UCLA, became the assigned media liaison for the whole Walkout coordinating committee.[53]

The Walkouts were scheduled across the high schools in a rolling fashion and lasted over ten days. On March 6, in addition to key East Los Angeles high schools, Jefferson High School in South Los Angeles and Hamilton High School in West Los Angeles also mobilized a large percentage of stu-dents to walk out in support of student empowerment in LAUSD. Roosevelt High School went out later in the day on March 6, but by this time the LAPD was ready, deploying a greater police presence focused on blocking non–high school students from entering the campus and keeping high school students inside the buildings. Indeed, the strike committee itself had antici-pated more significant repression and violence at Roosevelt because of its large black population.[54]

FIGURE 25. Student marching outside Roosevelt High School raises his fist in solidarity, March 1968. Photograph by Devra Weber. La Raza Collection, UCLA Chicano Studies Research Library.

Their prediction was correct. According to Sal Castro, the Roosevelt principal, William Dyer, had communicated with the nearby Hollenbeck Division of the LAPD to help him keep the students locked into the school to prevent them from walking out. As discussed in previous chapters of this book, the Hollenbeck Division had one of the worst reputations for violence against Mexican Americans in the city.[55] A tactical unit of forty officers entered the campus wearing riot gear with their batons drawn. Because the gates were closed and locked, some students tried to jump the fences, and Vickie Castro helped pull one fence down with her car. As the high school students emerged from the campus, police started to swing their batons, hitting them mercilessly, while arresting others who were caught in the melee nearby.[56]

The next day, Thursday March 7, Garfield walked out again and was joined by Belmont High School for the first time. Then on Friday, March 8, the largest coordinated Walkout occurred, with Lincoln, Roosevelt, and Garfield all walking out at the same time, totaling about 5,000 students. Many of the students were instructed to meet at Hazard Park, where they heard from a multitude of strike leaders but also from elected officials, who had begun to take notice of the enormous organized action. These included school board members, such as Julian Nava, as well as Congressman Roybal. The students

FIGURE 26. Students locked inside Roosevelt High School gates while others march outside, March 1968. La Raza Collection, UCLA Chicano Studies Research Library.

insisted that they meet with the school board in its entirety to discuss their demands. Ironically, the student leaders met every night that week with Sal Castro to try to identify what their demands even were, given the fact that the Walkout was happening two months ahead of schedule. Over the weekend, the strike committee heard that this meeting had been granted for Monday, March 11, and there were no more scheduled Walkouts from any school. The students, in short, had won their argument to be heard by the school board.[57]

The student demands, which were handed to the school board that Monday, listed solutions to the long-standing grievances that Mexican American activists had experienced as part of their substandard schooling in the LAUSD. The students demanded compulsory bilingual/bicultural education to be provided and requested that all administrators and staff become proficient in Spanish. They wanted relevant textbooks and curricula, and they demanded that Mexican American administrators be appointed at schools where Mexican American students were in the majority. A structure of teacher accountability was also high on their list, including the publication of "every teacher's ratio of failure per students in his classroom," as well as the removal of all administrators and teachers who displayed prejudice against

Mexican or Mexican American students. Students demanded an end to corporal punishment and to being tasked with janitorial duties at schools. They also wanted school facilities to be open to community activities and sought to have parents as teacher's aides. Students requested that vocational programs be updated, library facilities be expanded, and new high schools and junior high schools be built to reduce overcrowding on the Eastside. Most importantly, they demanded immunity: no student or teacher should be reprimanded or suspended for participating in efforts to improve educational quality through the Walkouts.[58]

AFTERMATH: TOWARD THE *MOVIMIENTO*, NATIONALISM, AND MIXED FUTURES

At this point, most histories on the Chicano Walkouts turn their attention away from the high school student activists and toward "the grownups" who took over the movement. Indeed, parental involvement increased with the growing role of the Educational Issues Coordinating Committee (EICC), and then with the firing of Sal Castro as the chief instigator behind the Walkouts. Two months later, when the FBI arrested and charged 13 non–high school activists with conspiracy, the focus was on Castro, older Brown Berets members, and the college organizers who were critical to the buildup of the March Chicano Walkouts. All 13 of those arrested were male and over eighteen years old, and their defense dominated the direction of the Walkout demands, as did the reinstatement of Sal Castro to his faculty position. In many ways, the defense of Castro and the East L.A. 13 reoriented the movement away from the local high schools and toward the growth of a larger, more radical movement for Chicano nationalism and ethnic identity formation.

The upsurge of racial pride that was generated by the East L.A. Walkouts, as well as the defense momentum, led the nascent movement toward a broader "Brown Power" and cultural nationalism. Even though the Brown Berets did not directly participate in the planning of the Walkouts, they "gained wide notoriety" for their protection of the student organizers from the LAPD, especially after five of their members were arrested and indicted by the L.A. County Grand Jury for felonies for conspiracy to disrupt public schools.[59] By March 1969, 1,500 Chicano youth from Los Angeles and all over the Southwest gathered in Denver, Colorado, for the first-ever Chicano Youth Liberation Conference, consolidating the goals of the movement under a document entitled "El Plan Espiritual de Aztlán," which presented the call for self-determination and advocated "nationalism" as the means to secure complete control of Chicano neighborhoods.[60] As the movement turned toward cultural nationalism, it also increasingly focused on opposition to Chicano participation in the Vietnam War, particularly among the youth, and this led directly to the Vietnam Moratorium Movement in Los Angeles, beginning in December 1969. Eventually the largest Chicano demonstration against the war, on August 29, 1970, would involve upwards of 30,000 participants, who were met with violent attacks by the Los Angeles Sheriff's Department in East Los Angeles' Laguna Park and the murder of journalist Ruben Salazar on Whittier Boulevard later that day.[61]

But I want to return to the meaning of the Walkout activities for the high school students involved, partly because it clarifies the local conditions facing high school activists. The weekend after the March 8 Walkout at every East Los Angeles high school, which all the participants agreed was the height of achievement for the Walkout Movement, was monumental for the main high school leaders because presidential candidate Robert F. Kennedy reached out to support and actually meet them during a layover at Los Angeles Airport when he was on his way to break a fast with labor leader César Chávez in Delano, California (a 25-day water-only protest fast that was part of his non-violent approach to gaining attention for migrant workers' rights). After grassroots community leaders sponsored a 500-person support rally for the student Walkouts at Obregon Park on Sunday afternoon, about 15 students were whisked away to the VIP section of the Los Angeles airport for the impromptu meeting. Kennedy met with the students for over an hour and told them he supported them because their cause was just. Harry Gamboa from Garfield High School remembers that "he was very generous with his words and offered us public support."[62] Sal Castro believed that because a major national leader "had the guts to publicly endorse their actions," it validated them, including in front of their parents. "It was a moment that none of them has ever forgotten."[63] Indeed, Paula Crisostomo could remember details of the encounter almost fifty years later: "He had a poster of Benito Juarez; he got off the plane and came down the stairs and we were taken to a small room. He had a farmworker button on. He was very well prepared, he knew all about the Walkouts, he asked us about our demands, he asked us how it was going. Made some small talk, said he really liked what we were doing, supported us, but he had to leave. We got a couple of photo opportunities. It was very exciting."[64]

FIGURE 27. Paula Crisostomo meets Robert F. Kennedy with other Walkout Leaders at L.A. Airport, March 10, 1968. With permission of Paula Crisostomo.

Despite this significant endorsement, it was not easy for the high school students to return to school and their daily lives, or to deal with the negative comments from teachers and classmates, after all that positive excitement. Paula remembers, "It was pretty crazy at the same time. I'm trying to graduate wondering what I'm going to do after I graduate. Plus, I'm still working, and I'm still going to class, right after the Walkouts." Fellow students were telling her, "I can't hang out with you anymore. My mom said you are a communist, so I can't be your friend anymore." Even her parents began receiving threatening phone calls late at night questioning their parenting behavior, which stirred internal tensions between them and drove her father to drink again. Paula received snide comments from teachers who thought that the students' actions were unnecessary, as well as from college counselors who told her that there was no money for her to go to college. Though Paula was the class valedictorian with the highest GPA at Lincoln High School—and though she had fought for greater college access as part of the demands of the Chicano Walkouts—Paula herself had not made any plans to apply for college at that point and was planning to attend the local community college.[65]

It is difficult to fathom how quickly the world was changing in the spring of 1968, and this pace of change could be disorienting. The Vietnam War was dramatically expanding and its violence increasing, which led to a disappointing finish for President Johnson in the New Hampshire primary and the announcement later that month, on March 31, 1968, that he would not seek reelection. Five days later, on April 4, 1968, Martin Luther King Jr. was assassinated, sending many urban communities throughout the United States into an uproar of flames and violence. As Paula Crisostomo was preparing for her senior prom as prom chair, the East L.A. 13 were arrested on the evening of May 31, forcing Sal Castro to miss the big dance as a volunteer chaperone. Paula turned 18 on June 6, 1968, the day after Robert F. Kennedy was shot and killed in Los Angeles after winning the California Democratic presidential primary. On June 6, Sal Castro and his wife came by Paula's house with birthday flowers and discussed "what a great president he would have been." At her graduation later that month, Paula delivered a speech, which she had written with help from her mother, through her own research, and from the inspiration and legacy of Martin Luther King Jr., and quoted the profound poem by Langston Hughes about "a dream deferred."[66]

Even after graduation, Paula's future was still unclear, and it took intervention from Moctezuma Esparza, the previous year's valedictorian from Lincoln High School, who lived right outside Ramona Gardens in Boyle Heights and had just completed his first year at UCLA. During the summer of 1968, he sat Paula down at her kitchen table with her mother, had Paula complete the UCLA application, and submitted it for her. As Paula admitted, "I didn't believe it for myself, I didn't believe that this could happen to me." Her father was fuming in a nearby room because he didn't want Paula to go to a school that was so far away. At UCLA, Paula remembers a difficult transition to being "the only dark-skinned girl" on her dorm floor and feeling less academically prepared than others. She got involved with MEChA, though she felt burnt out by her earlier activism, and eventually graduated with a degree in Chicano studies. Ironically, Paula felt that none of the student demands were met at East L.A. high schools, and it wasn't until the making of the movie *Walkout!* in the 1980s that she realized that others saw them as pioneers of the Chicano Movement.[67]

Student activists who were not yet seniors during the Walkouts had similarly difficult transitions. Seventeen-year-old Harry Gamboa was in a reflective mood when he applied in the spring of 1969 to East Los Angeles Community College through its Equal Opportunity Program (EOP). His application essay for the EOP program indirectly addressed his experiences as one of a handful of high school student leaders who had organized the first significant urban uprising among Mexican American youth in the United States. Gamboa, then a senior at Garfield High School in East Los Angeles, would eventually go on to a stellar career as a leading artist of the Chicano Movement in the 1970s and 1980s, but at this moment as a teenager he was still full of angst about his future and doubts about his role as a youth organizer of an urban rebellion.

"I am the oldest of my two brothers and two sisters," Gamboa wrote, beginning his essay. "My parents usually seem confused about the schools that their children attend . . . [and] see these institutions [as] too powerful to be criticized or condemned." Gamboa articulated that his parents, despite their "limited education," had kept them in school, encouraging their children "to go on with whatever we are . . . interested in." Gamboa went on to describe his own political involvement of the previous year as driven by the fact he "was deeply bothered and disgusted with the condition of his community and of Mexican-American people." He explained how he had gotten involved with a few committees and organizations, drawing for a newspaper called the *Chicano Student News,* and had eventually become the vice president of the Walkout committee of Garfield High School. In this work, "I learned to distrust and dislike everything that was pro-establishment." Although Gamboa confessed he had given these organizations priority over his high school education, he began to wonder, "Who would listen to a high school dropout?" This thinking changed his opinion of his potential college future from "a place where people would go and get their minds reshaped and processed to a point where White America would partially accept them in the mainstream" to a space that could enlarge his "general knowledge of life" and provide an education in subjects he knew little about. In this way, he rethought his attitude toward his future, and he admitted that he no longer belonged to any of his previous committees.[68]

At this point in his life, Gamboa had decided that he wanted to go to college so that he would "be able to come back to my community to teach and use all of my knowledge to help the people of my community, especially the students." When he was a high school senior his major interest was in music, though he admitted to interests in psychology and sociology as well. Though his grades had admittedly not always been high, and he had had trouble with some of his teachers, he had established himself as a committed reader. Gamboa hoped that EOP would give him access to a college education that would eventually get him back to the community he was committed to helping: East Los Angeles.

Harry Gamboa, like the other East Los Angeles youth who led and participated in the March 1968 Chicano Walkouts, was profoundly transformed by the political activity and the organizational skills he had developed while launching the urban Chicano Movement in Los Angeles. The students' personal futures, as well as their continued impact on East Los Angeles, would become clearer and mature over time as they entered adulthood and became the first professional class of Chicano college graduates. But as young adults, they had a difficult time realizing the influence they already possessed and the collective power they had displayed in 1968.

In short, the 1968 Chicano Walkouts marked an important transition in the growth of Boyle Heights, its racial relations, and its impact on the emerging empowerment movement of Mexican Americans in Los Angeles. The population of Boyle Heights increasingly became majority Latino like the rest of East Los Angeles. However, a changing population meant new tensions would now emerge between those second- and third-generation Mexican Americans and the newly arrived immigrants from Mexico and Central America. The Chicano urban movement spawned by the high school student activists would become an antiwar movement in East Los Angeles through the Chicano Moratorium Committee and would connect with other urban empowerment efforts of Chicanos throughout the Southwest during the 1970s.

Most writing on the East Los Angeles Walkouts of 1968 frames these events as the first major urban uprising of Chicana/os, shifting the center of activism from the countryside to the city. As historian Mario García analyzes this shift, political fronts would spread from "school protests such as the blowouts" to "the student movement in the universities, including the development of Chicano Studies; the Chicano antiwar movement; welfare rights struggles; the organization of La Raza Unida Party, an independent Chicano political party; the immigrant rights movement; and the origins of Chicana feminism; as well as many other more localized issues in numerous communities."[69] Moreover, this literature tends to credit the Walkouts with a rise in ethnic pride in the Mexican American community that would translate itself directly into the growth of Chicano cultural nationalism, primarily leading to the famous 1969 "Plan Espiritual de Aztlán," written the following year by the poet Alurista. Because the Walkouts led to the arrest of the all-male East L.A. 13 and the firing and then reinstatement of Sal Castro, the movement is too often remembered as inspired and spearheaded by male Chicanos alone.

But the actual origins of the 1968 East Los Angeles Walkouts lay in the discriminatory nature of the education system that was experienced by Mexican Americans, African Americans, and other students of color in Los Angeles. The Walkouts were the result of a multiracial effort to bring equity to the school system in Southern California. High school activists, both young women and men, drew from their own backgrounds growing up in Boyle Heights and East Los Angeles and from what they learned from the advanced civil rights movement, the Watts Riots, and the local efforts for racial justice that stretched across Mexican American and African American communities. And, as a movement for student justice, the Walkouts coupled with the parallel legal effort that was taking place to desegregate the Los Angeles school system.[70] Thus the Walkouts sprang from the larger efforts for racial justice in education that were being promoted by both Mexican Americans and African Americans in Boyle Heights. Even though developments after 1968 often led Chicano activists to reframe these efforts as emerging solely from Chicano history and ideologies, it was multiracial social justice organizing that propelled the student activists to demand dignity and fight for respect and equality.

NINE

Creating Sanctuary

IN MANY WAYS, GLORIA MOLINA should be considered part of the generation that came of age during the Chicano Movement, but her political context differed greatly, amid the rise of undocumented residents in Boyle Heights. Molina was born in 1948 in Montebello, California, the oldest of ten children. Her Mexican borderlands family had moved back and forth between Casas Grandes, Chihuahua, and Boyle Heights since the 1920s. In 1966, Molina graduated from El Rancho High School in Pico Rivera, about 11 miles from downtown L.A. in the San Gabriel Valley.[1] She worked full time as a legal secretary in a downtown Los Angeles law firm while attending night classes at East L.A. College in the early 1970s. As a night student, she learned about the issues confronting Chicano students and decided to volunteer at a student tutoring program at Maravilla public housing. At first, Molina "felt like they were just like me," but as she got to know them more, she admitted, "I didn't realize how huge their problems were, how big they were, how different they were from my family."[2]

Molina would rise in the political worlds of East Los Angeles after these humble beginnings, but the Boyle Heights that shaped her political ascent was different from the one that created the East Los Angeles Walkouts and the Chicano Moratorium. In 1970, in the thick of the Chicano Movimiento in East Los Angeles, it appeared to many outsiders that Boyle Heights was a unified community made up of exclusively Mexican Americans who had coalesced under the Chicano banner. While Molina was clearly influenced by the social and political lessons of the Chicano Movement, her political beginnings were also influenced by the changing dynamics of immigration and citizenship in Boyle Heights. And the rest of her career would be molded by Boyle Heights' growing undocumented population.

Gender discrimination at work, as well as nativist attacks on women's bodily autonomy, especially around the systematic sterilization of women who primarily spoke Spanish, led Gloria Molina to embrace politics and become president of the Los Angeles chapter of the Comisión Femenil Mexicana Nacional (CFMN), an organization dedicated to empowering Chicana women.[3] Elected to the California State Assembly in 1982, she also served on the Los Angeles City Council and, for 23 years, the Los Angeles Board of County Supervisors. On the board, she instituted programs that brought the high school graduation rates of children in foster care up from 58 percent to 80 percent, among many other accomplishments. She was also supportive of the efforts of the Mothers of East Los Angeles (MELA) to block the building of prisons on Santa Fe Avenue. She retired from the board because of term limits in 2014 and was awarded an honorary doctorate in humane letters from Whittier College.

At precisely the moment that generational mobility was taking hold in Boyle Heights, the economic rug was pulled out from under the community. Traditional industrial employment collapsed, and smaller scale, sweatshop-oriented, nonunionized manufacturing, particularly in textile production, replaced highly skilled union work.[4] These new employers were not interested in the solidly working-class Mexican American generation of union workers that had emerged after World War II, nor were they interested in the college-educated Chicano generation beginning to take shape after 1970. They wanted a steady stream of low-wage, often undocumented and exploitable, workers who were wary of organized labor. As urban planners Paul Ong and Evelyn Blumenberg put it, "Los Angeles, therefore, simultaneously underwent both industrial contraction and expansion."[5]

Over the next thirty years, Boyle Heights would undergo rapid and dramatic demographic transformation. Long-standing residents moved out and up to new Latino suburbs in eastern Los Angeles County, while immigrant newcomers from Mexico and other parts of Latin America poured in. The incorporation of undocumented immigrants into the Boyle Heights neighborhood would determine whether Boyle Heights could once again claim to be a "diverse community." With a well-established reputation for civic empowerment, new democratic practices emerged outside electoral politics to pull together different generations of Latinos, without regard to citizenship or legal status. These new ideas reconstructed "community" in Boyle Heights in ways that were unique to match the late twentieth-century political moment but that also built upon past histories of social movements in the area. Grassroots organizations developed that challenged the local political elite, often drawing the wrath of the larger society bent on slowing the entry of undocumented workers. This was the Boyle Heights that shaped the political rise of those like Gloria Molina in a changing Los Angeles—a Boyle Heights that would chart new ground because of the profound economic changes in the region and the newfound emphasis on the privileges of citizenship and legal entry.

ECONOMIC AND DEMOGRAPHIC TRANSFORMATIONS

After nearly 50 years of producing tires in the city of Commerce near East Los Angeles, the Uniroyal tire plant alongside the Santa Ana Freeway shut down and was boarded up in 1978. The imposing factory had been built just before the Great Depression to resemble an Assyrian palace full of turrets and a stylized façade to display the permanence of mighty industrial production with a Hollywood flair. Although it would be resurrected in 1990, ironically as the "Citadel," its closure in 1978 symbolized the collapse of auto manufacturing in Southern California. In its heyday, after World War II, the Los Angeles region was second to Detroit in this industry.[6]

Massive plant closures represented the rapid restructuring of industry that took place in South and East Los Angeles throughout the 1970s and 1980s. Between 1978 and 1982, five of six major auto assembly plants in California closed.[7] And when Bethlehem Steel shut down in the city of Vernon in December 1982, just south of Boyle Heights, over 2,000 men and women lost their jobs.[8] More than 70,000 well-paid mostly union jobs vanished between 1978 and 1983, 75 percent of local employment in the auto and aircraft industries.[9]

These industrial plants had been the heart of the Los Angeles labor movement and were critical to neighborhood empowerment, as exemplified by the union-trained leadership of the Community Service Organization (CSO) of the late 1940s and 1950s. It was these labor activists who trained and influenced their children to lead the Chicano Movement in the 1960s. However, while the Chicano Movement exploded in Boyle Heights and East Los Angeles after the 1968 Walkouts, many newcomers to Boyle Heights had little connection to the burgeoning Chicano Movimiento.

The transformation of the relationship between Mexican laborers and US labor opportunities would also have a profound effect on Boyle Heights in the last third of the twentieth century. In 1964, the US ended the Bracero Program, which had been originally instituted to counteract the labor shortages of World War II.[10] Four and a half million temporary workers, mostly seasonal farmhands, had come to the US as part of the program. The passage of the Immigration and Nationality Act of 1965 replaced the Bracero Program and for the first time set limits on the number of Latin American immigrants allowed to legally enter the United States. As a result, the number of Mexican citizens apprehended in the US for crossing without legal approval rose exponentially for the next two decades, from 55,340 in 1965 to 277,377 in 1970, and to a peak of 1,671,458 in 1986, a 3,000 percent overall increase. Some have estimated that approximately 28 million Mexicans entered the United States without papers between 1965 and 1986, compared to 1.3 million legal immigrants and 46,000 contract workers.[11]

California, and specifically Los Angeles, received the bulk of these workers. The cities and neighborhoods east and south of downtown Los Angeles became magnets for undocumented immigrants because of the low-wage job opportunities available in these reindustrialized areas and the increasingly accessible housing options in these neighborhoods. Much scholarly attention has been paid to the Latinization of southeastern Los Angeles County as white union workers moved out and newcomers, who often lacked papers, arrived from Mexico, and to a lesser extent, El Salvador and Guatemala.[12] However, the transformation of Boyle Heights and the rest of East Los Angeles is often overlooked because it involved long-term Mexican American residents moving out and new immigrants from Latin America moving in. In other words, the significant turnover was masked by the similar racialization of those leaving and entering. The 1970 US Census, for example, reported that only 46.6 percent of Boyle Heights' 82,000 residents were living in the same home as they had in 1965.[13] Indeed, the 1979 Boyle Heights Community Plan, prepared by the Department of City Planning for Los Angeles, discussed the unknown population of the neighborhood in this way: "These figures are the official estimates of population based on the 1970 Census, plus the Census undercount. These figures do not include a 1976 'estimate' of undocumented aliens which may range as high as 100,000 for this community, based on extrapolation of data from the Immigration and Naturalization Service."[14]

This demographic transition had profound implications on electoral politics and voter lists in Boyle Heights during the late 1960s and 1970s. The Ninth District that Edward Roybal had represented on the Los Angeles City

Council encompassed downtown Los Angeles, including Boyle Heights, and ended just north of Watts. When Roybal became a US congressman in 1962, District 9 elected Gilbert Lindsay, the first black council member. City Councilman Arthur Snyder, a fiery redhead of Irish descent, objected to a new reapportionment plan for 1970 because it linked the majority–Mexican American Boyle Heights (removing it from Gilbert Lindsay) with his mostly white Eagle Rock 14th council district. Although the new district was 68 percent Mexican American, 40 percent of those residents were noncitizens and could not vote. Even in the hotly contested 1969 mayoral race between Tom Bradley and Sam Yorty, only 13,618 residents of Boyle Heights were registered to vote, a strong indication of how few residents were eligible. Eagle Rock had more registered voters than Boyle Heights, even though its total resident population was under 29,000, or about one-third of the total resident population of Boyle Heights.[15]

This transformation of the resident Boyle Heights population in the late 1960s and 1970s was a function of many factors. The opening of suburbs in eastern Los Angeles County to Mexican Americans and the earlier exodus of Jews and other white ethnics from Boyle Heights allowed many to turn single-family homes into multiple rental units.[16] It was common for a former house built for a single family to be reconfigured with separate entrances to accommodate multiple renters on both the first and second floors. By 1970, these configurations led housing units in Boyle Heights to be 24.9 percent owner occupied: in other words, three-fourths of all residences in the neighborhood were occupied by renters.[17] In addition, actual apartment buildings and the public housing units in Boyle Heights had relatively rapid turnover, making them more available to newcomers. Finally, Boyle Heights was an overwhelmingly Spanish-speaking community, making it attractive to newcomers from Mexico or Latin America, many of whom were undocumented workers.

LIVING UNDOCUMENTED IN BOYLE HEIGHTS

In her book *Undocumented Lives,* which frames recent undocumented migration, historian Ana Raquel Minian has argued that migration from Mexico in this period was deeply gendered. "In the years between 1965 and 1986, approximately 80 percent of border crossers were men who left their families as part of a circular migration," with the majority of undocumented male migrants returning to Mexico within two years of their departure.[18]

These men frequently supported their families and communities with wages from the United States and had strong ties to US employers. A mobile, supportive community like Boyle Heights provided a secure landing place for migrants, but also an easy location to return to after a sojourn back from their native town or village.

Indeed, Minian makes clear that since the mid-1960s Boyle Heights has played a critical role in encouraging these Mexican male migrants to form *clubes sociales* (social clubs) to collectively send money to their hometowns. In the 1960s, about 30 percent of all Mexican migrants in the US moved to Los Angeles, and most club activists lived and worked in the Eastside enclaves of Boyle Heights, Lincoln Heights, and East Los Angeles. As one club from Zacatecas got established, others formed and began to meet at La Casa del Mexicano, a large building in eastern Boyle Heights bought by a Mexican charity organization, the Comité de Beneficencia Mexicana. By 1968, at least 20 clubs regularly met there, with an average of 35 members per club. The clubs organized lively parties on the weekends to raise funds, initially to aid needy individuals back home, but eventually to bankroll major infrastructure projects, such as hospitals and schools.[19]

The success of the *clubes sociales* gradually began to shift family orientation for these Mexican male migrants northward across the border. First, women were more likely to migrate to cities like Los Angeles than to other, more isolated areas of the United States. In one study of Mexican migrants from Las Animas, Zacatecas, 38 percent of urban migrants in Los Angeles were women, significantly higher than in smaller towns in the US.[20] Second, the men who started the social clubs in Boyle Heights and who were most active in the *clubes sociales* were more likely to be married and have families in the United States. According to Minian, initial activities by the *clubes sociales* tended to be "familial affairs"—because that was what attracted others to come—where women cooked and donated food that was sold to single men to raise money. As Minian states, "Most of the individuals who formed part of the club world had already established deep roots in the United States."[21] Third, these club activists became models for the other men who joined the *clubes sociales,* thereby encouraging them to bring their wives to Los Angeles. By the early 1970s, many Mexican migrant men had moved their families to Boyle Heights and had begun new lives as undocumented families north of the border; they were unlikely to return to Mexico unless deported.

The formation of families north of the border led to greater permanence of the undocumented in Boyle Heights; however, the shift of undocumented workers from primarily agricultural employment in the early 1960s to more urban employment and higher visibility by 1970 put Boyle Heights at the center of the growing anti-immigrant hostility. While the reaction against undocumented Mexican workers in the 1970s was connected to past forms of discrimination, a new virulence emerged in the post–civil rights era that included anti-Latino sentiment more broadly.

One of the earliest anti-immigrant and racist backlashes against Mexican undocumented workers came from within an encroaching Boyle Heights institution: the University of Southern California-Los Angeles (USC-LA) County Medical Center (LACMC). LACMC's partnership with the University of Southern California for the provision of medical care began in 1885 with a 100-bed hospital. It expanded with the opening of County General Hospital in 1932 in the northern part of Boyle Heights. When government grants to the poor increased after 1965 with the War on Poverty, and particularly with the Family Planning Services and Population Research Act in 1970, USC enlarged its family planning services for the poor, coercively sterilizing Mexican immigrant women who came into the hospital to deliver children. California had long led the nation in sterilization rates.[22] But with the new funding, amid nativist fears of high Mexican fertility and campaigns against "overpopulation" that identified it as a source of poverty, elective hysterectomy increased by 742 percent, elective tubal ligation by 470 percent, and tubal ligation after delivery by 151 percent.[23]

Two student residents at USC Medical School testified about systematic sterilization abuse by USC physicians. Resident Bernard Rosenfeld identified at least 180 Spanish-surnamed women who were coercively sterilized during childbirth, asked to sign consent forms while in labor and after being given large amounts of Demerol or Valium. Rosenfeld reported that staff doctors would congratulate residents on the number of postpartum tubal ligations they completed within a week's time, and that up to 20 percent of LACMC physicians actively pushed sterilization on women who did not understand what was happening to them.[24] Dr. Karen Benker, another USC medical student, recounted that the OB-GYN department put great emphasis on "cutting the birth rate of the Mexican and Negro populations" in their training of new physicians and had an "assembly-line approach" to sterilization that made women afraid of what would happen if they did not sign consent forms. Moreover, Benker acknowledged that non-English-speaking women were more likely to experience medical mistreatment because there were few interpreters available. Spanish-speaking women were often manipulated and sterilized on the basis of one question: "Mas niños?" Benker witnessed physicians making disparaging and prejudicial remarks about their Latina patients, degrading them on the basis of their sexual activity, commenting on their poverty and inability to provide for a large family, and threatening them with deportation if they did not agree to sterilization. The sociologist Elena Gutiérrez writes that "according to Dr. Benker, these biased attitudes and behaviors were common practice on the obstetrical floor."[25]

The experience of Jovita Rivera, a 28-year-old woman who spoke Spanish and could not speak or read in English, exemplified the pressure put on Mexican immigrant women. She was admitted to USC-LACMC on September 13, 1973, in advanced labor for the birth of her fifth child. In an affidavit, Rivera explained what happened next:

> I was given an anesthetic which made me groggy and numb. I was taken to the delivery room. . . . I spoke to a doctor who spoke some Spanish, the doctor said that it would be best to have my tubes tied as I had too many children and it would be too costly and burdensome for the government to have to support my family. . . . I was then brought some papers to sign which I could not read and no one explained them to me. I had a great deal of difficulty in signing the papers as I was heavily sedated. . . . I received no counselling or educational materials prior to being surgically sterilized, nor was the procedure explained to me, nor was the permanency of the operation explained to me.[26]

The experience for Mexican immigrant women of going into USC-LACMC to give birth and ending up sterilized was traumatic. LACMC doctors lied to Maria Hurtado, who was told that California state law allowed only three cesarean sections before sterilization was mandated, and then was given a tubal ligation without her consent while she lay unconscious following the delivery of her baby. It was only when she requested birth control at her six-week postpartum visit that a receptionist told Mrs. Hurtado that she would never be able to have any more children.[27]

Dolores Madrigal, who was separated from her husband after she refused to consent to sterilization, was told that her husband had agreed to have her undergo the procedure. Meanwhile he had been told falsely that she would die if she had another child.[28] Helena Orozco had repeatedly declined sterilization but finally signed papers after being "left alone" during intense labor pain because she thought the procedure could later be reversed. Mrs. Orozco did not realize until a year and a half later that she could never have children again. Orozco's son, born years before her sterilization, would later testify to

Gutiérrez about the emotional and mental health decline they witnessed in their mother, a "downward slope" that began with her coerced sterilization and continued for years afterward.[29]

Two court cases initially brought these systematic traumas to light and were pursued by lawyers who were products of the nascent Chicano Movement in Los Angeles. *Andrade et al. v. Los Angeles County–USC Medical Center* was filed on behalf of those forcibly sterilized between 1972 and 1973, but the case never made it to court. The second, more well-known case is *Madrigal v. Quilligan*, which was a wider class-action civil rights suit filed in 1975 in federal district court in Los Angeles, with ten selected plaintiffs representing women who had been coercively sterilized between 1968 and 1974. Two principal lawyers working for the Mexican American Legal Defense and Education Fund (MALDEF), Charles Nabarette and Antonia Hernández, charged USC–LACMC, 12 doctors, the State of California, and the US Department of Health, Education, and Welfare with violating the civil rights of these women and their constitutional right to bear children.[30] Even though many of those who suffered coercive sterilization were undocumented, these activist lawyers knew that they had made their case stronger by selecting ten women who were all citizens or legal residents.[31]

It took three years for this case to get to trial, and on June 8, 1978, Judge Jesse Curtis ruled against MALDEF and in favor of the defendant doctors, claiming they had acted in "good faith" with a "bona fide belief" that they had obtained proper authorization to sterilize, and, at worst, described the case as one of a "communication breakdown" rather than unlawful conduct.[32] Although disappointed in the judgment, the MALDEF lawyers could take some solace in the fact that the publicity had forced LACMC to begin to enforce compliance with new federal sterilization regulations. Early in the case, a preliminary injunction against the state forced health officials to stop using federal funds to sterilize minors and to rewrite existing Spanish-language guidelines at a sixth-grade level for comprehension. Because of the legal complaint, regulations regarding sterilization were revised at the state and federal levels, making it much more difficult to engage in the overt discriminatory behavior shown by the LACMC doctors and health personnel.[33]

Moreover, Chicana feminists and activists took on the issue of sterilization. Comisión Femenil Mexicana Nacional focused on sterilization abuse in the mid-1970s, when Gloria Molina was the president of the Los Angeles chapter.[34] Molina testified in 1977 to the California State Department of Health that politicians, hospitals, and doctors had no right to regulate the size of a Mexican family and instead asserted, "It is each woman's right to decide the number of children she will bear."[35] MALDEF created a Chicana Rights Project that focused on obtaining legal redress for those sterilized and new regulations to ensure this abuse would never happen again. In most cases, US-born Chicanas took the lead in pressing local officials to change their policies, and tactically, US citizens of Mexican descent often became the public face of those who testified to forced sterilization.[36] But as Gutiérrez makes clear, "There were many cases of undocumented Mexican women who were also coercively sterilized, but most feared that if they came forward, they or someone else in their family would be deported."[37]

FIGHTING ANTI-IMMIGRANT SENTIMENTS

By the mid-1970s Chicano organizations assumed the battle against anti-immigration policies in California. Beginning in the late 1960s, the Immigration and Naturalization Service began to reinstitute raids, and with the sharp recession of 1970 and 1971, many once again claimed that Mexicans were "stealing" US jobs.[38] Assemblyman Dixon Arnett of Redwood City introduced a bill in 1970 imposing sanctions on employers who knowingly hired an individual "not entitled to lawful residence in the United States." It turned potential employers into immigration officials, requiring them to determine the legal status of those they hired, and encouraged discrimination against hiring Latinos in general. While the bill originally passed, it was later ruled unconstitutional by the state supreme court. However, at the federal level, employer sanctions became a centerpiece of legislation sponsored by House Judiciary Committee chairman Peter Rodino (D-NJ) and would be debated in immigration policy for much of the 1970s and 1980s.[39]

At a local level in Los Angeles, the involvement of law enforcement in immigration enforcement was probably the most contentious issue, resurrecting concerns regarding a long history of police brutality toward minority youth dating back to the Zoot Suit Riots during World War II.[40] Chief of Police Ed Davis remembered that in 1969 almost 25 percent of the felony arrests had been for illegal entry, but because of community pushback in the 1970s the LAPD gradually stopped assisting federal agents in making such arrests. A report prepared by the Community Relations section of the LAPD for Chief Davis in January 1975 claimed that up to 100,000 undocumented "aliens" lived in the Hollenbeck Division, a significant portion of the estimated 250,000 undocumented population in Southern California as a whole.[41] And the report highlighted the local Chicano community's resentment over immigration raids: "The Mexican American community is concerned that police arrest of illegal aliens for their unlawful status in this country could result in general interrogation of citizens, not because they are suspected of being illegal aliens, but because of their ethnicity. For the Mexican-American, the spirit of kinship overrides other considerations."[42]

Among the leading local organizations that pressured the LAPD to disengage from the targeting of undocumented people for arrests because of legal status were La Hermandad Mexicana Nacional, which became known for their social service centers, and Centros de Acción Social Autónomo (CASA). La Hermandad, which expanded to Los Angeles in 1968, had been a long-standing organization that protected the rights of the undocumented in the San Diego area beginning in 1951.[43] Labor activist Bert Corona organized the first L.A. chapter with Soledad "Chole" Alatorre and other labor organizers who had been working with undocumented workers in the area since the 1950s. In addition to counseling undocumented workers about their rights under the US Constitution, such as due process, La Hermandad organized Mexican immigrants into mutual-benefit societies that met regularly and sponsored family social activities like picnics and potlucks. Because they provided much-needed counseling and information for undocumented immigrants, these societies spread rapidly throughout Southern California, including chapters in Boyle Heights and East Los Angeles. The labor backgrounds of the organizers also led La Hermandad of Los Angeles to connect immigrants with union organizers throughout Southern California.[44]

The Hermandades and CASAs were critical to pushing political organizations in California "to explore systematically the significance of the relationship between immigration, Chicano ethnicity, and the status of Mexican Americans in the United States."[45] With an organizing slogan of "Somos un Pueblo sin Fronteras" (We Are One People without Borders) and a newspaper titled *Sin Fronteras* (Without Borders), activists argued that Mexican immigrant workers had long been a critical part of the American working class. Even more important, Mexican Americans could see the connection between the rampant police brutality against American-born Chicano youth and the targeting and criminalization of undocumented immigrants in the barrio. These systematic, shared struggles reinforced the racial analysis that shaped Chicano identity in the 1970s and pushed organizations dominated by US-born activists to realize their intimate connections to the most recent newcomers, no matter their legal status.[46]

Starting with opposition to the Dixon Arnett bill, La Hermandad led efforts to oppose immigration bills that included employer sanctions and other anti-immigrant measures. On a local level, they pushed LAPD chief Ed Davis to stop arresting undocumented workers for simply being in the United States without papers; on a national level, they attacked the various versions of the Rodino bill that attempted to include employer sanctions across the country. Although CASA was overtaken by Marxist sectarian strife in the 1970s and collapsed, La Hermandad continued to be an effective vehicle for combating anti-immigrant efforts. Eventually, the League of United Latin American Citizens (LULAC) and the Mexican American Political Association (MAPA), two centrist organizations that had long prioritized the importance of naturalization and citizenship in the Mexican American community, started to reduce their own hostility to recent immigrants. This movement was even able to shift the position of the United Farm Workers (UFW), which had taken a largely anti-immigrant stance because of the use of undocumented workers to break labor strikes.[47]

When Democrat Jimmy Carter assumed the presidency in 1977, most Chicano organizations believed that their immigration positions would finally be elevated in the national discourse, but Carter adopted the Rodino bill as the basis of his immigration reform effort. The broad-based cohesion that had developed between Mexican American organizations across the political spectrum was best expressed at the landmark 1977 First National Chicano/Latino Conference on Immigration and Public Policy held in San Antonio in October 1977. Organized under the La Raza Unida Party of Texas, 2,000 participants from organizations as diverse as LULAC, the American G.I. Forum, MALDEF, the Crusade for Justice, La Hermandad Nacional, and the Socialist Workers Party came together to oppose the Carter plan. This consensus underscored the position of the wider Mexican American community that lasted throughout the Carter and Reagan years, well into the 1980s. It was not until the passage of the Immigration Reform and Control Act (IRCA) in 1986 under President Reagan that consensus crumbled, causing some organizations to push for compromise.[48]

Passage of IRCA marked the culmination of discussions that had begun in 1971 between lawmakers and the various organizations that wanted to find a "solution" to the "problem of illegal aliens" in the United States, including organized business structures, anti-immigrant nativist groups, labor unions, and Mexican American advocacy organizations. But the one group not directly included in any of these policy discussions was undocumented workers themselves. This meant that the piece of legislation that became IRCA was an amalgamation of several approaches wrapped in a compromise that included employer sanctions, enhanced border enforcement, expansion of temporary workers' programs, and an amnesty program for undocumented persons who had been in continuous residence in the US since January 1, 1982. It did not, however, address the central causes of undocumented Mexican migration to the United States, which included poverty and underemployment in Mexico and the growth of low-paying jobs in the US that American citizens would not take. Enhanced border enforcement fundamentally changed migration routes, making the journey much more hazardous. This, in turn, trapped migrants who had historically been engaged in circular migration but were now too scared to return to Mexico for fear of not being able to cross back into the US. So unauthorized migration was not curbed or even slowed down; instead, the number of undocumented in the US climbed from 3.2 million in 1986 to 5 million in 1996 and peaked at approximately 11 million in 2006.[49] Critically, the number of migrants who settled permanently in the US—because of the now deadly conditions of crossings and the implementation of harsh immigration laws—increased dramatically as well.

The amnesty provisions of IRCA did move immigrant rights organizations like La Hermandad and MALDEF to focus on helping the undocumented obtain legal status and citizenship. Approximately 2.3 million Mexicans legalized their status in the United States because of IRCA, and the largest group consisted of residents from Los Angeles County. But because of IRCA's other provisions, communities like Boyle Heights ended up more mixed in legal status after 1986. New populations of legalized migrants, settled undocumented migrants, and temporary contract workers increasingly made Boyle Heights home and put down roots next to long-term residents who were US citizens or permanent residents.[50] Mixed-status families proliferated in Boyle Heights, with marriages between recent newcomers and legal residents, and US-born children grew up with siblings and parents who were often born in Mexico or Central America. The community-based organizations of the late twentieth and early twenty-first centuries in Boyle Heights and East Los Angeles had to work with these mixed-status families and neighborhoods to be successful.

One of the most important groups of this era in Boyle Heights was the Mothers of East Los Angeles (MELA), which was started in 1985 by several longtime community activists to block a proposed state prison nearby in an industrial district on Santa Fe Avenue and Twelfth Street. In early May 1985, then California assemblywoman Gloria Molina asked her field representative Martha Molina to contact local activist Juana Gutiérrez and her husband Ricardo about these plans by Governor George Deukmejian and California legislative leaders. Juana Beatriz Gutiérrez was a Boyle Heights homemaker, a mother of nine, and a neighborhood watch program organizer. Born in Zacatecas, she had lived in Boyle Heights for 33 years. She knew her immediate neighbors well because of her neighborhood watch work and her church community because she had made tamales for fund-raisers for Santa Isabel Elementary School, beginning when her first child attended in 1962, and continuing with efforts to save Cathedral High School. On May 24, Juana and Ricardo Gutiérrez hosted a community meeting at their home where their local pastor and several neighbors heard from field representative Martha Molina about the prison plans. Very quickly, Juana gathered 900 signatures on a petition against the prison.[51]

Assemblywoman Gloria Molina called upon local activists because her power in the state legislature was limited without the direct support from own district. Assembly District 56 included Boyle Heights and part of downtown, the Eastside and Southeast portion of L.A., and, as such, was the most Latino district in the state. It also had the lowest number of registered voters in the entire Southwest.[52] Later on, in an interview about the issue of the prison, Molina reflected on her district's grassroots activism: "I brought in people to go up there and testify, and I always got it killed on the assembly side."[53]

Local activists in Boyle Heights had learned that their power lay in their ability to highlight an issue that affected their neighborhood, stay with it for years, including directly lobbying in Sacramento, and outlast those government officials who assumed East Los Angeles residents did not have enough money or influence to combat the powerful forces in the capital. They also knew that the immigrant status of most parishioners made many ineligible to vote and thus that electoral politics alone could not protect their community. As they enlisted other Catholic parishes, older Latinas who had long served their neighborhoods teamed with Catholic priests to create a network that could call up a much wider group of community members for lobbying or

FIGURE 28. Five hundred MELA marchers on Olympic Boulevard protest the siting of a prison in East L.A., 1986. Los Angeles Public Library.

protesting. Father John Morreta, pastor of Resurrection Church, joined the effort in 1986, suggesting that the women tie white scarves around their heads to draw attention to themselves, calling themselves Las Madres del Este de Los Angeles (MELA) after the more famous group Las Madres de la Plaza de Mayo (The Mothers of the Plaza de Mayo), which fought for information on "the disappeared" under the right-wing military in Argentina. He encouraged them to hold a massive march against the prison in the summer of 1986. After that, the local women continued to hold weekly marches to highlight their opposition to the prison and to keep local media focused on the issue.[54]

Unlike the earlier CSO, which concentrated on naturalization and voter registration, MELA dealt with large numbers of undocumented and noncitizen residents in the Boyle Heights community that did not (and could not) translate into immediate voter strength. For MELA, the visibility of mass protests, the claim of legitimacy through their identities as mothers with familial responsibilities, the direct lobbying of politicians, and the gathering of families by neighborhood parishes all worked to incorporate undocumented residents into community politics in safe and productive ways. Indeed, many foreign-born women made the trip by bus to lobby Sacramento politicians because the group fund-raised in their respective parishes to pay for the transportation and this activity did not depend on citizenship.[55] Scholar Kamala Pratt has called this "an alternative means of political participation" at a "vital nonelectoral juncture."[56] MELA membership grew close to 3,000 by the early 1990s.[57] When asked directly, leaders downplayed the differences between members in terms of legal status and citizenship, but a closer look at the nature of the membership reveals the importance of a cross-national, diverse organization that staked its legitimacy on the basis of residency and motherhood, not voting power.

All of the acknowledged leaders in MELA were long-standing residents of Boyle Heights who had been regular participants in community affairs, no matter their birthplace or citizenship status. What bound them together was a commitment to their community and bilingual abilities that allowed them to communicate with all their neighbors. Maria Roybal, for example, who lived down the street from Juana Gutiérrez, was a widow born in Guatemala City. She had lived in the same house in Boyle Heights since 1953, was a regular member of Resurrection Church, and had friends at many other parishes.[58] Another member of Resurrection Parish was Rosa Villaseñor, who lived in Wyvernwood Apartments. She had migrated to Boyle Heights from Cuba via Florida in the 1950s.[59] Aurora Castillo, daughter of a World War I navy veteran, was born in East Los Angeles, grew up in the Great Depression, worked for Douglas Aircraft in World War II, and never married. She lived in Boyle Heights with her sister Henrietta until she became president of MELA.[60] Other women, such as Erlinda Robles of Our Lady of Talpa Parish and Lucille Mendoza of Dolores Mission, were also active from the very start. Most, but not all, had married, and their husbands often held or had retired from union jobs in bakeries, construction, machine manufacturing plants, the armed services, and plant maintenance.[61]

As leaders who were long-term residents of Boyle Heights, these women, and their allies, vividly remembered the history of displacement and urban renewal in Los Angeles that too often ran roughshod over Mexican American neighborhoods. Many recalled the displacement of the Mexican community of Chavez Ravine for public housing and Dodger Stadium. Others pointed out the destruction of Bunker Hill as part of a plan for so-called urban renewal. Many of the activists personally remembered having to move out of their homes in the wake of the freeways built through Boyle Heights. The building of the Pomona Freeway (60) had led to the demolition of the Santa Isabel Church and its relocation in Boyle Heights.[62] With these memories intact, these leaders understood the vulnerability of largely immigrant Latino neighborhoods and the political strategies necessary to defend them.

What was key about these leaders was that they recognized that their respective constituencies contained large numbers of foreign-born immi-

FIGURE 29. Members of Mothers of East Los Angeles (MELA) oppose the building of a proposed state prison near Boyle Heights, 1986. Photograph by Javier Mendoza, Los Angeles Herald Examiner Photo Collection/Los Angeles Public Library.

grants, including many undocumented, who still had a right to voice their concerns, keep their communities safe, and improve their neighborhoods. This came through in the very nature of their protests. At all public forums, for example, they brought interpreters so that Spanish-speaking residents could fully follow and participate in the proceedings. This was the case even though at least half of the leadership were second-generation Mexican Americans, many of whom struggled with their own Spanish-language abilities.[63] Mary Pardo conveys the power of this commitment in the face of a state legislature that refused to provide translators, with a description of a hearing in the state office building auditorium, filled with Boyle Heights residents: "Councilwoman Gloria Molina approached the podium to speak against the prison project. She looked from side to side, seeking an interpreter. There was none. Facing the audience, she asked, 'Who needs a Spanish translation of the hearing proceedings?' The audience was silent for a moment; no one responded. Then someone called out, 'Ask that question in Spanish?' She did. About three-fourths of the audience raised their hands.

She read her entire statement in Spanish and then again in English, dismaying the hearing panel with the extra time that was required to deliver her comments twice."[64]

Commitment to bilingual communication and a shared history of neglect and displacement were not the only issues that helped shape a broader political agenda. Angie Flores, a second-generation Mexican American woman and Roosevelt class of 1941 graduate, learned about the issues confronting the undocumented in her neighborhood when she assisted her parish priest to counsel immigrants so they could fill out IRCA forms. She empathized with the poverty of the newcomers and their fear of separation from their families. At the same time, Flores noted a decline of public services, such as the loss of the local post office, and the declining quality of private businesses, such as supermarkets, that she connected with the influx of the most recent newcomers from Mexico and Latin America.[65] Despite the differences in legality and citizenship between the generations, these two groups came together because as a neighborhood collective they recognized they shared the same struggles and desires for the future of their children and grandchildren.

MELA was able to derail the state prison project near Boyle Heights by working with Assemblywoman Gloria Molina in Sacramento, building networks with other politicians, and forging coalitions with others in the neighborhood like the local chambers of commerce. However, their battle, which began in 1985, would not be won until July 1992, when California's deep fiscal crisis forced newly elected Republican California governor Pete Wilson to sign Senate Bill 97, which eliminated the Eastside prison project and redirected the funding to other prison expansion.[66] But MELA had also quickly taken on other community issues that threatened Boyle Heights.

During the eight-year prison project battle, MELA also publicized how continued attempts to dump hazardous materials in Boyle Heights reflected a view of residents as disposable—a form of dehumanization with deep roots in the area. First they participated in the Coalition Against the Pipeline —an oil pipeline to be built only three feet below the surface through downtown and Boyle Heights, close to several schools and actually underneath Hollenbeck Junior High School, despite the possibility of a gas leak. When one oil representative defended avoiding the coastline because "it would endanger the marine life," the activists shouted back, "You value the marine life more than human beings?" Through this activity—which led to the defeat of the pipeline—MELA was exposed to wider regional politics.[67]

Shortly after this victory, State Assemblywoman Lucille Roybal-Allard, daughter of Congressman Edward Roybal, alerted MELA that the adjacent small industrial city of Vernon had agreed to grant a permit to one of the first entirely commercial hazardous waste incinerators proposed for California, which would be located only three miles from the heart of Boyle Heights, Vernon officials did not wait for an environmental impact report, even though the incinerator would operate 24 hours a day and burn 125,000 pounds of waste daily. MELA immediately gathered more than 4,000 petition signatures and began to stage rallies at the Vernon site, forcing the company to abandon the project, who argued that community involvement had unraveled the six-year-old deal. Because of the community struggle, Roybal-Allard was able to secure passage of Assembly Bill 58, which gave all Californians the minimum protection of requiring that an environmental impact report be completed before construction of hazardous waste incinerators.[68]

MELA had a significant impact on a wide range of issues, but eventually those activists working in and near Resurrection Parish south of Santa Ana Freeway decided to stay focused on prison expansion, while a larger coalition north of the freeway near the Santa Isabel Parish broadened their concerns. Madres del Este de Los Angeles, Santa Isabel (MELA-SI) operated independently and carried the MELA mission into the 1990s, developing a graffiti cleanup project, a scholarship program, a Child Immunization Project in conjunction with White Memorial Hospital to promote community well-being, and a collaborative Water Conservation Project offering free low-flush toilets, which also generated 27 community jobs.[69]

HOMEBOY INDUSTRIES

By the mid-1980s Boyle Heights would become known as the gang capital of Los Angeles, which itself was the gang capital of the United States. The rise of violent gangs in Boyle Heights was connected to demographic change in the neighborhood, with the families of the undocumented experiencing increased poverty, a decline of youth programs, repressive police violence, and the incarceration of minority youth based on the zero-tolerance policies of the period.[70] Journalist Celeste Fremon described the situation: "With each immigration wave, the newest, poorest immigrants gravitated to the areas already most densely populated with other Mexican-Americans—areas such as the East L.A. housing projects. When the American economy drooped and joblessness rose in the seventies, and again in the eighties, the poverty of East L.A. began to calcify to form a permanent underclass. As some of their parents turned to drug use and alcoholism, the kids of this immigrant underclass fought feelings of exclusion and hopelessness by banding together."[71] The most intense area of gang activity in Boyle Heights was in the area of Pico Gardens and Aliso Village in the Flats, where in the 1980s there were eight active gangs, seven Latino and one African American.[72] Smack in the middle of that area of Boyle Heights was the Dolores Mission Church, which, like MELA, would generate a local solution to the neglect and abuse suffered by residents of the projects and nearby housing.

Father Gregory Boyle grew up near the Hancock Park area of Los Angeles in a middle-class household, attended Loyola High School, and was ordained in 1984, then was appointed as pastor of the Dolores Mission Church. Boyle had been an associate pastor at Dolores Mission before being placed in Bolivia in 1984–85, where he was "evangelicized" to serve the poor. When asked about the main issues confronting his parish, Father Boyle did not hesitate:

> Well, one of the main issues, I think, affecting the community when I first arrived was immigration. So you had the Simpson-Rodino Act, and you had eventually the Immigration Reform and Control Act. That was kind of a front burner for that community, because there were so many undocumented, then they had amnesty and people started qualifying for amnesty. Then you had issues of family separation, where the husband qualified but the wife didn't. So there was the possibility and sometimes the reality of families being separated, so that was the biggest issue, without question. But you had a lot of undocumented living in the projects in those days.[73]

Father Boyle knew he had to deliver a message of dignity for all people, despite their citizenship or legal status. In 1986, he began building the Homeboy Industries infrastructure to offer alternative pathways to gang members in the area. Boyle began by opening a school in 1988, Dolores Mission Alternative (DMA), to serve gang-involved middle school students who had been kicked out of regular schools because of violence or drug dealing. Later that year, Boyle and the affiliated women of the housing project opened "Jobs for a Future," which provided employment to gang members unable to secure jobs and as an alternative to gang life. The parish-led program created jobs ranging from the building of a child care center, to neighborhood cleanup and graffiti removal, to landscaping and maintenance. It

FIGURE 30. Father Gregory Boyle consoles gang members at grave, February 1990. Photograph by Anacleto Rapping. Copyright © 2012. Los Angeles Times. Used with Permission.

also placed gang members in a variety of businesses and nonprofits where they could gain skills, with Jobs for a Future paying their salaries.[74]

Boyle learned early on that the growing gang problem—though rooted in poverty and lack of opportunity for youth—was deeply connected to legal status, which was a major factor in diminishing opportunity, especially in these times of mounting anti-immigrant sentiment. He observed: "Here at Homeboy Industries, you get folks, gang members, who came to this country in their mother's arms, that's the profile, so they aren't legally here. So now they're being penalized across the board for a decision that they didn't make."[75] Boyle called immigration policy "outrageous" for its effect on young people in his community.[76] In an anthropological study of the Cuatro Flats gang that predominated in Pico Gardens in this period, scholar James Diego Vigil found that many gang members were part of a "1.5 generation," arriving in the US between the ages of four and seven years old. According to Vigil, "With eroding conventional opportunities for many of these youths, . . .

marginalization ensures gang membership," and the steady stream of undocumented continued to replenish gang membership in Pico Gardens.[77]

This meant that the Dolores Mission neighborhood that Father Boyle entered in the mid-1980s was struggling with a rapidly growing youth gang problem that was relatively new and dangerous. But Boyle was not alone in responding to these new circumstances. When some parishioners began to feel uneasy with gang members hanging out at the parish in 1989, a meeting was called in which parishioners packed the elementary school cafeteria to express their opinions. One community mother led a group of gang members into the room, and one by one they got up and talked: "We're human beings and we need help. And Father Greg is helping us."[78] According to Boyle, it was two powerful parish leaders, Teresa Navarro and Paula Hernández, who rose and exclaimed, "We help gang members at this parish because it is what Jesus would do."[79] Other parish mothers followed this and spoke: "These gang members are not the enemy. They are our children. And if we don't help them, no one will."[80] Those in attendance applauded and continued to follow these women leaders, often coordinating marches into and through the projects in the wake of ceaseless shootings to try to calm down the area. They formed the Comité Pro Paz (Committee for Peace) to take on hotspots in the community and to support larger efforts to expand opportunities for gang members through job creation, while also averting violence with gentle praying and singing. They began to operate as Christian base communities (*comunidades eclesiales de base*—CEBs), or communities that reflect on how the gospel should have an impact on their everyday lives—a development known throughout Latin America in connection with liberation theology. Parishioners, especially the mothers from the public housing complex, partnered with Father Boyle on behalf of the disaffected homeboys.[81]

The compassion of the resident parishioners extended not only to the children of undocumented parents but also to the newly arrived undocumented adults in their community. After the passage of IRCA in 1986, the Dolores Mission Church declared itself a sanctuary church for the undocumented in 1987, the second such declaration in the city of Los Angeles. Soon after, recently arrived undocumented men would sleep in the church, and women and children would sleep across the street in the convent. Mothers in the parish community organized meals. The number of men eventually housed and fed in the church in a project called Guadalupe Homeless Project rose quickly from 10 men each night to 100. The housing of women and children led parishioners to open Dolores Mission Women's Cooperative

Day Care Center in the stage area of the elementary school cafeteria. When hate messages and death threats followed, parishioners fought back. One night, when someone spray-painted "WETBACK CHURCH" across the front steps of the church, Petra Saldaña and other parish women refused to clean it up, saying, "If there are people in our community who are disparaged and hated and left out because they are *mojados* (wetbacks), . . . then we shall be proud to call ourselves a wetback church."[82]

Despite this growing activism and the church's commitment to all community members, gang violence continued to rise, peaking in 1992. The LAPD responded with increased repression of minority youth and antagonism toward Father Boyle, Dolores Mission Church, and others that had developed alternative methods to confront the increase of gang violence in the neighborhood. By January 1991, the Comité Pro Paz called a meeting with Captain Bob Medina, head of the Hollenbeck Division of the LAPD, to complain about the harassment of youth living in the projects, two weeks after a police raid led to the rounding up of 25 adolescents. When the mothers tried to stop the police from indiscriminately beating up the youth, they were told to get back into their apartments or they would be arrested. Lupe Loera, the president of the Comité Pro Paz, exclaimed, "The police think we are all criminals, just because we live in the projects."[83] These police raids were part of the LAPD antigang program known as Operation Hammer, intended to keep constant pressure on gang members, harassing and arresting them for minor violations. Operation Hammer in Pico-Aliso evolved into antagonism directed at Father Boyle and Dolores Mission Church by Captain Medina and the rest of the Hollenbeck division.[84]

It would take the release of the video showing LAPD officers beating motorist Rodney King, later in 1991, to end Operation Hammer, but it was the explosion of the Los Angeles Riots in response to the acquittal of four LAPD officers for that beating on April 29, 1992, and to decades of unfettered police brutality, that led to more profound changes in the relationship between the LAPD and the Boyle Heights community. Perhaps surprisingly, given the pervasive police brutality against residents in Boyle Heights, neither the Pico-Aliso neighborhood nor the larger Boyle Heights erupted in the wake of the Rodney King verdict. It did not make sense to most in Boyle Heights to attack and firebomb the local businesses owned by neighborhood parents and families. Indeed, even Asian-owned mom-and-pop stores were "adopted" by local gangs in Pico-Aliso because they might be the only store available for purchasing groceries in a protected gang neighborhood, based on a tightly-woven geography with firm gang lines.[85] In the wake of the city-wide riots, however, even greater attention was paid to the successful implementation of the jobs programs for gang members that Father Boyle had instituted as a solution to urban poverty and despair among young people. As Father Boyle himself acknowledged, "After the unrest of '92, where people said we need to have after school programs and we need to keep the schools open longer, and we need to have mentoring, . . . all these things were born right after that time."[86]

Father Boyle was required by the Jesuits to take a one-year retreat after serving in his post for six years, but after community activists advocated for his return, he was placed in a limited gang ministry in East Los Angeles. On January 2, 1994, Boyle set up a tiny storefront office for Homeboy Industries four blocks from the Dolores Mission Church and started employing home-boys from the local community.[87] From this storefront, Homeboy Industries would grow into being one of the leading and best-known gang intervention programs in the world. By 2000, Homeboy Industries moved to a rehabbed printing factory at 1916 East First Street and started serving gang members from outside Boyle Heights, reaching up to 1,000 young people a month. Its services expanded beyond employment to tattoo removal, mental health counseling, case management, and legal services. By 2007, it would move out of Boyle Heights altogether, including its headquarters, Homeboy Bakery, and would establish a new Homegirl Café near Chinatown in downtown Los Angeles. By now it included a full-blown silkscreen printing operation, a maintenance crew, and a merchandising department. It would be recognized by the city as a cultural asset, especially once Boyle Heights native Antonio Villaraigosa was elected mayor in 2005, and its programs began to be replicated all over the country and even outside the US.[88]

PICO-ALISO AND THE PRIVATIZATION
OF PUBLIC HOUSING

A relentless recession between 1990 and 1993, and media attention to gang killings that peaked in 1992, only intensified anti-immigrant scapegoating. In 1994, Proposition 187 was overwhelmingly passed by state voters. It sought to ban social services to illegal immigrants, criminalize undocumented status in the state, and force public service providers, such as teachers and social workers, to turn over information concerning the legal status of their clients and students. In 1996, the state voted in favor of Proposition 209, which prohibited affirmative action in state government hiring, contracting, and institutions of higher education, a measure aimed at the growing diversity among the state's population, largely fueled by increased immigration. Then in 1998, Proposition 227 eliminated bilingual education in California's public schools, even in curricula intended to transition newcomers to the English language.[89] Given their close working relationship with the undocumented in Boyle Heights, Homeboy Industries and MELA came out strongly against the punitive measures of Proposition 187, but long-term residents of Boyle Heights grew concerned with the negative stereotypes that had developed among non-Latinos who associated crime, gang violence, and illegality with all Latinos.[90]

Then, during the second half of the 1990s, new federal funds allowed local governments to put forward one solution to the gang problem in Pico-Aliso: razing the existing housing structures, moving families out, and building new public-private communities designed as mixed-class neighborhoods. Started by Housing and Urban Development (HUD) Secretary Jack Kemp under President George Bush Sr., the Home Opportunities for People Everywhere (HOPE) program was modeled after Margaret Thatcher's privatization of the public housing program in England. This neoliberal initiative saw the failure of most public housing complexes in the United States as a function of concentrating poor people into small, rigidly segregated areas like Pico-Aliso and thus proposed that it could be resolved by reducing the number of public housing units while introducing market-rate housing under private management. When President Bill Clinton took office in 1993, the HOPE IV program was expanded under new HUD secretary Henry Cisneros and was embraced by Los Angeles city leaders, eventually leading to the Pueblo del Sol mixed-income, transit-oriented community to replace Aliso Village.[91]

In 1993, Cisneros awarded a $50 million grant to the Los Angeles City Housing Authority, approving plans to tear down and rebuild the Pico Gardens and Aliso Extension public housing projects south of First Street and replace them with townhouse-like units in a gated community. "We're trying to make some dramatic changes," explained Cisneros.[92] As demolition began in 1997 after extensive community discussions, the process of relocating current resident families to temporary units or elsewhere with Section 8 housing subsidies went relatively smoothly, although it was still anxiety producing for displaced residents. Yet dreams of new homes replacing dilapidated structures did fuel hope.[93] As explained by City Councilman Richard

Alatorre, who replaced Art Snyder in 1985 as the second Latino, after Edward Roybal, to be elected to the Los Angeles City Council, and who served until 1999: "Times have changed. What agencies of government were able to get away with before they cannot get away with now."[94]

Indeed, the City Housing Authority was able to get the support for demolition and replacement from community leadership in Pico-Aliso and the Dolores Mission clergy, who had worked so hard to provide alternatives to gang membership. Breavon (Bebee) McDuffie, president of the Pico Gardens Resident Advisory Council, was clear that he had lost hope in the current circumstances and that change was needed. "I have seen the evolution ... where neighborhood support and community have all dilapidated. So I'm hoping that we can regain some of the things in the past."[95] McDuffie himself had been born in Pico Gardens to an African American migrant family from East Texas, had grown up immersed in gang life in Cuatro Flats, and had eventually spent time in prison in the mid-1970s for second-degree murder. But he had since established a reputation as a community leader and "as a reliable black Chicano," according to anthropologist Diego Vigil.[96] But McDuffie was willing to actively support the move for the betterment of the community by talking to neighbors. "We have to assure them [the residents] that it's the community that will benefit from this."[97]

Father Boyle also supported the reconstruction efforts in 1995, thinking that the upgrade was long overdue for the Pico-Aliso community. It helped that the City Housing Authority was willing to employ community members for the reconstruction, promising as many as 40 jobs through an apprenticeship program to local homeboys.[98] Lupe Loera, who had been president of Comité Pro Paz at Dolores Mission Church, also had faith in the change. "It was about time. We deserve something good. I'm willing to move around—as long as it's here."[99] There was actual enthusiasm for the demolition of the antiquated structures, built in the 1940s and 1950s, and their replacement by something newer. Father Mike Kennedy, who replaced Boyle as the pastor in charge of Dolores Mission Parish, went as far as carrying a replica of the Virgin de Guadalupe to bless the demolition of Aliso Village in 1998.[100]

By the time that residents were moving back into Pico-Aliso in 1998 and 1999, and plans were under way with an additional $83 million in HOPE IV funding to tear down Aliso Village north of First Street in 1998, a larger number of residents were skeptical. A new group formed, Unión de Vecinos Pico Aliso, headed by Leonardo Vilchis, that wanted demolition of Aliso Village to be postponed and most residences to be repaired, not destroyed. Vilchis organized more than 300 Aliso Village residents to sign a petition opposing the demolition, stoking fears that many residents would not be allowed back into the neighborhood when construction was complete. Still, the new demolition plan for Aliso Village continued to have the support of the Aliso Village Tenants Committee, headed by David Ochoa, and from Father Boyle and the rest of the Dolores Mission Catholic hierarchy. Father Boyle was critical of the new group's approach, calling Vecinos "irresponsible" for needlessly "fomenting" people's fears. "I don't think having poor people piled on top of poor people is what God had in mind," expressed Boyle as he endorsed the plan to create a mixed-income community. Boyle continued that "if I thought anyone was going to be left out [of new housing], I'd be at the top of the march."[101]

As the demolition of Aliso Village finally began, families moved into the reconstructed Pico Gardens, and Pueblo del Sol eventually replaced Aliso Village at the beginning of the twenty-first century. These transformations made it clear that the neighborhood had fundamentally changed and that a different community was being established. Lower-density, mixed-income housing was coupled with the opening of the Metro Gold Line into Boyle Heights, as well as the completion of Felicitas and Gonzalo Mendez High School in the Flats in 2009, named after the path-breaking pioneers who had challenged segregated schooling in California in the 1940s. Gang killings in the neighborhood, although still a factor, never returned to the predemolition numbers because known gang members were prohibited from returning to the Flats.[102] Lupe Loera remarked upon moving into her new townhouse in Pico-Aliso, "You feel all this privacy. It feels like a real house. It feels like mine." Her neighbor Felix García knew that more work was ahead: "It's not just the casitas that are going to change us. We have to change ourselves. It depends on us to change our neighborhood." His wife, Claudia Martinon, summed up the situation when she said, "It's the beginning of a new community. We have high hopes."[103]

> At Homeboy, we often say, "Community trumps gang." Only by offering a real, live community are you able to shine a light on the empty, shallow, and false "belonging" of a gang.
>
> FATHER GREGORY BOYLE, FOUNDER OF HOMEBOY INDUSTRIES, *Barking to the Choir* (2017)

The struggle of neighborhoods in Boyle Heights in the late twentieth century was felt throughout the area. The diversity of legal statuses among the population and the oppressive nature of the anti-immigrant policies strained efforts to achieve neighborhood stability and progress. Even though Boyle Heights had never been more Latino, and Mexican American politicians were rising to new heights in the city of Los Angeles, undocumented residents, their children, mixed-status families, and other individuals could not simply participate electorally to become part of the resident citizen population.

The politics of MELA and the Homeboy Industries in the late twentieth century showed how community-based organizations could engage the entire community without regard to legal status. But while the transformation of the Pico-Aliso neighborhood in the 1990s would fundamentally change the social dynamics for families in that part of Boyle Heights, it would also ignite a process that questioned the very nature of community, especially around gentrification in Boyle Heights. Even Father Boyle, who had been a strong advocate for the reconstruction of Pico Gardens and Aliso Village, began to have doubts. "For all the problems in the projects, there was also a sense of community that was so strong it was palpable," remembered Father Boyle. "As advocates for the poor, we had for years demanded more humane living conditions. And then one day, much to our surprise, the federal government said, 'Okay.' Should we have said, 'No, thanks'? My mind still isn't made up about it."[104]

TEN

Remembering Boyle Heights

The challenge of history is to recover the past and introduce it
to the present. It is the same challenge that confronts memory.

DAVID THELEN, *"Memory and
American History," 1989*

IN HIS TURN-OF-THE-TWENTY-FIRST-CENTURY political campaigns
for mayor, Boyle Heights–born Antonio Villaraigosa had to overcome the
sense that he was simply representing newcomers to the city, even though his
own family's history in the area had begun in 1903, when his grandfather
moved from Mexico and bought a house overlooking Hollenbeck Park. In
one of his most effective commercials of the successful 2005 mayoral campaign, Villaraigosa highlighted his relationship with a former counselor and
English teacher at Roosevelt High School in a television ad entitled
"Mentorship." Then known as Tony Villar, the future mayor credited
Herman Katz, a Jewish American teacher who himself was a former student
at Roosevelt, for helping make a difference in his life and putting him on a
path away from local gangs and educational failure. The campaign commercial clearly made the point that the now grown-up Antonio Villaraigosa
understood how working across racial and economic lines could help the city
prosper and overcome its great challenges.[1]

This new narrative of multiracialism in Boyle Heights can be credited
with helping to elect Villaraigosa as mayor of Los Angeles after the bruising
defeat he had suffered four years earlier to white candidate James Hahn in
2001. Indeed, Hahn had stoked fear of growing Latino political power and
emphasized his father Kenneth Hahn's legacy of advocating for black residents as Los Angeles County supervisor to garner 80 percent of the black
vote in 2001.[2] Although from the beginning of his political career Villaraigosa
had often talked about his high school teacher Katz and his own experience
of diverse connections, he had to overcome the perception that he would
represent only Latino interests and the needs of the Eastside of the city if he
was to become the first Latino elected mayor of Los Angeles since the 1870s.

He now used this story and his upbringing in Boyle Heights to its greatest political effect, displaying the cultural exchange that was often at work on the Eastside, even if it meant framing it as a form of white paternalism. Describing the harmonious mix of Latinos, Jews, blacks, and Japanese Americans, he told a group of Asian American leaders meeting in Little Tokyo in May 2005 that "we lived side by side . . . It was a harbinger of the future."[3] What Villaraigosa, in effect, would promise to the rest of the city was a candidate trained in fostering unity amid diversity, fulfilling the desire for a new Los Angeles that so much of the public yearned for.

Over the past two decades of working on the history of Boyle Heights, I have learned that many people care deeply about it, not only current residents but those who moved out of the neighborhood decades ago. In constructing and reconstructing the history of Boyle Heights, I realized that I was providing a window into the complexity of making meaning from history in contemporary Los Angeles, a task in which varied organizations and individuals had a stake. I witnessed this over and over again through my own process of engagement with a wider public who cared deeply about their own memories of multiracial Boyle Heights, and another set of developers and protectors who saw in contemporary Boyle Heights an opening for a multiracial future. The individual desires for a blueprint of a multiracial past in Los Angeles are today filtered through organizations and cultural institutions that reflect twenty-first-century Los Angeles, including a deeply segregated city, divided politics, and vast economic inequities.

RECOVERING A TRULY MULTIRACIAL PAST

In December of 1998, First Lady Hillary Rodham Clinton kicked off the West Coast version of a White House initiative dedicated to preserving historic American sites by visiting a run-down, largely abandoned synagogue in Boyle Heights. The selection of the Breed Street Synagogue for preservation was intended to evoke a particular kind of historical remembrance, one that would connect generations of immigrants and immigrant children from different backgrounds. While Clinton addressed a crowd of about 500 local politicians, academics, and representatives of Los Angeles' dispersed Jewish community, local Mexican American residents stood on the sidelines curious and somewhat bemused.[4] The synagogue site was available because it was no longer in use in Boyle Heights; some of the most significant sites of Jewish

Boyle Heights have become reintegrated into the changing ethnic landscape of the neighborhood. Smaller houses of Jewish worship, strewn throughout the streets of Boyle Heights, are actually more typical of the community-based congregations of Boyle Heights, and they have been turned over largely to small Latino Protestant congregations. My favorite, on Mathews Street, continues to be decorated by the Jewish star and metalwork, as well as by the designation *Iglesia Hebreo*. Likewise, formerly Jewish businesses have been transformed to shops and restaurants serving a predominantly Latino clientele, while the ownership continues to be multiracial, although largely Latino or Asian. Indeed, the lack of attention to sites that were once critical to actual interaction between Jews, Mexicans, Japanese Americans, and others caused one to be destroyed without community approval in March 2006. The Soto-Michigan Jewish Community Center, iconic for its early midcentury style, was central to multiracial engagement in the 1960s and 1970s. When it was destroyed in 2006, city council member Jose Huizar, president of the Boyle Heights Neighborhood Council Robert Jimenez, president of the Jewish Historical Society Steven Sass, and other neighborhood and Jewish community leaders expressed outrage over the demolition, but it was clear that none had moved quickly enough to have it named a historic landmark, something that might have prevented its destruction.[5]

On the other hand, the choice of a synagogue to symbolize the Jewish past of Boyle Heights reinforces an unfortunate discussion that is difficult to dislodge: the sense that a predominantly Jewish community has been replaced by a largely Mexican population. While one cannot deny that Latinos now make up the vast majority of Boyle Heights residents, this formulation of change fails to recognize that the Boyle Heights population was *never* majority Jewish and that Mexicans and other ethnic groups have always lived alongside the Jewish population of the past. For example, historian Scott Kurashige has identified Boyle Heights as the single largest Japanese American prewar neighborhood in Southern California, and Japanese Americans, after being released from the internment camps, returned to Boyle Heights, though they too began to move to the suburbs during the postwar period, without the rapidity of Jewish out-migration.[6] During the 1950s, out-migration of the Japanese American population of Boyle Heights led to a significant decline of 11.5 percent in this residential community; however, some of the traditional churches, Buddhist temples, and language schools remained situated in Boyle Heights, with parishioners and participants now regularly migrating into the city of Los Angeles from inner-ring suburbs to attend services or classes at Tenrikyo Church or Nichiren Buddhist Temple.[7] Since 1970, immigration from other parts of Asia has skyrocketed because of new immigration legislation and changing economic patterns, thereby producing an exponential growth dominated by new immigrant families from the Philippines, Korea, China, Vietnam, India, Taiwan, and other parts of South and Southeast Asia. Predictions are that the Asian American population in Southern California, having already surpassed the number of African Americans, is destined to catch up with whites around the mid-twenty-first century.[8]

It was in this changing demographic and cultural landscape of Los Angeles, and therefore the changing terrain of historical remembrance, that former Boyle Heights resident Bruce Kaji, a major real estate developer and banker in Little Tokyo, joined forces with two World War II veterans in 1982 to explore the prospect of a museum about Japanese Americans that would preserve and teach about the heritage of that group, especially their contributions to World War II as soldiers and their unjust incarceration. In 1985, the Japanese American National Museum was officially incorporated as a private, nonprofit institution, and its scheduled opening on April 30, 1992, had to be postponed for ten days following the verdict in the Rodney King trials and its backlash. This political moment pushed the National Museum to quickly broaden its mission "to include the intragroup diversity with the Japanese American community, as well as the interactions with Europeans, Africans, Latinos/Latinas, and Native Americans that have shaped our (Japanese Americans) experiences and perspectives."[9] I would also argue that the relative shrinking of the population of Japanese Americans in Southern California, coupled with the group's distinctive history in the region, moved museum organizers to experiment with new forms of collaboration across racial and ethnic groups, particularly in the museum's local setting in downtown Los Angeles.

During the exhibition at the Japanese American National Museum, for all the talk of Boyle Heights as "a laboratory of democracy," another undercurrent of discussion was under way. As one visitor explained in the comment books on the exhibition, "Unfortunately Boyle Heights as we knew it—will never happen again."[10] Except for rare occasions, such as the multigenerational forum at the International Institute, the older, nostalgic Boyle Heights rarely interacted with the contemporary Mexican-dominated Boyle Heights in serious conversation about their similarities and differences. As various social scientists have reminded us, in the 30 years beginning in the mid-1950s, various Eastside neighborhoods, including Boyle Heights, coalesced in a process of "superbarrioization" to create a single, dominant East Los Angeles, though it was far from monolithic. And by the mid-1980s, with the Latino population in the four-county Los Angeles metropolitan area surging past four million, this growth expanded widely in all directions, fueled by high birthrates and soaring immigration. By the onset of the twenty-first century, it was not just Boyle Heights that was dominated by a Latino majority; the city, county, and region as a whole now verged on a Latino majority.[11]

Without comparable regional or national institutions like the Jewish Historical Society of Southern California or the Japanese American National Museum, the Mexican American community of Los Angeles, including the recently arrived Mexican immigrant community, relied on new narratives of multiracialism, born in the heat of the political process, to frame much of their knowledge of the Boyle Heights past. Nowhere was this process more revealing than in the renaming of the central thoroughfare of the neighborhood in 1995. Brooklyn Avenue, which had evoked for generations of former residents a connection to New York's European immigrant communities, was renamed Avenida César Chávez by the Los Angeles City Council upon the death of the famed Chicano labor leader. Many former residents wrote to the city council protesting this decision, and the media portrayed the conflict as a racial one, pitting Jewish residents of the past against the current Latino population of the area. The Jewish Historical Society's Newsletter reprinted letters to then city councilman Richard Alatorre that described the renaming as "diminishing the cultural heritage that we all shared" and "erasing from our maps the name of an historic Los Angeles street . . . which through all these years, has been the heart and soul of the Eastside community of Boyle Heights."[12] What struck me, however, was how both sides in the conflict failed to consistently recognize the Mexican presence in Boyle Heights from the beginning of the twentieth century, and the role that that presence played in the history of racial interaction and community development. The narrative tended to cast Mexicans as simply the latest newcomers on the scene, vying for attention now through the political process and working against the memories of those who had come before. It was this dynamic that plagued Villaraigosa's first unsuccessful mayoral campaign, though the conflict mirrors others in a city that tends to pit the remembrance of the past against the current Latino majority.

The struggle over historical memory in Boyle Heights faces new challenges in the twenty-first century. With the exodus of so many middle-income residents after World War II, and the subsequent in-migration of the poor, mostly immigrant and Mexican, to Boyle Heights, this racial and economic transformation of the diversity of the Boyle Heights community left its residents with minimized economic control of the neighborhood as renters came to replace homeowners throughout the Heights. Estimates are that up to 75 percent of Boyle Heights residents currently rent, although some of those renters have lived in the community for decades. Because rents and housing prices have skyrocketed in recent years—double the rate of growth in all of Los Angeles County in 2005, for example—many community leaders worry that gentrification will force the remaining long-term residents to leave. With the profound transformation of other city neighborhoods nearby, such as Echo Park and downtown, community leaders are pushing "for City officials and developers to practice responsible planning in order to prevent exclusion of working families in Boyle Heights and the breaking of the historical fabric of this community."[13] With the expansion of the light rail system to Boyle Heights and East L.A. in 2009 and the expansion of both the USC Medical Center and White Memorial Hospital, pressures on the rental market have increased as the stakes in gentrification have soared.

As sociologist Alfredo Huante has argued, the seeds of gentrification in Boyle Heights were planted under the tenure of progrowth mayor Tom Bradley from 1973 to 1993.[14] As the first African American mayor of Los Angeles, Bradley hoped to nurture a growth economy that would lift all residents of the city to new economic heights, but segregated and historically "Caucasian" parts of the city on the Westside and the San Fernando Valley stymied these efforts. Redevelopment efforts, therefore, became largely concentrated in the central business district (CBD) of downtown Los Angeles and, after several false starts, began to finally take off in the late twentieth century.

In Boyle Heights, Huante makes clear that urban planners' vision of the neighborhood decidedly shifted during the Bradley administration. In the 1970s, the Boyle Heights Community Plan concentrated on the "use value" of the neighborhood, fighting off any sense that this was a blighted community that should be destroyed, and instead stressing the stable nature of the community's working-class residents, its attractive walking urban culture, and its proximity to downtown Los Angeles. This argument was shaped by local planners who had witnessed other urban neighborhoods like Bunker Hill and Chavez Ravine described as damaged and unwanted, and made available to wholesale replacement and urban redevelopment for downtown interests.[15]

By the end of the 1980s, however, urban planners in the Bradley administration increasingly turned to assessing the community through "exchange value," stressing the possibility of expansion and improvement of social and transportation services in Boyle Heights because of how the community could develop with investment in its crumbling infrastructure and housing stock. Having suffered through the disinvestment period of the 1980s and the Reagan administration, Bradley hoped that new capital could be leveraged by the Eastside Economic Development Council, which he instituted to consider community concerns alongside economic development.[16] Indeed, it was this philosophy that allowed the Mothers of East Los Angeles to protect the Boyle Heights neighborhood from prisons and nearby toxic waste facilities, as well as Homeboy Industries to leverage the city's gang problems toward a refashioning of public housing options in the neighborhood.[17]

Boyle Heights leaders thought they had found a developer they could work with when Mark Weinstein, CEO of the Santa Monica–based firm MJW Investments, Inc., bought the historic Sears Roebuck & Co. building and its 23-acre site at Olympic Boulevard and Soto for $40 million in 2004. An active philanthropist in Los Angeles' Jewish community, Weinstein's grandparents and great-grandparents all had lived in Boyle Heights, while Weinstein himself had grown up in Canoga Park in the San Fernando Valley. He met extensively with community groups to craft a mixed-use project that met the retail and office needs of the neighborhood while providing plans for townhomes, condominiums, and rental apartments, with 20 percent reserved for low-income families. But in May 2006, MJW Investments announced it was seeking to sell the site, and local leaders remained skeptical that the sale would not again set in motion the forces of gentrification. Maria Cabildo, executive director of East Los Angeles Community Corporation (ELACC), expressed the concern that "we're really on the verge of changing as a community in a very dramatic way."[18]

Some of the forces most critical to the current gentrification trends in Boyle Heights are Latino urban planners and developers who have long been involved in movements to protect the community from destruction, as well as Latino politicians interested in ensuring that the Eastside benefits from urban reinvestment and growth. Frank Villalobos, whose own family had been displaced by the freeway construction of the 1950s, founded Barrio

Planners in the early 1970s to reflect a socially conscious approach to urban planning and development on the Eastside. One of their first projects was to confront the California Department of Transportation (CalTrans) over the construction of the El Monte busway through East Los Angeles, fighting on behalf of the community by suing for the design of sound barrier walls to protect residents along the Pomona Freeway.[19] In the late 1980s, Villalobos would join with MELA to further protect the neighborhood from prison building and environmental contamination.

Yet Villalobos and Barrio Planners also were hired to design the new configuration of Pico-Aliso and the downsizing of public housing units in the Aliso Village area, probably the first example of organized gentrification in the Boyle Heights community in the 1990s. They designed one of the master plans for this transition and were the architects of some of the projects there. They were also hired to create the blueprints for the expansion of USC Medical Center and White Memorial Hospital, as well as designing the new Mendez High School in the Flats neighborhood.[20] According to Frank Villalobos, "By far the best thing we've [Barrio Planners] done is to be the lead architect of the metro rail Gold Line . . . giving our people a chance to link up to the rest of the city."[21] The Gold Line extension of 2009, which most note as the fundamental turning point toward gentrification in Boyle Heights, had to be fought for after the monies to build the Red Line through East Los Angeles were diverted to the North Hollywood Line in the early 1990s.

What made the upgrading of transportation, public housing, and other amenities in Boyle Heights possible was the newfound political vibrancy of Eastside politicians, such as Mayor Antonio Villaraigosa, County Supervisor Gloria Molina, and City Councilmen Richard Alatorre and Jose Huizar. In the twenty-first century, they made sure that Boyle Heights and East Los Angeles benefited from growth and development politics that had taken root in the post-Bradley period, leading to an economic resurgence of downtown Los Angeles and the creation of the new Arts District alongside the Los Angeles River. In many ways, they were linked to the economic development plans crafted by the East Los Angeles Community Union (TELACU), founded in 1968 to counter the internal colonialism of East Los Angeles but also to foster political and economic growth on the Eastside and bring capital improvements to the region.[22] In the twenty-first century, TELACU, along with Barrio Planners and other Latino corporate developers, was often integrated into new plans for economic development in Boyle Heights that led directly to gentrification.

After the financial meltdown and Great Recession of 2008–9, two unique forms of gentrification dictated discussions of the phenomenon in Boyle Heights. The first was the long-term rise of the cost of housing in the neighborhood, particularly the rise of rents in a community that was now dominated by a renting public. With rent-controlled units in Boyle Heights under intense pressure because of public-private ventures such as Pueblo del Sol and the decline of available public housing, Boyle Heights was susceptible to the rapid rise in rents enabled by the broader lack of low-income housing in Southern California at large. The second form of gentrification focused on a transformation of businesses and visible public spaces in Boyle Heights, especially the movement of storefronts like art galleries and coffeehouses into the neighborhood to take advantage of comparatively lower rents. This reshaping of the business environment was the most detectible form of gentrification in Boyle Heights as the visual markers revealed how capital in the community was concentrated in the hands of whites and other non-Latinos, as opposed to internal Latino entrepreneurs.

FIGHTING RISING RENTS

The rent crisis that has plagued Southern California hit Boyle Heights particularly hard. Los Angeles joins with New York, Miami, and San Francisco as the cities in the US with the highest percentages of renters, and Boyle Heights surpasses the city average, as 75 percent of its residents are renters. But in 2013, Los Angeles also became the most rent-burdened city in the entire nation, with 62 percent of the city's renters spending more than 30 percent of their household income on rent. The median apartment rent in Los Angeles in 2017 was $2,483 per month, the highest in the country, with double-digit increases in rental costs becoming the norm in recent years. Moreover, the city's poorest individuals pay the highest percentage of their incomes toward rent, with the majority paying more than 50 percent of their wages, and often much more. Almost all of the 10,000 new units of rental housing built in the 2017 fiscal year were high-end units in downtown Los Angeles, so little development will help the poorer residents of Boyle Heights and Los Angeles.[23]

Another way to think about how the poor are priced out of the Southern California renters' market is to take a long view of the crisis. Since 2000, inflation-adjusted household income in Los Angeles County has decreased by 3 percent, and rents soared by 32 percent by 2017.[24] This rapid rise in rents has unfolded even given the city's rent control regimen, which is supposed to limit most multiunit rental housing increases to no more than 3 percent a year. But violations of the city's Rent Stabilization Ordinance (RSO), which outlines rent-control for multiunit rental housing that was built in 1978 or earlier, are widespread in Boyle Heights, as language barriers and undocumented status often play a role in keeping residents unaware of their rights or in fear of advocating for them. Even though 88 percent of the approximately 16,000 units in Boyle Heights should be protected against high-rent increases by the RSO, violations are common with new owners, who often threaten immigrant residents with deportation in an effort to force them to vacate units.[25]

Two of the most infamous examples of rental conflicts in Boyle Heights, however, do not directly violate the RSO but still display the fears of displacement for low-income residents that have become commonplace in the twenty-first century. The first is the potential razing of the rent-stabilized Wyvernwood apartment complex between Olympic Boulevard and Eighth Street in the southern part of Boyle Heights near the Vernon border. Originally built in 1939, Wyvernwood is known as a prime example of a "garden apartments" complex and is a registered landmark in the California Register of Historical Preservation. With close to 6,000 residents, it is a community that struggled with intense gang involvement during the 1980s and 1990s, and low-income, mostly Latino residents have fought to live there in peace. Moreover, with rents in 2018 averaging around $1,184, the complex has attracted low-income residents wanting to take advantage of the below-market rents (the surrounding neighborhood's rental prices average over $300 more per month). In 1998 the Fifteen Group Land and Development LLC, a Miami-based developer led by cofounder and principal Mark Sanders, acquired the 70-acre site, and in 2008 it established plans to convert the property into a much more dense "21st century, sustainable community that increases the amount of rental and for-sale housing, retail office, and commercial space in Boyle Heights."[26] Plans called to raze the 1,200 two-story garden apartments and build one of the largest housing complexes in the West, 4,400 new units in 24-story high-rises, with 660 apartments designated as affordable housing for 30 years.[27]

But the community that currently lives there has fought against "The New Wyvernwood" for 20 years, often led by El Comité de la Esperanza, a community-based tenant rights organization dedicated to fighting gentrification and saving the "Old Wyvernwood." Residents such as Silvia Cabrera, who moved her family there in 1996, believes that the new development plans are "not fair to those that have been living here for a long time."[28] By fighting the out-of-town developers at Los Angeles City Hall and enlisting the Los Angeles Conservancy to help designate "The Old Wyvernwood" as a protected site for historical preservation in 2012, local residents have kept the redevelopment at bay for two decades.[29] The strength of the neighborhood is that it shows exceptional stability for a multifamily property, having been almost fully occupied for the last 20 years, with residents staying an average of nearly 14 years.[30] The young people who have grown up there also display an enormous attachment to the beauty they see in their low-income community. Mario Serrano, a student at Roosevelt High School in 2013, explained, "Boyle Heights may be depicted as a bad area, but in reality the people in the area are really friendly and respect one another."[31]

While the Wyvernwood struggle shows how the RSO does not prevent a developer from destroying an entire complex to rebuild for another rental clientele, the story of the Mariachi Crossing apartments displays the complex arrangements that can occur when properties that have been built since 1978 fall outside the boundaries of the rent stabilization regimen in Los Angeles. In 1983, a 24-unit Boyle Heights apartment complex was built on Second Street, just a block away from the crossroads intersection of Boyle Avenue and First Street, which had long been known as Mariachi Plaza. Since the 1930s, mariachi musicians had come to this corner to secure day labor playing for baptisms, birthdays, weddings, *quinceañeras,* or other festive occasions for the growing Mexican American community.[32] The new apartment complex quickly became homes for low-income residents, including many mariachis looking to take advantage of the location for selling their skills at Mariachi Plaza.

When the building on Second Street was sold in December 2016, the new owner, Frank B. J. Turner, sent seven tenants—five of them mariachi musicians—notices in January 2017 through the Crescent Canyon Management Company that their rents would rise in April by as much as 80 percent. Francisco Gonzalez, a 12-year resident of the building, said, "We didn't know what to do. We would have had to move out, but everything we could afford was in Riverside or far away."[33] Ironically and tellingly, the intended renovation at the apartment complex was to be called "Mariachi Crossing," taking advantage of the complex's location while forcing out actual mariachis who lived there. Tyler Anderson, codirector of the Los Angeles Center for Community Law and Action (LACCLA), who helped the tenants in this case, explained, "The company that bought this property is branding itself, choosing the mariachi name and logo, they're next to the Mariachi Plaza and they're

FIGURE 31. Mariachi stands in front of Our Lady of Guadalupe mural in Plaza de Mariachi, 1998. Photograph by Virgil Murano. Los Angeles Public Library.

using mariachi in their corporate marketing. But the actual mariachis who live and work there . . . are going to leave and lose their jobs."[34]

The tenants reached out to La Unión de Vecinos, who had originally fought the renovations at Pico-Aliso that led to Pueblo del Sol. They were encouraged to join the newly formed Los Angeles Tenants Union and also received support from LACCLA, a nonprofit that provides free legal services for issues related to affordable housing. With this assistance, the tenants decided to refuse to pay the new April rents through an organized rent strike, a tool from the turn of the twentieth century when European immigrants were battling stunning inequality manifested in unfair rent hikes and evictions by unscrupulous landlords. The vulnerable mariachis became a very public face against gentrification in 2017, speaking at various functions about their situation and joining with residents of other multiunit buildings fighting similar rent hikes across Southern California. The mariachi tenants were given eviction notices, even as they were joined by residents of six other units in the complex fearing that they might face similar increases in rent. In constant negotiation with Turner, the LA Tenants Union organized an overnight protest in front of Turner's Westside home in December 2017. Taking the protest to the landlord's home in the affluent Westside, the demonstrators camped out, chanting and handing out leaflets to Turner's neighbors. In a tactic first used in sprawling Los Angeles, all the way back to the time of organizer Rose Pesotta during the 1933 dressmakers' strike, the LA Tenants Union and the mariachi protesters finally received attention from the city.[35]

Apparently, Turner agreed to negotiate a deal soon after his Westside home was targeted for a demonstration. Almost one year after this confrontation began, renters in the Second Street apartment complex reached an agreement with the building's owner and the property management company that allowed them to remain in their residences. The tenants agreed to a roughly 14 percent price increase and agreed to pay back a portion of the rent that had been withheld during the rent strike. In return, they received a new 42-month lease with yearly rent hikes capped at no more than 5 percent. They also received agreement to their demand that they be able to collectively bargain for new leases as a renters' union. "Mariachi Crossing" became a symbol of what is possible when labor union strategy is applied to the housing crisis, especially in confronting real estate speculators and land gamblers flooding the market. While there have been at least a half-dozen rent strikes in Los Angeles since 2016, "Mariachi Crossing" has special significance, as it gained national attention.[36]

DEFENDING BOYLE HEIGHTS
FROM GENTRIFICATION

The traditional Flats area of Boyle Heights along the Los Angeles River has become a central battleground in the transformation of the public face of businesses in the neighborhood, as it acts as both a barrier and a gateway between the developing Arts District on the east side of the downtown district and the heart of Boyle Heights proper. One of the first skirmishes between community members and capitalizing outsiders occurred in 2015, when realtors associated with the Adaptive Realty Company promoted a bike tour through what they called the "charming, historic, walkable and bikeable neighborhood" of Boyle Heights. They did this by inundating the downtown LA Arts District with flyers that asked: "Why Rent Downtown When You Could Own in Boyle Heights?" Organizers of the bike tour had to quickly cancel, however, when the realtor received messages to "stay outta my hood," forecasting that the bike ride would be a total disaster.[37] The battle over whether the Flats would become a gateway to or barrier for Boyle Heights from the gentrified L.A. Arts District downtown had begun.

At least 17 art galleries opened in Boyle Heights in 2015 and 2016, mostly along Anderson Street and Third Street in the Flats area, south of the new public-private developments of Pueblo del Sol and the former Pico-Aliso housing projects. As the downtown Arts District developed on the other side of the Los Angeles River, then gentrified to the extent that it became price-prohibitive for artists' lofts, studios, and gallery spaces, the arts industry looked east for expansion.[38] Among the many galleries that opened at this time was PSSST Gallery, which set up shop in May 2016 on Third Street in a building that had once housed a Halloween costume factory. In one of the sweetheart deals that so often characterizes the gentrification process, PSSST signed a lease that gave them that space for free for 20 years, facilitated by an anonymous donor who invested $2 million to purchase and renovate the building. PSSST was set up as an experimental art space for marginalized populations that was supposed to be accessible and inviting to the community. Chicano/Latino artists were put on the governing board of the gallery, and local artists were among the first to exhibit there and serve as artists in residence, particularly reaching out to queer artists from the Latino community.[39]

But local groups Defend Boyle Heights and La Unión de Vecinos both rejected the claim that the PSSST Gallery or the other galleries that moved in at this time were open to serious community involvement and leadership. They claimed that "queer-friendliness in the name of redevelopment or revitalization [was] simply a tactic of gentrification known as pink-washing, similar to art-washing, both of which have been used to ignore or mask serious socio-economic issues that affect the livelihood of longstanding locals."[40] These organizations broadened to form the Boyle Heights Alliance Against Art-Washing and Displacement, or BHAAAD. The new alliance marched

FIGURE 32. Union de Vecinos cofounder Elizabeth Blaney speaks on the steps of Nicodim Gallery in Boyle Heights, November 5, 2016. Photograph by Matt Stromberg.

in September 2016 through the neighborhood, handing out mock eviction notices to the galleries for being community "gentrifiers." This group even took on Self-Help Graphics, a centerpiece of Eastside Latino culture and art-making since 1973, for aiding and abetting the movement of other galleries across the Los Angeles River. In October 2016, three acts of vandalism occurred targeting new art galleries in Boyle Heights that the LAPD investigated as possible "hate crimes." Since "Fuck White Art" was spray-painted on the Nicodim Gallery and was interpreted as "anti-white," the Hollenbeck Division called for an emergency dialogue meeting of all interested parties and began extra surveillance at gallery events. The vandalism even prompted district councilman Jose Huizar to denounce the act, under the invocation of Boyle Heights' history, which "has always been inclusionary."[41]

The continued protests began to have an impact over the last few years, with half of the art galleries closing or relocating by the end of 2018 because both artists and patrons "grew skittish" about working in or buying work from a gallery in Boyle Heights. In February 2017, the PSSST Gallery closed its doors over gentrification tensions and the difficult tightrope that community-based artists had to walk to participate in their experimental art space.[42]

One year later, four other galleries—Venus Los Angeles, 356 Mission, UTA Artist Space, and Museum as Retail Space (MaRS)—also announced that they were closing their doors for good or moving to other parts of Los Angeles. These three were followed closely by Chimento Contemporary, whose owner Eva Chimento felt "the location wasn't working for me anymore." Chimento still had two years on her lease when she announced the closing. Many of these galleries, unlike PSSST Gallery, had not even attempted to dialogue with local artists and activists.[43]

The success of BHAAAD and Defend Boyle Heights in encouraging art galleries to leave Boyle Heights and dissuading others from moving in emboldened these groups to expand their efforts toward other entrepreneurs trying to start businesses with capital from outside Boyle Heights. From barbershops to coffeehouses, various businesses have been targeted that seem to represent outside influences on the Boyle Heights community and that critics feel bring little—besides higher prices or outside capital—to the neighborhood. When Weird Wave Coffee Brewers opened on César Chávez Avenue in June 2017 next to a *cambio de cheques* store and a pawnshop, protesters showed up almost immediately. Defend Boyle Heights sponsored regular marches on the sidewalk and called for a boycott. Protesters remembered and highlighted how trendy specialty coffee shops in Highland Park and Echo Park had marked the turning point of gentrification in those neighborhoods. In addition, the previous business on that site had been one of the few black-operated businesses in Boyle Heights and had had its rent raised dramatically, forcing it to close. Three men from outside the community had opened this new business, and they posted a "Latino Owned Business" sign in the window because one of them, Mario Chavarria, was a Latino born in El Salvador and raised in Inglewood. Over the next two years, at least nine acts of vandalism occurred at the site, including a brick thrown through a window and blue paint splattered on the storefront sign. The protests and the vandalism also generated a certain level of sympathy and support from other Boyle Heights residents, including fellow businesses along César Chávez Avenue and a loyal customer base that felt the new coffeehouse provided more options for residents.[44]

The community response to gentrification, or perceived gentrification, can be complicated and uneven. Lino Campos, 41, opened Boyle Heights' newest barbershop in July 2016, and the business, "The Cream Shop" on César Chávez Avenue, was immediately labeled as a gentrifying business on

Facebook. Campos was surprised because he had grown up in Boyle Heights and had attended Roosevelt High School, but he knew he charged $20 for the standard stylish cut at the Cream Shop when other barbers in the neighborhood were charging prices from $8 to $12 on average. Though his prices meant he had fewer customers than other barbershops in the neighborhood, he also drew more customers from outside Boyle Heights. Campos worked hard to let community members know that he lived in the neighborhood, and after his first year in business he became largely accepted. "I want to be [the] first Chicano to have a chain of barbershops where we can continue to support other communities as well," explained Campos, thankful that protesters eventually left him alone.[45]

GENTE-FICATION: THE MANY FACES OF COMMUNITY DISPLACEMENT

This pattern of homegrown businesses emerging from a generation of Boyle Heights Latino residents has expanded dramatically over the past ten years and created confusion among those who typically define gentrification as an influx of white people from outside the neighborhood invading the barrio/ghetto, leading to racial minority and longtime resident displacement. When Juan Romero opened Primera Taza Coffee on First Street in 2009, he did it to give his own community "the kind of place he wanted as a college student, when he drove miles from Boyle Heights to find a comfortable place to study."[46] Although Primera Taza does sell $4 lattes, it also sells Café Americano under the name Café Chicano and features specialty coffees from Mexico. Similarly, Capuyo Café opened in July 2018 as a "sensitive" coffee shop, featuring Latin American coffees only, and owned by one of the only Latina business owners in the neighborhood, Daisy Iniguez. Iniguez, the daughter of two Mexican immigrants, explained, "I wanted to continue my ancestors' roots and culture. Here in Boyle Heights, we're so rich in this essence of beauty, so I wanted to keep that going."[47] Or as Romero declared, "We grew up always talking about being a part of something bigger. We've learned just how to create it for ourselves. Making it doesn't mean moving out."[48]

Like coffeehouses becoming community-oriented hubs of activity, businesses emerging from young, upwardly mobile, often college-educated Latinos back from school usually were quicker to connect with the modern—some would say more Americanized—tastes and preferences of young Latinos than the immigrant-owned shops that had dominated Boyle Heights. When the popular taco restaurant Guisados opened in Boyle Heights in 2010, it stood out from other restaurants along César Chávez Avenue and attracted a wider clientele, some that came from outside the neighborhood. Offering an "Armando Palmero" to drink and advertising its selection of tacos as "gluten-free," Guisados has become quite successful for owner Armando de la Torre, who grew up in the suburbs east of Los Angeles. Likewise, La Monarca Bakery opened in 2014 as a Latino-owned coffee shop and bakery that sells café de olla, pan dulce, and a vegetarian chorizo quiche but clearly is attracting a mixed clientele of the old and new. Opposite Mariachi Plaza on the corner of Boyle Avenue and First Street, La Monarca was described as "an upscale Mexican café and *panaderia*" by the *Los Angeles Times* but is trying to appeal both to local residents from the renovated market-rate apartment building, where it is located on the bottom floor, and to the low-income housing complex across the street.[49]

These new Latino-owned businesses reflect a pattern that some have called "self-gentrification" or "homegrown gentrification." Guillermo Uribe, owner of Eastside Luv, a self-described *pocho* bar in Boyle Heights (the term *pocho* is generally used to denigrate Americanized Mexicans who have lost their Spanish) coined the term *gente*-fication in 2007 to describe what he called "the potential of improving the community from the inside out." Uribe, who grew up in East Los Angeles, explained, "If gentrification is happening, it might as well be from people who care about the existing culture. In the case of Boyle Heights, it would be best if the *gente* decide to invest in improvements because they are more likely to preserve its integrity."[50] Uribe opened his bar in 2006 along First Street and instituted sign-ups to participate in MariachiOke, which allows patrons to engage in karaoke but with a catalog of traditional songs played by a live mariachi band. Others from this generation of college-educated Chicanos who have returned to Boyle Heights embrace the term *gente*-fication as "being part of a neighborhood revitalization effort that protects the area from invasion by richer (and whiter) outsiders."[51]

But the antigentrification activists in Boyle Heights largely reject all gentrifiers regardless of race, seeing little distinction between *gente*-fication and its white-faced counterpart. Leonardo Vilchis, an organizer with La Unión de Vecinos, explained that if poor renters suffer from the changes of *gente*-fication, then those businesses responsible should be boycotted. "People want to pretend that their actions don't have an impact on the people already living here, but when the prices go up, the poor have to go someplace else," explained Vilchis. "Coming back is emblematic of some kind of opportunism. We had children going to college two decades ago, but back then it wasn't cool to live here."[52] Community organizer Asiyahola Sankara is even more pointed in his criticism: "When someone leaves the community but returns with a different mindset it's no longer beneficial to the community. . . . You know if the person comes back and they have the same mindset as a gentrifier who's never lived there before, then it's just as bad."[53]

The controversy between those who believe in *gente*-fication and the antigentrifying protesters in Boyle Heights is so passionate and full of contradictions that it was ripe for a Hollywood treatment. In 2018, the STARZ network launched the show *Vida*, which revolves around two well-to-do sisters who return to Boyle Heights after the death of their mother to take over a building owned by the mother and a neighborhood bar managed by her lesbian wife.[54] Very quickly, the two daughters become targets of antigentrification activists and old battles that center on personal and political differences in approaches to identity, race, class, and sexuality. The show itself was developed by Latina creator Tanya Saracho, who leads a nearly all-Latina writers' room, something unheard of on any English-language TV network in 2018. In 2020, Netflix took on the phenomenon with the series *Gentefied,* also based in Boyle Heights.[55]

Despite the controversy and tensions attached to gentrification in Boyle Heights, the overall demographic changes in the population so far have been minimal. In the year 2000, Boyle Heights was almost exclusively Latino, with the population reaching 96 percent. Fifteen years later, Boyle Heights has remained 96 percent Latino.[56] Moreover, while the median percent change in home value in Boyle Heights in those 15 years has increased by 43 percent, that figure was still less than for the entire Los Angeles County, which saw a 52 percent increase in the same period. Five of the 25 census tracts in Boyle Heights did have an increase in home values above the median, indicating substantial investment in certain areas of Boyle Heights.[57] The percentage change in educational attainment for Latinos also indicates the lack of substantial gentrification. Although the Boyle Heights Latino population with a bachelor's degree did increase by 2.3 percent in the last 15 years, that figure is almost half the size of the median increase for the overall Latino population in Los Angeles, at 4.2 percent, and well behind the median increase in educational attainment for all populations in Los Angeles, at 5.4 percent.[58]

On the other hand, it does seem that certain aspects of *gente*-fication have begun to affect the population in Boyle Heights. Because Boyle Heights remains three-quarters renters, as opposed to homeowners, the fact that rents went up in the neighborhood by $800 on average from 2000 to 2015 is sure to have priced out some low-income families, especially those who had historically been drawn to Boyle Heights for its affordability. Altogether, the one study that statistically tried to determine the current patterns of gentrification "determined that *gente*-fication did occur in Boyle Heights between 2000 and 2015, although not substantially."[59] With the reality of this dynamic, regardless of scale, some lawyers and Latino professionals who flock to Boyle Heights as homeowners and residents are trying to pair their movement with advocacy for the neighborhood. "It's really easy to say no to things, but the harder question is how do we change things and empower people at the same time," said lawyer Alfred Fraijo. Indeed, he captured the dilemma facing Boyle Heights when he explained, "If we're closed to outsiders, we're going to be stuck in the past. If we can figure out how to say yes to development and history at the same time, we can really be a model for this city that hasn't had one yet."[60]

Despite media depictions of race relations in Southern California that focus on conflict, competition, and riots, Boyle Heights residents—past and present—hope for a future in which individuals of different races live and work side by side in solidarity, even if that means struggling for survival together. This includes honoring Boyle Heights' multiracial past. For example, students at Roosevelt High School have even tried to right past wrongs by advocating that former Japanese American students receive the diplomas they were denied when they were incarcerated in America's concentration camps. And one group of students took it upon themselves to rebuild the school's Japanese garden, which was destroyed by vandals during World War II. These students have reached across generations and ethnicities to embrace and amplify the contributions of others, positioning themselves as part of the political and multiracial legacy that this book has sought to unearth. Calling attention to the Japanese American students whose futures were thwarted by incarceration also resonates for current Roosevelt students, who want all races to receive the educational opportunities that are so often lacking in a school of over 5,000, especially one with deteriorating funding, shrinking personnel, and an escalating dropout rate. Unfortunately, such conditions are far too often the norm in schools where the student body is majority people of color.

Boyle Heights residents who moved away have felt the absence of this multiracial spirit since they left the neighborhood—and it is something they've never been able to recreate elsewhere as adults in Southern California. Most of the personal testimonials gathered by historical recovery projects on Boyle Heights come from former residents who have not lived there for over forty years, yet still refer to the community as "their home." It has been common for me to engage in intense conversations about Boyle Heights with someone who has not ventured into the actual Boyle Heights area for more than three or four decades. Various informal groups, such as the "Saxons" or the "Jasons," which started as clubs for young people in the 1930s and 1940s, have continued to meet every week. With participants in their 70s and 80s, these groups never meet in East Los Angeles but rather attract former Boyle Heights residents to weekly get-togethers in homes and diners in the San Fernando Valley or San Gabriel Valley. Why hasn't Tujunga or Beverly Hills or Palm Springs become "home" for those who were once Roosevelt's Rough Riders? And why does so much of their social lives continue to revolve around friendships and relationships that began when they were children and adolescents in Boyle Heights? They explain that they often don't know their neighbors in the towns and cities they moved into as young adults or are currently living in as elderly residents. As they have moved up the economic ladder, as most of these expatriates usually have done, they have lost the connectivity that a working-class community like Boyle Heights celebrated. Moreover, these personal connections often involved friendships across racial lines, something they are much less likely to experience in the stratified suburbs of contemporary Los Angeles. While certainly some of this may be nostalgia, I believe there is more here regarding loss of community and connection in greater Los Angeles.

Of course, what draws others to research and writing on Boyle Heights—those who never lived in the neighborhood and have no personal connection to the region—is also this desire for solidarity, for knowing a community that seemingly worked across the racial divide even during war and depression. Even though I was born in Boyle Heights, this is still clearly part of my own motivation to research this history, as a way to provide insights for the Los Angeles I envision today and for the future. But this intense desire and passion for a working multiracialism in Los Angeles can also serve as blinders that keep one from fully investigating both what has and hasn't worked in the past in Boyle Heights, by neglecting the very real tensions and glossing over the failures. Working on this project, I have learned that we must resist the very natural tendency to highlight only the positive, because only by unearthing the complexity of multiracialism in the past will we be able to fight for new multiracial communities that work in the present and future.

What will happen to Boyle Heights in the future is unclear. It is certain that antigentrification activists have, for the moment, pushed back against the onslaught of traditional white-dominated forces of change such as art galleries, while Latino *gente*-fication is occurring throughout Boyle Heights, but perhaps not at significant levels that encourage fear of widespread displacement. Rather, it seems that the return of Latino college graduates to East Los Angeles has pushed rents up while transforming the range of businesses that cater to a younger, more upwardly mobile Latino clientele. One cannot ignore the possibility that this form of *gente*-fication may just be one stage in the more traditional process of gentrification, in which a new Latino population are intermediaries before a white influx, with longtime residents still vulnerable to being priced out. In this scenario, "*Gentefiers* can thus operate as middlemen that set up the foundation for top-down gentrification and push out poor Latinos from their communities while giving way to racial change."[61]

But Boyle Heights has also demonstrated resiliency against gentrification. And the key will be whether Boyle Heights remains a place that low-income Latinos, particularly recent immigrants of all legal statuses, can find shelter and establish their families. The neighborhood has a host of activist groups dedicated to protecting the rights of low-income residents, but also committed organizations like the East Los Angeles Community Corporation (ELACC), whose mission since its founding in 1995 has been economic and social justice on the Eastside through affordable housing for low- and moderate-income families. Although unable to ensure that current residents will not be displaced, ELACC, having leveraged about $135 million of investment to the Eastside and facilitated over 500 units of affordable housing as of mid-2018, has often been very successful at partnering with other developers to underwrite affordable housing as part of the future of Boyle Heights.[62]

Advancing city housing policy is also critical to the availability of affordable housing and to the development of plans that do not lead to displacement and homelessness, and the city council is still a crucial arm with the power to mandate that low-income housing be part of whatever plans eventually do get implemented. In this way, the upcoming election of the next Boyle

Heights city council person in 2020 is crucial to the future direction of local housing policy and the protection of current residents in the neighborhood.

While I believe the availability of affordable housing is key to maintaining a recognizable Boyle Heights, so is ensuring local residents' ability to begin new businesses. Generations of street vendors and small shops have been allowed to flourish in the neighborhood, serving a diverse clientele of Boyle Heights residents and providing new opportunities for individuals to provide for their families and loved ones. The decision by the Los Angeles City Council to legalize street vendors in the city in 2018 is a critical start to supporting small entrepreneurs, especially among the undocumented, while strengthening the local economy.[63] The formation of other incubators that will allow vendors to have greater access to capital, and small businesses to rent affordable commercial space to expand their enterprises, is important to sustaining the locally rich street life that has long marked Boyle Heights.

There is no reason that young Latinos who grew up in Boyle Heights and return to the neighborhood after college should not be seen as assets to the community. Their homecoming marks a significant development for the community that should be welcomed rather than feared. New businesses that this generation founds to serve their needs can also add a new level of inclusion to Boyle Heights history, from LGBTQ-friendly environments to technologically advanced operations that have the capacity to excite schoolchildren about the possibilities of higher learning. What is vital is that these new businesses work collaboratively with older shops and longtime residents in the neighborhood to ensure equal access, affordable products, and diverse options for the multiple generations and socioeconomic classes that continue to make up the neighborhood.

The multiracial history of Boyle Heights must continue to play a role in the development of the neighborhood, connecting those who currently live east of the river with the offspring of former residents who left long ago. This past is also a blueprint amid a drastically changing Los Angeles and a model of hope for a present and future city that includes new multiracial communities. The current struggles of neighborhoods like Koreatown, Inglewood, and South Los Angeles to bring residents together amid diversity and change can see the histories of multiracial sites like Crenshaw, downtown, and Boyle Heights as resources and examples of local coalition and community building.

But we must remember this history in full—that the destruction of the polyglot community of Boyle Heights of the mid-twentieth century was a function of a growing white suburban privilege that pulled some families away from the neighborhood, while continued racial discrimination against Mexicans and others confined most people of color to this neighborhood, leaving them vulnerable to government urban renewal policies that directly targeted multiracial communities for public housing, freeway construction, and discriminatory mortgage lending policies. Our personal nostalgia must not blind us to the forces that pulled the community apart or to the ones that bound us together. Only by confronting the multiple histories and contemporary conditions of Boyle Heights may the true power of the multiracial past in Los Angeles be recognized for its importance and its continued impact on the lives of us all.

TIME LINE

1781 Pueblo of Los Angeles is founded at Tongva-Gabrielino village of Yang-Na. El Paredón Blanco (White Bluffs) within pueblo boundaries; Tongva-Gabrielino servitude.

1800–1850 Californio ranchos: Spanish and Mexican land grants; secularization of mission lands. Rancho San Antonio and Mission San Gabriel lands encircle the mesa of what becomes Boyle Heights.

1824 Mexico liberalizes immigration laws for Europeans and Anglo-Americans; by 1840 Anglos and Europeans dominate local business.

1846–48 US conquest of California; 1848 Treaty of Guadalupe Hidalgo ends the Mexican-American War (1846–48). Mexico cedes California to the United States.

1850 California becomes a US state.

1858 Irish immigrant Andrew Boyle purchases land on El Paredón Blanco, plants vineyards, and builds a home on what becomes Boyle Avenue.

1851–1860s 1851 Land Act (whereby Spanish-Mexicans must prove ownership of their land), land speculation, floods, and drought end "age of ranchos"; violence against both Mexican newcomers and Californios increases as they are lumped together racially by the new Anglo elite.

1870s–1920s African Americans migrate to Los Angeles from the South and Southwest; Los Angeles Forum, the People's Independent Church, the Black Masons, Shriners, and Odd Fellows emerge in Los Angeles.

1871 Andrew Boyle dies, leaving his property in the hands of his son-in-law, William Henry Workman.

1876 Workman renames El Paredón Blanco "Boyle Heights" in honor of father-in-law; subdivides Boyle Heights into residential communities and brings water, bridges, and horse-drawn interurban rail system to Boyle Heights.

1876–1914	Four million Sicilians, Calabrians, and others from southern Italy migrate to the US amid global disruptions in the Italian citrus and wine industries; families settle into Boyle and Lincoln Heights.
1879	California constitution of 1879 allows incorporated cities and towns to remove and prohibit the creation of Chinese neighborhoods.
1882	Chinese Exclusion Act prohibits immigration of Chinese laborers. Japanese immigrants are recruited to fill the need for cheap labor.
1885	Railway fare wars bring down price of transcontinental travel; population booms; opulent homes built in Boyle Heights, marking its elite standing.
1889	Real estate bubble bursts, opens Boyle Heights to racial and ethnic residents.
1890–1903	Suppression of strikes by telegraph and railway unions; antiunion "open shop" promoted by the Merchants and Manufacturing Association (M&M) and the *Los Angeles Times*.
1890–1910	Boxcar communities of Mexican railway workers in Boyle Heights.
1896	First Catholic parish created in Boyle Heights; St. Mary's Church dedicated one year later.
1902	Residential racial covenants funnel racial and ethnic "undesirables" into neighborhoods such as Boyle Heights.
1902–7	38,000 Japanese move first to Hawai'i, then to the US West amid Meiji repression in Japan.
1903	Interurban railway connects Boyle Heights to factories, agriculture, and retail; railway strikes suppressed.
1905	Russian Molokans, a pacifist sect of the Russian Orthodox Church, flee Russia to avoid conscription into the Russo-Japanese War. Many settle in the Flats of Boyle Heights. Russian Revolution of 1905 fails; Jews flee increase in anti-Semitic pogroms.
1906	San Francisco Earthquake; relocation of many Japanese Americans to Los Angeles. Little Tokyo becomes the center of community life.
1907	Ricardo and Enrique Flores Magón, exiled from Mexico in 1903, move their Partido Liberal Mexicano (PLM) to Los Angeles and continue protests against semifeudal conditions and capitalism in fiery speeches in the Plaza.
1908	Race-based zoning laws create residential versus industrial zones, protecting the Westside from industrial development. Eastside Boyle Heights remains open to industrial development, and by 1915 the industrial district encompasses the Flats area of Boyle Heights.
1910	Sicilian anarchist Ludovico Caminita of the Gruppo L'Era Nuova (New Era Group) relocates to Los Angeles to be closer to the PLM.

1910–20	Mexican Revolution; many displaced individuals and families migrate to Los Angeles.
1910s	Los Angeles becomes the largest manufacturing city in the West; Industrial Workers of the World (IWW, "Wobblies") attempts to organize all workers, regardless of race, nationality, gender, or skill.
1912	Anti-Italian brutalization in the general strike in 1912 in Lawrence, Massachusetts, and subsequent labor conflicts bridge divisions between northern and southern Italians and forge a new national ethnic identity across the United States.
1913	California Alien Land Law prevents ownership of land by "aliens ineligible for citizenship."
1914	Congregation Talmud Torah purchase property on Breed Street in Boyle Heights, where they eventually build the Breed Street Shul, the largest and longest-running synagogue in the neighborhood.
1914–18	World War I mobilizes industry; more than a third of Los Angeles factories are located in largely working-class districts in the central city near Boyle Heights; war forces many Europeans to flee homelands and immigrate to the United States; the persecution and 1915 massacre of 1.5 million Armenians in Turkey precipitates exodus to other countries.
1919	St. Peter's Church in Lincoln Heights is designated the Italian national church of Los Angeles.
1920	Pan-African "National Convention of Peoples of African Descent" is held in Los Angeles, which produces Division 156 of the Universal Negro Improvement Association (UNIA); in 1922 Pan-African activist Marcus Garvey visits Los Angeles.
1920s	Significant numbers of Jewish immigrants move to Los Angeles from the East Coast and Midwest, eventually making Boyle Height home to the largest Jewish community west of Chicago; working-class Boyle Heights builds *folkschule,* Vladeck Center, Cooperative Center to promote Yiddish *kultur* and leftist ideals.
1923	Theodore Roosevelt Senior High School opens doors as a "multiethnic utopia."
1924	"National origins" principle of Immigration Act of 1924 prohibits immigration from Asia and limits immigration from southern and eastern Europe.
1924	Modern Talmud Torah and Social Center opens, renamed Soto-Michigan Jewish Community Center in 1934, renamed Eastside Jewish Community Center in 1952.
1929	Japanese American Citizens League established; stock market crashes; Great Depression begins.

1930	Citizens Committee creates job placement service for unemployed city residents, is quickly overwhelmed; ethnic organizations support indigent Jews and keep Japanese employed, but Catholic Charities introduces anti-Mexican policy; International Workers Organization (IWO), a Jewish fraternity affiliated with the Communist Party, provides mutual aid for working-class immigrants, organizes "Work for Wages" march, and begins monthly protests; LAPD "Red Squad" created to brutalize activists and protesters.
1930–60	Middle-income housing developed on the Westside prompts Boyle Heights Jews to consider moving west; Jewish migration to the Westside accelerates in the forties and fifties.
1931–34	Mexican Repatriation Campaign, relying on Spanish speaking social workers, targets racially segregated neighborhoods, especially the Flats of Boyle Heights.
1932	Franklin Delano Roosevelt elected; encourages workers to stand up for a decent wage; unions make progress in organizing workers as part of Roosevelt's New Deal.
1933	El Monte Berry Strike becomes an international incident; ILGWU organizes in Los Angeles; Dressmakers Strike of Mexican American and Jewish women paves way for stronger links between industrial unionism and community-based efforts; Anti-Defamation League organizes Community Relations Committee (CRC) to monitor Nazi activities in the US and combat anti-Semitism; fascist organizations discovered in Los Angeles.
1934	Tenrikyo Church established in Boyle Heights.
1937	Congress of Industrial Organizations (CIO) organizes in the steel, automobile, rubber, garment, and construction industries in Los Angeles. In Boyle Heights, the rise of the CIO generation meant that US-born ethnics from immigrant families would take leadership roles in the developing political and cultural context of the New Deal, especially in the Mexican and Jewish communities.
1938	Kristallnacht (the Night of Broken Glass) in Germany marks the beginning of open and intensified violence against Jewish people, culminating in the Holocaust.
1939	El Congreso, the first national Latino civil rights assembly, convenes in East Los Angeles with over 1,000 delegates; platform calls for an end to segregation, the right to join unions, and the right for immigrants to work without fear of deportation.
1941	Japan bombs Pearl Harbor, prompting US entry into World War II (1941–45); Executive Order 8802 outlaws defense industry discrimination on the basis of race, creed, or national origins as labor shortages make equal employment hiring a national priority.

1941–42	Following the passage of the United States Housing Act of 1937 (Wagner–Steagall Act) funding public housing agencies, public housing is built in Boyle Heights: Ramona Gardens (1941), Estrada Courts (1942), Pico Gardens (August 1942), and Aliso Village (1942). Aliso Village is the first integrated public housing; priority for public housing is given to war-industry workers, and later to returning servicemen.
1941–49	The anticommunist California Committee, created under right-wing state senator Jack Tenney (Tenney Committee), utilizes same tactics of humiliating and red-baiting as the federal House Un-American Activities Committee (HUAC). Tenney often equates communism with Judaism and accuses the Soto-Michigan Center of promoting "communist propaganda." By the end of 1948, the Jewish Centers Association tightens control over the Soto-Michigan Center and expels the Jewish People's Fraternal Order for its affiliation with the communist-linked IWO.
1942–43	American Jewish Congress sponsors the World War II bomber *The Spirit of Boyle Heights*, offering "proof of their patriotism"; Los Angeles becomes "Arsenal of Democracy."
1942–44	Japanese American removal and incarceration.
1943	Zoot Suit Riots explode in downtown Los Angeles and surrounding barrios, including Boyle Heights.
1943–64	Bracero Program fills agricultural labor shortage from World War II and replaces the now-incarcerated Japanese Americans with Mexican *braceros*.
1944	Two hundred thousand African Americans move to Los Angeles for employment in war industries; Little Tokyo nicknamed "Bronzeville."
1944	Sleepy Lagoon Murder convictions overturned through defense efforts from El Congreso and the Sleepy Lagoon Defense Committee (SLDC); CRC moves from a principally Jewish "defense" agency to an agency dedicated to fighting bigotry against any Los Angeles residents.
1945	Jewish community centers become the centerpiece of Jewish community life.
1945, 1946	Edward Roybal travels to Chicago to study community organizing at independent radical Saul Alinsky's Chicago-based Industrial Area Foundation (IAF).
1947	Community Service Organization (CSO) founded to advocate for Latino civil rights and to elect Edward Roybal to Los Angeles City Council. CSO creates the Health Committee, the Housing

Committee, the Civil Rights Committee; organizes massive voter registration effort.

1947–52   Legislation targets activists and unions: 1947 Taft-Hartley Act; 1950 Smith Act; 1952 McCarran-Walter Act establishing quota system for immigrants.

1948   Congress passes the "Truman Directive," which prioritizes immigration of "displaced persons" from World War II. "White" begins to apply to those of European descent; white ethnics gain access to "white" residential options; Supreme Court overturns racial restrictive covenants, though residential discrimination against blacks and Mexican Americans continues.

1949   Soto-Michigan Center organizes first Festival of Friendship to "bring together Mexican, Japanese, Negro, and Jewish youth in a cooperative venture."

1949–53   Collapse of support for public housing. 1950 Los Angeles Committee to Protect the Foreign Born (LACPFB) is founded in response to growing anti-immigrant sentiments; activists targeted for deportation.

1951   Bloody Christmas incident, LAPD brutalizes jailed Latinos, resulting in broken bones and ruptured organs.

1952–62   Expansion of the freeway system by five major freeways, including Golden State Freeway, Santa Ana Freeway, and Pomona Freeway; 15 percent of Boyle Heights is taken up by freeways, largely to serve suburban commuters traveling through metropolitan Los Angeles rather than local residents.

1956   Destruction of Bunker Hill neighborhood as part of urban renewal, serving the commercial interests of private developers, including creation of a cultural district downtown.

1958   Eastside Jewish Community Center (Soto-Michigan Center) sold to All Nations Church.

1959   Chavez Ravine homes bulldozed for development of Dodger Stadium.

1960s   Mexican male migrants form *clubes sociales* (social clubs) to collectively send money to their hometowns.

1964   War on Poverty's Economic Opportunity Act is passed by Congress; Boyle Heights youth create Young Citizens for Community Action, later renamed Young Chicanos for Community Action (remaining YCCA).

1965   Watts Riots; creation of the Economic and Youth Opportunities Agency of Greater Los Angeles (EYOA); antipoverty funds approved for Los Angeles. Immigration and Nationality Act of 1965 replaces the Bracero Program and for the first time sets limits on the number of Latin American immigrants allowed to legally enter the United States, creating surge in undocumented workers.

1966   YCCA organize Brown Berets, modeled after Black Panthers.

1967   César Chávez, United Farm Workers (UFW) leader, speaks to students about his organizing techniques, and students join UFW picket lines.

1968   Chicano Student Walkouts in East Los Angeles protest discrimination in the school system.

1968   The East Los Angeles Community Union (TELACU), Barrio Planners, and other Latino corporate developers create plans for economic development in Boyle Heights, leading in directly to gentrification.

1968–72   Five of six major auto assembly plants in California close; auto manufacturing collapses in L.A.

1968–74   1970 Family Planning Services and Population Research Act used to support systematic coercive sterilization of poor, Spanish-speaking women at Los Angeles County–USC Medical Center. Media attention brings an end to practice.

1970   National Chicano Moratorium is organized to protest the Vietnam War.

1970s   Immigration skyrockets from the Philippines, Korea, China, Vietnam, India, Taiwan, and other parts of South and Southeast Asia because of new immigration legislation; economic conditions and civil strife in Mexico and Central America lead to increased immigration to the United States.

1970–90   Long-standing Mexican American residents move to new Latino suburbs in eastern Los Angeles County.

1981   Artist-In-Residence (AIR) bill allows artists to live legally in the areas that can no longer be put to industrial use as long as they obtain a business license; Arts District created alongside the Los Angeles River, threatens to spill over and gentrify Boyle Heights.

1986   Las Madres del Este de Los Angeles / Mothers of East Los Angeles (MELA) protest plans to build a prison in East Los Angeles; Immigration Reform and Control Act of 1986 ends up creating a more mixed-legal-status Boyle Heights community.

1987   Dolores Mission Church declares itself a sanctuary church for the undocumented.

1992   Rodney King Riots; Homeboy Industries created to offer alternative pathways to gang members in the area.

1994–98   California Votes for Anti-Immigrant Policies: Proposition 187 (1994) bans social services for illegal immigrants; Proposition 209

(1996) prohibits affirmative action in state hiring; Proposition 227 (1998) eliminates bilingual education.

1995   Brooklyn Avenue, which evoked for generations of former residents a connection to New York's European immigrant communities, is renamed Avenida César Chávez

1997   Demolition of Aliso Village and Pico Gardens, replaced by Pueblo del Sol, a mixed-income, transit-oriented community.

2000   Breed Street Synagogue declared a Los Angeles Historic-Cultural Monument.

2006   Eastside (Soto-Michigan) Jewish Community Center, iconic for its California midcentury style, destroyed.

2007   Term *gente*-fication emerges to describe "homegrown gentrification" by Latino-owned businesses.

2009   The Metro Gold Line created by Barrio Planners to give "our people a chance to link up to the rest of the city" spurs gentrification efforts.

2013   Los Angeles becomes the most rent-burdened city in the entire nation, with 62 percent of the city's renters spending more than 30 percent of their household income on rent.

2015   Defend Boyle Heights and Boyle Heights Alliance Against Art-Washing and Displacement (BHAAAD) founded to combat gentrification from the L.A. Arts District downtown.

2017   Los Angeles Tenants Union established to protest rent increases at Mariachi Crossing apartments; rent strikes and protests.

2017   Ten thousand new units of high-end rental housing built in downtown Los Angeles.

2017–18   Art gallery exodus from Boyle Heights (PSSST, Venus Los Angeles, 356 Mission, UTA Artist Space, and Museum as Retail Space/MaRS) over tension around gentrification.

MAYOR AND CITY COUNCIL LISTS

LOS ANGELES MAYORS SINCE 1930

John Porter (1929–33)
Frank Shaw (1933–38)
Fletcher Bowron (1938–53)
Norris Poulson (1953–61)
Sam Yorty (1961–73)
Tom Bradley (1973–93)
Richard Riordan (1993–2001)
James Hahn (2001–5)
Antonio Villaraigosa (2005–13)
Current: Eric Garcetti, (elected 2013)

BOYLE HEIGHTS CITY COUNCIL
REPRESENTATIVES SINCE 1925*

Winfred J. Sanborn (1925–31)
Howard E. Dorsey (1931–35)
Parley P. Christensen (1935–37)
Howard E. Dorsey (1937)
Winfred J. Sanborn (1937–39)
Parley P. Christensen (1939–49)
Edward Roybal (1949–62)
Gilbert Lindsay (1962–70)

*The Boyle Heights District was created in a 15-district system under the 1925 Charter.

Arthur Snyder (1970–85)
Richard Alatorre (1985–99)
Nick Pacheco (1999–2003)
Antonio Villaraigosa (2003–5)
Current: Jose Huizar (elected 2005)

NOTES

1. INTRODUCTION: A MULTIRACIAL MAP FOR AMERICA

1. For one of my earliest attempts to contextualize the 1992 Los Angeles Riots, see George J. Sánchez, "Face the Nation: Race, Immigration, and the Rise of Nativism in Late Twentieth Century America," *International Migration Review* 31:4 (Winter 1997): 1009–30.

2. Mollie Murphy, Mary Nishi, and Sandie Okada, life history interview conducted by Sojin Kim and Darcie Iki for Re-examining Boyle Heights Project, January 18, 2001, Los Angeles, transcript, Japanese American National Museum, Los Angeles.

3. These letters are now in the possession of the Japanese American National Museum and were used in an exhibition on racial interaction in the Boyle Heights neighborhood that opened in Los Angeles at the museum in fall 2002.

4. Murphy, Nishi, and Okada, interview, p. 16.

5. See, for example, Arnold R. Hirsch, *Making the Second Ghetto: Race and Housing in Chicago, 1940–1960*, 3rd ed. (Chicago: University of Chicago Press, 1998). For the classic story of barrioization, see Albert Camarillo, *Chicanos in a Changing Society: From Mexican Pueblos to American Barrios in Santa Barbara and Southern California, 1848 to 1930* (Cambridge, MA: Harvard University Press, 1979). For a recent discussion of the development of the idea of the ghetto, see Mitchell Duneier, *Ghetto: The Invention of a Place, the History of an Idea* (New York: Farrar, Straus and Giroux, 2017).

6. See Robert E. Park and Ernest W. Burgess, *Introduction to the Science of Sociology* (Chicago: University of Chicago Press, 1921), and Robert E. Park, Ernest W. Burgess, and Roderick D. McKenzie, *The City* (Chicago: University of Chicago Press, 1925). For a wider analysis of the role of Park in broad social science theory, see R. Fred Wacker, *Ethnicity, Pluralism, and Race: Race Relations Theory in America before Myrdal* (Westport, CT: Greenwood Press, 1983), 41–59.

7. Henry Yu, *Thinking Orientals: Migration, Contact, and Exoticism in Modern America* (New York: Oxford University Press, 2001), 38–42.

8. This phrase is taken from "The New Colossus," a sonnet written in 1883 by the poet Emma Lazarus to raise money for the pedestal for the Statue of Liberty, and eventually memorialized on a bronze plaque on the inside of the pedestal in 1903. For the continued salience of spatial assimilation theory in sociology, see John R. Logan, Richard D. Alba, and Wenquan Zhang, "Immigrant Enclaves and Ethnic Communities in New York and Los Angeles," *American Sociological Review* 67:2 (April 2002): 299–322.

9. Thomas Lee Philpott, *The Slum and the Ghetto: Neighborhood Deterioration and Middle-Class Reform, Chicago, 1880–1930* (New York: Oxford University Press, 1978), 137–45.

10. Logan, Alba, and Zhang, "Immigrant Enclaves," 304–5.

11. One significant exception to this pattern is the work of my colleague Leland Saito in *Race and Politics: Asian Americans, Latinos, and Whites in a Los Angeles Suburb* (Urbana: University of Illinois Press, 1998).

12. The inspiration for many of these works is the important theoretical text of Michael Omi and Howard Winant, *Racial Formation in the United States: From the 1960s to the 1980s* (New York: Routledge, 1986), and its second edition, *Racial Formation in the United States: From the 1960s to the 1990s* (New York: Routledge, 1994). For smart analyses of racial formation theory since this classic work, see Daniel Martinez HoSang, Oneka LaBennett, and Laura Pulido, eds., *Racial Formation in the Twenty-First Century* (Berkeley: University of California Press, 2012).

13. George Lipsitz, *The Possessive Investment in Whiteness: How White People Profit from Identity Politics*, rev. and enl. ed. (Philadelphia: Temple University Press, 2009), 6.

14. See George J. Sánchez, *Becoming Mexican American: Ethnicity, Culture and Identity in Chicano Los Angeles, 1900–1945* (New York: Oxford University Press, 1993).

15. Douglas S. Massey and Nancy A. Denton, *American Apartheid: Segregation and the Making of the Underclass* (Cambridge, MA: Harvard University Press, 1993), 15.

16. George Lipsitz, *How Racism Takes Place* (Philadelphia: Temple University Press, 2011), 6.

17. See George J. Sánchez, "Generations of Segregation: Immigrant Dreams and Segregated Lives in Metropolitan Los Angeles," in *New World Cities: Globalization, Urbanization, and Popular Participations in the Americas*, ed. John Tutino and Martin V. Melosi (Chapel Hill: University of North Carolina Press, 2018), 210–41.

18. Karen Brodkin, *How Jews Became White Folks and What That Says about Race in America* (New Brunswick, NJ: Rutgers University Press, 1998); Michael Rogin, *Blackface, White Noise: Jewish Immigrants in the Hollywood Melting Pot* (Berkeley: University of California Press, 1996); Neal Gabler, *An Empire of Their Own: How the Jews Invented Hollywood* (New York: Crown, 1988).

19. See George J. Sánchez, "'What's Good for Boyle Heights Is Good for the Jews': Creating Multiracialism on the Eastside during the 1950s," *American Quarterly* 56:3 (September 2004): 633–62.

20. For a wider discussion of the links between these historical events, see George J. Sánchez, "Disposable People, Expendable Neighborhoods: Repatriation, Internment and Other Population Removals," in *A Companion to Los Angeles,* ed. William Deverell and Greg Hise (Malden, MA: Wiley-Blackwell, 2010), 129–46.

2. MAKING LOS ANGELES

1. "Boyle Heights Bones Divide Metro Officials," *Los Angeles Times,* October 27, 2005, B1; Hector Becerra, "Crews Unearth Forgotten Graves," *Los Angeles Times,* November 22, 2005, B1, B9; Ching-Ching Ni, "No Longer Forgotten; An L.A. Memorial Honors Chinese Laborers Buried in a Potters' Field," *Los Angeles Times,* March 9, 2010, AA1; Julie Cart, "Chinese Laborers Finally Rest in Peace in New Soil," *Los Angeles Times,* September 5, 2010, A37.

2. Robert M. Fogelson, *The Fragmented Metropolis: Los Angeles, 1850–1930* (Cambridge, MA: Harvard University Press, 1967), 7.

3. John D. Weaver, *El Pueblo Grande: A Non-fiction Book about Los Angeles* (Los Angeles: Ward Ritchie Press, 1973), 15–16.

4. Greg Hise, "Border City: Race and Social Distance in Los Angeles," in *Los Angeles and the Future of Urban Cultures,* ed. Raul Homero Villa and George J. Sánchez (Baltimore: Johns Hopkins University Press, 2005), 52.

5. See Michael J. González, *This Small City Will Be a Mexican Paradise: Exploring the Origins of Mexican Culture in Los Angeles, 1821–1846* (Albuquerque: University of New Mexico Press, 2005), 30.

6. H. D. Barrows, "Don Antonio Maria Lugo: A Picturesque Character of California," *Annual Publication of the Historical Society of Southern California* 3:4 (1896): 28–29.

7. Lynn Bowman, *Los Angeles: Epic of a City* (Berkeley, CA: Howell-North Books, 1974), 114; Works Project Administration (WPA), *Los Angeles: A Guide to the City and Its Environs,* compiled by Workers of the Writers' Program of the WPA in Southern California, American Guide Series (New York: Hastings House, 1941), 28.

8. Douglas Monroy, *Thrown among Strangers: The Making of Mexican Culture in Frontier California* (Berkeley: University of California Press, 1990), 117–34; WPA, *Los Angeles,* 32–33; Bowman, *Los Angeles,* 44–46.

9. "Introducing the Lopez Family," *The Lopez Adobe* (blog), November 4, 2012, https://lopezadobe.wordpress.com/2012/11/04/introducing-the-lopez-family/.

10. Barrows, "Don Antonio Maria Lugo," 33.

11. Monroy, *Thrown among Strangers,* 154–62; Weaver, *El Pueblo Grande,* 18–19; WPA, *Los Angeles,* 33–34.

12. Monroy, *Thrown among Strangers,* 163–76; Donald E. Rowland, *John Rowland and William Workman: Southern California Pioneers of 1841* (Los Angeles: Arthur H. Clark and Historical Society of Southern California, 1999), 49–52.

13. Rowland, *Rowland and William Workman,* 89–106.

14. Juan Gómez-Quiñones, "An East Side Profile in Historical Sequence," in *Cultural Needs Assessment: Metro East Side Extension* (Los Angeles: Los Angeles County Metropolitan Transportation Authority, February 1995), IV-5–6; Andrew A. Boyle, "The Battle of Coleto and the Goliad Massacre: From the Republic Pension Application of Andrew A. Boyle," n.d., in *The Goliad Massacre*, online exhibit, Texas State Library and Archives Commission, accessed June 7, 2017, www.tsl.texas.gov/treasures/republic/goliad/boyles.html; Los Angeles Education Partnership, "Our Place Called Home: A History of Boyle Heights," n.d., accessed June 7, 2017, http://laep.org/access/change/histbh/index.html; Robert Glass Cleland and Frank B. Putnam, *Isaias W. Hellman and the Farmers and Merchants Bank* (San Marino, CA: Huntington Library, 1965), 21.

15. For one of the best descriptions of the adjustments to conquest made by one ranchero, Mariano Vallejo, and his extended family, see Rosina Lozano, *An American Language: The History of Spanish in the United States* (Berkeley: University of California Press, 2018), 30–37, 67–76.

16. Monroy, *Thrown among Strangers*, 225–30; Weaver, *El Pueblo Grande*, 29–30; Harris Newmark, *Sixty Years in Southern California, 1853–1913*, ed. Maurice H. and Marco R. Newmark (1916; repr., Los Angeles: Zeitlin and Ver Brugge, 1970), 220, 374.

17. Monroy, *Thrown among Strangers*, 222–32; Richard Griswold del Castillo, *The Los Angeles Barrio, 1850–1890: A Social History* (Berkeley: University of California Press, 1979), 30–61. William Deverell goes so far as calling the 1850s part of "the unending Mexican War"; William Deverell, *Whitewashed Adobe: The Rise of the Los Angeles and the Remaking of Its Mexican Past* (Berkeley: University of California Press, 2004), 11–25.

18. Gómez-Quiñones, "East Side Profile," IV-5–6; Los Angeles Education Partnership, "Our Place Called Home"; Wendy Elliott-Scheinberg, "Boyle Heights: Jewish Ambiance in a Multicultural Neighborhood" (PhD diss., Claremont Graduate University, 2001), 30–31; Blake Gumprecht, *The Los Angeles River: Its Life, Death, and Possible Rebirth* (Baltimore: Johns Hopkins University Press, 1999), 60.

19. David Roediger, *The Wages of Whiteness: Race and the Making of the American Working Class* (London: Verso, 1991), 133–63; Noel Ignatiev, *How the Irish Became White* (New York: Routledge, 1995).

20. Quoted in Roediger, *Wages of Whiteness*, 137.

21. Allison Varzally, *Making a Non-white America: Californians Coloring outside Ethnic Lines, 1925–1955* (Berkeley: University of California Press, 2008), 22.

22. Elliot-Scheinberg, "Boyle Heights," 35; Cleland and Putnam, *Isaias W. Hellman*, 9–13.

23. Elliot-Scheinberg, "Boyle Heights," 40–41.

24. George Hansen's 1868 "Official Map No. 2" of Los Angeles, Los Angeles City Archives, charted this land ownership pattern. See Elliot-Scheinberg, "Boyle Heights," 35–44.

25. Rowland, *Rowland and William Workman*, 136–38.

26. Elliot-Scheinberg, "Boyle Heights," 42–43; Boyle Workman, *The City That Grew* (Los Angeles: Southland, 1936), 20, 102.

27. Cleland and Putnam, *Isaias W. Hellman,* 20; Workman, *City That Grew,* 108.

28. Elliot-Scheinberg, "Boyle Heights," 46.

29. Workman, *City That Grew,* 182.

30. Elliot-Scheinberg, "Boyle Heights," 50–79.

31. Elliot-Scheinberg, "Boyle Heights," 77.

32. Elliot-Scheinberg, "Boyle Heights," 53–53; Workman, *City That Grew,* 90.

33. Workman, *City That Grew,* 182–83.

34. Elliot-Scheinberg, "Boyle Heights," 58–62; Robert C. Post, *Street Railways and the Growth of Los Angeles* (San Marino, CA: Golden West Books, 1989), 36–39.

35. Kevin Starr, *Inventing the Dream: California through the Progressive Era* (New York: Oxford University Press, 1985), 15.

36. Elliot-Scheinberg, "Boyle Heights," 44.

37. Elliot-Scheinberg, "Boyle Heights," 83–87, 94–96; Starr, *Inventing the Dream,* 49.

38. Walter Nugent, *Into the West: The Story of Its People* (New York: Alfred A. Knopf, 1999), 89–91.

39. Nugent, *Into the West,* 91–94.

40. From Nathan Masters, "A Brief History of Bridges in Los Angeles County," web content for *Lost L.A.* series, by L.A. as Subject research alliance, KCET, July 18, 2012. www.kcet.org/shows/lost-la/a-brief-history-of-bridges-in-los-angeles-county.

41. Los Angeles Department of City Planning, "Recommendation Report: Application by the Boyle Heights Historical Society to Designate the Gless Farmhouse as a Historic Cultural Landmark in Los Angeles," 2010, https://planning.lacity.org/StaffRpt/CHC/1-21-10/CHC-2010-71.pdf.

42. US Commission on Civil Rights, *Hearings before the United States Commission on Civil Rights, 1960, Los Angeles, California* (Washington, DC: Government Printing Office, 1960), 207–78; Christopher Jimenez y West, "More Than My Color: Space, Politics and Identity in Los Angeles, 1940–1973" (PhD diss., University of Southern California, 2007), chap. 2; Natalia Molina, *Fit to Be Citizens? Public Health and Race in Los Angeles, 1879–1939* (Berkeley: University of California Press, 2006), 15–31.

43. Robert M. Fogelson, *Bourgeois Nightmares: Suburbia, 1870–1930* (New Haven, CT: Yale University Press, 2005), 43–59.

44. US Commission on Civil Rights, "Hearings," 207–78; Jimenez y West, "More Than My Color," chap. 2. For a full analysis of the role of Los Angeles in the development of racially restrictive covenants, see Sánchez, "Generations of Segregation."

45. Carey McWilliams, *Southern California: An Island on the Land* (Salt Lake City, UT: Peregrine Smith Books, 1946), 121.

46. Mansel G. Blackford, *The Lost Dream: Businessmen and City Planning on the Pacific Coast, 1890–1920* (Columbus: Ohio State University Press, 1993), 84, 92–93; Jon A. Peterson, *The Birth of City Planning in the United States, 1840–1917* (Johns Hopkins University Press, 2003), 309.

47. Molina, *Fit to Be Citizens?,* 36.

48. Molina, *Fit to Be Citizens?*, 35–43.

49. Mark Wild, *Street Meeting: Multiethnic Neighborhoods in Early Twentieth-Century Los Angeles* (Berkeley: University of California Press, 2005), 18–56; Sánchez, "Generations of Segregation."

50. Douglas Flamming, *Bound for Freedom: Black Los Angeles in Jim Crow America* (Berkeley: University of California Press, 2005), 221–25.

51. McWilliams, *Southern California*, 130–31.

52. See Hise, "Border City."

53. Paul R. Spitzzeri, "Historic Photos of Boyle Heights: The Cummings Block, circa 1889," *Boyle Heights History Blog*, September 17, 2014, http://boyleheightshistoryblog.blogspot.com/2014/09/historic-photos-of-boyle-heights.html.

54. Though the official opening of L.A. County General Hospital was in early 1934, Los Angeles officials opened the maternity ward four months earlier at the end of 1933. See Nic John Ramos, "From Home to Hospital, Hospital to Home: The State, the Family, and the Nation" (unpublished paper, University of Southern California, Department of American Studies and Ethnicity, 2011), 2–3; and Nic John Ramos, "City of Health: Race, Gender, and Public Hospital Construction in Los Angeles" (unpublished paper, University of Southern California, Department of American Studies and Ethnicity, 2011), 10.

55. Los Angeles Department of City Planning, "Recommendation Report"; Catherine Kurland, "A Brief History of the Lopez and Cummings Families in Boyle Heights, Los Angeles," December 7, 2006, attachment V to Application by Boyle Heights Historical Society to Designate Boyle Hotel-Cummings Block as a Historic-Cultural Monument in Los Angeles, September 21, 2007, https://clkrep.lacity.org/onlinedocs/2007/07-3028_rpt_chc_9-21-07.pdf.

56. See Spitzzeri, " Historic Photos." See also Catherine L. Kurland and Enrique R. Lamadrid, *Hotel Mariachi: Urban Space and Cultural Heritage in Los Angeles*, photographs by Miguel A. Gandert (University of New Mexico Press, 2013).

57. Manuel M. Martin-Rodriguez, "Mexican American Literature," in *A History of California Literature*, ed. Blake Allmendinger (Cambridge University Press, 2015), 145–46; "Pioneer Meets Awful Death, Cremated in Burning of Kern Hotel," *Los Angeles Herald*, December 8, 1903, 1; "Plan Rites for Woman Pioneer," *Los Angeles Express*, August 1, 1930, obituary.

58. McWilliams's famous subtitle was borrowed from a line by the nineteenth-century novelist Helen Hunt Jackson. See McWilliams, *Southern California*, 1–8; Helen Hunt Jackson, *Ramona* (Boston: Little, Brown, 1884).

3. FROM GLOBAL MOVEMENTS TO URBAN APARTHEID

1. Leo Frumkin, life history interview by Ken Burt and Sojin Kim for Reexamining Boyle Heights Project, December 19, 2001, Tarzana, CA, transcript, Japanese American National Museum, Los Angeles, pp. 1–2, 35, 39.

2. Frumkin, interview, p. 24.

3. Frumkin, interview, pp. 2–3.

4. Frumkin, interview, p. 28.

5. Mollie Murphy, Mary Nishi, and Sandie Okada, life history interview by Sojin Kim and Darcie Iki for Re-examining Boyle Heights Project, January 18, 2001, Los Angeles, transcript, Japanese American National Museum, Los Angeles, p. 10.

6. Gerald Sorin, *Tradition Transformed: The Jewish Experience in America* (Baltimore: Johns Hopkins University Press, 1997), 34.

7. Deborah Dash Moore, *To the Golden Cities: Pursuing the American Jewish Dream in Miami and L.A.* (Cambridge, MA: Harvard University Press, 1994), 4; Max Vorspan and Lloyd P. Garner, *History of the Jews of Los Angeles* (San Marino, CA: Huntington Library, 1970), 109–12.

8. Caroline Luce, "Reexamining Los Angeles' 'Lower East Side': Jewish Bakers Union Local 453 and Yiddish Food Culture in 1920s Boyle Heights," in *Jews in the Los Angeles Mosaic,* ed. Karen S. Wilson (Los Angeles: Autry National Center of the American West; Berkeley: University of California Press, 2013), 29–30; Caroline Elizabeth Luce, "Visions of a Jewish Future: the Jewish Bakers Union and Yiddish Culture in East Los Angeles, 1908–1942" (PhD diss., University of California, Los Angeles, 2013), 57.

9. Kate Boletin and Paul Zolnekoff, life history interview by Wendy Elliott for Re-examining Boyle Heights Project, August 15, 2000, Los Angeles, transcript, Japanese American National Museum, Los Angeles, pp. 1–2.

10. Douglas Monroy, *Rebirth: Mexican Los Angeles from the Great Migration to the Great Depression* (Berkeley: University of California Press, 1999), 217–21; Kelly Lytle Hernández, *City of Inmates: Conquest, Rebellion, and the Rise of Human Caging in Los Angeles, 1771–1965* (Chapel Hill: University of North Carolina Press, 2017), 92–130; John H. M. Laslett, *Sunshine Was Never Enough: Los Angeles Workers, 1880–1910* (Berkeley: University of California Press, 2012), 63–70; David Marshall Struthers, "World in a City: Transnational and Inter-racial Organizing in Los Angeles, 1900–1930" (PhD diss., Carnegie Mellon University, 2010), 124–34.

11. See, for example, Otis's son-in-law Harry Chandler's land syndicate ownership of C&M ranch in Baja California in Laslett, *Sunshine Was Never Enough,* 65–67. For a wider analysis of this phenomenon, see Jessica M. Kim, *Imperial Metropolis: Los Angeles, Mexico, and the Borderlands of American Empire, 1865–1941* (Chapel Hill: University of North Carolina Press, 2019).

12. Struthers, "World in a City," 193–239.

13. Flamming, *Bound for Freedom,* 44–50.

14. Atoy Wilson Jr., interview by Paul Spitzerri and Lisa Itagaki for Re-examining Boyle Heights Project, January 25, 2001, Los Angeles, transcript, Japanese American National Museum, Los Angeles, pp. 1–3. Atoy Wilson Jr. and Mollie Wilson Murphy are brother and sister.

15. Flamming, *Bound for Freedom,* p. 37.

16. Emory J. Tolbert, *The UNIA and Black Los Angeles* (Los Angeles: UCLA Center for Afro-American Studies, 1980), 50–52, 63.

17. Eiichiro Azuma, *Between Two Empires: Race, History, and Transnationalism in Japanese America* (New York: Oxford University Press, 2005), 29.

18. Yuji Ichioka, *The Issei: The World of the First Generation Japanese Immigrants, 1885–1924* (New York: Free Press, 1988), 102–13; See also Yushi Yamasaki, "Buried Strands: From Peasant Rebellions to Internationalist Multiracial Labor Organizing among Japanese Immigrant Communities in Hawaii and California, 1885–1941" (PhD diss., University of Southern California, 2015), 172–242.

19. Ronald Takaki, *A Different Mirror: A History of Multicultural America* (Boston: Little, Brown, 1993), 251–66; Ronald Takaki, *Strangers from a Different Shore: A History of Asian Americans* (Boston: Little, Brown, 1989), 147–55.

20. Donna R. Gabaccia, "Worker Internationalism and Italian Labor Migration, 1870–1914," *International Labor and Working-Class History* 45 (Spring 1994): 64.

21. Gabaccia, "Worker Internationalism"; Thomas Kessner, *The Golden Door: Italian and Jewish Immigrant Mobility in New York City, 1880–1915* (New York: Oxford University Press, 1977), 15.

22. Struthers, "World in a City," 183, 202–3.

23. Marcella Bencivenni, *Italian Immigrant Radical Culture: The Idealism of the Sovversivi in the United States, 1890–1940* (New York: New York University Press, 2011), 10.

24. Laslett, *Sunshine Was Never Enough,* 16–17.

25. Laslett, *Sunshine Was Never Enough,* 25.

26. Laslett, *Sunshine Was Never Enough,* 25, 28–31, 33–35; Struthers, "World in a City," 105–15; David M. Struthers, *The World in a City: Multiethnic Radicalism in Early Twentieth Century Los Angeles* (Urbana: University of Illinois Press, 2019), 74–78; William B. Friedricks, "Capital and Labor in Los Angeles: Henry E. Huntington vs. Organized Labor, 1900–1920," *Pacific Historical Review* 59:3 (1990): 375–95; Charles Wollenberg, "Working on El Traque: The Pacific Electric Strike of 1903," *Pacific Historical Review* 42:3 (1973): 358–69.

27. See Paul Buhle, *Marxism in the United States: A History of the American Left,* 3rd ed. (London: Verso, 2013).

28. For an approach similar to mine in this radical tradition, see Marcella Bencivenni, *Italian Immigrant Radical Culture,* 2.

29. Varzally, *Making a Non-white America,* 24.

30. See Sánchez, *Becoming Mexican American,* 119–23, and Stephanie Lewthwaite, *Race, Place, and Reform in Mexican Los Angeles: A Transnational Perspective, 1890–1940* (Tucson: University of Arizona Press, 2009), 106–11.

31. Andrea Geiger, *Subverting Exclusion: Transpacific Encounters with Race, Caste, and Borders, 1885–1928* (New Haven, CT: Yale University Press, 2011), 46–49.

32. Sánchez, *Becoming Mexican American,* 122–23; Monroy, *Rebirth,* 62–65.

33. Azuma, *Between Two Empires,* 18–27.

34. See John Modell, *The Economics and Politics of Racial Accommodation: The Japanese of Los Angeles, 1900–1942* (Urbana: University of Illinois Press, 1977), 79–88; Sánchez, *Becoming Mexican American,* 113–18, 122–24; Francisco E. Balder-

rama, *In Defense of La Raza: The Los Angeles Mexican Consulate and the Mexican Community, 1929–1936* (Tucson: University of Arizona Press, 1982).

35. Dino Cinel, *From Italy to San Francisco: The Immigrant Experience* (Stanford, CA: Stanford University Press, 1982), 228–55.

36. Michael Miller Topp, *Those without a Country: The Political Culture of Italian American Syndicalists* (Minneapolis: University of Minnesota Press, 2001), 109–11.

37. This term comes from Varzally, *Making a Non-white America*, 23.

38. See Struthers, "World in a City," introduction.

39. See Gary Gerstle, *American Crucible: Race and Nation in the Twentieth Century* (Princeton, NJ: Princeton University Press, 2001), for more on this contradictory nature of Americanism in the early twentieth century.

40. Blackford, *Lost Dream*, 84, 92–93; Peterson, *Birth of City Planning*, 309.

41. Wild, *Street Meeting*, 54. See Isabella Seong-Leong Quintana, "National Borders, Neighborhood Boundaries: Gender, Space and Border Formation in Chinese and Mexican Los Angeles, 1871–1938" (PhD diss., University of Michigan, 2010), for a thorough description of the development of downtown ethnic communities in this era west of the Los Angeles River.

42. Luce, "Visions of a Jewish Future," 65–66; Vicki L. Ruiz, *Cannery Women, Cannery Lives: Mexican Women, Unionization, and the California Food Processing Industry, 1930–1950* (Albuquerque: University of New Mexico Press, 1987), 71.

43. See Modell, *Economics and Politics*, 113–21.

44. Struthers, *World in a City*, 45–50.

45. California Commission of Immigration and Housing (CCIH), "Community Survey," 23, in Lewthwaite, *Race, Place and Reform*, 71.

46. Wild, *Street Meeting*, 55–56.

47. CCIH, Community Survey, 23, in Lewthwaite, *Race, Place and Reform*, 71.

48. Wild, *Street Meeting*, 18–56.

49. Massey and Denton, *American Apartheid*, 15.

50. Luce, "Visions of a Jewish Future," 66; Cloyed Gustafson, "An Ecological Survey of the Hollenbeck Area" (Master's thesis, University of Southern California, 1940), 104.

51. Albert Johnson II, life history interview by Paul Spitzzeri and Sojin Kim for "Re-examining Boyle Heights" Project, July 3, 2002, Los Angeles, transcript, Japanese American National Museum, Los Angeles, p. 7.

52. Johnson, interview; Lawrence B. de Graff, "The City of Black Angels: Emergence of the Los Angeles Ghetto, 1890–1930," *Pacific Historical Review* 39:3 (August 1970): 323–52; J. Max Bond, "The Negro in Los Angeles" (PhD diss., University of Southern California, 1936).

53. Azuma, *Between Two Empires*, 77–78; Modell, *Economics and Politics*, 56–66.

54. Modell, *Economics and Politics*, 72–73.

55. Boletin and Zolnekoff, interview, pp. 12, 25.

56. Gloria Ricci Lothrop, "Italians of Los Angeles: An Historical Overview," *Southern California Quarterly* 85:3 (Fall 2003): 263.

57. Ray Aragon, life history interview by Joanne Koenig Reyes for "Re-examining Boyle Heights" Project, August 12, 2000, Los Angeles, transcript, Japanese American National Museum, Los Angeles, p. 7.

58. Hershey Eisenberg, life history interview by Darcie Iki and Sojin Kim for "Re-examining Boyle Heights" Project, December 18, 2000, Los Angeles, transcript, Japanese American National Museum, Los Angeles, p. 1.

59. Eddie Ramirez, life history interview by Raul Vasquez and Sojin Kim for "Re-examining Boyle Heights" Project, January 11, 2002, Los Angeles, transcript, Japanese American National Museum, Los Angeles, p. 3.

60. Claire (Orlosoroff) Stein, life history interview by Dan Gebler for "Re-examining Boyle Heights" Project, November 11, 2000, Laguna Niguel, CA, transcript, Japanese American National Museum, Los Angeles, p. 7.

61. Luce, "Visions of a Jewish Future," 108–10.

62. See Ruiz, *Cannery Women,* 31–32, 34–36, 70–71.

63. Frumkin, interview, p. 23.

64. Elliot-Scheinberg, "Boyle Heights," 144–53.

65. Elliott-Scheinberg, "Boyle Heights," 139.

66. Modell, *Economics and Politics,* 75–78.

67. Lothrop, "Italians of Los Angeles," 268.

68. Mike Nelson, "St. Mary Church: The 'Grand Lady' of Boyle Heights," *Angelus News,* August 7, 2014; Dolores Mission Church, Archdiocese of Los Angeles, "About," n.d., accessed August 13, 2020, www.dolores-mission.org/about; Resurrection Church, Archdiocese of Los Angeles, "About Us," n.d., accessed August 13, 2020, www.resurrectionla.com/about-us/.

69. Luce, "Visions of a Jewish Future," 99.

70. International Institute of Los Angeles, "Our History," n.d., accessed August 13, 2020, www.iilosangeles.org/about/our-history/.

71. Valerie Matsumoto, *City Girls: The Nisei Social World in Los Angeles, 1920–1950* (New York: Oxford University Press, 2014).

72. Francis Polytechnic Senior High School, "Brief History of Poly," n.d., accessed June 14, 2019, www.polyhigh.org/apps/pages/About_Us.

73. David Frum, *How We Got Here: The 1970s: The Decade That Brought You Modern Life (for Better or Worse)* (New York: Basic Books, 2000), 267.

74. Matt García, *A World Of Its Own: Race, Labor, and Citrus in the Making of Greater Los Angeles, 1900–1970* (Chapel Hill: University of North Carolina Press, 2001), 206. For some of this work focusing on youth culture, see Varzally, *Making a Non-white America,* esp. chap. 2; Wild, *Street Meeting*; Anthony Macías, *Mexican American Mojo: Popular Music, Dance, and Urban Culture in Los Angeles, 1935–1968* (Durham, NC: Duke University Press, 2008).

75. See Boletin, interview, p. 22; Stein, interview, p. 7.

76. Freda Maddow, life history interview by Paul Spitzzeri for "Re-examining Boyle Heights" Project, July 27, 2000, Los Angeles, transcript, Japanese American National Museum, Los Angeles, p. 21.

77. Aragon, interview, p. 22; Murphy, Nishi, and Okada, interview, pp. 32–34.

78. According to one survey at Roosevelt in 1938, the Mexican-descent student population was 800, while Jewish youngsters almost doubled that at 1,500. The only other groups with large contingents were 400 Russians and 200 Japanese. William E. Zazueta, Reunion Chairman, Roosevelt High School 50th Year Class of 1937, 1938, and 1939 Reunion, "A Letter from the Committee," February 13, 1988, "Re-examining Boyle Heights" Project, Japanese American National Museum, Los Angeles. Also see Eisenberg, interview, p. 25.

79. Although many Jewish and Japanese teenagers also dropped out to help their family economies during the 1930s, these ventures into the factory world were usually temporary. As Vicki Ruiz has pointed out in her work on the United Cannery and Packing Allied Workers of America (UCAPAWA), Jewish and Mexican women from Boyle Heights, many of them young adults, banded together and formed the backbone of the garment and food-packing unions, which grew in strength in the decade. However, Mexican women were much more likely to find themselves in the factories for decades. Ruiz, *Cannery Women*, 34–39; John H. M. Laslett and Mary Tyler, *The ILGWU in Los Angeles, 1907–1988* (Inglewood, CA: Ten Star Press, 1989), 26–44; Beatrice Griffith, "Viva Roybal—Viva America," *Common Ground*, Autumn 1949, p. 62.

80. Ramirez, interview, pp. 10–11.

81. Aragon, interview, p. 21.

82. Eisenberg, interview, p. 21; Daniel Kawahara, life history interview by Sojin Kim and Darcie Iki for "Re-examining Boyle Heights" Project, December 18, 2000, Los Angeles, transcript, Japanese American National Museum, Los Angeles, p. 10.

83. Cedrick Shimo, life history interview by Sojin Kim and Erick Molinar for "Re-examining Boyle Heights" Project, March 19, 2001, Los Angeles, transcript, Japanese American National Museum, Los Angeles, p. 19.

84. Frumkin, interview, p. 26.

85. See Maddow, interview, pp. 17, 22.

86. The big difference is that those gangs that developed in Mexican American sections were usually made up of youth that had left schooling behind and were now struggling to help support their families with some sort of supplemental income. And as we now know, their histories would veer radically apart with police targeting that came after the Zoot Suit Riots during World War II and the subsequent racialization of Mexican youth. See Kawahawa, interview, p. 14. For the racialization of Mexican American gangs, see Edward J. Escobar, *Race, Police, and the Making of a Political Identity: Mexican Americans and the Los Angeles Police Department, 1900–1945* (Berkeley: University of California Press, 1999), 211–15.

87. Stein, interview, p. 19.

88. Murphy, Okada, and Nishi, interview.

89. Wild, *Street Meeting*, 139.

90. See Vicki L. Ruiz, "'Star Struck': Acculturation, Adolescence, and Mexican American Women, 1920–1940," in *Small Worlds: Children and Adolescents in America,* ed. Elliot West and Paula Petrik (Lawrence: University of Kansas Press, 1992), 61–80; Luce, "Visions of a Jewish Future"; Ruiz, *Cannery Women.*

91. Juan Flores, "Que Assimilated, Brother, *Yo Soy Asimilao:* The Structuring of Puerto Rican Identity in the U.S.," *Journal of Ethnic Studies* 13:3 (Fall 1985): 11. I want to thank George Lipsitz for pointing me toward this key work.

92. For examples of relational and transnational histories of Los Angeles, see Molina, *Fit to Be Citizens?*; Genevieve Carpio, *Collisions at the Crossroads: How Place and Mobility Make Race* (Berkeley: University of California Press, 2019); and Jessica M. Kim, *Imperial Metropolis: Los Angeles, Mexico, and the Borderlands of American Empire, 1865–1941* (Chapel Hill: University of North Carolina Press, 2019).

4. DISPOSABLE PEOPLE, EXPENDABLE NEIGHBORHOODS

1. Emilia Castañeda de Valenciana, interview by Christine Valenciana de Balderrama, transcript, O.H. 700, Oral History Collection, California State University at Fullerton, pp. 1–6.

2. Leonard Leader, *Los Angeles and the Great Depression* (New York: Garland, 1991), 6.

3. Valenciana, interview, pp. 3–14.

4. Valenciana, interview, p. 16.

5. Molina, *Fit to Be Citizens?*, 26.

6. See Natalia Molina, *How Race Is Made in America: Immigration, Citizenship, and the Historical Power of Racial Scripts* (Berkeley: University of California Press, 2014), esp. 5.

7. Quote from *B'nai B'rith Messenger,* February 28, 1930.

8. Modell, *Economics and Politics,* 133. See 94–121 for a full description of the Japanese American ethnic economy in Los Angeles during this period.

9. Leader, *Los Angeles,* 36–37.

10. Luce, "Visions of a Jewish Future," 95–98, 159–80; William H. Mullins, *The Depression and the Urban West Coast, 1929–1933: Los Angeles, San Francisco, Seattle and Portland* (Bloomington: Indiana University Press, 1991), 25–27; Cedrick Shimo, life history interview by Sojin Kim and Erick Molinar for Re-examining Boyle Heights Project, March 19, 2001, Los Angeles, transcript, Japanese American National Museum, Los Angeles, p. 8.

11. Steven J. Ross, *Hitler in Los Angeles: How Jews Foiled Nazi Plots against Hollywood and America* (New York: Bloomsbury, 2017), 32.

12. Ross, *Hitler in Los Angeles.*

13. Luce, "Visions of a Jewish Future," 169–70; Mullins, *Depression,* 26–27.

14. Abraham Hoffman, *Unwanted Mexican Americans in the Great Depression: Repatriation Pressures, 1929–1939* (Tucson: University of Arizona Press, 1974), 41–42.

15. Hoffman, *Unwanted Mexican Americans,* 39.

16. Western Union telegram from C. P. Visel, Coordinator of Los Angeles Citizens Committee of Unemployment Relief, to Col. Arthur M. Woods, United States

Government Coordinator of Unemployment Relief, Washington, D.C., January 6, 1931, UCLA Department of Special Collections.

17. Hoffman, *Unwanted Mexican Americans,* 43–66.

18. Frank Shaw was also a member of the city's Citizens Committee on Coordination of Unemployment Relief.

19. Hoffman, *Unwanted Mexican Americans,* 42, 86–87.

20. Figures from Hoffman, *Unwanted Mexican Americans,* 172–73.

21. Jerry Gonzalez, *In Search of the Mexican Beverly Hills: Latino Suburbanization in Postwar Los Angeles* (New Brunswick, NJ: Rutgers University Press, 2018), 25; Francisco E. Balderrama and Raymond Rodríguez, *Decade of Betrayal: Mexican Repatriation in the 1930s,* rev. ed. (Albuquerque: University of New Mexico Press, 2006), 129.

22. Shaw's estimates of savings from the repatriations of $200,000 a month, or over $2 million total, were wildly exaggerated. A better estimate is a modest half million dollars, which barely made a dent in relief needs.

23. Pauline V. Young, *The Pilgrims of Russian-Town* (Chicago: University of Chicago Press, 1932), 19.

24. All data in the database developed from linking names of repatriates in the Secretariat of Foreign Relations archives, Mexico City, to the 1930 US Census and the 1931 Los Angeles City Directory.

25. Eddie Ramirez, life history interview by Raul Vasquez and Sojin Kim for Re-examining Boyle Heights Project, January 11, 2002, Los Angeles, transcript, Japanese American National Museum, Los Angeles, p. 43.

26. All data taken from the database described in note 24.

27. Balderrama and Rodriguez, *Decade of Betrayal,* 266.

28. Marla Andrea Ramirez, "Contested Illegality: Three Generations of Exclusion through Mexican 'Repatriation' and the Politics of Immigration Law, 1920–2005" (PhD diss., University of California at Santa Barbara, 2015).

29. Hoffman, *Unwanted Mexican Americans,* 106.

30. Two scholars, in particular, have influenced my thinking on the development of this counterscript. Gary Gerstle's description of the power of civic nationalism from below during the 1930s is critical; see *American Crucible,* particularly 129–31, 140–48. Michael Denning discusses the power of the populist rhetoric of Americanism among the Left in the Popular Front era in *The Cultural Front: The Laboring of American Culture in the Twentieth Century* (London: Verso, 1996), esp. 128–32.

31. Dorothy Tomer, interview by Stephanie Maya for "The Other Los Angeles" Project, History 101.6, University of California, Los Angeles (UCLA), February 19, 1990, Montebello, CA. See Gerstle, *American Crucible,* 136–37, regarding the impact of the radio fireside chats in softening the image of the role of the president.

32. Michael Paul Rogin and John L. Shover, *Political Change in California: Critical Elections and Social Movements, 1890–1966* (Westport, CT: Greenwood, 1970), 112–17; Laslett, *Sunshine Was Never Enough,* 129; Leader, *Los Angeles,* 246.

33. Yu Tokunaga, "Making Transborder Los Angeles: Japanese and Mexican Immigration, Agriculture, and Labor Relations, 1924–1942" (PhD diss., University

of Southern California, 2018), 136–80; Laslett, *Sunshine Was Never Enough,* 136–38.

34. Telegram from Flores to Roosevelt, June 14, 1933, /136, in Abraham Hoffman, "El Monte Berry Strike, 1933: International Involvement in a Local Labor Dispute," *Journal of the West* 12:1 (1973): 76.

35. John Laslett and Mary Tyler, *The ILGWU in Los Angeles, 1907–1988* (Inglewood, CA: Ten Star Press, 1989), 15–17.

36. These comments were made by ILGWU West Coast director Louis Levy. See Laslett, *Sunshine Was Never Enough,* 134; Laslett and Tyler, *ILGWU in Los Angeles,* 30; Rose Pesotta, *Bread upon the Waters* (New York: Dodd, Mead, 1945), 21.

37. Isaias James McCaffery, "Organizing Las Costureras: Life, Labor and Unionization among Mexicana Garment Workers in Two Borderland Cities—Los Angeles and San Antonio, 1933–1941" (PhD diss., University of Kansas, 1999), 78.

38. Laslett and Tyler, *ILGWU in Los Angeles,* 31.

39. Pesotta, *Bread upon the Waters,* 1–4; Laslett and Tyler, *ILGWU,* 30–31.

40. Pesotta, *Bread upon the Waters,* 24–29.

41. Pesotta, *Bread upon the Waters,* 29–34.

42. Pesotta, *Bread upon the Waters,* 34–63; Louis B. Perry and Richard S. Perry, *The History of the Los Angeles Labor Movement, 1911–1941* (Berkeley: University of California Press, 1963), 251–58.

43. Luce, "Visions of a Jewish Future," 183. See 180–84 for a wider description of the impact of industrial unionism on the Boyle Heights Jewish bakers and their unions.

44. Vicki Ruiz, *Cannery Women,* 31–39, 69–71; Gary Gerstle, *Working-Class Americanism: The Politics of Labor in a Textile City, 1914–1960* (Cambridge: Cambridge University Press, 1989).

45. James N. Gregory, "California's EPIC Turn: Upton Sinclair's 1934 Campaign and the Reorganization of California Politics" (paper presented at the Los Angeles History Research Group, May 2, 1995); Errol Wayne Stevens, *Radical L.A.: From Coxey's Army to the Watts Riots, 1894–1965* (Norman: University of Oklahoma Press, 2009), 221–31.

46. Stevens, *Radical L.A.,* 233.

47. Stevens, *Radical L.A.,* 223–36.

48. Douglas Guy Monroy, "Mexicanos in Los Angeles, 1930–1941: An Ethnic Group in Relation to Class Forces" (PhD diss., University of California, Los Angeles, 1978), 124, 139–41; Laslett, *Sunshine Was Never Enough,* 147.

49. Monroy, "Mexicanos in Los Angeles," 138.

50. Laslett, *Sunshine Was Never Enough,* 148.

51. Stevens, *Radical L.A.,* 235; Denning, *Cultural Front,* esp. 16–19.

52. Luce, "Visions of a Jewish Future," 196–245. For more on the rise of Nazism in Los Angeles, see Ross, *Hitler in Los Angeles.*

53. Dana Cuff, *The Provisional City: Los Angeles Stories of Architecture and Urbanism* (Cambridge, MA: MIT Press, 2000), 135–38.

54. Cuff, *Provisional City,* 158–59.

55. Cuff, *Provisional City*, 151.

56. Cuff, *Provisional City*, 156–57.

57. James Tomalsov, life history interview by Sojin Kim for Re-examining Boyle Heights Project, April 17, 2001, Los Angeles, transcript, Japanese American National Museum, Los Angeles, pp. 1–2.

58. Don Parson, *Making a Better World: Public Housing, the Red Scare, and the Direction of Modern Los Angeles* (Minneapolis: University of Minnesota Press, 2005), 13–43.

59. See Parson, *Making a Better World*, and Eric Avila, *Popular Culture in the Age of White Flight: Fear and Fantasy in Suburban Los Angeles* (Berkeley: University of California Press, 2004).

60. Ira Katznelson, *When Affirmative Action Was White: An Untold History of Racial Inequality in Twentieth-Century America* (New York: Norton, 2005).

61. See Area D-53, Los Angeles 1939, 7, Home Owners Loan Corporation City Survey Files, National Archives, Washington, DC, quoted in George Lipsitz, *Time Passages: Collective Memory and American Popular Culture* (Minneapolis: University of Minnesota Press, 1990), 137.

62. See Gary Y. Okihiro, *Margins and Mainstreams: Asians in American History and Culture* (Seattle: University of Washington Press, 1994); Mae N. Ngai, *Impossible Subjects: Illegal Aliens and the Making of Modern America* (Princeton, NJ: Princeton University Press, 2004); Neil Gotanda, "Multiculturalism and Racial Stratification," in *Mapping Multiculturalism*, ed. Avery Fisher and Christopher Newfield (Minneapolis: University of Minnesota Press, 1996); and Angelo N. Ancheta, *Race, Rights, and the Asian American Experience* (New Brunswick, NJ: Rutgers University Press, 1998).

63. See Ngai, *Impossible Subjects*.

64. See Kevin Allen Leonard, "Years of Hope, Days of Fear: The Impact of World War II on Race Relations in Los Angeles" (PhD diss., University of California, Davis, 1992), 69–73; Hillary Jenks, "'Home Is Little Tokyo': Race, Community, and Memory in Twentieth-Century Los Angeles" (PhD diss., University of Southern California, 2008).

65. See Roger Daniels, *The Politics of Prejudice: The Anti-Japanese Movement in California and the Struggle for Japanese Exclusion* (Berkeley: University of California Press, 1999, 1973); Okihiro, *Margins and Mainstreams;* Greg Robinson, *By Order of the President: FDR and the Internment of Japanese Americans* (Cambridge, MA: Harvard University Press, 2001); Greg Robinson, *A Tragedy of Democracy: Japanese Confinement in North America* (New York: Columbia University Press, 2009); Brian Masaru Hayashi, *Democratizing the Enemy: The Japanese American Internment* (Princeton, NJ: Princeton University Press, 2004); and the first analysis produced by the US Commission on Wartime Relocation and Internment of Civilians, *Personal Justice Denied* (Washington, DC: Civil Liberties Public Education Fund; Seattle: University of Washington Press, 1997).

66. For the most thorough analysis of the losing battle of egalitarians against exclusionists, including the call for "selective internment," see Lon Kurashige, *Two*

Faces of Exclusion: The Untold History of Anti-Asian Racism in the United States (Chapel Hill: University of North Carolina Press, 2016), 171–83.

67. Lon Kurashige, *Japanese American Celebration and Conflict: A History of Ethnic Identity and Festival, 1934–1990* (Berkeley: University of California Press, 2002).

68. Fernando Saul Alanis Enciso, *They Should Stay There: The Story of Mexican Migration and Repatriation during the Great Depression,* trans. Russ Davidson (Chapel Hill: University of North Carolina Press, 2017; originally published in Spanish as *Que se queden allá: El gobierno de México y la repatriación de mexicanos en Estados Unidos (1934–1940)* (Tijuana: El Colegio de la Frontera Norte, 2007), 97–98.

69. John Anson Ford Papers, Box 75, Folder dd (1941), Huntington Library, San Marino, CA.

70. For Bowron's testimony before the infamous congressional hearings of the Tolan Committee, see L. Kurashige, *Two Faces of Exclusion,* 177–78.

71. John Anson Ford, interview by Christine Valenciana, September 4, 1971, transcript, O.H. 759, Mexican American History Collection, Center for Oral and Public History, California State University at Fullerton. Ford's description of a "failure of human rights" is likely a result of postwar recognition of these rights through the United Nations Declaration of Human Rights that included racial injustice, including Japanese American internment.

72. Ruth Toshiko Matsuo Brandt, life history interview by Sojin Kim and Raul Vasquez for Re-examining Boyle Heights Project, August 17, 2001, Los Angeles, transcript, Japanese American National Museum, Los Angeles, pp. 21–23.

73. See discussion earlier in this chapter, and Modell, *Economics and Politics,* 86, 133.

74. Wayne Allen, Chief Administrative Officer, to Board of Supervisors, January 26, 1942, John Anson Ford Papers, Box 74, Folder i, bb, 7 (1942), Huntington Library, San Marino, CA.

75. Sugahara to John Anson Ford, May 21, 1942, John Anson Ford Papers, Box 74, Folder i, bb, 7 (1942), Huntington Library, San Marino, CA.

76. Sugahara to Ford, May 21, 1942.

77. Sugahara to Ford, May 21, 1942.

78. Ford to Sugahara, May 26, 1942, John Anson Ford Papers, Box 74, Folder i, bb, 7 (1942), Huntington Library, San Marino, CA.

79. Castañeda de Valenciana, interview, pp. 16–56.

80. See Gary Gerstle's discussion of the tension between civic and racial nationalism in the World War II period in *American Crucible.*

5. WITNESSES TO INTERNMENT

1. Claire (Orlosoroff) Stein, life history interview by Dan Gebler for Re-examining Boyle Heights Project, November 11, 2000, Laguna Niguel, CA, transcript, Japanese American National Museum, Los Angeles, pp. 8–9.

2. Mollie Murphy, Mary Nishi, and Sandie Okada, life history interview by Sojin Kim and Darcie Iki for Re-examining Boyle Heights Project, January 18, 2001, Los Angeles, transcript, Japanese American National Museum, Los Angeles, pp. 80–81.

3. Leo Frumkin, life history interview by Ken Burt and Sojin Kim for Re-examining Boyle Heights Project, December 19, 2001, Tarzana, CA, transcript, Japanese American National Museum, Los Angeles, p. 45.

4. Edward Duran Ayres, "Statistics," Sleepy Lagoon Defense Committee Papers, Box 5, UCLA Special Collections, cited in Matt S. Meier and Feliciano Rivera, *Readings on La Raza: The Twentieth Century* (New York: Hill and Wang, 1974), 127–32. The deputy sheriff's quote is in Eduardo Obregón Pagán, *Murder at the Sleepy Lagoon: Zoot Suits, Race, and Riot in Wartime L.A.* (Chapel Hill: University of North Carolina Press, 2003), 183.

5. Daniel Kawahara, life history interview by Sojin Kim and Darcie Iki for Re-examining Boyle Heights Project, December 18, 2000, Los Angeles, transcript, Japanese American National Museum, Los Angeles, pp. 24–26.

6. Ruth Toshiko Matsuo Brandt, life history interview by Sojin Kim and Raul Vasquez for Re-examining Boyle Heights Project, August 17, 2001, transcript, Los Angeles, Japanese American National Museum, Los Angeles, 23.

7. Kevin Allen Leonard, *The Battle for Los Angeles: Racial Ideology and World War II* (Albuquerque: University of New Mexico Press, 2006), 55.

8. Leonard, *Battle for Los Angeles,* 56–64.

9. Leonard, *Battle for Los Angeles,* 65–66.

10. For a comprehensive review of this expansive literature, see Gary Y. Okihiro, *The Columbia Guide to Asian American History* (New York: Columbia University Press, 2001), 100–127.

11. US Army, Western Defense Command and Fourth Army, *Final Report—Japanese Evacuation from the West Coast* (Washington, DC, 1943), 34, quoted in Arthur C. Verge, *Paradise Transformed: Los Angeles during the Second World War* (Dubuque, IA: Kendall/Hunt, 1993), 41.

12. See John Dower, *War without Mercy: Race and Power in the Pacific War* (New York: Pantheon Books, 1986). See also Gerstle, *American Crucible,* 201–10.

13. Verge, *Paradise Transformed,* 23–24.

14. Verge, *Paradise Transformed,* 32–34. See Kevin Starr, *Embattled Dreams: California in War and Peace, 1940–1950* (New York: Oxford University Press, 2002), 34–65, for the best account of this growing anxiety in wartime.

15. Kawahara, interview, p. 54.

16. Atoy Wilson Jr., life history interview by Paul Spitzerri and Lisa Itagaki for Re-examining Boyle Heights Project, January 25, 2001, Los Angeles, transcript, Japanese American National Museum, Los Angeles, pp. 24–25.

17. Conversation with son of female minister, Tenrikyo Church, at the Boyle Heights History Walk in June 2015.

18. James Tolmasov, life history interview by Sojin Kim for Re-examining Boyle Heights Project, April 17, 2001, Los Angeles, transcript, Japanese American National Museum, Los Angeles, pp. 56–57.

19. Matthew M. Briones, *Jim and Jap Crow: A Cultural History of 1940s Interracial America* (Princeton, NJ: Princeton University Press, 2012), 66; Lawrence P. Jackson, *Chester B. Himes: A Biography* (New York: Norton, 2017), 157; Japanese American National Museum, "Boyle Heights: Neighborhood Sites and Insights" project application to the National Endowment for the Humanities, February 5, 2001, p. 4.

20. Chester Himes, *If He Hollers Let Him Go* (1945; repr., New York: Thunder's Mouth Press, 1986), 3.

21. Brandt, interview, p. 23.

22. See the documentary film *East LA Interchange* (2015) for a poignant scene where her son, Cedrick Shimo, recovers one of those items from a Mexican family who now lives in the home in the twenty-first century; Cedrick Shimo and Saul Ness, tour and sit-down interview by Betsy Kalin for her documentary film *East LA Interchange*, June 18, 2008, transcript, pp. 36–38.

23. Cedrick Shimo, interview by Sojin Kim and Erick Molinar for Re-examining Boyle Heights Project, March 19, 2001, Los Angeles, transcript, Japanese American National Museum, Los Angeles, pp. 43–45.

24. Joey Ryoyei Kitayama, interview by Glen Ikuo Kitayama for "The Other Los Angeles" Project, History 101.6, University of California, Los Angeles (UCLA), February 24, 1990.

25. Kate Bolotin and Paul Zolnekoff, life history interview by Wendy Elliott for Re-examining Boyle Heights Project, August 15, 2000, Los Angeles, transcript, Japanese American National Museum, Los Angeles, p. 23.

26. Starr, *Embattled Dreams*, 91.

27. Earl Warren testimony at House Select Committee Investigating National Defense Migration hearings (Tolan Committee), quoted in David O'Brien and Stephen Fugita, *The Japanese American Experience* (Bloomington: University of Indiana Press, 1991), 47.

28. Kitayama, interview, February 24, 1990; Katz Kunitsugu, interview by Teresa Kay Williams for "The Other Los Angeles" Project, History 101.6, University of California, Los Angeles (UCLA), February 8, 1990; Malcolm Kambayashi, "Issei Women: Life Histories of Six Issei Women Who Participated in Social and Other Activities in Los Angeles" (Master's thesis, University of California, Los Angeles, 1984), 197–99; Takaki, *Strangers from a Different Shore*, 379–405.

29. Donald Hata and Nadine Hata, "Indispensable Scapegoats: Asians and Pacific Islanders in Pre-1945 Los Angeles," in *City of Promise: Race and Historical Change in Los Angeles*, ed. Martin Schiesl and Mark M. Dodge (Claremont, CA: Regina Books, 2006), 51.

30. Guy Gabaldon, life history interview by Darcie Iki, Sojin Kim, and Dean Hayasaka for Re-examining Boyle Heights Project, February 13, 2001, Los Angeles, transcript, Japanese American National Museum, Los Angeles, pp. 19, 22–28. The military career of Guy Gabaldon was made famous in the Hollywood movie *Hell to Eternity*, released in 1960.

31. Bud Weber, life history interview by Jim Gatewood for Re-examining Boyle Heights Project, July 21, 2000, Los Angeles, transcript, Japanese American National Museum, Los Angeles, p. 35.

32. Weber, interview, pp. 36–37.

33. Moore, *To the Golden Cities*, 10–11.

34. Beverly Beyette, "The Saxons of Wabash: Together Once Again," *Los Angeles Times*, December 11, 1989, E1.

35. Beyette, "Saxons of Wabash," E2.

36. Florence Zimmerman Coutin, interview by Sarah Gelb Felman for "The Other Los Angeles" Project, History 101.6, University of California, Los Angeles (UCLA), February 14, 1990.

37. Stein, interview, pp. 12–13, 19–26.

38. Hershey Eisenberg, life history interview by Darcie Iki and Sojin Kim for Re-examining Boyle Heights Project, December 18, 2000, Los Angeles, transcript, Japanese American National Museum, Los Angeles, pp. 14–15.

39. William M. Kramer, "The Man behind 'The Spirit of Boyle Heights,'" *Western States Jewish History Quarterly* 20:3 (April 1988): 238–41.

40. Elizabeth R. Escobedo, *From Coveralls to Zoot Suits: The Lives of Mexican American Women on the World War II Home Front* (Chapel Hill: University of North Carolina Press, 2013), 74.

41. Leonard, *Battle for Los Angeles*, 28–48.

42. Escobedo, *From Coveralls to Zoot Suits*, 75.

43. Sherna B. Gluck, *Rosie the Riveter Revisited: Women, the War, and Social Change* (Boston: Twayne, 1987), 71–72, 87.

44. Escobedo, *From Coveralls to Zoot Suits*, 79.

45. Escobedo, *From Coveralls to Zoot Suits*, 75.

46. Albert Johnson II, life history interview by Paul Spitzzeri and Sojin Kim for Re-examining Boyle Heights Project, July 3, 2002, Los Angeles, transcript, Japanese American National Museum, Los Angeles, pp. 1–4.

47. Wilson, interview, pp. 23–24.

48. Escobedo, *From Coveralls to Zoot Suits*, 75.

49. Scott Tadeo Kurashige, *The Shifting Grounds of Race: Black and Japanese Americans in the Making of Multiethnic Los Angeles* (Princeton, NJ: Princeton University Press, 2008), 144.

50. Laslett, *Sunshine Was Never Enough*, 205.

51. Escobedo, *From Coveralls to Zoot Suits*, 96, 135–36; Hope Mendoza Schechter, oral history interview by Malca Chall, 1977–78, transcript, BANC MSS 81/73, Bancroft Library Regional History Office, University of California, Berkeley, pp. 28–29.

52. Josh Sides, *L.A. City Limits: African American Los Angeles from the Great Depression to the Present* (Berkeley: University of California Press, 2003), 44–45; also see Jenks, "'Home Is Little Tokyo.'"

53. Quoted in Graaf, "Negro Migration," 189.

54. Mario T. García, *Memories of Chicano History: The Life and Narrative of Bert Corona* (Berkeley: University of California Press, 1994), 155–56.

55. Laslett, *Sunshine Was Never Enough,* 179.

56. Escobedo, *From Coveralls to Zoot Suits,* 98; Naomi Quiñonez, "Rosita the Riveter: Welding Tradition with Wartime Transformations," in *Mexican Americans and World War II,* ed. Maggie Rivas-Rodriguez (Austin: University of Texas Press, 2005), 264.

57. Carey McWilliams, *North from Mexico: The Spanish Speaking People of the United States* (1948; repr., New York: Greenwood Press, 1968), 206.

58. "'Zoot Suit' Gangsters," editorial from *Manzanar Free Press,* n.d., Records of the War Relocation Authority, Record Group 210, National Archives, Washington, DC, quoted in Leonard, "Years of Hope," 182.

59. Janice Shyer, life history interview by Dan Gebler for Re-examining Boyle Heights Project, October 2000, Los Angeles, transcript, Japanese American National Museum, Los Angeles, p. 12.

60. Pagán, *Murder at the Sleepy Lagoon,* 11, 39, 108; Luis Alvarez, *The Power of the Zoot: Youth Culture and Resistance during World War II* (Berkeley: University of California Press, 2008), 83–84. For an alternative interpretation of the origin of the zoot suit stressing roots at the US-Mexican border, see Gerardo Licón, "Pachucas, Pachucos, and Their Culture: Mexican American Youth Culture of the Southwest, 1910–1950" (PhD diss., University of Southern California, 2009).

61. Stuart Cosgrove, "The Zoot-Suit and Style Warfare," *History Workshop,* no. 18 (Autumn 1984): 78.

62. Cosgrove, "Zoot-Suit," 78.

63. Escobar, *Race, Police,* 180.

64. Escobedo, *From Coveralls to Zoot Suits,* 25.

65. Escobedo, *From Coveralls to Zoot Suits,* 27–28.

66. Escobar, *Race, Police,* 162–66, 188.

67. Escobar, *Race, Police,* 186–96.

68. Escobar, *Race, Police,* 207–10. Probably the best account of this hysteria is in Pagán, *Murder at the Sleepy Lagoon,* 45–68.

69. Escobedo, *From Coveralls to Zoot Suits,* 22–23.

70. Escobar, *Race, Police,* 224–27.

71. Escobar, *Race, Police,* 227–28.

72. Escobar, *Race, Police,* 229–31.

73. Pagán, *Murder at the Sleepy Lagoon,* 145–66.

74. Dorothy Tomer, interview by Stephanie Maya for "The Other Los Angeles" Project, History 101.6, University of California, Los Angeles (UCLA), February 19, 1990, Montebello, CA; Pete Martinez, interview by Laura Olague for "The Other Los Angeles" Project, History 101.6, University of California, Los Angeles (UCLA), February 22, 1990; Interview with Robert Rodriguez, interview by Raul Gomez for "The Other Los Angeles" Project, History 101.6, University of California, Los Angeles (UCLA), March 1, 1990; Mauricio Mazón, *The Zoot-Suit Riots: The Psychology of Symbolic Annihilation* (Austin: University of Texas Press, 1984).

75. Escobar, *Race, Police,* 233.

76. Escobar, *Race, Police,* 234–36.

77. *Los Angeles Daily News,* June 7, 1943; Escobar, *Race, Police,* 236–37.

78. Escobar, *Race, Police,* 240–41, 244.

79. For the spread of violence to surrounding suburbs, see Gonzalez, *In Search,* 34–36.

80. Leonard, *Battle for Los Angeles,* 160, 174–75.

81. Leonard, *Battle for Los Angeles,* 184–94; Escobar, *Race, Police,* 272–84; Shana Bernstein, *Bridges of Reform: Interracial Civil Rights Activism in Twentieth-Century Los Angeles* (New York: Oxford University Press, 2011) 76–99.

82. Frumkin, interview, pp. 4–7.

83. Shana Bernstein, "From Civic Defense to Civil Rights: The Growth of Jewish American Interracial Civil Rights Activism in Los Angeles," in *A Cultural History of Jews in California: The Jewish Role in American Life, An Annual Review,* vol. 7, ed. Bruce Zuckerman, William Deverell, and Lisa Ansell (West Lafayette, IN: Purdue University Press for the University of Southern California Casden Institute for the Study of the Jewish Role in American Life, 2009), 56–60.

84. Ross, *Hitler in Los Angeles,* 161.

85. See Ross, *Hitler in Los Angeles.*

86. Ross, *Hitler in Los Angeles,* 316–22.

87. Ross, *Hitler in Los Angeles,* 312–13; see also Bernstein, *Bridges of Reform,* 97–98.

88. For a wider national analysis of this transition, see Stuart Svonkin, *Jews against Prejudice: American Jews and the Fight for Civil Liberties* (New York: Columbia University Press, 1997), esp. chap. 1, "From Self-Defense to Intergroup Relations," 11–40.

89. Leon Lewis, various letters to heads of Jewish organizations in places including Seattle, Minneapolis, Pittsburgh, San Francisco, and Florida, Summer 1942, Civil Rights Congress (CRC) Collection, Folder 22, Box 5, Series II, Southern California Library for Social Studies and Research, cited in Bernstein, *Bridges of Reform,* 91.

90. Bernstein, *Bridges of Reform,* 92.

91. Bernstein, *Bridges of Reform,* 90–98.

92. Leonard, *Battle for Los Angeles,* 223–26.

93. Leonard, *Battle for Los Angeles,* 233.

94. "Ickes Assails Coast Stand on Japanese," *Los Angeles Examiner,* April 14, 1944, pt. 1, 1.

95. Leonard, *Battle for Los Angeles,* 233–34.

96. "'Poll Conductor' Led Off Campus in Nisei Rumpus," *Los Angeles Times,* September 28, 1944, pt. 2, 1; Leonard, *Battle for Los Angeles,* 237–42.

97. Leonard, *Battle for Los Angeles,* 242–43.

98. Leonard, *Battle for Los Angeles,* 246–47.

99. Shimo, interview, p. 55.

100. Toshiko Ito, life history interview by Darcie Iki for Re-examining Boyle Heights Project, April 2, 2001, Los Angeles, transcript, Japanese American National Museum, Los Angeles, pp. 18–20.

101. Shimo, interview, pp. 8–9.

102. Murphy, Nishi, and Okada, interview, pp. 16, 72.

103. Anthony Macías, "Multicultural Music, Jews, and American Culture: The Life and Times of William Phillips," in *Beyond Alliances: The Jewish Role in Reshaping the Racial Landscape of Southern California/The Jewish Role in American Life: An Annual Review of the Casden Institute for the Study of the Jewish Role in American Life,* ed. Bruce Zuckerman, George J. Sánchez, and Lisa Ansell (West Lafayette, IN: Purdue University Press for the USC Casden Institute for the Study of the Jewish Role in American Life, 2012), 45.

104. See Phil Ethington, Anne Marie Kooistra, and De Young, "Los Angeles County Unified Census Data Series, 1949–1990" (data prepared with the support of the John Randolph Hayes and Dora Haynes Foundation, Los Angeles).

105. S. Kurashige, *Shifting Grounds of Race,* 168.

106. Ito, interview, pp. 20–26.

107. Frumkin, interview, p. 19.

108. Frumkin, interview, p. 46.

6. THE EXODUS FROM THE EASTSIDE

1. Ida B. Fiering, interview by Leslye Sneider for "The Other Los Angeles" Project, History 101.6, University of California, Los Angeles (UCLA), February 23, 1990.

2. See, for example, Neal Gabler, *An Empire of Their Own: How the Jews Invented Hollywood* (New York: Crown, 1988); Rogin, *Blackface, White Noise.*

3. Eric L. Goldstein, "Contesting the Categories: Jews and Government Racial Classification in the United States," *Jewish History Quarterly* 19:1 (2005): 95.

4. Eric L. Goldstein, *The Price of Whiteness: Jews, Race, and American Identity* (Princeton, NJ: Princeton University Press, 2006), 200–201.

5. Moore, *To the Golden Cities,* 42–44; Jackson Mayers, *The San Fernando Valley* (Walnut, CA: John D. McIntyre, 1976), 172; James Thomas Keane, *Fritz B. Burns and the Development of Los Angeles: The Biography of a Community Developer and Philanthropist* (Los Angeles: Thomas and Dorothy Leavey Center for the Study of Los Angeles, 2001), 70–71; Greg Hise, *Magnetic Los Angeles: Planning the Twentieth-Century Metropolis* (Baltimore: Johns Hopkins University Press, 1997), 186–215.

6. Gerald Sorin, *Tradition Transformed: The Jewish Experience in America* (Baltimore: Johns Hopkins University Press, 1997), 197–99; Albert Gordon, *Jews in Suburbia* (Boston: Beacon Press, 1959).

7. Sorin, *Tradition Transformed,* 197.

8. Lipsitz, *Possessive Investment in Whiteness,* 5.

9. Kenneth T. Jackson, *Crabgrass Frontier: The Suburbanization of the United States* (New York: Oxford University Press, 1985), 213.

10. Vorspan and Gartner, *History of the Jews,* 204; Moore, *To the Golden Cities,* 56–57; Elliott-Scheinberg, "Boyle Heights," 11.

11. Ralph Friedman, "U.N. in Microcosm: Boyle Heights: An Example of Democratic Progress," *Frontier*, March 1955, 11; Vorspan and Gartner, *History of the Jews*, 297; Moore, *Golden Cities*, 58; Elliot-Schienberg, "Boyle Heights," 11.

12. Starr, *Embattled Dreams*, 193.

13. Approximately 850,000 veterans settled in California after the war; Starr, *Embattled Dreams*, 194.

14. Kevin Leonard, "'Brothers under the Skin'?: African Americans, Mexican Americans, and World War II in California," in *The Way We Really Were: The Golden State in the Second World War*, ed. Roger W. Lotchin (Urbana: University of Illinois Press, 2000), 192–93.

15. Starr, *Embattled Dreams*, 191.

16. Lynn C. Kronzek, "Fairfax . . . A Home, a Community, a Way of Life," *Legacy: Journal of the Jewish Historical Society of Southern California*, 1:4 (Spring 1990), 15, 23–36; Eshref Shevky and Marilyn Williams, *The Social Areas of Los Angeles: Analysis and Typology* (Berkeley: University of California Press, 1949), 157–59.

17. Morris J. Kay, Publisher, *Valley Jewish News*, to John Anson Ford, February 9, 1950, John Anson Ford Papers, Box 75, Folder B IV 5i cc(15), Huntington Library, San Marino, CA.

18. Milton A. Senn, Director, Anti-Defamation League of B'nai B'rith, "Report on Efforts in the Los Angeles Area to Circumvent the United States Supreme Court Decisions on Restrictive Covenants," memorandum, December 31, 1948, 8. John Anson Ford Papers, Box 75, Folder B IV 5i cc(13), Huntington Library, San Marino, CA.

19. Senn, "Report on Efforts," 3.

20. Moore, *Golden Cities*, 23.

21. Kronzek, "Fairfax," 36–37.

22. William Phillips, interview by Tamara Zwick for "The Other Los Angeles" Project, History 101.6, University of California, Los Angeles (UCLA), February 22, 1990; Mateo Gold, "Era Ends as 78-Year-Old Men's Store Calls It Quits; Neighborhoods: Zellman's Menswear in Boyle Heights Closes," *Los Angeles Times*, October 4, 1999, Home ed., 1.

23. Text in museum exhibition, *Boyle Heights: The Power of Place*, Japanese American National Museum, Los Angeles, September 2002–February 2003; "Bill Phillips Elected to Head Citizens Committee to Re-elect Roybal," *Eastside Sun*, February 1, 1951; Anthony Macías, "Multicultural Music," 33–69.

24. Jewish Centers Association, *Facts about the Eastside Jewish Community Center of the Jewish Centers Association*, pamphlet prepared for Budget Subcommittee #10, Community Chest—Welfare Federation of L.A., February 1954, Jewish Centers Association file, Jewish Federation of Los Angeles.

25. My thanks to George Lipsitz for pointing out the fundamental material benefits accrued by this transfer of population and capital accumulation.

26. Herbert Morris Biskar, "A History of the Jewish Centers Association of Los Angeles with Special Reference to Jewish Identity" (PhD diss., University of Southern California, 1972), 42–45.

27. Hershey Eisenberg, life history interview by Darcie Iki and Sojin Kim for Re-examining Boyle Heights Project, December 18, 2000, Los Angeles, transcript, Japanese American National Museum, Los Angeles, p. 21.

28. Eisenberg, interview, pp. 32–33.

29. Eisenberg, interview, p. 31.

30. Biskar, "Jewish Centers Association," 46–51.

31. Biskar, "Jewish Centers Association," 54–58; Jewish Centers Association, *A Decade of Service . . . The First Ten Years, 1943–1953: A Report to the Jewish Community of Los Angeles* (Los Angeles, 1954), Histories file, Jewish Centers Association, Los Angeles.

32. Edward L. Barrett Jr., *The Tenney Committee: Legislative Investigation of Subversive Activities in California* (Ithaca, NY: Cornell University Press, 1951), 37–39; Moore, *To the Golden Cities*, 201–2.

33. Transcript, vol. 48, p. 55, quoted in Barrett, *Tenney Committee*, 38.

34. Moore, *To the Golden Cities*, 201.

35. See Biskar, "Jewish Centers Association," 67–68.

36. Minutes of the Board Meeting of the Soto-Michigan Jewish Community Center, September 14, 1948, Box 9, Jewish Centers Association, Histories file, Archives, Jewish Community Library, Jewish Federation Council of Los Angeles (hereafter JCA).

37. Moore, *To the Golden Cities*, 201–2; Barrett, *Tenney Committee*, 38–39; Minutes of the Board Meeting of the Soto-Michigan Jewish Community Center, December 14, 1948, Box 9, JCA.

38. Minutes of the Board Meeting of the Soto-Michigan Jewish Community Center, December 14, 1948, Box 9, JCA; Biskar, "Jewish Centers Association," 68–69; Moore, *To the Golden Cities*, 202–5.

39. Moore, *To the Golden Cities*, 210.

40. Minutes of the Board Meeting of the Soto-Michigan Jewish Community Center, November 10, 1949, Box 9, JCA.

41. Minutes of the Board Meeting of the Soto-Michigan Jewish Community Center, February 14, 1950, and March 14, 1950, Box 9, JCA.

42. Biskar, "Jewish Centers Association," 61.

43. Minutes of the Board Meeting of the Soto-Michigan Jewish Community Center, May 18, 1949, Box 9, JCA.

44. Minutes of the Board Meeting of the Soto-Michigan Jewish Community Center, June 13, 1950, and January 8, 1952, Box 9, JCA. Indeed, Keats would go on to photograph many of the most progressive and intercultural activities of the 1960s, as evidenced by his photographic collection now available at the Southern California Library for Social Studies Research, Los Angeles (hereafter Southern California Library).

45. Minutes of the Board Meeting of the Soto-Michigan Jewish Community Center, November 14, 1950, January 9, 1951, and October 30, 1951, Box 9, JCA.

46. Minutes of the Board Meeting of the Soto-Michigan Jewish Community Center, June 13, 1950 and October 10, 1950, Box 9, JCA.

47. Moore, *To the Golden Cities*, 210–11; Minutes of the Board Meeting of the Soto-Michigan Jewish Community Center, October 30, 1951, Box 9, JCA.

48. Minutes of the Board Meeting of the Soto-Michigan Jewish Community Center, January 8, 1952, Box 9, JCA.

49. Phillips, interview; Minutes of the Board Meeting of the Soto-Michigan Jewish Community Center, April 12, 1950, Box 9, JCA.

50. Minutes of the Board Meeting of the Soto-Michigan Jewish Community Center, January 9, 1951, and February, 12, 1952, Box 9, JCA.

51. Minutes of the Board Meeting of the Soto-Michigan Jewish Community Center, June 12, 1951, September 11, 1951, Box 9, JCA.

52. Minutes of the Board Meeting of the Soto-Michigan Jewish Community Center, November 27, 1951, January 8, 1952, and February 12, 1952, Box 9, JCA. For more on the life of Walter Hilborn, see Walter Hilborn, *Reflections on Legal Practice and Jewish Community Leadership: New York and Los Angeles, 1907–1973* (Los Angeles: University of California, Berkeley, Regional Oral History Office, 1974), esp. 161–62.

53. Biskar, "Jewish Centers Association," 60.

54. Resolution from the Menorah Center Board, July 10, 1952, in Minutes of the Board Meeting of the Soto-Michigan Jewish Community Center, July 14, 1952, Box 9, JCA.

55. Minutes of the Board Meetings of the Soto-Michigan Jewish Community Center, September 9, 1952, October 14, 1952, November 11, 1952, December 9, 1952, Box 9, JCA; Roster of Board of Directors of the Soto-Michigan Jewish Community Center, 1951–52, United Way of Los Angeles Collection, Box 52, Urban Archives Center, University Library, California State University, Northridge.

56. The one book dedicated to the ACPFB until recently, which directly calls the organization "a tool of American communism" (1), is John W. Sherman, *A Communist Front at Mid-century: The American Committee for Protection of the Foreign Born, 1933–1959* (Westport, CT: Praeger, 2001); Litwin, "'How Could a Woman,'" 26. More recently, Rachel Ida Buff calls the ACPFB a broad-based "popular front" organization began as an immigrant rights organization "by and for the foreign born." See *Against the Deportation Terror: Organizing for Immigrant Rights in the Twentieth Century* (Philadelphia: Temple University Press, 2018), 13–15, for an analysis of this historiography.

57. For the best description of the formation of the LACPFB, see Jeffrey M. Garcilazo, "McCarthyism, Mexican Americans, and the Los Angeles Committee for the Protection of the Foreign-Born, 1950–1954," *Western Historical Quarterly* 32:3 (Autumn 2001): 273–95, especially 280–83. See also Buff, *Against the Deportation Terror*, 108–37, 203.

58. Kim Chernin, *In My Mother's House: A Daughter's Story* (New Haven, CT: Ticknor and Fields, 1983), 161–62, 177–78; Dorothy Healey and Maurice Isserman, *Dorothy Healey Remembers: A Life in the American Communist Party* (New York: Oxford University Press, 1990), 135. For a focused discussion of the development of Rose Chernin as a Los Angeles radical, see Litwin, "'How Could a Woman'"

59. *The Torchlight,* May 1953, 7, "Correspondence and Publicity: 1953," Labadie Collection, Folder, Box 14, American Committee for the Protection of the Foreign Born, Department of Special Collections, University of Michigan Library, Ann Arbor.

60. LACPFB, "A Call to the People of Los Angeles!!," Labadie Collection, "LACPFB: Correspondence & Publicity, 1954" folder, Box 14, ACPFB, Department of Special Collections, University of Michigan Library, Ann Arbor. See also Garcilazo, "McCarthyism," 293.

61. LACPFB, "Call to the People."

62. Yanez quoted in Buff, *Against the Deportation Terror,* 192.

63. *The Torchlight,* May 1954, "LACPFB: Correspondence & Publicity: 1954" folder, and Program for "Festival of Nationalities," June 7, 1953, "LACPFB: Correspondence & Publicity: 1953" folder, both in Box 14, ACPFB, Labadie Collection, Department of Special Collections, University of Michigan Library, Ann Arbor; Festival of Nationalities poster, June 14, 1964, Folder 21, and press release for the 3rd Annual Festival of Nationalities conference, 1954, Folder 22, both in LACPFB Papers, Box 1, Southern California Library; Jeffrey M. Garcilazo, "McCarthyism, Mexican Americans, and the Los Angeles Committee for the Protection of the Foreign-Born, 1950–1954," *Western Historical Quarterly* 32:3 (Autumn 2001): 283–84.

64. Flyer for Edo Mita Victory celebration, LACPFB Papers, Folder 22, Box 1, Southern California Library.

65. One of the best studies of this kind in Southern California is Lisa McGirr, *Suburban Warriors: The Origins of the New American Right* (Princeton, NJ: Princeton University Press, 2001), which focuses on Orange County, California. See also Sarah Schrank, *Art and the City: Civic Imagination and Cultural Authority in Los Angeles* (Philadelphia: University of Pennsylvania Press, 2009), 64–96.

66. See Litwin, "'How Could a Woman,'" 28–29; Barbara K. Soliz, "Rosalind Wiener Wyman and the Transformation of Jewish Liberalism in Cold War Los Angeles," in *Beyond Alliances: The Jewish Role in Reshaping the Racial Landscape of Southern California,* ed. Bruce Zuckerman, George J. Sánchez, and Lisa Ansell (West Lafayette, IN: Purdue University Press for the USC Casden Institute for the Study of the Jewish Role in American Life, 2012), 85–86.

67. Hershel Gluck, "City Council Honors Marion and Paul Miller: Jewish Couple 'Led 6 Lives' for Their Country," *B'nai B'rith Messenger,* February 7, 1958, 4.

68. For the best analysis of the career of Rosalind Wiener Wyman, see Soliz, "Rosalind Wiener Wyman."

69. See Neil J. Sullivan, *The Dodgers Move West* (New York: Oxford University Press, 1987), and John H. M. Laslett, *Shameful Victory: The Los Angeles Dodgers, the Red Scare, and the Hidden History of Chavez Ravine* (Tucson: University of Arizona Press, 2015).

70. Charlotta A. Bass to the Honorable City Council, Att. Mrs. Rosalind Wyman, n.d., LACPFB Papers, Folder 25, Box 1, Southern California Library.

71. Rose Chernin to Los Angeles City Council, February 11, 1958, LACPFB Papers, Folder 25, Box 1, Southern California Library.

72. Frumkin, interview, pp. 7–8.

73. Frumkin, interview, p. 9.

74. Minutes of the Eastside Jewish Community Center, 1954 to 1958, Box 9, JCA.

75. Frumkin, interview, pp. 35–36.

76. Richard and Barbara Duran, interview by Stephanie Duran, for "The Other Los Angeles" Project, History 101.6, University of California, Los Angeles (UCLA), February 18, 1990, Chino Hills, CA.

7. EDWARD R. ROYBAL AND THE POLITICS OF MULTIRACIALISM

1. Kenneth C. Burt, *The Search for a Civic Voice: California Latino Politics* (Claremont, CA: Regina Books, 2007), 55, 59, 69, 95–96.

2. Burt, *Search,* 100; Katherine Underwood, "Process and Politics: Multiracial Electoral Coalition Building and Representation in Los Angeles' Ninth District, 1949–1962" (PhD diss., University of California, San Diego, 1992), 167–68.

3. Burt, *Search,* 100; Underwood, "Process and Politics," 168; "Won't Sell to Mexicans GI Developer Tells Roybal," *California Eagle,* September 8, 1949, 1. Frank Javier García Berumen has a slightly different version of this story in *Edward R. Roybal: The Mexican American Struggle for Political Empowerment* (Los Angeles: Bilingual Educational Services, 2015), 108–9.

4. Berumen, *Edward R. Roybal,* 27–77; David R. Ayon and George L. Pla, *Power Shift: How Latinos in California Transformed Politics in America* (Berkeley: Berkeley Public Policy Press, Institute of Governmental Studies, University of California, Berkeley, 2018), 25–38.

5. Burt, *Search,* 54.

6. Kenneth C. Burt, "The Power of a Mobilized Citizenry and Coalition Politics: The 1949 Election of Edward R. Roybal to the Los Angeles City Council," *Southern California Quarterly* 85:4 (Winter 2003): 416–17; Rosina Lozano, "The Struggle for Inclusion: A Study of the Community Service Organization in East Los Angeles, 1947–1951" (Stanford University senior thesis, 2000), 14; Bernstein, *Bridges of Reform,* 149. For a fuller description of the generational change brought about by repatriation, see Sánchez, *Becoming Mexican American,* chap. 11, 227–52.

7. Burt, *Search,* 55–59; Lozano, "Struggle for Inclusion," 15; Mark Brilliant, *The Color of America Has Changed: How Racial Diversity Shaped Civil Rights Reform in California, 1941–1978* (New York: Oxford University Press, 2010), 133; Berumen, *Edward R. Roybal,* 79–83.

8. Lozano, "Struggle for Inclusion," 16; Gabriel Thompson, *America's Social Arsonist: Fred Ross and Grassroots Organizing in the Twentieth Century* (Berkeley: University of California Press, 2016), 86.

9. Thompson, *America's Social Arsonist,* 9–24.

10. Thompson, *America's Social Arsonist,* 32–82.

11. Lozano, "Struggle for Inclusion," 18.

12. Thompson, *America's Social Arsonist,* 72–73, 87–88.

13. Lozano, "Struggle for Inclusion," 24–28.

14. This biographical material is drawn from Hope Mendoza Schecter, "Activist in the Labor Movement, the Democratic Party and the Mexican-American Community: Oral History Transcript," interview by Malca Chall, transcript, BANC MSS 81/73, Regional Oral History Office, Bancroft Library, University of California, Berkeley).

15. Mendoza Schecter, interview, p. 7.

16. Mendoza Schecter, interview, p. 71.

17. Brilliant, *Color of America,* 133; Lozano, "Struggle for Inclusion," 28–31; Berumen, *Edward R. Roybal,* 91–92.

18. Edward Roybal, introduction to Mendoza Schecter, interview, p. vii.

19. See Denning, *Cultural Front.*

20. Lozano, "Struggle for Inclusion," 27.

21. Bernstein, *Bridges of Reform,* 148.

22. Burt, *Search,* 75–76; Bernstein, *Bridges of Reform,* 148–49. For a description of Leon Lewis shifting the focus of the Community Relations Committee, see Ross, *Hitler in Los Angeles,* 338–39.

23. Bernstein, *Bridges of Reform,* 146.

24. Burt, "Power of a Mobilized Citizenry," 417–19.

25. See, for example, the exploration of fear of violence as a rationale for coalition building in Bernstein, *Bridges of Reform,* 151–56.

26. Underwood, "Process and Politics," 108–9; Berumen, *Edward R. Roybal,* 98–99.

27. Richard A. Donovan, "Roybal Rouses the Ninth: A Los Angeles Mexican-American District Learns How to Make Its Political Voice Heard," *The Reporter,* January 17, 1950, 7–9, quoted in Underwood, "Process and Politics," 118. Also quoted in Burt, *Search,* 108; Berumen, *Edward R. Roybal,* 124.

28. Underwood, "Process and Politics," 116–18; Berumen, *Edward R. Roybal,* 122–24; *Eastside Sun,* February 22, 1951, 1.

29. Underwood, "Process and Politics," 119; *Eastside Sun,* March 29, 1951, Roybal Newspaper Scrapbook, L.A. County Library, East L.A. branch (hereafter RNS).

30. Berumen, *Edward R. Roybal,* 125–26.

31. Fred Ross, unpublished manuscript, 17, Fred Ross Collection, M812, Box 21, Folder 18, Stanford University Archives, Stanford, CA.

32. Ross, unpublished manuscript, 14–25. For a more extensive analysis of Bowron's time in office, see Tom Sitton, *Los Angeles Transformed: Fletcher Bowron's Urban Reform Revival, 1938–1953* (Albuquerque: University of New Mexico Press, 2005).

33. See Underwood, "Process and Politics," 164–74.

34. Joe Kovner, *Eastside Sun,* March 15, 1951, RNS; Underwood, "Process and Politics," 164–74.

35. Vern Partlow, "Bypassed 'Islands' of L.A. Experience Awakening," *Los Angeles Daily News,* December 27, 1950, Fred Ross Collection, M812, Box 11, Folder 11.

36. Health issues are generally marginalized in civil rights histories, but they have always been important. The CSO campaigns in Boyle Heights against tuberculosis and diphtheria would help explain why pesticide use later became a focal point for Fred Ross in his work with the United Farm Workers (UFW).

37. Lozano, "Struggle for Inclusion," 32–33.

38. See Ayon and Pla, *Power Shift,* 36–37; Berumen, *Edward R. Roybal,* 62–63.

39. See Burt, *Search,* chap. 6, "The Tony Rios and Bloody Christmas Police Beatings," 117–34, for the most complete analysis of this issue.

40. *Los Angeles Times,* September 23, 1949, pt. 2, 4.

41. Underwood, "Process and Politics," 175–79; Berumen, *Edward R. Roybal,* 107–8.

42. Underwood, "Process and Politics," 184–96; Berumen, *Edward R. Roybal,* 111–12.

43. Ed Roybal, "A Week Ago Today . . .," 2, Edward Roybal Collection, MS 847, Box 8, Folder "Communism," UCLA Special Collections.

44. Lillian Roybal-Rose, Interview by Frank Javier García Berumen, April 29, 2005, quoted in Berumen, *Edward R. Roybal,* 113.

45. *Eastside Sun,* September 14, 1950, RNS; *Los Angeles Daily News,* September 15, 1950, RNS.

46. George E. Rundquist to Councilman Edward R. Roybal, October 6, 1950, and Edward R. Roybal to Mr. George E. Rundquist, October 17, 1950, both in Edward Roybal Collection, MS 847, Box 8, Folder "Communism," UCLA Department of Special Collections, Los Angeles.

47. Lozano, "Struggle for Inclusion," 82–92.

48. Burt, *Search,* 133–34; Lozano, "Struggle for Inclusion," 99.

49. See Soliz, "Rosalind Wiener Wyman."

50. See Sitton, *Los Angeles Transformed,* 165–90.

51. Underwood, "Process and Politics," 239–45; Berumen, *Edward R. Roybal,* 133–35.

52. Underwood, "Process and Politics," 217–18, 239–45; Berumen, *Edward R. Roybal,* 150–54.

53. See Laslett, *Shameful Victory,* 80–122.

54. See Cuff, *Provisional City,* 161–63.

55. Underwood, "Process and Politics," 227–31.

56. See Edward Roybal Collection, MS 847, Box 13, Folders "Freeways," UCLA Department of Special Collections, Los Angeles.

57. Joseph Kovner, *Eastside Sun,* November 14, 1957, 1; Underwood, "Process and Politics," 231–38; Berumen, *Edward R. Roybal,* 135–37.

58. See Jerry Gonzalez, "'A Place in the Sun': Mexican Americans, Race, and the Suburbanization of Los Angeles, 1940–1980" (PhD diss., University of Southern California, 2009); Gonzalez, *In Search*; and Leland T. Saito, *Race and Politics: Asian*

Americans, Latinos, and Whites in a Los Angeles Suburb (Urbana: University of Illinois Press, 1998).

59. Berumen, *Edward R. Roybal,* 179.

60. Underwood, "Process and Politics," 49; Berumen, *Edward R. Roybal,* 179.

61. Sides, *L.A. City Limits,* 153.

62. Berumen, *Edward R. Roybal,* 96, 144–46, 178.

63. For the origins of MAPA, see García, *Memories of Chicano History,* 195–208.

64. Underwood, "Process and Politics," 253.

65. Ruben Salazar, "Negro May Win Roybal Seat in City Council," *Los Angeles Times,* December 16, 1962, reprinted in *Ruben Salazar: Border Correspondent; Selected Writings, 1955–1970,* ed. Mario T. García (Berkeley: University of California Press, 1995), 80–82.

66. *Los Angeles Times,* November 1, 2005, pt. B, 1.

8. BLACK AND BROWN POWER IN THE BARRIO

1. Paula Crisostomo, interview by George Sánchez and María José Plascencia, July 31, 2014, Los Angeles, transcript, pp. 13–14; Mario T. García, *The Chicano Generation: Testimonios of the Movement* (Berkeley: University of California Press, 2015), 42–44.

2. Mollie Murphy, Mary Nishi, and Sandie Okada, life history interview by Sojin Kim and Darcie Iki for Re-examining Boyle Heights Project, January 18, 2001, Los Angeles, transcript, Japanese American National Museum, Los Angeles, p. 10.

3. Tolbert, *UNIA,* 27–29.

4. Daniel Widener, *Black Arts West: Culture and Struggle in Postwar Los Angeles* (Durham, NC: Duke University Press, 2010), 57.

5. See S. Kurashige, *Shifting Grounds of Race*; Jenks, "'Home Is Little Tokyo.'"

6. Sides, *L.A. City Limits,* 19, 109.

7. Parson, *Making a Better World,* 42.

8. "Aliso Village Grows Up," *Now,* 2nd half March 1945, 13, in the Roger Johnson Collection, Box 1, Aliso Village—Printed Material 1942–45, quoted in Parson, *Making a Better World,* 68.

9. Parson, *Making a Better World,* 69–71. One exception to this pattern in Boyle Heights was Estrada Courts, which had no black residents in December of 1944 or 1945.

10. Sitton, *Los Angeles Transformed,* 165–90.

11. Crisostomo, interview, pp. 1–2.

12. Crisostomo, interview.

13. Vickie Castro, interview by George Sánchez and María José Plascencia, November 24, 2014, East Los Angeles, transcript, pp. 4–5.

14. Castro, interview.

15. Erick Galindo, "How Dolores Huerta and Cesar Chavez Started the Chicano Civil Rights Movement from a Kitchen in Boyle Heights," *L.A. Taco*, September 7, 2018, www.lataco.com/how-dolores-huerta-and-cesar-chavez-started-the-chicano-civil-rights-movement-from-a-kitchen-in-boyle-heights/.

16. Castro, interview, p. 2.

17. Dolores Delgado Bernal, "Chicana School Resistance and Grassroots Leadership: Providing an Alternative History of the 1968 East Los Angeles Blowouts" (PhD diss., University of California, Los Angeles, 1997), 96–97; Vicki L. Ruiz, *From Out of the Shadows: Mexican Women in Twentieth-Century America* (New York: Oxford University Press, 1998), 101–2.

18. Crisostomo, interview, pp. 3–5.

19. Katsuyo Tsuchiya, *Reinventing Citizenship: Black Los Angeles, Korean Kawasaki, and Community Participation* (Minneapolis: University of Minnesota Press, 2014), 6, 27–29.

20. Tsuchiya, *Reinventing Citizenship*, 66–72. See also Robert Bauman, *Race and the War on Poverty: From Watts to East L.A.* (Norman: University of Oklahoma Press, 2008), 21–25.

21. Tsuchiya, *Reinventing Citizenship*, 71–72; Bauman, *Race and the War*, 27–28.

22. Crisostomo, interview, p. 3.

23. Crisostomo, interview, pp. 3–4.

24. Don Nakanishi, interview by Natasha Miller for "The Other Los Angeles" Project, History 101.6, University of California, Los Angeles (UCLA), February 26, 1990, Los Angeles; quote from artist Patssi Valdez in the video documentary *Chicano! History of the Mexican American Civil Rights Movement: Part 3—Taking Back the Schools,* produced by Susan Racho (United States: NLCC Educational Media, 1996), VHS.

25. See Ray Santana and Mario Esparza, "East Los Angeles Blowouts," in *Parameters of Institutional Change: Chicano Experiences in Education,* edited by Armando Váldez (Hayward, CA: Southwest Network, 1974), 2.

26. Castro, interview, p. 6.

27. Nakanishi, interview.

28. Castro, interview, p. 6.

29. Castro, interview, p. 6.

30. Mario T. García and Sal Castro, *Blowout! Sal Castro and the Chicano Struggle for Educational Justice* (Chapel Hill: University of North Carolina Press, 2011), 5–6.

31. Gustavo Arellano, "How a Jewish Youth Camp Birthed the 1968 East L.A. Chicano Student Walkouts," *Tablet Magazine,* March 2, 2018, www.tabletmag.com/scroll/256617/how-a-jewish-youth-camp-birthed-the-1968-east-l-a-chicano-student-walkouts.

32. Castro, interview, pp. 7–8.

33. See Gerald Horne, *Fire This Time: The Watts Uprising and the 1960s* (Charlottesville: University Press of Virginia, 1995), 3, 54–115; Tsuchiya, *Reinventing Citizenship,* 72–78.

34. Crisostomo, interview, p. 5.

35. Tsuchiya, *Reinventing Citizenship*, 72–78.

36. García and Castro, *Blowout!*, 132.

37. Castro, interview, pp. 7–8.

38. Crisostomo, interview, p. 6.

39. García and Castro, *Blowout!*, 98–102.

40. McWilliams, *North from Mexico*.

41. Crisostomo, interview, p. 6.

42. Crisostomo, interview, pp. 7–8; Castro, interview, pp. 8–10.

43. Crisostomo, interview, p. 8; García and Castro, *Blowout!*, 67.

44. Castro, interview, pp. 8, 12.

45. García and Castro, *Blowout!*, 140; Crisostomo, interview, p. 10.

46. García and Castro, *Blowout!*, 156.

47. García and Castro, *Blowout!*, 147–48.

48. Castro, interview; see also Gustavo Licón, "'La Union Hace la Fuerza!' (Unity Creates Strength!): M.E.Ch.A. and Chicana/o Student Activism in California, 1967–1999" (PhD diss., University of Southern California, 2009).

49. García and Castro, *Blowout!*, 149–151.

50. Castro, interview, pp. 10–11.

51. Crisostomo, interview, pp. 13–14.

52. See Bernal, "Chicana School Resistance," for a discussion of the need for a reconceptualization of leadership in the Blowouts. For a wider discussion of the need to do this reconceptualization for the entire Chicano Movement, see Maylei Blackwell, *!Chicana Power! Contested Histories of Feminism in the Chicano Movement* (Austin: University of Texas Press, 2011), 34–37.

53. Esparza would go on to have a fifty-year career in the film industry and is considered the leading Latino film producer of his generation. See Elda María Román, "From Walking Out to Walking In: Activist Goals, Neoliberal Constraints, and the Discourse of Latino Entrepreneurship," *Latino Studies* 17 (2019): 5–26.

54. Roosevelt High School had more African American students enrolled in 1968 than any other high school in East Los Angeles.

55. For tensions between the Hollenbeck Division and Mexican American zoot suiters during World War II, see chapter 5 above. For run-ins between a young Edward Roybal and police from the Hollenbeck Division, see chapter 7 above.

56. García and Castro, *Blowout!*, 160–61; García, *Chicano Generation*, 44–45.

57. García and Castro, *Blowout!*, 172–86; García, *Chicano Generation*, 44.

58. "Student Demands," Walkouts Archives, Sal Castro Educational Foundation; "Student Demands," *Chicano Student News*, March 15, 1968, 3, Harry Gamboa Papers, Stanford University Libraries, Department of Special Collections.

59. Ernesto Chávez, *!Mi Raza Primero! (My People First!): Nationalism, Identity, and Insurgency in the Chicano Movement in Los Angeles, 1966–1978* (Berkeley: University of California Press, 2002), 47–48.

60. Lorena Oropeza, *!Raza Si! !Guerra No! Chicano Protest and Patriotism during the Viet Nam War Era* (Berkeley: University of California Press, 2005), 85–88.

61. Oropeza, *!Raza Si!,* 145–82; E. Chávez, *!Mi Raza Primero!,* 61–79.

62. Harry Gamboa quote taken from the video documentary *Chicano!*.

63. García and Castro, *Blowout!,* 180–82.

64. Crisostomo, interview, p. 15.

65. Crisostomo, interview, pp. 12, 15–16.

66. Crisostomo, interview, pp. 15–16.

67. Crisostomo, interview, pp. 12, 17–19.

68. "Autobiography," by Harry Gamboa, Garfield High, Harry Gamboa Papers, 1968–2010, RG M0753, Box 2, Folder 26, Stanford University, Department of Special Collections.

69. García and Castro, *Blowout!,* 8.

70. See Henry Joseph Gutierrez, "The Chicano Education Rights Movement and School Desegregation: Los Angeles, 1962–1970" (PhD diss., University of California, Irvine, 1990).

9. CREATING SANCTUARY

1. See Gloria Molina, oral history interview by Carlos Vasquez for the California State Archives, State Government Oral History Program, 1990, transcript, pp. 1–34.

2. Molina, interview, p. 34.

3. For more on the founding and growth of the Comisión Femenil Mexicana, see Anna NietoGomez, "Francisca Flores, the League of Mexican American Women, and the Comisión Femenil Mexicana Nacional, 1958–1975," in *Chicana Movidas: New Narratives of Activism and Feminism in the Movement Era,* ed. Dionne Espinoza, Maria Eugenia Cotera, and Maylei Blackwell (Austin: University of Texas Press, 2018), 44–50.

4. Manuel Pastor, *State of Resistance: What California's Dizzying Descent and Remarkable Resurgence Mean for America's Future* (New York: New Press, 2018), 67.

5. Paul Ong and Evelyn Blumenberg, "Income and Racial Inequality in Los Angeles," in *The City: Los Angeles and Urban Theory at the End of the Twentieth Century,* ed. Allen J. Scott and Edward W. Soja (Berkeley: University of California Press, 1996), 317.

6. Rick Holguin, "Tire Plant Recapped: Uniroyal Landmark Revived as $120-Million Complex," *Los Angeles Times,* November 30, 1990, B7; Harry Anderson, "Tire Makers Quit L.A.—Top U.S. Market: Reasons Perplex Workers," *Los Angeles Times,* January 31, 1978, Section III, 8, 10.

7. Pastor, *State of Resistance,* 67.

8. Raymond A. Rocco, "Latino Los Angeles: Reframing Boundaries/Borders," in Scott and Soja, *City,* 375.

9. Roger Keil, *Los Angeles: Globalization, Urbanization and Social Struggles* (Chichester: John Wiley and Sons, 1998), 96.

10. See Ana Elizabeth Rosas, *Abrazando el Espiritu: Bracero Families Confront the U.S.-Mexico Border* (Berkeley: University of California Press, 2014); Mireya

Loza, *Defiant Braceros: How Migrant Workers Fought for Racial, Sexual, and Political Freedom* (Chapel Hill: University of North Carolina Press, 2016); and Deborah Cohen, *Braceros: Migrant Citizens and Transnational Subjects in the Postwar United States and Mexico* (Chapel Hill: University of North Carolina Press, 2011), for some of the best examples of this growing literature on *braceros,* their migration to the US, and the program that structured their migration.

11. Ana Raquel Minian, *Undocumented Lives: The Untold Story of Mexican Migration* (Cambridge, MA: Harvard University Press, 2018), 3–5.

12. See, for example, Becky M. Nicolaides, *My Blue Heaven: Life and Politics in the Working-Class Suburbs of Los Angeles, 1920–1965* (Chicago: University of Chicago Press, 2002); and Karen Brodkin, *Power Politics: Environmental Activism in South Los Angeles* (New Brunswick, NJ: Rutgers University Press, 2009).

13. US 1970 Census and City of Los Angeles, Department of City Planning, Boyle Heights Community Background. Summary, January 1974, and 1970 US Census, figures, in Rodolfo F. Acuña, *A Community under Siege: A Chronicle of Chicanos East of the Los Angeles River, 1945–1975,* Monograph No. 11 (Chicano Studies Research Center Publications: University of California Los Angeles, 1984), 184.

14. City of Los Angeles, Department of City Planning, "Boyle Heights Community Plan," 1979, 2, Mary Pardo Collection, Box 1, Folder 24, Urban Archives, Oviatt Library, California State University at Northridge.

15. Acuña, *Community under Siege,* 249–50.

16. See Gonzalez, *In Search,* especially 62–63, 81–83; City of Los Angeles, Department of City Planning, "Boyle Heights Community Plan," 2–3.

17. Acuña, *Community under Siege,* 184. The figure of 24.9 percent owner-occupied residences was even substantially lower than that for East Los Angeles, which was 39.2 percent owner occupied, the same as for the city of Los Angeles overall.

18. Minian, *Undocumented Lives,* 7, 87.

19. Minian, *Undocumented Lives,* 128–41.

20. Richard Mines, *Developing a Community Tradition of Migration: A Field Study in Rural Zacatecas, Mexico, and California Settlement Areas,* Monographs in US-Mexican Studies 3 (La Jolla: Program in United States-Mexican Studies, University of California, San Diego, 1981), table A-4a, 166; Minian, *Undocumented Lives,* 117.

21. Minian, *Undocumented Lives,* 131.

22. Alexandra Stern, *Eugenic Nation: Faults and Frontiers of Better Breeding in Modern America* (Berkeley: University of California Press, 2005), 208–9.

23. Elena R. Gutiérrez, *Fertile Matters: The Politics of Mexican-Origin Women's Reproduction* (Austin: University of Texas Press, 2008), 37.

24. E. Gutiérrez, *Fertile Matters,* 35, 40–41.

25. E. Gutiérrez, *Fertile Matters,* 40–41, 44.

26. Plaintiff Affidavit of Jovita Rivera, executed on April 29, 1975, at Los Angeles, Mexican American Legal Defense and Education Fund (MALDEF) Records, M673, Stanford University Archives, Special Collections, Legal Program Department, Chicana Rights Project, RG#5, Box 10, Folder 6.

27. E. Gutiérrez, *Fertile Matters,* 43. See the documentary film *No Más Bebés,* dir. Renee Tajima-Pena (United States: Moon Canyon Films, 2015), DVD, for a fuller, more personal depiction of the long-term impact on these women.

28. E. Gutiérrez, *Fertile Matters,* 42.

29. E. Gutiérrez, *Fertile Matters,* 42, 123–25.

30. *Madrigal v. Quilligan* was one of Antonia Hernández's first cases out of UCLA Law School when she was employed by the Los Angeles Center for Law and Justice. Having grown up in Maravilla Public Housing after immigrating from Mexico at age seven, Hernández would go on to serve as president and general counsel of the Mexican American Legal Defense and Education Fund (MALDEF) from 1985 to 2004.

31. E. Gutiérrez, *Fertile Matters,* 44–45.

32. E. Gutiérrez, *Fertile Matters,* 49.

33. E. Gutiérrez, *Fertile Matters,* 50–51.

34. For a broader history of the founding and growth of the Comisión Femenil, see NietoGomez, "Francisca Flores."

35. Gloria Molina, testimony, February 14, 1977, at Los Angeles hearing, MALDEF Records, M673, Stanford University Archives, RG#5, Box 54, Folder 8: Sterilization, transcript, p. 132.

36. E. Gutiérrez, *Fertile Matters,* 94–108. In particular, see the role of Mrs. Consuelo Vasquez, US citizen, writing to Governor Jerry Brown about complications resulting from sterilization (96–97).

37. E. Gutiérrez, *Fertile Matters,* 97.

38. García, *Memories of Chicano History,* 288–93. Regarding the increase of home and workplace raids in the period, see Adam Goodman, *The Deportation Machine: America's Long History of Expelling Immigrants* (Princeton, NJ: Princeton University Press, 2020), 121–33.

39. García, *Memories of Chicano History,* 300–303; David G. Gutiérrez, *Walls and Mirrors: Mexican Americans, Mexican Immigrants, and the Politics of Ethnicity* (Berkeley: University of California Press, 1995), 188–89. Also see Jimmy Patino, *Raza Sí, Migra No: Chicano Movement Struggles For Immigrant Rights in San Diego* (Chapel Hill: University of North Carolina Press, 2017), 52.

40. See discussion in previous chapters of this book. For the most incisive history of this interaction, see Escobar, *Race, Police.*

41. Lieutenant Ronald D. Nelson, Commanding Officer, Community Relations, "Illegal Aliens: Composite Profile," report prepared at the direction of Chief E. M. Davis, Los Angeles Police Department, January 1975, Frank del Olmo Collection, Box 53, Folder 12, California State University at Northridge Archives.

42. Nelson, "Illegal Aliens," 22, 26.

43. Patino, *Raza Sí, Migra No,* 41–44.

44. García, *Memories of Chicano History,* 290–97.

45. D. Gutiérrez, *Walls and Mirrors,* 190–91.

46. D. Gutiérrez, *Walls and Mirrors,* 190–93; E. Chávez, *"Mi Raza Primero!,"* 104–6.

47. D. Gutiérrez, *Walls and Mirrors,* 192–99; García, *Memories of Chicano History,* 300–315; E. Chávez, *"Mi Raza Primero!,"* 106–16.

48. D. Gutiérrez, *Walls and Mirrors,* 200–202; García, *Memories of Chicano History,* 315–18.

49. Minian, *Undocumented Lives,* 183–207.

50. Minian, *Undocumented Lives,* 208–30; García, *Memories of Chicano History,* 318–20.

51. Gabriel Gutierrez, "The Founding of the Mothers of East Los Angeles" (unpublished paper, December 1989), Mothers of East LA Collection, Box 1, Folder 2, California State University, Northridge; MELA-SI Scholarship Fund—Tamale Drive, Mothers of East LA Collection, Box 1, Folder 4; Juana Gutierrez, interview by Mary Pardo, July 15, 1988, transcript, Mary Pardo Collection, Box 1, Folder 41, California State University, Northridge Archives, pp. 1–3; Mary S. Pardo, *Mexican American Women Activists: Identity and Resistance in Two Los Angeles Communities* (Philadelphia: Temple University Press, 1998), 110–11.

52. Molina, interview, p. 244.

53. Molina, interview, p. 412.

54. Louis Sahagun, "The Mothers of East L.A. Transform Themselves and Their Neighborhood," *Los Angeles Times,* August 13, 1989, 1, 6; Pardo, *Mexican American Women Activists,* 117.

55. Pardo, *Mexican American Women Activists,* 127–28.

56. Kamala Pratt, "Chicana Strategies for Success and Survival: Cultural Poetics of Environmental Justice from the Mothers of East Los Angeles," *Frontiers: A Journal of Women Studies* 18:2 (1997): 54.

57. Mary Pardo, the academic who integrated herself into MELA in the late 1980s and early 1990s, would regularly observe the involvement of Mexican women in the organization who she believed were undocumented residents. Yet when she asked the leadership about this, they typically shrugged off their differences with each other, stressing their collective commitment to the community. See J. Gutierrez, interview, pp. 5–6; Maria Roybal, interview by Mary Pardo, July 15, 1989, transcript, Mary Pardo Collection, Box 2, Folder 8, California State University, Northridge Archives, pp. 5–6; James Vigil Jr., interview by Mary Pardo, September 27, 1989, transcript, Mary Pardo Collection, Box 2, Folder 20, California State University, Northridge Archives, p. 3. See also G. Gutierrez, "Founding of the Mothers," 4.

58. Roybal, interview, pp. 1–2, 7.

59. Rosa Villaseñor, interview by Mary Pardo, March 7, 1990, transcript, Mary Pardo Collection, Box 2, Folder 21, California State University, Northridge Archives, pp. 1–4.

60. Michael Quinanilla, "The Earth Mother," *Los Angeles Times,* April 24, 1995, E1, E5.

61. Pardo, *Mexican American Women Activists,* 190.

62. Frank Villalobos, interview by Betsy Kalin for documentary film *East LA Interchange,* February 14, 2012, Los Angeles, transcript, p. 2.

63. Pardo, *Mexican American Women Activists,* 119–21.

64. Pardo, *Mexican American Women Activists,* 121.

65. Pardo, *Mexican American Women Activists,* 169–72; Scott Harris, "Community Crusaders: Three Groups Wage Hard-Nosed Struggle for Social Change," *Los Angeles Times,* November 29, 1987, Part II, 1.

66. Pardo, *Mexican American Women Activists,* 53–57.

67. Pardo, *Mexican American Women Activists,* 132–33.

68. Pardo, *Mexican American Women Activists,* 133–35.

69. Pardo, *Mexican American Women Activists,* 136–38.

70. See Edward Orozco Flores, *God's Gangs: Barrio Ministry, Masculinity, and Gang Recovery* (New York: New York University Press, 2014), 43–51.

71. Celeste Fremon, *G-Dog and the Homeboys: Father Greg Boyle and the Gangs of East Los Angeles,* updated and rev. ed. (Albuquerque: University of New Mexico Press, 2008), 24.

72. Gregory Boyle, *Tattoos on the Heart: The Power of Boundless Compassion* (New York: Free Press, 2010), 3; Fremon, *G-Dog,* 2–3.

73. Father Gregory Boyle, interview by Betsy Kalin for documentary film *East LA Interchange,* February 14, 2012, Los Angeles, transcript, p. 1.

74. Boyle, *Tattoos on the Heart,* 1–5.

75. Boyle, interview, p. 7.

76. Boyle, interview, p. 7.

77. James Diego Vigil, *The Projects: Gang and Non-Gang Families in East Los Angeles* (Austin: University of Texas Press, 2007), 24.

78. Freeman, *G-Dog,* 46.

79. Boyle, *Tattoos on the Heart,* 4.

80. Freeman, *G-Dog,* 46.

81. Freeman, *G-Dog,* 45–46; Boyle, *Tattoos on the Heart,* 2–5.

82. Boyle, *Tattoos on the Heart,* 71–75; Freeman, *G-Dog,* 46–49. See also Mario T. García, *Father Luis Olivares, a Biography: Faith Politics and the Origins of the Sanctuary Movement in Los Angeles* (Chapel Hill: University of North Carolina Press, 2018), 343–89, for a description of the expansion of the sanctuary movement protecting Central American refugees to all undocumented from Latin America.

83. Boyle, *Tattoos on the Heart,* 41–43.

84. Freeman, *G-Dog,* 47–49; E. Flores, *God's Gangs,* 52–55; Max Felker-Kantor, *Policing Los Angeles: Race, Resistance, and the Rise of the LAPD* (Chapel Hill: University of North Carolina Press, 2018), 208–11.

85. Father Gregory Boyle, "On The Streets: 'These Problems Aren't about Race; They're about Class,'" *Los Angeles Times,* May 13, 1992.

86. Boyle, interview, p. 3.

87. Freeman, *G-Dog,* 285–87.

88. Boyle, *Tattoos on the Heart,* 7–8.

89. See Daniel Martinez HoSang, *Racial Propositions: Ballot Initiatives and the Making of Postwar California* (Berkeley: University of California Press, 2010), on the racial implications of the state propositions; Lisa García Bedolla, *Fluid Borders:*

Latino Power, Identity, and Politics in Los Angeles (Berkeley: University of California Press, 2005), 94–95.

90. García Bedolla, *Fluid Borders,* 166.

91. Gloria Ohland, "Renaissance in the Barrio," *LA Weekly,* November 18, 2004.

92. Mary Anne Perez, "Pico-Aliso Residents Hopeful over Renovation Plans," *Los Angeles Times,* February 5, 1995; George Ramos, "Housing Project Overhaul Raises Eastside Hopes," *Los Angeles Times,* May 26, 1996.

93. Angie Chuang, "As Eastside Building Falls, So Do Tears," *Los Angeles Times,* January 17, 1997; "Demolition of Pico-Aliso Housing Project Begins," *Los Angeles Times,* August 8, 1997.

94. Ramos, "Housing Project Overhaul," A27.

95. Perez, "Pico-Aliso Residents Hopeful," 3.

96. Vigil, *Projects,* 94, 94–105.

97. Perez, "Pico-Aliso Residents Hopeful," 4.

98. Ramos, "Housing Project Overhaul," A27.

99. Chuang, "As Eastside Building Falls."

100. Ohland, "Renaissance in the Barrio," 4.

101. Hector Becerra, "Aliso Village Residents Divided over Demolition Plan," *Los Angeles Times,* August 7, 1998. See also Hector Becerra, "Building Confidence in a New Project," *Los Angeles Times,* August 23, 1998, B2–B3, and George Ramos, "A Work in Progress," *Los Angeles Times,* July 17, 1999, A12–A13.

102. On the continuation of gang violence in the neighborhood, see Anna Gorman, "Hope Is Reborn in Promise of Security," *Los Angeles Times,* April 12, 2004, B1, B9; and Hector Becerra, "Hope, Reality Collide on Eastside," *Los Angeles Times,* August 8, 2004, B1, B7.

103. Matea Gold, "Reviving Pride in the Projects," *Los Angeles Times,* September 20, 1999, A1, A16.

104. Ohland, "Renaissance in the Barrio," 11.

10. REMEMBERING BOYLE HEIGHTS

1. Jessica Garrison, "Candidate Portraits: A Second Chance," *Los Angeles Times,* February 8, 2005, A1; Robin Abcarian, "Spotlight on a Longtime Villaraigosa Supporter," *Los Angeles Times,* July 2, 2005, E1; and Tina Daunt, "Early Challenges, Different Paths, Same Goals," *Los Angeles Times,* May 8, 2005, A1.

2. Bauman, *Race and the War,* 140.

3. Daunt, "Early Challenges," A1.

4. Joseph Trevino and Caitlin Liu, "First Lady Visits Historic Synagogue, Movie House," *Los Angeles Times,* December 11, 1998, Metro, B1.

5. Lynn Doan, "Demolition of Cultural Icon Spurs Anger," *Los Angeles Times,* March 16, 2006, B2.

6. Scott Kurashige, "Transforming Los Angeles: Black and Japanese American Struggles for Racial Equality in the 20th Century" (PhD diss., University of California, Los Angeles, 2000), 471.

7. Scott Kurashige, "Transforming Los Angeles," 481–82.

8. For basic figures on the transformation of the Asian American population, see Roger Daniels, "United States Policy towards Asian Immigrants: Contemporary Developments in Historical Perspective," in *New American Destinies: A Reader in Contemporary Asian and Latino Immigration,* ed. Darrell Y. Hamamoto and Rodolfo D. Torres (New York: Routledge, 1997), 73–90; Lucie Cheng and Philip Q. Yang, "Asians: The 'Model Minority' Deconstructed," in *Ethnic Los Angeles,* ed. Roger Waldinger and Mehdi Bozorgmehr (New York: Russell Sage Foundation, 1996), 305–44; and James Allen and Eugene Turner, *Changing Faces, Changing Places: Mapping Southern California* (Northridge, CA: Center for Geographical Studies, Department of Geography, California State University, Northridge, 2002), 33–45.

9. Akemi Kikumura-Yano, Lane Ryo Hirabayashi, and James A. Hirabayashi, preface to *Common Ground: The Japanese American National Museum and the Culture of Collaboration* (Boulder: University Press of Colorado, 2004), viii. For a quite different perspective, see L. Kurashige, *Japanese American Celebration,* 209–12.

10. From *Boyle Heights: The Power of Place*, exhibition comment books, Japanese American National Museum, October 11, 2002, 9.

11. See, for example, James R. Curtis, "Barrio Space and Place in Southeast Los Angeles, California," in *Hispanic Spaces, Latino Places: Community and Cultural Diversity in Contemporary America,* ed. Daniel D. Arreola (Austin: University of Texas Press, 2004), 132–33.

12. Letters from Jerome B. Polloch and William Usher, Mailbox, *Newsletter of the Jewish Historical Society of Southern California,* Summer 1993/5753, 2.

13. Quote from "Progress at What Costs? Comunidades Unidas de Boyle Heights Developing Principles for Responsible Development," *LatinoLA*, June 16, 2006, www.latinola.com.

14. Alfredo Huante, "A Lighter Shade of Brown? Gentrification, *Gente*-fication, and Latina/o Urbanism in Los Angeles" (PhD diss., University of Southern California, 2018), 27–73.

15. Huante, "Lighter Shade of Brown," 40–46.

16. Huante, "Lighter Shade of Brown," 46–56.

17. See chapter 9 above for a fuller description of these efforts on a localized scale.

18. Michelle Keller, "Major Eastside Redevelopment Project Will Have to Wait Longer," *Los Angeles Times,* May 22, 2006, C1; Andy Fixmer, "Mixed-Use Project Is Planned for Sears' Boyle Heights Site," *Los Angeles Business Journal,* June 21, 2004; Marc Ballon, "Builder to Fashion a Lofty Downtown," *Jewish Journal of Greater Los Angeles,* December 20, 2002; Gloria Ohland, "Renaissance in the Barrio," *LA Weekly,* November 18, 2004.

19. Frank Villalobos, interview by Betsy Kalin for documentary film *East LA Interchange*, February 14, 2012, Los Angeles, transcript, p. 3.

20. Villalobos, interview, pp. 4–5.

21. Villalobos, interview, p. 5.

22. See John R. Chávez, *Eastside Landmark: A History of the East Los Angeles Community Union, 1968–1993* (Stanford, CA: Stanford University Press, 1998), and Bauman, *Race and the War*, 90–109, for a description of the first twenty-five years of this economic relationship.

23. USC Sol Price Center for Social Innovation, "Rising Rent Burden in Los Angeles," web content for *City Rising* broadcast series and multimedia project, KCET, October 29, 2017. October 29, 2017, www.kcet.org/shows/city-rising /rising-rent-burden-in-los-angeles.

24. Daniela Barranco, "Housing Squeeze in Boyle Heights Makes for Tough Choices," *Boyle Heights Beat,* July 23, 2017.

25. Malerie Wilkins, "Rent Control in Boyle Heights," *University Times* (California State University, Los Angeles), November 17, 2017, www.csulauniversity-times.com/11099/news/rent-control-in-boyle-heights/.

26. Alex Medina, "Historic Boyle Heights' 'Wyvernwood' Complex Facing New Threat from Developer," *Boyle Heights Beat,* August 9, 2018, https://boyle-heightsbeat.com/wyvernwood-developer-secures-155-million-loan/.

27. Carmen González, "Most Boyle Heights Development Out of Reach for Current Residents," *Boyle Heights Beat,* December 18, 2018, https://boyleheights-beat.com/most-boyle-heights-development-out-of-reach-for-current-residents/.

28. Wendy Cabrera, "Wyvernwood: Community within Community," in Roosevelt High School, *La Vida Diferente: Interviews, Biographies, Poems and Narratives; Celebrating Boyle Heights' Community Treasures, Written in the Spring of 2013 by Ms. Alva's and Mr. Lopez's Students at Roosevelt High School* (Los Angeles: 826LA, California Endowment, 2013), 37–38.

29. Lauren Walser, "The Fight to Save Wyvernwood, L.A.'s First Large-Scale Garden Apartment," article with video, National Trust for Historic Preservation website, December 9, 2015, https://savingplaces.org/stories/wyvernwood-las-first-large-scale-garden-apartment#.

30. See A. Medina, "Historic Boyle Heights' 'Wyvernwood'"

31. Mario Serrano, "A Store Van: A Fruity Blessing," in Roosevelt High School, *La Vida Diferente,* 128–29. Threats continued to be expressed as the developer secured a $155 million loan in late 2018 to refinance his plans to raze and rebuild. See A. Medina, "Historic Boyle Heights' 'Wyvernwood'."

32. See Kurland and Lamadrid, *Hotel Mariachi,* for a fuller history of this corner and mariachi culture in Los Angeles.

33. Elijah Chiland, "Boyle Heights Mariachis Agree to 14 Percent Rent Hike but Win New Leases Ending Months-Long Strike," *Curbed Los Angeles,* February 16, 2018, https://la.curbed.com/2018/2/16/17018298/boyle-heights-mariachi-gentrification-rent-strike.

34. Ruben Vives, "As Rents Soar in L.A., Even Boyle Heights Mariachis Sing the Blues," *Los Angeles Times,* September 9, 2017.

35. Vives, "As Rents Soar"; Chiland, "Boyle Heights Mariachis"; Rob Kuznia, "Los Angeles Tenants Increasingly Engaging in Rent Strikes amid Housing Crisis," *Washington Post,* June 2, 2018.

36. Chiland, "Boyle Heights Mariachis"; Kuznia, "Los Angeles Tenants."

37. Gilbert Estrada, "The Historical Roots of Gentrification in Boyle Heights," web content for *City Rising* broadcast series and multimedia project, KCET, September 13, 2017, www.kcet.org/shows/city-rising/the-historical-roots-of-gentrification-in-boyle-heights/.

38. One report indicated that rents in the Arts District rose 140 percent between 2000 and 2014. See Andrew Romano and Garance Franke-Ruta, "A New Generation of Anti-gentrification Radicals Are on the March in Los Angeles—and around the Country," *Huffington Post* (originally published on *Yahoo News*), March 5, 2018, 16, www.huffpost.com/entry/a-new-generation-of-anti-gentrification-radicals-are-on-the-march-in-los-angeles-and-around-the-country_n_5a9d6c45e4b0479c0255adec.

39. Carribean Fragoza, "Art and Complicity: How the Fight against Gentrification in Boyle Heights Questions the Role of Artists," web content for *Artbound* series, KCET, July 20, 2016, www.kcet.org/shows/artbound/boyle-heights-gentrification-art-galleries-pssst/.

40. Fragoza, "Art and Complicity."

41. Fragoza, "Art and Complicity"; G. Estrada, "Historical Roots"; Brittany Mejia, "Boyle Heights Vandalism Seen as Possible Hate Crimes," *Los Angeles Times,* November 4, 2016, B1, B5; Saul Soto, "Defend Boyle Heights Sparks Controversy with Anti-gentrification Push," *Boyle Heights Beat,* July 17, 2017.

42. G. Estrada, "Historical Roots," 11; Carolina A. Miranda, "The Art Gallery Exodus from Boyle Heights and Why More Anti-gentrification Battles Loom on the Horizon," *Los Angeles Times,* August 8. 2018.

43. Miranda, "Art Gallery Exodus"; Abe Ahn, "More Galleries Are Leaving the Contested Los Angeles Neighborhood of Boyle Heights," *Hyperallergic,* May 4, 2018.

44. G. Estrada, "Historical Roots"; Soto, "Defend Boyle Heights"; Ruben Vives, "Vandal Targets Coffee Shop at Center of Anti-gentrification Protests in Boyle Heights," *Los Angeles Times,* July 19, 2017; Steve Lopez, "Protesting a Coffee House over Gentrification Fears Is Silly—and Misses the Point of L.A.," *Los Angeles Times,* July 22, 2017; Diana Kruzman, "Weird Wave Coffee Reports Ninth Vandalism," *Boyle Heights Beat,* February 15, 2019.

45. Alex Medina, "The Cream Shop's $20 'Dos Spark Gentrifier Label," *Boyle Heights Beat,* July 18, 2017.

46. Jennifer Medina, "Los Angeles Neighborhood Tries to Change, but Avoid the Pitfalls," *New York Times,* August 17, 2013.

47. Sarah Soutoul, "From Gentrification to *Gentefication;* The Change of a Neighborhood by Latinos" (capstone project for USC Annenberg Media,

Annenberg School for Communication and Journalism, 2019), https://ascjcapstone.com/terms/spring-2019/soutoul/.

48. J. Medina, "Los Angeles Neighborhood." See also Emma G. Gallegos, "*NY Times* Explores the 'Gentefication' of Boyle Heights by 'Chipsters,'" *LAist,* August 19, 2013.

49. J. Medina, "Los Angeles Neighborhood"; Natalie Delgadillo, "Defining 'Gentefication' in Latino Neighborhoods," *CityLab,* August 15, 2016; Karen Cruz-Orduna, "From Gentrification to Gente-fication: Boyle Heights Residents Reclaim Their Neighborhood," *Latino Reporter: The 2018 NAHJ Student Project,* July 19, 2018.

50. Julia Herbst, "Guillermo Uribe on the "Gentefication" of East L.A.," *Los Angeles Magazine,* September 9, 2014. Though Uribe coined the term in 2007, it did not gain widespread popularity until the *New York Times* used it in an article in 2013. See J. Medina, "Los Angeles Neighborhood."

51. Delgadillo, "Defining 'Gentefication.'"

52. J. Medina, "Los Angeles Neighborhood."

53. Alex Medina, "In One LA Neighborhood, A Fight over Homegrown Gentrification," *Boyle Heights Beat,* January 24, 2018.

54. *Vida,* created by Tanya Saracho (United States: Big Beach/Chingona Productions, Network: Starz, 2018–present), dramatic television series.

55. *Gentefied,* created by Marvin Lemus and Linda Yvette Chávez (United States: MACRO/Sector 7/Anchor Baby/Take Fountain Productions, Network: Netflix, 2020-present), comedy-drama television series.

56. Ubaldo Escalante, "There Goes the Barrio: Measuring *Gentefication* in Boyle Heights, Los Angeles" (Master's thesis, Columbia University, 2017), 30.

57. Escalante, "There Goes the Barrio," 26–27.

58. Escalante, "There Goes the Barrio," 28–29.

59. Escalante, "There Goes the Barrio," 45.

60. J. Medina, "Los Angeles Neighborhood."

61. See Escalante, "There Goes the Barrio," 49, for this possibility.

62. See the ELACC-produced People's Plan for Boyle Heights (El Plan del Pueblo), English Version, May 18, 2015, https://issuu.com/eastlacommunitycorporation/docs/plandelpueblo_english_digitalversio. See also Alison Salazar, "When Affordable Housing Gentrifies," *LA Progressive,* April 29, 2018, and Gregory Cornfield, "Affordable Housing Developer's New Mixed-Complex Adds to Growing List in Boyle Heights," *Real Deal,* April 19, 2019.

63. Noemi Pedraza, "Los Angeles City Council Agrees to Legalize Street Vending," *Boyle Heights Beat,* November 28, 2018.

BIBLIOGRAPHY

PRIMARY SOURCES

Manuscript Collections

Ann Arbor, Michigan. University of Michigan Library, Special Collections
Labadie Collection

East Los Angeles, California. Los Angeles County Library, East Los Angeles Branch
Roybal Newspaper Scrapbook (RNS)

Fullerton, California. California State University, Fullerton
Oral History Program

Los Angeles, California. Boyle Heights Historical Society
California State University at Los Angeles, University Archives
Boyle Heights Archive
Japanese American National Museum, Archives
Boyle Heights: The Power of Place Exhibition Comment Books
Molly Wilson Murphy Papers
Re-examining Boyle Heights Project
Jewish Federation of Los Angeles
Jewish Community Centers, Los Angeles, Collection
Los Angeles City Archives
Sal Castro Foundation
Walkouts Archives
Southern California Library for Social Studies and Research
Civil Rights Congress (CRC) Collection

Los Angeles Committee for the Protection of the Foreign Born (LACPFB) Collection
    Mark Keats Photographic Collection
University of California, Los Angeles (UCLA), Special Collections
    Edward Roybal Collection
    George C. Clements Papers
    Sleepy Lagoon Defense Committee Papers
University of Southern California, Special Collections
    Works Progress Administration (WPA) Card Collection

Mexico City, DF, Mexico. Secretariat of Foreign Relations, Archives
    Los Angeles, California Consulate Papers

Northridge, California. California State University at Northridge, Urban Archives Center, University Library
    Frank del Olmo Collection
    Mary Pardo Collection
    Mothers of East L.A. Collection
    United Way of Los Angeles Collection

San Marino, California. Huntington Library
    John Anson Ford Papers

Stanford, California. Stanford University, Special Collections
    Harry Gamboa Papers
    Fred Ross Collection
    Mexican American Legal Defense and Education Fund Records, 1967–1983

Washington, D.C. National Archives
    Home Owners Loan Corporation City Survey Files
    Records of the War Relocation Authority
    US Census Manuscript Schedules, 1930

Newspapers, Magazines, and Online Journals

Angelus News
B'nai B'rith Messenger
Boyle Heights Beat
California Eagle
CityLab
Common Ground

Curbed Los Angeles
The Eastsider
Eastside Sun
Fortnight
The Forward
Frontier: The Voice of the New West
Huffington Post
Hyperallergic
Jewish Journal of Greater Los Angeles
LAist
LA Progressive
L.A. Taco
LatinoLA
Latino Reporter
LA Weekly
Los Angeles Business Journal
Los Angeles Daily News
Los Angeles Examiner
Los Angeles Magazine
Los Angeles Times
New York Times
Pacific Citizen
The Real Deal
The Reporter
Tablet Magazine
University Times (California State University, Los Angeles)
Urbanize Los Angeles
Vice
Washington Post

Oral Histories and Firsthand Accounts

Aragon, Ray. Life history interview by Joanne Koenig Reyes for Re-examining Boyle Heights Project, August 12, 2000, Los Angeles. Transcript, Japanese American National Museum, Los Angeles.

Boletin, Kate, and Paul Zolnekoff. Life history interview by Wendy Elliott for Re-examining Boyle Heights Project, August 15, 2000, Los Angeles. Transcript, Japanese American National Museum, Los Angeles.

Boyle, Gregory. *Barking to the Choir: The Power of Radical Kinship.* New York: Simon and Schuster, 2017.

Boyle, Father Gregory. Interview by Betsy Kalin for her *East LA Interchange* documentary film, February 14, 2012, Los Angeles. Transcript.

Boyle, Gregory. *Tattoos on the Heart: The Power of Boundless Compassion.* New York: Free Press, 2010.

Brandt, Ruth Toshiko Matsuo. Life history interview by Sojin Kim and Raul Vasquez for Re-examining Boyle Heights Project, August 17, 2001, Los Angeles. Transcript, Japanese American National Museum, Los Angeles.

Castañeda de Valenciana, Emilia. Interview by Christine Valenciana on February 24 and March 9, 1972. Transcript, O.H. 700, Mexican American History Collection, Center for Oral and Public History, California State University at Fullerton.

Castro, Vickie. Interview by George Sánchez and María José Plascencia, November 24, 2014, East Los Angeles. Transcript.

Chernin, Kim. *In My Mother's House: A Daughter's Story.* New Haven, CT: Ticknor and Fields, 1983.

Coutin, Florence Zimmerman. Interview by Sarah Gelb Felman for "The Other Los Angeles" Project, History 101.6, University of California, Los Angeles (UCLA), February 14, 1990.

Crisostomo, Paula. Interview by George J. Sánchez and María José Plascencia, July 31, 2014, Los Angeles. Transcript.

Duran, Richard, and Barbara Duran. Interview by Stephanie Duran for "The Other Los Angeles" Project, History 101.6, University of California, Los Angeles (UCLA), February 18, 1990, Chino Hills, CA.

Eisenberg, Hershey. Life history interview by Darcie Iki and Sojin Kim for Re-examining Boyle Heights Project, December 18, 2000, Los Angeles. Transcript, Japanese American National Museum, Los Angeles.

Fiering, Ida B. Interview by Leslye Sneider for "The Other Los Angeles" Project, History 101.6, University of California, Los Angeles (UCLA), February 23, 1990.

Ford, John Anson. Interview by Christine Valenciana, September 4, 1971. Transcript, O.H. 759, Mexican American History Collection, Center for Oral and Public History, California State University at Fullerton.

Frumkin, Leo. Life history interview by Ken Burt and Sojin Kim for Re-examining Boyle Heights Project, December 19, 2001, Tarzana, CA. Transcript, Japanese American National Museum, Los Angeles.

Gabaldon, Guy. Life history interview by Darcie Iki, Sojin Kim, and Dean Hayasaka for Re-examining Boyle Heights Project, February 13, 2001, Los Angeles. Transcript, Japanese American National Museum, Los Angeles.

Gutiérrez, Juana. Interview by Mary Pardo, July 15, 1988. Transcript, Mary Pardo Collection, Box 1, Folder 41, University Library, Urban Archives Center, California State University, Northridge.

Hilborn, Walter. *Reflections on Legal Practice and Jewish Community Leadership: New York and Los Angeles, 1907–1973.* Los Angeles: University of California, Berkeley, Regional Oral History Office, 1974.

Hoffman, Abraham. "My Boyle Heights Childhood, Los Angeles, 1940–50s." *Western States Jewish History* 35:1 (Fall 2002): 81.

Ito, Toshiko. Life history interview by Darcie Iki for Re-examining Boyle Heights Project, April 2, 2001, Los Angeles. Transcript, Japanese American National Museum, Los Angeles.

Johnson, Albert, II. Life history interview by Paul Spitzzeri and Sojin Kim for Re-examining Boyle Heights Project, July 3, 2002, Los Angeles. Transcript, Japanese American National Museum, Los Angeles.

Kawahara, Daniel. Life history interview by Sojin Kim and Darcie Iki for Re-examining Boyle Heights Project, December 18, 2000, Los Angeles. Transcript, Japanese American National Museum, Los Angeles.

Kitayama, Joey Ryoyei. Interview by Glen Ikuo Kitayama for "The Other Los Angeles" Project, History 101.6, University of California, Los Angeles (UCLA), February 24, 1990.

Kunitsugu, Katsumi. Interview by Teresa Kay Williams for "The Other Los Angeles" Project, History 101.6, University of California, Los Angeles (UCLA), February 8, 1990.

Maddow, Freda. Life history interview by Paul Spitzzeri for Re-examining Boyle Heights Project, July 27, 2000, Los Angeles. Transcript, Japanese American National Museum, Los Angeles.

Martinez, Pete. Interview by Laura Olague for "The Other Los Angeles" Project, History 101.6, University of California, Los Angeles (UCLA), February 22, 1990, Los Angeles.

Mendoza Schechter, Hope. "Activist in the Labor Movement, the Democratic Party and the Mexican-American Community: Oral History Transcript." Interview by Malca Chall, 1977–78. Transcript, BANC MSS 81/73, Regional Oral History Office, Bancroft Library, University of California, Berkeley.

Molina, Gloria. Oral History Interview by Carlos Vasquez for the California State Archives' State Government Oral History Program, 1990. Transcript.

Murphy, Mollie, Mary Nishi, and Sandie Okada. Life history interview by Sojin Kim and Darcie Iki for Re-examining Boyle Heights Project, January 18, 2001, Los Angeles. Transcript, Japanese American National Museum, Los Angeles.

Nakanishi, Don. Interview by Natasha Miller for "The Other Los Angeles" Project, History 101.6, University of California, Los Angeles (UCLA), February 26, 1990, Los Angeles.

Newmark, Harris. *Sixty Years in Southern California, 1853–1913.* Edited by Maurice H. and Marco R. Newmark. 1916. Reprint, Los Angeles: Zeitlin and Ver Brugge, 1970.

Pesotta, Rose. *Bread upon the Waters.* New York: Dodd, Mead, 1945.

Phillips, William. Interview by Tamara Zwick for "The Other Los Angeles" Project, History 101.6, University of California, Los Angeles (UCLA), February 22, 1990.

Ramirez, Eddie. Life history interview by Raul Vasquez and Sojin Kim for Re-examining Boyle Heights Project, January 11, 2002, Los Angeles. Transcript, Japanese American National Museum, Los Angeles.

Rodriguez, Robert. Interview by Raul Gomez for "The Other Los Angeles" Project, History 101.6, University of California, Los Angeles (UCLA), March 1, 1990.

Roosevelt High School. *La Vida Diferente: Interviews, Biographies, Poems and Narratives; Celebrating Boyle Heights' Community Treasures, Written in the Spring of
2013 by Ms. Alva's and Mr. Lopez's Students at Roosevelt High School.* Los Angeles:
826LA, California Endowment, 2013.

Roybal, Maria. Interview by Mary Pardo, July 15, 1989. Transcript, Mary Pardo Collection, Box 2, Folder 8, University Library, Urban Archives Center, California
State University, Northridge.

Sanchez, Luis. Life history interview by Sojin Kim, Ruben Guevara, and Ann
Kaneko for Re-examining Boyle Heights Project, July 21, 2002, Los Angeles.
Transcript, Japanese American National Museum, Los Angeles.

Satow, Fumiko (Nishihara). Life history interview by Sojin Kim for Re-examining
Boyle Heights Project, October 23, 2000, Los Angeles. Transcript, Japanese
American National Museum, Los Angeles.

Shimo, Cedrick. Life history interview by Sojin Kim and Erick Molinar for Re-
examining Boyle Heights Project, March 19, 2001, Los Angeles. Transcript, Japanese American National Museum, Los Angeles.

Shimo, Cedrick, and Saul Ness. Tour and sit-down interview by Betsy Kalin for *East
LA Interchange* documentary film, June 18, 2008, Los Angeles. Transcript.

Shyer, Janice. Life history interview by Dan Gebler for Re-examining Boyle Heights
Project, October 2000, Los Angeles. Transcript, Japanese American National
Museum, Los Angeles.

Stein, Claire (Orlosoroff). Life history interview by Dan Gebler for Re-examining
Boyle Heights Project, November 11, 2000, Laguna Niguel, CA. Transcript, Japanese American National Museum, Los Angeles.

Tolmasov, James. Life history interview by Sojin Kim for Re-examining Boyle
Heights Project, April 17, 2001, Los Angeles. Transcript, Japanese American
National Museum, Los Angeles.

Tomer, Dorothy. Interview by Stephanie Maya for "The Other Los Angeles" Project,
History 101.6, University of California, Los Angeles (UCLA), February 19, 1990,
Montebello, CA.

Vigil, James, Jr. Interview by Mary Pardo, September 27, 1989. Transcript, Mary
Pardo Collection, Box 2, Folder 20, University Library, Urban Archives Center,
California State University, Northridge.

Villalobos, Frank. Interview by Betsy Kalin for documentary film *East LA Interchange*, February 14, 2012, Los Angeles. Transcript.

Villaseñor, Rosa. Interview by Mary Pardo, March 7, 1990. Transcript, Mary Pardo
Collection, Box 2, Folder 21, University Library, Urban Archives Center, California State University, Northridge.

Weber, Bud. Life history interview by Jim Gatewood for Re-examining Boyle
Heights Project, July 21, 2000, Los Angeles. Transcript, Japanese American
National Museum, Los Angeles.

Wilson, Atoy, Jr. Life history interview by Paul Spitzerri and Lisa Itagaki for Re-
examining Boyle Heights Project, January 25, 2001, Los Angeles. Transcript,
Japanese American National Museum, Los Angeles.

Government Documents and Reports

Branfman, Judy. "Boyle Heights: A Jewish History." In *Cultural Needs Assessment: Metro Red Line East Side Extension*. Los Angeles County Metropolitan Transportation Authority, February 1995.

City of Los Angeles, Department of City Planning. "Boyle Heights Community Background: Summary." January 1974.

City of Los Angeles, Department of City Planning. "Boyle Heights Community Plan." 1979.

City of Los Angeles, Department of City Planning. "Recommendation Report. Application by the Boyle Heights Historical Society to Designate the Boyle Hotel-Cummings Block as a Historic Cultural Monument in Los Angeles." September 21, 2007. https://clkrep.lacity.org/onlinedocs/2007/07-3028_rpt_chc_9-21-07.pdf

City of Los Angeles, Department of City Planning. "Recommendation Report: Application by the Boyle Heights Historical Society to Designate the Gless Farmhouse as a Historic Cultural Landmark in Los Angeles." 2010. https://planning.lacity.org/StaffRpt/CHC/1-21-10/CHC-2010-71.pdf.

Gómez-Quiñones, Juan. "An East Side Profile in Historical Sequence." In *Cultural Needs Assessment: Metro East Side Extension*. Los Angeles County Metropolitan Transportation Authority, February 1995.

Lieutenant Ronald D. Nelson, Commanding Officer, Community Relations. "Illegal Aliens: Composite Profile." Report prepared at the direction of Chief E. M. Davis, Los Angeles Police Department, January 1975.

Los Angeles City Directories, 1931, 1932, 1933.5US Army, Western Defense Command and Fourth Army. *Final Report—Japanese Evacuation from the West Coast*. Washington, DC, 1943.

US Census. Manuscript Schedules for Los Angeles, Boyle Heights, 1930.

US Commission on Civil Rights. *Hearings before the United States Commission on Civil Rights, 1960, Los Angeles, California*. Washington, DC: Government Printing Office, 1960.

US Commission on Wartime Relocation and Internment of Civilians. *Personal Justice Denied*. Washington, DC: Civil Liberties Public Education Fund; Seattle: University of Washington Press, 1997.

Works Projects Administration. *Los Angeles: A Guide to the City and Its Environs*. Compiled by Workers of the Writers' Program of the Work Projects Administration (WPA) in Southern California. American Guide Series. New York: Hastings House, 1941.

Film and Multimedia Sources

Boyle, Andrew A. "The Battle of Coleto and the Goliad Massacre: From the Republic Pension Application of Andrew A. Boyle." n.d. In *The Goliad Massacre*, online exhibit, Texas State Library and Archives Commission. Accessed June 7, 2017. www.tsl.texas.gov/treasures/republic/goliad/boyles.html.

"Boyle Heights: Power of Place." Website at the Japanese American National Museum, Los Angeles. Accessed July 15, 2019. www.janm.org/exhibits/bh /exhibition/exhibition.htm.

Chicano! History of the Mexican American Civil Rights Movement: Part 3—Taking Back the Schools. Produced by Susan Racho. United States: NLCC Educational Media, 1996. VHS Video documentary.

East LA Interchange. Directed by Betsy Kalin. United States: Bluewater Media Productions, 2015. DVD documentary film.

Estrada, Gilbert. "The Historical Roots of Gentrification in Boyle Heights." Web content for *City Rising* broadcast series and multimedia project. KCET, September13,2017.www.kcet.org/shows/city-rising/the-historical-roots-of-gentrification-in-boyle-heights/.

Fragoza, Carribean. "Art and Complicity: How the Fight against Gentrification in Boyle Heights Questions the Role of Artists." KCET, July 20, 2016. www.kcet .org/shows/artbound/boyle-heights-gentrification-art-galleries-pssst/.

Gentefied. Created by Marvin Lemus and Linda Yvette Chávez. United States: MACRO/Sector 7/Anchor Baby/Take Fountain Productions, Network: Netflix, 2020–present. Comedy-drama television series.

Hell to Eternity. Directed by Phil Karlson. United States: Allied Artists, 1960. Motion picture film.

Jewish Life in the American West: Generation to Generation. Exhibition, Autry Museum of Western Heritage, Los Angeles. 2002–3.

Los Angeles Education Partnership. "Our Place Called Home: A History of Boyle Heights." n.d. Accessed June 7, 2017. http://laep.org/access/change/histbh/ index.html.

Masters, Nathan. "A Brief History of Bridges in Los Angeles County." Web content for *Lost L.A.* series, by "L.A. as Subject" research alliance. KCET, July 18, 2012. www.kcet.org/shows/lost-la/a-brief-history-of-bridges-in-los-angeles-county.

Meet Me at Brooklyn and Soto. Directed by Ellie Kahn. United States: Jewish Historical Society of Southern California; Huell Howser Productions, 1996. VHS documentary film.

No Más Bebés. Directed by Renee Tajima-Pena. United States: Moon Canyon Films, 2015. DVD documentary film.

The People's Plan for Boyle Heights (El Plan del Pueblo). English Version. May 18, 2015. East LA Community Corporation. https://issuu.com/eastlacommunitycorporation/docs/plandelpueblo_english_digitalversio.

Spitzzeri, Paul R. "Historic Photos of Boyle Heights: The Cummings Block, circa 1889." *Boyle Heights History Blog*, September 17, 2014. http://boyleheightshistoryblog.blogspot.com/2014/09/historic-photos-of-boyle-heights.html.

USC Sol Price Center for Social Innovation. "Rising Rent Burden in Los Angeles." Web content for *City Rising* broadcast series and multimedia project. KCET, October 29, 2017. www.kcet.org/shows/city-rising/rising-rent-burden-in-los-angeles.

Vida. Created by Tanya Saracho. United States: Big Beach/Chingona Productions, Network: Starz, 2018–present. Dramatic television series.

Walser, Lauren. "The Fight to Save Wyvernwood, L.A.'s First Large-Scale Garden Apartment." Article with video. National Trust for Historic Preservation website, December 9, 2015. https://savingplaces.org/stories/wyvernwood-las-first-large-scale-garden-apartment#. XzG3Ey2ZMlU.

SECONDARY SOURCES

Acuña, Rodolfo F. *A Community under Siege: A Chronicle of Chicanos East of the Los Angeles River, 1945–1975.* Monograph No. 11. Los Angeles: Chicano Studies Research Center Publications, University of California Los Angeles, 1984.

Acuña, Rodolfo F. *Occupied America: A History of Chicanos.* 3rd ed. New York: Harper and Row, 1988.

Alanis Enciso, Fernando Saul. *They Should Stay There: The Story of Mexican Migration and Repatriation during the Great Depression.* Translated by Russ Davidson. Chapel Hill: University of North Carolina Press, 2017. Originally published in Spanish as *Que se queden allá: El gobierno de México y la repatriación de mexicanos en Estados Unidos (1934–1940)* (Tijuana: El Colegio de la Frontera Norte, 2007).

Allen, James P., and Eugene Turner. *Changing Faces, Changing Places: Mapping Southern California.* Northridge, CA: Center for Geographical Studies, Department of Geography, California State University, Northridge, 2002.

Almaguer, Tomas. *Racial Fault Lines: The Historical Origins of White Supremacy in California.* Berkeley: University of California Press, 2009.

Alvarez, Luis. "Eastside Imaginaries: Toward a Relational and Transnational Chicana/o Cultural History." In *A Promising Problem: The New Chicana/o History,* edited by Carlos Kevin Blanton, chap. 7. Austin: University of Texas Press, 2016.

Alvarez, Luis. *The Power of the Zoot: Youth Culture and Resistance during World War II.* Berkeley: University of California Press, 2008.

Ancheta, Angelo N. *Race, Rights, and the Asian American Experience.* New Brunswick, NJ: Rutgers University Press, 1998.

Arredondo, Gabriela F. *Mexican Chicago: Race, Identity, and Nation, 1916–39.* Urbana: University of Illinois Press, 2008.

Avila, Eric. *Popular Culture in the Age of White Flight: Fear and Fantasy in Suburban Los Angeles.* Berkeley: University of California Press, 2004.

Ayon, David R., and George L. Pla. *Power Shift: How Latinos in California Transformed Politics in America.* Berkeley: Berkeley Public Policy Press, Institute of Governmental Studies, University of California, Berkeley, 2018.

Azuma, Eiichiro. *Between Two Empires: Race, History, and Transnationalism in Japanese America.* New York: Oxford University Press, 2005.

Balderrama, Francisco E. *In Defense of La Raza: The Los Angeles Mexican Consulate and the Mexican Community, 1929–1936.* Tucson: University of Arizona Press, 1982.

Balderrama, Francisco E., and Raymond Rodríguez. *Decade of Betrayal: Mexican Repatriation in the 1930s.* Rev. ed. Albuquerque: University of New Mexico Press, 2006.

Barrett, Edward L., Jr. *The Tenney Committee: Legislative Investigation of Subversive Activities in California.* Ithaca, NY: Cornell University Press, 1951.

Barrett, James R., and David Roediger. "Inbetween Peoples: Race, Nationality, and the 'New Immigrant' Working Class." *Journal of American Ethnic History* 16:3 (Spring 1997): 3–45.

Barrows, H. D. "Don Antonio Maria Lugo: A Picturesque Character of California." *Annual Publication of the Historical Society of Southern California* 3:4 (1896): 28–78.

Bauman, Robert. *Race and the War on Poverty: From Watts to East L.A.* Norman: University of Oklahoma Press, 2008.

Bencivenni, Marcella. *Italian Immigrant Radical Culture: The Idealism of the Sovversivi in the United States, 1890–1940.* New York: New York University Press, 2011.

Bernstein, Shana. *Bridges of Reform: Interracial Civil Rights Activism in Twentieth-Century Los Angeles.* New York: Oxford University Press, 2011.

Bernstein, Shana. "From Civic Defense to Civil Rights: The Growth of Jewish American Interracial Civil Rights Activism in Los Angeles." In *A Cultural History of Jews in California: The Jewish Role in American Life, An Annual Review,* vol. 7, edited by Bruce Zuckerman, William Deverell, and Lisa Ansell, 55–80. West Lafayette, IN: Purdue University Press for the University of Southern California, Casden Institute for the Study of the Jewish Role in American Life, 2009.

Berumen, Frank Javier García. *Edward R. Roybal: The Mexican American Struggle for Political Empowerment.* Los Angeles: Bilingual Educational Services, 2015.

Biskar, Herbert Morris. "A History of the Jewish Centers Association of Los Angeles with Special Reference to Jewish Identity." PhD diss., University of Southern California, 1972.

Blackford, Mansel G. *The Lost Dream: Businessmen and City Planning on the Pacific Coast, 1890–1920.* Columbus: Ohio State University Press, 1993.

Blackwell, Maylei. *!Chicana Power! Contested Histories of Feminism in the Chicano Movement.* Austin: University of Texas Press, 2011.

Bond, J. Max. "The Negro in Los Angeles." PhD diss., University of Southern California, 1936.

Bonilla-Silva, Eduardo. *Racism without Racists: Color-Blind Racism and the Persistence of Racial Inequality in the United States.* Lanham, MD: Rowman and Littlefield, 2003.

Bowman, Lynn. *Los Angeles: Epic of a City.* Berkeley: Howell-North Books, 1974.

Brilliant, Mark. *The Color of America Has Changed: How Racial Diversity Shaped Civil Rights Reform in California, 1941–1978.* New York: Oxford University Press, 2010.

Briones, Matthew M. *Jim and Jap Crow: A Cultural History of 1940s Interracial America.* Princeton, NJ: Princeton University Press, 2012.

Brodkin, Karen. *How Jews Became White Folks and What That Says about Race in America.* New Brunswick, NJ: Rutgers University Press, 1998.

Brodkin, Karen. *Power Politics: Environmental Activism in South Los Angeles.* New Brunswick, NJ: Rutgers University Press, 2009.

Buff, Rachel Ida. *Against the Deportation Terror: Organizing for Immigrant Rights in the Twentieth Century.* Philadelphia: Temple University Press, 2018.

Buhle, Paul. *Marxism in the United States: A History of the American Left.* 3rd ed. London: Verso, 2013.

Burt, Kenneth C. "The Power of a Mobilized Citizenry and Coalition Politics: The 1949 Election of Edward R. Roybal to the Los Angeles City Council." *Southern California Quarterly* 85:4 (Winter 2003): 413–38.

Burt, Kenneth C. *The Search for a Civic Voice: California Latino Politics.* Claremont, CA: Regina Books, 2007.

Camarillo, Albert M. *Chicanos in a Changing Society: From Mexican Pueblos to American Barrios in Santa Barbara and Southern California, 1848 to 1930.* Cambridge, MA: Harvard University Press, 1979.

Camarillo, Albert M. "Navigating Segregated Life in America's Racial Borderhoods, 1910s–1950s." *Journal of American History* 100:3 (December 2013): 645–62.

Carpio, Genevieve. *Collisions at the Crossroads: How Place and Mobility Make Race.* Berkeley: University of California Press, 2019.

Chávez, Ernesto. *"Mi Raza Primero!": Nationalism, Identity, and Insurgency in the Chicano Movement in Los Angeles, 1966–1978.* Berkeley: University of California Press, 2002.

Chávez, John R. *Eastside Landmark: A History of the East Los Angeles Community Union, 1968–1993.* Stanford, CA: Stanford University Press, 1998.

Chávez-García, Miroslava. *Negotiating Conquest: Gender and Power in California, 1770s–1880s.* Tucson: University of Arizona Press, 2004.

Cheng, Lucie, and Philip Q. Yang. "Asians: The 'Model Minority' Deconstructed." In *Ethnic Los Angeles,* edited by Roger Waldinger and Mehdi Bozorgmehr, 305–44. New York: Russell Sage Foundation, 1996.

Cinel, Dino. *From Italy to San Francisco: The Immigrant Experience.* Stanford, CA: Stanford University Press, 1982.

Cleland, Robert Glass, and Frank B. Putnam. *Isaias W. Hellman and the Farmers and Merchants Bank.* San Marino, CA: Huntington Library, 1965.

Cohen, Deborah. *Braceros: Migrant Citizens and Transnational Subjects in the Postwar United States and Mexico.* Chapel Hill: University of North Carolina Press, 2011.

Cohen, Lizabeth. *Making a New Deal: Industrial Workers in Chicago, 1919–1939.* Cambridge: Cambridge University Press, 1990.

Cosgrove, Stuart. "The Zoot-Suit and Style Warfare." *History Workshop,* no. 18 (Autumn 1984): 77–91.

Cuff, Dana. *The Provisional City: Los Angeles Stories of Architecture and Urbanism.* Cambridge, MA: MIT Press, 2000.

Curtis, James R. "Barrio Space and Place in Southeast Los Angeles, California." In *Hispanic Spaces, Latino Places: Community and Cultural Diversity in Contemporary America,* edited by Daniel D. Arreola, 125–42. Austin: University of Texas Press, 2004.

Daniels, Roger. *The Politics of Prejudice: The Anti-Japanese Movement in California and the Struggle for Japanese Exclusion*. 1973. Reprint, Berkeley: University of California Press, 1999.

Daniels, Roger. "United States Policy towards Asian Immigrants: Contemporary Developments in Historical Perspective." In *New American Destinies: A Reader in Contemporary Asian and Latino Immigration*, edited by Darrell Y. Hamamoto and Rodolfo D. Torres, 73–90. New York: Routledge, 1997.

de Certeau, Michel. *The Practice of Everyday Life*. 3rd ed. Translated by Steven Rendall. 1984. Reprint, Berkeley: University of California Press, 2011.

Delgado Bernal, Dolores. "Chicana School Resistance and Grassroots Leadership: Providing an Alternative History of the 1968 East Los Angeles Blowouts." PhD diss., University of California, Los Angeles, 1997.

Denning, Michael. *The Cultural Front: The Laboring of American Culture in the Twentieth Century*. London: Verso, 1996.

Deverell, William. *Whitewashed Adobe: The Rise of Los Angeles and the Remaking of Its Mexican Past*. Berkeley: University of California Press, 2004.

Dower, John. *War without Mercy: Race and Power in the Pacific War*. New York: Pantheon Books, 1986.

Duneier, Mitchell. *Ghetto: The Invention of a Place, The History of an Idea*. New York: Farrar, Straus and Giroux, 2016.

Elliott-Scheinberg, Wendy. "Boyle Heights: Jewish Ambiance in a Multicultural Neighborhood." PhD diss., Claremont Graduate University, 2001.

Escalante, Ubaldo. "There Goes the Barrio: Measuring *Gentefication* in Boyle Heights, Los Angeles." Master's thesis, Columbia University, 2017.

Escobar, Edward J. *Race, Police, and the Making of a Political Identity: Mexican Americans and the Los Angeles Police Department, 1900–1945*. Berkeley: University of California Press, 1999.

Escobedo, Elizabeth R. *From Coveralls to Zoot Suits: The Lives of Mexican American Women on the World War II Home Front*. Chapel Hill: University of North Carolina Press, 2013.

Estrada, William David. *The Los Angeles Plaza: Sacred and Contested Space*. Austin: University of Texas Press, 2008.

Felker-Kantor, Max. *Policing Los Angeles: Race, Resistance, and the Rise of the LAPD*. Chapel Hill: University of North Carolina Press, 2018.

Flamming, Douglas. *Bound for Freedom: Black Los Angeles in Jim Crow America*. Berkeley: University of California Press, 2005.

Flores, Edward Orozco. *God's Gangs: Barrio Ministry, Masculinity, and Gang Recovery*. New York: New York University Press, 2014.

Flores, Juan. "Que Assimilated, Brother, *Yo Soy Asimilao:* The Structuring of Puerto Rican Identity in the U.S." *Journal of Ethnic Studies* 13:3 (Fall 1985): 1–16.

Fogelson, Robert M. *Bourgeois Nightmares: Suburbia, 1870–1930*. New Haven, CT: Yale University Press, 2005.

Fogelson, Robert M. *The Fragmented Metropolis: Los Angeles, 1850–1930*. Cambridge, MA: Harvard University Press, 1967.

Foley, Neil. *The White Scourge: Mexicans, Blacks, and Poor Whites in Texas Cotton Culture*. Berkeley: University of California Press, 1997.

Fremon, Celeste. *G-Dog and the Homeboys: Father Greg Boyle and the Gangs of East Los Angeles*. Updated and rev. ed. Albuquerque: University of New Mexico Press, 2008.

Friedricks, William B. "Capital and Labor in Los Angeles: Henry E. Huntington vs. Organized Labor, 1900–1920." *Pacific Historical Review* 59:3 (1990): 375–95.

Frum, David. *How We Got Here: The 70's: The Decade That Brought You Modern Life (for Better or Worse)*. New York: Basic Books, 2000.

Gabaccia, Donna R. "Worker Internationalism and Italian Labor Migration, 1870–1914." *International Labor and Working-Class History* 45 (Spring 1994): 63–79.

Gabler, Neal. *An Empire of Their Own: How the Jews Invented Hollywood*. New York: Crown, 1988.

García, Mario T. *The Chicano Generation: Testimonios of the Movement*. Berkeley: University of California Press, 2015.

García, Mario T. *Father Luis Olivares, a Biography: Faith Politics and the Origins of the Sanctuary Movement in Los Angeles*. Chapel Hill: University of North Carolina Press, 2018.

García, Mario T. *Memories of Chicano History: The Life and Narrative of Bert Corona*. Berkeley: University of California Press, 1994.

García, Mario T., ed. *Ruben Salazar: Border Correspondent; Selected Writings, 1955–1970*. Berkeley: University of California Press, 1995.

García, Mario T., and Sal Castro. *Blowout! Sal Castro and the Chicano Struggle for Educational Justice*. Chapel Hill: University of North Carolina Press, 2011.

García, Matt. *A World of Its Own: Race, Labor, and Citrus in the Making of Greater Los Angeles, 1900–1970*. Chapel Hill: University of North Carolina Press, 2001.

García Bedolla, Lisa. *Fluid Borders: Latino Power, Identity, and Politics in Los Angeles*. Berkeley: University of California Press, 2005.

Garcilazo, Jeffrey M. "McCarthyism, Mexican Americans, and the Los Angeles Committee for the Protection of the Foreign-Born, 1950–1954." *Western Historical Quarterly* 32:3 (Autumn 2001): 273–95.

Geiger, Andrea. *Subverting Exclusion: Transpacific Encounters with Race, Caste, and Borders, 1885–1928*. New Haven, CT: Yale University Press, 2011.

Gerstle, Gary. *American Crucible: Race and Nation in the Twentieth Century*. Princeton, NJ: Princeton University Press, 2001.

Gerstle, Gary. *Working-Class Americanism: The Politics of Labor in a Textile City, 1914–1960*. Cambridge: Cambridge University Press, 1989.

Gluck, Sherna B. *Rosie the Riveter Revisited: Women, the War, and Social Change*. Boston: Twayne, 1987.

Goldstein, Eric L. "Contesting the Categories: Jews and Government Racial Classification in the United States." *Jewish History Quarterly* 19:1 (2005): 79–107.

Goldstein, Eric L. *The Price of Whiteness: Jews, Race, and American Identity*. Princeton, NJ: Princeton University Press, 2006.

Gonzalez, Jerry. *In Search of the Mexican Beverly Hills: Latino Suburbanization in Postwar Los Angeles*. New Brunswick, NJ: Rutgers University Press, 2018.

Gonzalez, Jerry. "'A Place in the Sun': Mexican Americans, Race, and the Suburbanization of Los Angeles, 1940–1980." PhD diss., University of Southern California, 2009.

González, Michael J. *This Small City Will Be a Mexican Paradise: Exploring the Origins of Mexican Culture in Los Angeles, 1821–1846.* Albuquerque: University of New Mexico Press, 2005.

Goodman, Adam. *The Deportation Machine: America's Long History of Expelling Immigrants.* Princeton, NJ: Princeton University Press, 2020.

Gordon, Albert. *Jews in Suburbia.* Boston: Beacon Press, 1959.

Gordon, Linda. *The Great Arizona Orphan Abduction.* Cambridge, MA: Harvard University Press, 1999.

Gotanda, Neil. "Multiculturalism and Racial Stratification." In *Mapping Multiculturalism,* edited by Avery Fisher and Christopher Newfield, 238–52. Minneapolis: University of Minnesota Press, 1996.

Gotham, Kevin Fox. *Race, Real Estate, and Uneven Development: The Kansas City Experience, 1900–2000.* Albany: State University of New York Press, 2002.

Graaf, Lawrence B. de. "The City of Black Angels: Emergence of the Los Angeles Ghetto, 1890–1930." *Pacific Historical Review* 39:3 (August 1970): 323–52.

Graaf, Lawrence B. de. "Negro Migration to Los Angeles, 1930–1950." PhD diss., University of California, Los Angeles, 1962.

Gregory, James N. "California's EPIC Turn: Upton Sinclair's 1934 Campaign and the Reorganization of California Politics." Unpublished paper presented at the Los Angeles History Research Group, May 2, 1995.

Griswold del Castillo, Richard. *The Los Angeles Barrio, 1850–1890: A Social History.* Berkeley: University of California Press, 1979.

Guerin-Gonzales, Camille. *Mexican Workers and American Dreams: Immigration, Repatriation, and California Farm Labor, 1900–1939.* New Brunswick, NJ: Rutgers University Press, 1994.

Guglielmo, Thomas A. *White on Arrival: Italians, Race, Color, and Power in Chicago, 1890–1945.* New York: Oxford University Press, 2004.

Gumprecht, Blake. *The Los Angeles River: Its Life, Death, and Possible Rebirth.* Baltimore: Johns Hopkins University Press, 1999.

Gustafson, Cloyed. "An Ecological Survey of the Hollenbeck Area." Master's thesis, University of Southern California, 1940.

Gutiérrez, David G. *Walls and Mirrors: Mexican Americans, Mexican Immigrants, and the Politics of Ethnicity.* Berkeley: University of California Press, 1995.

Gutiérrez, Elena R. *Fertile Matters: The Politics of Mexican-Origin Women's Reproduction.* Austin: University of Texas Press, 2008.

Gutiérrez, Henry Joseph. "The Chicano Education Rights Movement and School Desegregation: Los Angeles, 1962–1970." PhD diss., University of California, Irvine, 1990.

Hale, Grace Elizabeth. *Making Whiteness: The Culture of Segregation in the South, 1890–1940.* New York: Vintage, 1999.

Hata, Donald, and Nadine Hata. "Indispensable Scapegoats: Asians and Pacific Islanders in Pre-1945 Los Angeles." In *City of Promise: Race and Historical Change in Los Angeles,* edited by Martin Schiesl and Mark M. Dodge, 39–58. Claremont, CA: Regina Books, 2006.

Hayashi, Brian Masaru. *Democratizing the Enemy: The Japanese American Internment.* Princeton, NJ: Princeton University Press, 2004.

Healey, Dorothy, and Maurice Isserman. *Dorothy Healey Remembers: A Life in the American Communist Party.* New York: Oxford University Press, 1990.

Hernández, Kelly Lytle. *City of Inmates: Conquest, Rebellion, and the Rise of Human Caging in Los Angeles, 1771–1965.* Chapel Hill: University of North Carolina Press, 2017.

Himes, Chester. *If He Hollers Let Him Go.* 1945. Reprint, New York: Thunder's Mouth Press, 1986.

Hirsch, Arnold R. *Making the Second Ghetto: Race and Housing in Chicago, 1940–1960.* 3rd ed. Chicago: University of Chicago Press, 1998.

Hise, Greg. "Border City: Race and Social Distance in Los Angeles." In *Los Angeles and the Future of Urban Cultures,* edited by Raul Homero Villa and George J. Sánchez, 45–60. Baltimore: Johns Hopkins University Press, 2005.

Hise, Greg. *Magnetic Los Angeles: Planning the Twentieth-Century Metropolis.* Baltimore: Johns Hopkins University Press, 1997.

Hoffman, Abraham. "El Monte Berry Strike, 1933: International Involvement in a Local Labor Dispute." *Journal of the West* 12:1 (1973): 71–84.

Hoffman, Abraham. *Unwanted Mexican Americans in the Great Depression: Repatriation Pressures, 1929–1939.* Tucson: University of Arizona Press, 1974.

Horne, Gerald. *Fire This Time: The Watts Uprising and the 1960s.* Charlottesville: University Press of Virginia, 1995.

HoSang, Daniel Martinez. *Racial Propositions: Ballot Initiatives and the Making of Postwar California.* Berkeley: University of California Press, 2010.

HoSang, Daniel Martinez, Oneka LaBennett, and Laura Pulido, eds. *Racial Formation in the Twenty-First Century.* Berkeley: University of California Press, 2012.

Huante, Alfredo. "A Lighter Shade of Brown? Gentrification, *Gente*-fication, and Latina/o Urbanism in Los Angeles." PhD diss., University of Southern California, 2018.

Ichioka, Yuji. *The Issei: The World of the First Generation Japanese Immigrants, 1885–1924.* New York: Free Press, 1988.

Ignatiev, Noel. *How the Irish Became White.* New York: Routledge, 1995.

Ishizuka, Karen L. "Coming to Terms: America's Concentration Camps." In *Common Ground: The Japanese American National Museum and the Culture of Collaborations,* edited by Akemi Kikumura-Yano, Lane Ryo Hirabayashi, and James A. Hirabayashi, 101–22. Boulder: University Press of Colorado, 2005.

Jackson, Helen Hunt. *Ramona.* Boston: Little, Brown, 1884.

Jackson, Kenneth T. *Crabgrass Frontier: The Suburbanization of the United States.* New York: Oxford University Press, 1985.

Jackson, Lawrence P. *Chester B. Himes: A Biography.* New York: Norton, 2017.

Jacobson, Matthew Frye. *Roots Too: White Ethnic Revival in Post–Civil Rights America.* Cambridge, MA: Harvard University Press, 2006.

Jacobson, Matthew Frye. *Whiteness of a Different Color: European Immigrants and the Alchemy of Race.* Cambridge, MA: Harvard University Press, 1999.

Jenks, Hillary. "'Home Is Little Tokyo': Race, Community, and Memory in Twentieth-Century Los Angeles." PhD diss., University of Southern California, 2008.

Jimenez y West, Christopher. "More Than My Color: Space, Politics and Identity in Los Angeles, 1940–1973." PhD diss., University of Southern California, Department of History, 2007.

Kambayashi, Malcolm. "Issei Women: Life Histories of Six Issei Women Who Participated in Social and Other Activities in Los Angeles." Master's thesis, University of California, Los Angeles, 1984.

Kasun, Jacqueline. *Some Social Aspects of Business Cycles in the Los Angeles Area, 1920–1950.* Los Angeles: Haynes Foundation, 1954.

Katznelson, Ira. *When Affirmative Action Was White: An Untold History of Racial Inequality in Twentieth-Century America.* New York: Norton, 2006.

Keane, James Thomas. *Fritz B. Burns and the Development of Los Angeles: The Biography of a Community Developer and Philanthropist.* Los Angeles: Thomas and Dorothy Leavey Center for the Study of Los Angeles, 2001.

Keil, Roger. *Los Angeles: Globalization, Urbanization and Social Struggles.* Chichester: John Wiley and Sons, 1998.

Kelley, Robin D. G. *Hammer and Hoe: Alabama Communists during the Great Depression.* Chapel Hill: University of North Carolina Press, 1990.

Kelley, Robin D. G. "The Rest of Us: Rethinking Settler and Native." *American Quarterly* 69:2 (June 2017): 267–76.

Kessner, Thomas. *The Golden Door: Italian and Jewish Immigrant Mobility in New York City, 1880–1915.* New York: Oxford University Press, 1977.

Kikumura-Yano, Akemi, Lane Ryo Hirabayashi, and James A. Hirabayashi, eds. *Common Ground: The Japanese American National Museum and the Culture of Collaboration.* Boulder: University Press of Colorado, 2004.

Kim, Jessica M. *Imperial Metropolis: Los Angeles, Mexico, and the Borderlands of American Empire, 1865–1941.* Chapel Hill: University of North Carolina Press, 2019.

Kim, Jessica M. "Oilmen and Cactus Rustlers: Metropolis, Empire, and Revolution in the Los Angeles-Mexico Borderlands." PhD diss., University of Southern California, Department of History, 2012.

Kim, Sojin. "All Roads Lead to Boyle Heights: Exploring a Los Angeles Neighborhood." In *Common Ground: The Japanese American National Museum and the Culture of Collaboration,* edited by Akemi Kikumura-Yano, Lane Ryo Hirabayashi, and James A. Hirabayashi, 149–66. Boulder: University Press of Colorado, 2004.

Konno, Yuko. "Transnational Localism: Emigration, Adaptation, and Nationalism among Japanese Immigrants to California, 1890–1940." PhD diss., University of Southern California, Department of History, 2012.

Kramer, William M. "The Man behind 'The Spirit of Boyle Heights.'" *Western States Jewish History Quarterly* 20:3 (April 1988): 238–46.

Kronzek, Lynn C. "Fairfax ... A Home, a Community, a Way of Life." In *Legacy: Journal of the Jewish Historical Society of Southern California* 1:4 (Spring 1990): 15, 23–36.

Kurashige, Lon. *Japanese American Celebration and Conflict: A History of Ethnic Identity and Festival, 1934–1990.* Berkeley: University of California Press, 2002.

Kurashige, Lon. *Two Faces of Exclusion: The Untold History of Anti-Asian Racism in the United States.* Chapel Hill: University of North Carolina Press, 2016.

Kurashige, Scott Tadao. *The Shifting Grounds of Race: Black and Japanese Americans in the Making of Multiethnic Los Angeles.* Princeton, NJ: Princeton University Press, 2008.

Kurashige, Scott Tadao. "Transforming Los Angeles: Black and Japanese American Struggles for Racial Equality in the 20th Century." PhD diss., University of California, Los Angeles, 2000.

Kurland, Catherine L., and Enrique R. Lamadrid. *Hotel Mariachi: Urban Space and Cultural Heritage in Los Angeles.* Photographs by Miguel A. Gandert. Albuquerque: University of New Mexico Press, 2013.

Laslett, John H. M. *Shameful Victory: The Los Angeles Dodgers, the Red Scare, and the Hidden History of Chavez Ravine.* Tucson: University of Arizona Press, 2015.

Laslett, John H. M. *Sunshine Was Never Enough: Los Angeles Workers, 1880–2010.* Berkeley: University of California Press, 2012.

Laslett, John H. M., and Mary Tyler. *The ILGWU in Los Angeles, 1907–1988.* Inglewood, CA: Ten Star Press, 1989.

Leader, Leonard. *Los Angeles and the Great Depression.* New York: Garland, 1991.

Leonard, Kevin Allen. *The Battle for Los Angeles: Racial Ideology and World War II.* Albuquerque: University of New Mexico Press, 2006.

Leonard, Kevin Allen. "'Brothers under the Skin'? African Americans, Mexican Americans, and World War II in California." In *The Way We Really Were: The Golden State in the Second World War,* edited by Roger W. Lotchin, 187–214. Urbana: University of Illinois Press, 2000.

Leonard, Kevin Allen. "Years of Hope, Days of Fear: The Impact of World War II on Race Relations in Los Angeles." PhD diss., University of California, Davis, 1992.

Leuchtenberg, William E. *Franklin D. Roosevelt and the New Deal, 1932–1940.* New York: Harper and Row, 1963.

Lewthwaite, Stephanie. *Race, Place, and Reform in Mexican Los Angeles.* Tucson: University of Arizona Press, 2009.

Licón, Gerardo. "Pachucas, Pachucos, and Their Culture: Mexican American Youth Culture of the Southwest, 1910–1950." PhD diss., University of Southern California, Department of History, 2009.

Licón, Gustavo. "'La Union Hace la Fuerza!' (Unity Creates Strength!): M.E.Ch.A. and Chicana/o Student Activism in California, 1967–1999." PhD diss., University of Southern California, 2009.

Lipsitz, George. "Blood Lines and Blood Shed: Intersectionality and Differential Consciousness in Ethnic Studies and American Studies." In *A Concise Companion to American Studies*, edited by John Carlos Rowe, 153–71. New York: Blackwell, 2010.

Lipsitz, George. *How Racism Takes Place*. Philadelphia: Temple University Press, 2011.

Lipsitz, George. *The Possessive Investment in Whiteness: How White People Profit from Identity Politics*. Rev. and enl. ed. Philadelphia: Temple University Press, 1998.

Lipsitz, George. *Time Passages: Collective Memory and American Popular Culture*. Minneapolis: University of Minnesota Press, 1990.

Litwin, Patricia. "'How Could a Woman . . . Not Even Five Feet Tall, Change the World?': Rose Chernin and the Los Angeles Committee for the Protection of the Foreign-Born." Master's thesis, Sarah Lawrence College, 2007.

Logan, John R., Richard D. Alba, and Wenquan Zhang. "Immigrant Enclaves and Ethnic Communities in New York and Los Angeles." *American Sociological Review* 67:2 (April 2002): 299–322.

López, Ronald. "The El Monte Berry Strike of 1933." *Aztlan: Chicano Journal of the Social Sciences and the Arts* 1:1 (Spring 1970): 101–15.

Lotchin, Roger W. *Fortress California, 1910–1961: From Warfare to Welfare*. New York: Oxford University Press, 1992.

Lothrop, Gloria Ricci. "Italians of Los Angeles: An Historical Overview." *Southern California Quarterly* 85:3 (Fall 2003): 249–300.

Lott, Eric. *Love and Theft: Blackface Minstrelsy and the American Working Class*. New York: Oxford University Press, 1995.

Lowe, Lisa. *Immigrant Acts: On Asian American Cultural Politics*. Durham, NC: Duke University Press, 1996.

Loza, Mireya. *Defiant Braceros: How Migrant Workers Fought for Racial, Sexual, and Political Freedom*. Chapel Hill: University of North Carolina Press, 2016.

Lozano, Rosina. *An American Language: The History of Spanish in the United States*. Berkeley: University of California Press, 2018.

Lozano, Rosina. "The Struggle for Inclusion: A Study of the Community Service Organization in East Los Angeles, 1947–1951." Senior honors thesis, Stanford University, 2000.

Luce, Caroline Elizabeth. "Reexamining Los Angeles' 'Lower East Side': Jewish Bakers Union Local 453 and Yiddish Food Culture in 1920s Boyle Heights." In *Jews in the Los Angeles Mosaic*, edited by Karen S. Wilson, 25–42. Los Angeles: Autry National Center of the American West; Berkeley: University of California Press, 2013.

Luce, Caroline Elizabeth. "Visions of a Jewish Future: the Jewish Bakers Union and Yiddish Culture in East Los Angeles, 1908–1942." PhD diss., University of California, Los Angeles, 2013.

Luce, Caroline Elizabeth. "Yiddish Writers in Los Angeles and the Jewish Fantasy Past." *American Jewish History Quarterly* 102:4 (2018): 481–509.

Macías, Anthony. *Mexican American Mojo: Popular Music, Dance, and Urban Culture in Los Angeles, 1935–1968*. Durham, NC: Duke University Press, 2008.

Macías, Anthony. "Multicultural Music, Jews, and American Culture: The Life and Times of William Phillips." In *Beyond Alliances: The Jewish Role in Reshaping the Racial Landscape of Southern California,* edited by Bruce Zuckerman, George J. Sánchez, and Lisa Ansell, 33–69. West Lafayette, IN: Purdue University Press for the USC Casden Institute for the Study of the Jewish Role in American Life, 2012.

Martin-Rodriguez, Manuel M. "Mexican American Literature." In *A History of California Literature,* edited by Blake Allmendinger, 145–46. New York: Cambridge University Press, 2015.

Massey, Douglas S., and Nancy A. Denton. *American Apartheid: Segregation and the Making of the Underclass.* Cambridge, MA: Harvard University Press, 1993.

Matsumoto, Valerie. *City Girls: The Nisei Social World in Los Angeles, 1920–1950.* New York: Oxford University Press, 2014.

Mayers, Jackson. *The San Fernando Valley.* Walnut, CA: John D. McIntyre, 1976.

Mazón, Mauricio. *The Zoot-Suit Riots: The Psychology of Symbolic Annihilation.* Austin: University of Texas Press, 1984.

McCaffery, Isaias James. "Organizing Las Costureras: Life, Labor and Unionization among Mexicana Garment Workers in Two Borderland Cities—Los Angeles and San Antonio, 1933–1941." PhD diss., University of Kansas, 1999.

McGirr, Lisa. *Suburban Warriors: The Origins of the New American Right.* Princeton, NJ: Princeton University Press, 2001.

McWilliams, Carey. *North from Mexico: The Spanish-Speaking People of the United States.* 1948. Reprint, New York: Greenwood Press, 1968.

McWilliams, Carey. *Southern California: An Island on the Land.* Salt Lake City, UT: Peregrine Smith Books, 1946.

Meier, Matt S., and Feliciano Rivera. *Readings on La Raza: The Twentieth Century.* New York: Hill and Wang, 1974.

Menchaca, Celeste. "Borderland Visualities: Technologies of Sight and the Production of the Nineteenth-Century U.S.-Mexico Borderlands." PhD diss., University of Southern California, 2016.

Mines, Richard. *Developing a Community Tradition of Migration: A Field Study in Rural Zacatecas, Mexico, and California Settlement Areas.* Monographs in US-Mexican Studies 3. La Jolla: Program in United States-Mexican Studies, University of California, San Diego, 1981.

Minian, Ana Raquel. *Undocumented Lives: The Untold Story of Mexican Migration.* Cambridge, MA: Harvard University Press, 2018.

Modell, John. *The Economics and Politics of Racial Accommodation: The Japanese of Los Angeles, 1900–1942.* Urbana: University of Illinois Press, 1977.

Molina, Natalia. "Examining Chicana/o History through a Relational Lens." *Pacific Historical Review* 82:4 (2013): 645–62.

Molina, Natalia. *Fit to Be Citizens? Public Health and Race in Los Angeles, 1879–1939.* Berkeley: University of California Press, 2006.

Molina, Natalia. *How Race Is Made in America: Immigration, Citizenship, and the Historical Power of Racial Scripts.* Berkeley: University of California Press, 2013.

Molina, Natalia, Daniel Martinez HoSang, and Ramon A. Gutierrez, eds. *Relational Formations of Race: Theory, Method and Practice*. Berkeley: University of California Press, 2019.

Monroy, Douglas. "Mexicanos in Los Angeles, 1930–1941: An Ethnic Group in Relation to Class Forces." PhD diss., University of California, Los Angeles, 1978.

Monroy, Douglas. *Rebirth: Mexican Los Angeles from the Great Migration to the Great Depression*. Berkeley: University of California Press, 1999.

Monroy, Douglas. *Thrown among Strangers: The Making of Mexican Culture in Frontier California*. Berkeley: University of California Press, 1990.

Moore, Deborah Dash. *To the Golden Cities: Pursuing the American Jewish Dream in Miami and L.A.* New York: Free Press, 1994.

Moreno, Alexis. "African Americans in Boyle Heights." Unpublished paper submitted to Instructor Carol Goldstein in Urban Planning 277: Historic Preservation, Spring Quarter 1999, UCLA School of Public Policy and Social Research.

Mullins, William H. *The Depression and the Urban West Coast, 1929–1933: Los Angeles, San Francisco, Seattle and Portland*. Bloomington: Indiana University Press, 1991.

Ngai, Mae N. *Impossible Subjects: Illegal Aliens and the Making of Modern America*. Princeton, NJ: Princeton University Press, 2004.

Nicolaides, Becky M. *My Blue Heaven: Life and Politics in the Working-Class Suburbs of Los Angeles, 1920–1965*. Chicago: University of Chicago Press, 2002.

NietoGomez, Anna. "Francisca Flores, the League of Mexican American Women, and the Comisión Femenil Mexicana Nacional, 1958–1975." In *Chicana Movidas: New Narratives of Activism and Feminism in the Movement Era*, edited by Dionne Espinoza, Maria Eugenia Cotera, and Maylei Blackwell, 33–50. Austin: University of Texas Press, 2018.

Nieto-Phillips, John. *The Language of Blood: The Making of Spanish-American Identity in New Mexico, 1880s–1930s*. Albuquerque: University of New Mexico Press, 2004.

Norman, E. Herbert. *Japan's Emergence as a Modern State: Political and Economic Problems of the Meiji Period*. 1940. Reprint, Westport, CT: Greenwood Press, 1973.

Nugent, Walter. *Into the West: The Story of Its People*. New York: Alfred A. Knopf, 1999.

O'Brien, David, and Stephen Fugita. *The Japanese American Experience*. Bloomington: University of Indiana Press, 1991.

Okihiro, Gary Y. *The Columbia Guide to Asian American History*. New York: Columbia University Press, 2001.

Okihiro, Gary Y. *Margins and Mainstreams: Asians in American History and Culture*. Seattle: University of Washington Press, 1994.

Okihiro, Gary Y. *A Social History of the Bakwena and Peoples of the Kalahari of Southern Africa, 19th Century*. Lewiston, NY: Edwin Mellen Press, 2000.

Omi, Michael, and Howard Winant. *Racial Formation in the United States: From the 1960s to the 1980s*. New York: Routledge, 1986.

Omi, Michael, and Howard Winant. *Racial Formation in the United States: From the 1960s to the 1990s*. 2nd ed. New York: Routledge, 1994.

Ong, Paul, and Evelyn Blumenberg. "Income and Racial Inequality in Los Angeles." In *The City: Los Angeles and Urban Theory at the End of the Twentieth Century*, edited by Allen J. Scott and Edward W. Soja, 311–35. Berkeley: University of California Press, 1996.

Ornelas-Higdon, Julia. "A Cultivating Enterprise: Wine, Race, and Conquest in California, 1769–1920." PhD diss., University of Southern California, 2014.

Oropeza, Lorena. *!Raza Si! !Guerra No! Chicano Protest and Patriotism during the Viet Nam War Era*. Berkeley: University of California Press, 2005.

Orsi, Jared. *Hazardous Metropolis: Flooding and Urban Ecology in Los Angeles*. Berkeley: University of California Press, 2004.

Pagán, Eduardo Obregón. *Murder at the Sleepy Lagoon: Zoot Suits, Race, and Riot in Wartime L.A.* Chapel Hill: University of North Carolina Press, 2003.

Painter, Nell Irvin. *The History of White People*. New York: Norton, 2010.

Pardo, Mary S. *Mexican American Women Activists: Identity and Resistance in Two Los Angeles Communities*. Philadelphia: Temple University Press, 1998.

Park, Robert E., and Ernest W. Burgess. *Introduction to the Science of Sociology*. Chicago: University of Chicago Press, 1921.

Park, Robert E., Ernest W. Burgess, and Roderick D. McKenzie. *The City*. Chicago: University of Chicago Press, 1925.

Parson, Don. *Making a Better World: Public Housing, the Red Scare, and the Direction of Modern Los Angeles*. Minneapolis: University of Minnesota Press, 2005.

Pastor, Manuel. *State of Resistance: What California's Dizzying Descent and Remarkable Resurgence Mean for America's Future*. New York: New Press, 2018.

Patino, Jimmy. *Raza Sí, Migra No: Chicano Movement Struggles for Immigrant Rights in San Diego*. Chapel Hill: University of North Carolina Press, 2017.

Perry, Louis B., and Richard S. Perry. *The History of the Los Angeles Labor Movement, 1911–1941*. Berkeley: University of California Press, 1963.

Peterson, Jon A. *The Birth of City Planning in the United States, 1840–1917*. Baltimore: Johns Hopkins University Press, 2003.

Philpott, Thomas Lee. *The Slum and the Ghetto: Neighborhood Deterioration and Middle-Class Reform, Chicago, 1880–1930*. New York: Oxford University Press, 1978.

Plascencia, María José, and George J. Sánchez. "Living in the Transpacific Borderlands: Expressions of Japanese Latino Culture and Identity." In *Transpacific Borderlands: The Art of Japanese Diaspora in Lima, Los Angeles, Mexico City, and Sao Paulo*, edited by Emily Anderson, 6–21. Los Angeles: Japanese American National Museum, 2017.

Post, Robert C. *Street Railways and the Growth of Los Angeles*. San Marino, CA: Golden West Books, 1989.

Pratt, Kamala. "Chicana Strategies for Success and Survival: Cultural Poetics of Environmental Justice from the Mothers of East Los Angeles." *Frontiers: A Journal of Women Studies* 18:2 (1997): 48–72.

Quiñonez, Naomi. "Rosita the Riveter: Welding Tradition with Wartime Transformations." In *Mexican Americans and World War II*, edited by Maggie Rivas-Rodriguez, 245–68. Austin: University of Texas Press, 2005.

Quintana, Isabella Seong-Leong. "National Borders, Neighborhood Boundaries: Gender, Space and Border Formation in Chinese and Mexican Los Angeles, 1871–1938." PhD diss., University of Michigan, 2010.

Ramirez, Marla Andrea. "Contested Illegality: Three Generations of Exclusion through Mexican 'Repatriation' and the Politics of Immigration Law, 1920–2005." PhD diss., University of California at Santa Barbara, 2015.

Ramos, Nic John. "City of Health: Race, Gender, and Public Hospital Construction in Los Angeles." Unpublished paper, University of Southern California, Department of American Studies and Ethnicity, 2011.

Ramos, Nic John. "From Home to Hospital, Hospital to Home: The State, the Family, and the Nation." Unpublished paper, University of Southern California, Department of American Studies and Ethnicity, 2011.

Robinson, Greg. *By Order of the President: FDR and the Internment of Japanese Americans.* Cambridge, MA: Harvard University Press, 2001.

Robinson, Greg. *A Tragedy of Democracy: Japanese Confinement in North America.* New York: Columbia University Press, 2009.

Rocco, Raymond A. "Latino Los Angeles: Reframing Boundaries/Borders." In *The City: Los Angeles and Urban Theory at the End of the Twentieth Century,* edited by Allen J. Scott and Edward W. Soja, 365–89. Berkeley: University of California Press, 1996.

Roediger, David. *The Wages of Whiteness: Race and the Making of the American Working Class.* New York: Verso, 1991.

Rogin, Michael Paul. *Blackface, White Noise: Jewish Immigrants in the Hollywood Melting Pot.* Berkeley: University of California Press, 1996.

Rogin, Michael Paul, and John L. Shover. *Political Change in California: Critical Elections and Social Movements, 1890–1966.* Westport, CT: Greenwood, 1970.

Roman, Elda Maria. "From Walking Out to Walking In: Activist Goals, Neoliberal Constraints, and the Discourse of Latino Entrepreneurship." *Latino Studies* 17 (2019): 5–26.

Rosas, Ana Elizabeth. *Abrazando el Espiritu: Bracero Families Confront the U.S.-Mexico Border.* Berkeley: University of California Press, 2014.

Ross, Steven J. *Hitler in Los Angeles: How Jews Foiled Nazi Plots against Hollywood and America.* New York: Bloomsbury, 2017.

Rowland, Donald E. *John Rowland and William Workman: Southern California Pioneers of 1841.* Los Angeles: Arthur H. Clark and Historical Society of Southern California, 1999.

Ruiz, Vicki L. *Cannery Women, Cannery Lives: Mexican Women, Unionization, and the California Food Processing Industry, 1930–1950.* Albuquerque: University of New Mexico Press, 1987.

Ruiz, Vicki L. *From Out of the Shadows: Mexican Women in Twentieth-Century America.* New York: Oxford University Press, 1998.

Ruiz, Vicki L. "'Star Struck': Acculturation, Adolescence, and Mexican American Women, 1920–1940." In *Small Worlds: Children and Adolescents in America*, edited by Elliot West and Paula Petrik, 61–80. Lawrence: University of Kansas Press, 1992.

Saito, Leland. *Race and Politics: Asian Americans, Latinos, and Whites in a Los Angeles Suburb.* Urbana: University of Illinois Press, 1998.

Salerno, Salvatore. "*I Delitta della Razza Bianca* (Crimes of the White Race): Italian Anarchists' Racial Discourse as Crime." In *Are Italians White? How Race Is Made in America*, edited by Jennifer Guglielmo and Salvatore Salerno, 111–23. New York: Routledge, 2003.

Sánchez, George J. *Becoming Mexican American: Ethnicity, Culture and Identity in Chicano Los Angeles, 1900–1945.* New York: Oxford University Press, 1993.

Sánchez, George J. "Disposable People, Expendable Neighborhoods: Repatriation, Internment and Other Population Removals." In *A Companion to Los Angeles*, edited by William Deverell and Greg Hise, 129–46. Malden, MA: Wiley-Blackwell, 2010.

Sánchez, George J. "Face the Nation: Race, Immigration, and the Rise of Nativism in Late Twentieth Century America." *International Migration Review* 31:4 (Winter 1997): 1009–30.

Sánchez, George J. "Generations of Segregation: Immigrant Dreams and Segregated Lives in Metropolitan Los Angeles." In *New World Cities: Challenges of Urbanization and Globalization in the Americas*, edited by John Tutino and Martin V. Melosi, 210–41. Chapel Hill: University of North Carolina Press, 2019.

Sánchez, George J. "'What's Good for Boyle Heights Is Good for the Jews': Creating Multiracialism on the Eastside during the 1950s." *American Quarterly* 56:3 (September 2004): 633–62.

Sánchez, George J. "Why Are Multiracial Communities So Dangerous? Hawai'i, Cape Town South Africa, and Boyle Heights, California in Comparison." *Pacific Historical Review* 86:1 (February 2017): 153–70.

Santana, Ray, and Mario Esparza. "East Los Angeles Blowouts." In *Parameters of Institutional Change: Chicano Experiences in Education*, edited by Armando Váldez, 1–9. Hayward, CA: Southwest Network, 1974.

Schiffman, Paula M. "The Los Angeles Prairie." In *Land of Sunshine: An Environmental History of Metropolitan Los Angeles*, edited by William Deverell and Greg Hise, 38–51. Pittsburgh, PA: University of Pittsburgh Press, 2005.

Schrank, Sarah. *Art and the City: Civic Imagination and Cultural Authority in Los Angeles.* Philadelphia: University of Pennsylvania Press, 2009.

Sherman, John W. *A Communist Front at Mid-century: The American Committee for Protection of the Foreign Born, 1933–1959.* Westport, CT: Praeger, 2001.

Shevky, Eshref, and Marilyn Williams. *The Social Areas of Los Angeles: Analysis and Typology.* Berkeley: University of California Press, 1949.

Shorr, Howard J. "The Boyle Heights Project: Linking Students with Their Community." *History Teacher* 18:4 (August 1985): 489–99.

Sides, Josh. *L.A. City Limits: African American Los Angeles from the Great Depression to the Present.* Berkeley: University of California Press, 2003.

Sitton, Thomas Joseph. *Los Angeles Transformed: Fletcher Bowron's Urban Reform Revival, 1938–1953.* Albuquerque: University of New Mexico Press, 2005.

Sitton, Thomas Joseph. "Urban Politics and Reform in the New Deal Los Angeles Recall of Mayor Frank L. Shaw." PhD diss., University of California, Riverside, 1983.

Soliz, Barbara K. "Rosalind Wiener Wyman and the Transformation of Jewish Liberalism in Cold War Los Angeles." In *Beyond Alliances: The Jewish Role in Reshaping the Racial Landscape of Southern California,* edited by Bruce Zuckerman, George J. Sánchez, and Lisa Ansell, 71–110. West Lafayette, IN: Purdue University Press for the USC Casden Institute for the Study of the Jewish Role in American Life, 2012.

Sonenshein, Raphael F. *Politics in Black and White: Race and Power in Los Angeles.* Princeton, NJ: Princeton University Press, 1993.

Sorin, Gerald. *Tradition Transformed: The Jewish Experience in America.* Baltimore: Johns Hopkins University Press, 1997.

Soutoul, Sarah. "From Gentrification to *Gentefication*: The Change of a Neighborhood by Latinos." Capstone project for USC Annenberg Media, Annenberg School for Communication and Journalism, 2019. https://ascjcapstone.com/terms/spring-2019/soutoul/.

Starr, Kevin. *Embattled Dreams: California in War and Peace, 1940–1950.* New York: Oxford University Press, 2002.

Starr, Kevin. *Inventing the Dream: California through the Progressive Era.* New York: Oxford University Press, 1985.

Steinberg, Janice. *The Tin Horse: A Novel.* New York: Random House, 2013.

Stern, Alexandra. *Eugenic Nation: Faults and Frontiers of Better Breeding in Modern America.* Berkeley: University of California Press, 2005.

Stevens, Errol Wayne. *Radical L.A.: From Coxey's Army to the Watts Riots, 1894–1965.* Norman: University of Oklahoma Press, 2009.

Struthers, David Marshall. *The World in a City: Multiethnic Radicalism in Early Twentieth-Century Los Angeles.* Urbana: University of Illinois Press, 2019.

Struthers, David Marshall. "The World in a City: Transnational and Inter-racial Organizing in Los Angeles, 1900–1930." PhD diss., Carnegie Mellon University, 2010.

Sugrue, Thomas J. *The Origins of the Urban Crisis: Race and Inequality in Postwar Detroit.* Princeton, NJ: Princeton University Press, 1996.

Sullivan, Neil J. *The Dodgers Move West.* New York: Oxford University Press, 1987.

Svonkin, Stuart. *Jews against Prejudice: American Jews and the Fight for Civil Liberties.* New York: Columbia University Press, 1997.

Takaki, Ronald. *A Different Mirror: A History of Multicultural America.* Boston: Little, Brown, 1993.

Takaki, Ronald. *Strangers from a Different Shore: A History of Asian Americans.* Boston: Little, Brown, 1989.

Thelen, David. "Memory and American History." *Journal of American History* 75:4 (March 1989): 1117–29.

Thompson, Gabriel. *America's Social Arsonist: Fred Ross and Grassroots Organizing in the Twentieth Century.* Berkeley: University of California Press, 2016.

Tokunaga, Yu. "Making Transborder Los Angeles: Japanese and Mexican Immigration, Agriculture, and Labor Relations, 1924–1942." PhD diss., University of Southern California, 2018.

Tolbert, Emory J. *The UNIA and Black Los Angeles.* Los Angeles: UCLA Center for Afro-American Studies, 1980.

Topp, Michael Miller. *Those without a Country: The Political Culture of Italian American Syndicalists* Minneapolis: University of Minnesota Press, 2001.

Tsuchiya, Katsuyo. *Reinventing Citizenship: Black Los Angeles, Korean Kawasaki, and Community Participation.* Minneapolis: University of Minnesota Press, 2014.

Tucker, Sherrie. *Dance Floor Democracy: The Social Geography of Memory at the Hollywood Canteen.* Durham, NC: Duke University Press, 2014.

Underwood, Katherine. "Process and Politics: Multiracial Electoral Coalition Building and Representation in Los Angeles' Ninth District, 1949–1962." PhD diss., University of California, San Diego, 1992.

Varzally, Allison. *Making a Non-white America: Californians Coloring outside Ethnic Lines, 1925–1955.* Berkeley: University of California Press, 2008.

Verge, Arthur C. *Paradise Transformed: Los Angeles during the Second World War.* Dubuque, IA: Kendall/Hunt, 1993.

Vigil, James Diego. *The Projects: Gang and Non-gang Families in East Los Angeles.* Austin: University of Texas Press, 2007.

Vorspan, Max, and Lloyd P. Garner. *History of the Jews of Los Angeles.* San Marino, CA: Huntington Library, 1970.

Wacker, R. Fred. *Ethnicity, Pluralism, and Race: Race Relations Theory in America before Myrdal.* Westport, CT: Greenwood Press, 1983.

Wallach, Ruth, Dace Taube, Claude Zachary, Linda McCann, and Curtis S. Roseman. *Los Angeles in World War II: Images of America.* Charleston, SC: Arcadia, 2011.

Weaver, John D. *El Pueblo Grande: A Non-fiction Book about Los Angeles.* Los Angeles: Ward Ritchie Press, 1973.

Weber, Devra Anne. "The Organization of Mexicano Agricultural Workers, the Imperial Valley and Los Angeles, 1928–1934: An Oral History Approach." *Aztlan: Chicano Journal of the Social Sciences and the Arts* 3:2 (Fall 1972): 307–47.

Weise, Julie M. "Strange Familiarity: Jewish and Mexican Immigrants in Los Angeles, 1890–1933." Unpublished paper for undergraduate history course with Professor Paula Hyman, "Jewish Immigration and American Society," Yale University, 1999.

Widener, Daniel. *Black Arts West: Culture and Struggle in Postwar Los Angeles.* Durham, NC: Duke University Press, 2010.

Wild, Mark. *Street Meeting: Multiethnic Neighborhoods in Early Twentieth-Century Los Angeles.* Berkeley: University of California Press, 2005.

Wollenberg, Charles. "Working on El Traque: The Pacific Electric Strike of 1903." *Pacific Historical Review* 42:3 (1973): 358–69.

Workman, Boyle. *The City That Grew*. Los Angeles: Southlan, 1936.

Yamasaki, Yushi. "Buried Strands: From Peasant Rebellions to Internationalist Multiracial Labor Organizing among Japanese Immigrant Communities in Hawaii and California, 1885–1941." PhD dissertation, University of Southern California, 2015.

Young, Pauline. *The Pilgrims of Russian-Town*. Chicago: University of Chicago Press, 1932.

Yu, Henry. *Thinking Orientals: Migration, Contact, and Exoticism in Modern America*. New York: Oxford University Press, 2001.

INDEX

Chicano Youth Liberation Conference, 206
Child Immunization Project, 231
Chimento Contemporary, 256
Chimento, Eva, 256
Chinatown, 31, 33, 50, 126, 236
Chinatown, 7
Chinese: discrimination, 31, 48, 137; exclusion, 31; families, 37; immigrants, 7, 24; laborers 17; laundries, 33; neighborhoods, 31, 266; population, 7, 68, 188
Chinese Historical Society of Southern California, 17
Christian base communities, 234
Christensen, Parley P., 160, 167–168
Church of the Epiphany, 199
Cinel, Dino, 47
circular migration, 217, 225
Cisneros, Henry, 237
Citizens' Committee for the Defense of Mexican-American Youth, 118
Citizens Committee to Re-Elect Roybal, 168
Citizenship: and Alien Land Laws; and CIO, 83; changing dynamics, 213–215; Gloria Molina, 213; IRCA, 224–225; and Japanese Americans, 91, 104; McCarran-Walter Act, 149; and MELA, 227–228, 232; racialization of, 88, 131, 152; repatriation of Mexicans, 74
Citrus Belt, 161
City Hall Grill, 125
City Housing Authority. *See* Los Angeles Housing Authority
City Terrace, 53, 92, 99, 102, 130, 134, 139, 146, 150
City Terrace Cultural Center, 130
civic: action, 162; empowerment, 160, 214; engagement, 163–164; leadership, 164
Civilian Conservation Corps (CCC) 159
Civilian Defense Corps, 109
civil rights: activism, 111, 113, 191; Boyle Heights residents, 127; and CIO, 83; and CSO, 112, 170, 192, 303n35; and emerging consciousness, 99; future of, 120; high school activists, 212; immigrants, 151; and Japanese Americans,125, 127–128, 131; and Jews 131, 152; Latino, 112, 151, 219, 268–269; leaders, 111, 113, 192; and liberalism, 153; and Paula Crisos-

tomo, 193, 196; *Madrigal v. Quilligan,* 221; movement: 186, 190–191, 212; multiracial coalitions, 123; organizations, 123–125; racial civil rights, 121; *See also* African American(s) civil rights
Civil Rights Congress, 83
classism, 193, 198
Claudio and Anita, 36
Clinton, Bill, 237
Clinton, Hillary Rodham, 242
clubes sociales, 218, 270
Coalition Against the Pipeline, 230
Coleman, John Wesley, 43, 46
Coleman Flats, 43
College of Medical Evangelists, 180
Collins, Leroy, 197
colonialism, 248
Combs, R.E., 142
Comisión Femenil Mexicana Nacional (CFMN), 214, 221, 307n3
Comité de Beneficencia Mexicana, 218
Comité Pro Paz (Committee for Peace), 234–235, 238
Committee Against Socialist Housing (CASH), 176
Committee of Civic Unity, 121
Committee to Elect Edward Roybal, 160
Communist: and CSO, 166; IWO, 269; and Jews, 81, 138, 147, 154; and LAPD, 70; Left, 96, 138; and Leo Frumkin, 39, 154; and multicultural activities, 152; organizers, 111, 165–166; Paula Crisostomo, 208; public housing, 87, 146, 188; radical communists,117; registration, 173; Soto-Michigan Center, 142–143, 146–147, 269; sympathizers, 149; working-class neighborhoods,149; Yiddish, 58, 69
Communist Party: communist registration, 173; International Workers Order (IWO) and, 70, 143, 268; Italian, 47; Leo Frumkin, 39; McCarran Internal Security Act of 1950, 149; Rose Chernin, 150
Communist Party Los Angeles (CPLA), 70
community: activist, 163, 199, 226, 236; building, 13, 263; coalition, 159
Community Action Program (CAP), 192

Mexican American Political Association (MAPA), 224
Mexican American Youth Leadership, 198
Mexican-American War, 17, 265, 278n17
Mexican Constitution 1917, 58
Mexican Farm Labor Agreement, 1942, 12
Mexican Independence Day, 145
Mexican Repatriation Campaign, 68, 84, 91, 98, 103, 268
Mexican Revolution, 42, 45, 47, 58, 267
Mexican Subcommittee of the CIO Industrial Council, 113
migrant workers' rights, 207
Mexican War of Independence, 20
Mills, Billy, 183
Mills College, 195
Minian, Ana Raquel, 217–218
minority communities, 113
minority youth, 196
Medina, Bob, 235
Mexican American Political Association (MAPA), 182, 191, 224
Mexico, 225, 230, 241
migration, 111
military recruitment, 105
Missoula, 92
Mita, Edo, 152
mixed-status families, 225
MJW Investments, Inc., 247
Modern Talmud Torah and Social Center, 139
Mojave Desert, 39
Molina, Gloria: beginnings, 213; California assemblywoman, 226, 230; Comisión Femenil Mexicana Nacional (CFMN), 214, 221; Councilwoman, 229; County Supervisor, 248; interview, 307n1; political rise, 215
Molina, Irene, 109
Molina, Martha, 226
Molina, Natalia, 33, 68
Monroy, Douglas, 82
Montebello, 213
Monterey Park, 7, 181
Moreno, Luisa, 81
Morreta, John, 227
mothers, 234–235

Mothers of East Los Angeles (MELA): Dolores Mission Church, 232; hazardous materials, 230–231; leaders, 228, 310n57; membership, 227*fig.;* pipeline, 230; politics, 240; prisons, 214, 226–227*fig.,* 230–231, 248, 271; Proposition 187, 237; undocumented, 227, 310; water conservation, 229*fig.*
Movimiento Estudiantil Chicano de Aztlán (MEChA), 201, 209
multicultural, 152
multiethnic, 157
multiracial: activists, 149; civil rights, 123; committee, 163; community, 4, 7, 40, 64, 88, 99, 171, 184, 262–264; democracy, 81; enclave, 38; engagement, 243; future, 242, 246; history, 7, 263; interaction, 3; labor struggles, 44, 84; multiracialism 148–149, 152, 156, 245, 261–262; neighborhoods, 4, 12, 49, 65, 83, 99, 176, 187, 261; past, 242, 260, 264; political coalition, 60, 158, 166, 168, 183–184; politics, 149, 183; population, 58, 73; residents, 1, 133, 261; schools, 60, 211; social justice, 212; traditions, 75; union organizations, 47, 80, 163; working class, 48, 134
Murakami, Mary, 93
Museum as Retail Space (MaRS), 256
Myer, Dillon S., 125

Nabarette, Charles, 221
Nakanishi, Don, 194
National Association for the Advancement of Colored People (NAACP), 83, 109, 168, 182
National Convention of Peoples of African Descent, 43
National Industrial Recovery Act, 77, 81
National Jewish Welfare Board, 140
national patriotism, 98
Nava, Henry, 169
Nava, Julian, 204
Navarro, Teresa, 234
Nazi(s): activities, 122, 268; Community Relations Committee (CRC), 122; fight against, 98, 128; Germany, 82; local, 123;

Founded in 1893,
UNIVERSITY OF CALIFORNIA PRESS
publishes bold, progressive books and journals
on topics in the arts, humanities, social sciences,
and natural sciences—with a focus on social
justice issues—that inspire thought and action
among readers worldwide.

The UC PRESS FOUNDATION
raises funds to uphold the press's vital role
as an independent, nonprofit publisher, and
receives philanthropic support from a wide
range of individuals and institutions—and from
committed readers like you. To learn more, visit
ucpress.edu/supportus.